LET THE READER UNDERSTAND

LET THE READER UNDERSTAND

READER-RESPONSE CRITICISM and the GOSPEL OF MARK

ROBERT M. FOWLER

FORTRESS PRESS   MINNEAPOLIS

LET THE READER UNDERSTAND
Reader-Response Criticism and the Gospel of Mark

Library of Congress Cataloging-in-Publication Data

Fowler, Robert M.
   Let the reader understand : reader-response criticism and the
Gospel of Mark / Robert M. Fowler.
     p.   cm.
   Includes bibliographical references and index.
   ISBN 0-8006-2491-2 (alk. paper)
   1. Bible. N.T. Mark—Reading. I. Title.
BS2585.5.F68   1991
   226.3'066—dc20   91-12714
                                                     CIP

Manufactured in the U.S.A.   AF 1-2491

95   94   93   92   91   1   2   3   4   5   6   7   8   9   10

To Wayne and
Jo Anne Fowler

CONTENTS

ACKNOWLEDGMENTS

In writing a book that has taken as long as this one has, an author piles up a considerable debt to institutions and to friends, colleagues, and family. This project began with—and would have been impossible without—a year-long fellowship from the National Endowment for the Humanities. Generous gifts from Robert and Mary Lou Thomson allowed me to participate for five years in a seminar in the Studiorum Novi Testamenti Societas. Generous support from Baldwin-Wallace College and Robert Brown gave me the time to finish my manuscript in a sabbatical year.

As I wrote the following pages, I often visualized the faces of my colleagues in seminars at the regional level (in the Working Group on Rhetorical and Narrative Criticism of the Bible of the Eastern Great Lakes Biblical Society), national level (in the Group on the Literary Aspects of the Gospels and Acts of the Society of Biblical Literature), and international level (in the Seminar on the Role of the Reader in the Interpretation of the New Testament of the Studiorum Novi Testamenti Societas). Early drafts of portions of this book were presented to each of these seminars and published in some form or another in the *Proceedings* of the EGLBS, the *Seminar Papers* of the SBL, and in the journal *Semeia*. I owe a great debt to my colleagues in all of these scholarly societies for their comments, suggestions, and encouragement.

Closer to home, I extend my thanks to a host of individuals who assisted and encouraged me through the years: to Kathy Meneely and others at Ritter Library, for help with mountains of interlibrary loans; to Chris Sullivan, Mary Wilson, and other Computer Center staff, for help with word processing; to Fred Blumer, Hugh Burtner, and Hank Knight, my unfailingly supportive departmental colleagues; to Lynn Poland and Jim Voelz, for trying out my manuscript in the classroom and for asking me to speak to their students; to the late John Hollar, for his commitment to the manuscript, and to Timothy G. Staveteig, Kyle Halverson, and others at Fortress Press, for so graciously and capably seeing the project through to completion; to Werner Kelber and

David Rhoads, for their assistance at a crucial time; to countless college students and church audiences, who allowed me to introduce them to the experience of reading Mark's Gospel; to Susie, my wife, and Geoffrey and Amanda, my children, who gave me time to write; and to my parents, Wayne and Jo Anne Fowler, who gave me roots and wings.

One index of the reader for whom I am writing is that the text of Mark that I read is the Greek text in the 26th edition of the Nestle-Aland *Novum Testamentum Graece;* another index is that I never cite the Greek text of Mark without also providing an English translation, usually from the Revised Standard Version, sometimes from other translations, and frequently from my own translation.

Excerpt from "Qualitative Anarthrous Predicate Nouns: Mark 15:39 and John 1:1" by Philip B. Harner from *Journal of Biblical Literature* 92 (1973), pp. 75-87. Reprinted by permission.

Excerpt from *Selected Essays* by T. S. Eliot, copyright © 1950 by Harcourt Brace Jovanovich, Inc. and renewed 1978 by Esme Valerie Eliot. Reprinted by permission of Harcourt Brace Jovanovich, Inc. and Faber & Faber, Ltd.

Diagram from *Story and Discourse: Narrative Structure in Fiction and Film,* by Seymour Chatman. Copyright © 1978 Cornell University. Used by permission of the publisher, Cornell University Press.

Diagram from *The Mirror and the Lamp: Romantic Theory and the Critical Tradition,* by M. H. Abrams. Copyright © 1953 Oxford University Press. Used by permission.

Diagrams from *Style in Language,* ed. Thomas A. Sebeok. Copyright © 1960 Massachusetts Institute of Technology. Used by permission.

Diagram from *Critical Inquiry,* Vol. 3, Winter 1976, p. 370. Copyright © 1976 by the University of Chicago. Used by permission.

ABBREVIATIONS

AnBib	Analecta Biblica
BAGD	W. Bauer, W. F. Arndt, F. W. Gingrich, and F. W. Danker, *Greek-English Lexicon of the New Testament*
BDF	F. Blass, A. Debrunner, and R. W. Funk, *A Greek Grammar of the New Testament*
BETL	Bibliotheca ephemeridum theologicarum lovaniensium
CBQ	*Catholic Biblical Quarterly*
CI	*Critical Inquiry*
CP	Collection Poétique
CR	*Centennial Review*
EKKNT	Evangelisch-katholischer Kommentar zum Neuen Testament
Forum	*Foundations and Facets Forum*
FRLANT	Forschungen zur Religion und Literatur des Alten und Neuen Testaments
GNS	Good News Studies
HTR	*Harvard Theological Review*
Int	*Interpretation*
JAAR	*Journal of the American Academy of Religion*
JBL	*Journal of Biblical Literature*

JLS	*Journal of Literary Semantics*
JR	*Journal of Religion*
JTS	*Journal of Theological Studies*
LD	Lectio Divina
MLN	*Modern Language Notes*
Neophil	*Neophilologus*
Neot	*Neotestamentica*
NLH	*New Literary History*
NovT	*Novum Testamentum*
NTS	*New Testament Studies*
par.	parallel(s)
PEGLMBS	*Proceedings of the Eastern Great Lakes and Midwest Biblical Societies*
PR	*Partisan Review*
PT	*Poetics Today*
R&M	The translation of Mark's Gospel in David Rhoads and Donald Michie, *Mark as Story: An Introduction to the Narrative of a Gospel* (Philadelphia: Fortress, 1982)
RMF	The author's translation
RSV	Revised Standard Version
SBLDS	Society of Biblical Literature Dissertation Series
SBLSP	*Society of Biblical Literature Seminar Papers*
SBLSS	Society of Biblical Literature Semeia Series
SLI	*Studies in the Literary Imagination*
TDNT	G. Kittel and G. Friedrich (eds.), *Theological Dictionary of the New Testament*
THL	Theory and History of Literature
TLS	*Times Literary Supplement*
TToday	*Theology Today*

UBS	Greek text of the United Bible Societies, 3d ed.
YFS	*Yale French Studies*
YR	*Yale Review*
ZNW	*Zeitschrift für die neutestamentliche Wissenschaft*
ZTK	*Zeitschrift für Theologie und Kirche*

THE READING EXPERIENCE

This book intends to hasten the metamorphosis of my critical guild. This guild is still predominantly philological-historical in its presuppositions and practices, although in recent years significant movements into a formalist-structuralist phase and in some quarters to a poststructuralist-deconstructive phase have occurred. Here I take up the enduring legacy of philological-historical biblical criticism and more recent formalist literary criticism of the Bible to demonstrate one way we can move on from there.

Despite appearances, this book is not about the Gospel of Mark. Rather, it is a book about the experience of reading the Gospel of Mark. I shall try to demonstrate what a difference this distinction can make for biblical criticism.

My central move is to take up the critical comments made by generations of biblical critics as disguised reports of the critics' own experience of reading biblical texts. I learned this strategy especially from the early reader-response criticism of Stanley Fish. Analogous to what Fish used to say about the legacy of criticism associated with texts such as *Paradise Lost,* I claim that we have always talked about our experience of reading Mark's Gospel but have usually done so under the guise of talking about the intentions of the evangelist, the historical events or theological ideas toward which the Gospel points, or the literary structure of the Gospel, in short, in terms of almost everything except our own encounter with the text in the act of reading. By redirecting our critical focus away from the text per se and toward the reading of the text, we shall not only better understand what we have been doing all along as we were reading and talking about our reading but also gain new sensitivities that should enable us to read in new ways and achieve new insights. I am proposing the adoption of a new reader-language into which the old familiar insights into the Gospel can be translated and with which new and unfamiliar experiences of reading may become possible.

When we translate the legacy of biblical criticism into the language of readers and reading, then the history of biblical interpretation is transformed into a history of reading, that is, a reception history. We who know the history of the reception of the Gospel of Mark cannot help but read Mark within and by means of that weighty, accumulated legacy of reading experience, which extends all the way back to the first known readings of Mark—the Gospels of Matthew, Luke, and John. For me the history of the reception of the canonical Gospels is far more interesting and important than philological-historical criticism's professed interest in the history of the production of the Gospels. The Synoptic Problem, for example, has been defined classically as a problem of production history, a question of who borrowed what from whom in order to produce the Gospels. For me the more interesting and definitely more fruitful activity is reconsidering the relationship of the Gospels as a matter of reading experience, a question of which text overshadows another as we ourselves read them. In keeping with my central interpretive move in this book, I shall be pointing out how the relationship between the Gospels, as experienced in the act of reading, has frequently been discussed under the guise of a discussion about the history of the production of the Gospels. The philological-historical critic who seeks the world behind the Gospels, the world that produced the Gospels, dwells in the world in front of the Gospels and is actively contributing to an ongoing reception history. The world I explore in this book is the world that lies in front of the biblical texts—the world I live in and the world in which readers have always lived, the world of the reception of the Gospels—rather than the world of their production. My expression "the experience of reading Mark's Gospel" should always be understood as shorthand for "the experience of reading Mark's Gospel in and through the accumulated legacy of nineteen hundred years of reading history, stretching from the modern, academic criticism of the Gospels, back to the first known revisionary readings of Mark, the Gospels of Matthew, Luke, and John."

I shall not point out at every juncture how my discussion of the reading of Mark's Gospel is enmeshed in the history of reading Mark. Sometimes I shall explicitly acknowledge my precursors, but usually the critical readers whose readings of the Gospel I am interrogating at every step will have to remain unnamed. Specialists in Markan studies will have little difficulty in detecting these muted echoes of the voices of our common forebears.

NARRATIVE RHETORIC

The shift from talking about the Gospel per se to talking about the experience of reading the Gospel brings with it a number of related shifts. One is a shift away from the story of the Gospel narrative to the discourse of the narrative. Most modern readers of the Gospel have focused upon the *story level* of the narrative—the characters, events, and settings within the narrative. Consequently, they have failed to reckon adequately with the *discourse level* or the *rhetoric* of the narrative—the ways in which the language of the narrative attempts to weave its spell over the reader. To be sure, the discourse has always been there, trying to weave its spell over us, and all along we have been responding to its direct and indirect leadings, but we have not been attentive to what it was trying to do to us or to how we were responding to it. Therefore, I will focus on the much too neglected discourse level of the Gospel. As I hope to demonstrate, in the history of reading Mark's Gospel its rhetoric has been obscured by the shadows of the longer and more illustrative Gospels of Matthew, Luke, and John. Discovering the rhetoric of Mark's Gospel requires discovering simultaneously the competing discourses of its strong successors.

A shift in focus from story to discourse encourages at the same time a shift away from looking for a static structure in the text and toward an awareness of the dynamic, temporal experience of reading the text. Reading takes place through time, and the rhetorical effects of narrative are often the cumulative effects of the temporal experience of reading. Then, once this experience is the focus of criticism, the meaning of meaning also needs to be reinterpreted. No longer can meaning be understood to be a stable, determinate content that lies buried within the text, awaiting excavation. Rather, meaning becomes a dynamic event in which we ourselves participate. Furthermore, the shift from meaning-as-content to meaning-as-event leads us to understand the workings of the language of the Gospel in new ways. No longer can the language of the Gospel be regarded as primarily referential or informative; it has become rhetorical, affective, and powerful.

To attempt to orchestrate all of these shifts in biblical criticism, I have forged a critical amalgam of reader-response criticism, narratology, rhetorical criticism, and insights from orality and textuality studies. To some, these approaches are already familiar, but for others this book will be their introduction to a foreign set of tools. To some this may appear to be bricolage, a jumble of literary-critical odds and ends. My response is simple and pragmatic: I use this assortment of critical tools because I find that they complement each other nicely and especially because they work well on the problems with which I have to deal.

A BRIDGE-BUILDING EFFORT

Obviously, this project is a contribution to the larger dialogue taking place today between biblical scholarship and literary theory and criticism. I have dreamed that these separate realms might one day be fused into a single continuous realm stretching to the distant horizon, but this dream is not likely to be realized anytime soon. The gulf that separates us is wider than I once thought. On the one hand, the biblical scholar who ventures over to the literary-critical shore may be chided for not following the latest critical fashion or for mixing up literary-critical apples and oranges. On the other hand, the literary critic who ventures onto the turf of the biblical critic is likely to make

similarly egregious blunders in the eyes of that guild through not knowing
their modus operandi. Our respective guilds are different cultures, separated
by different histories, languages, and concerns. Nevertheless, I am eager to
build a bridge, one that will be most useful to fellow biblical scholars seeking
access to the rhetorical and reader-oriented district on the literary-critical side
of the gulf, but one that literary critics as well may use, especially if they
would like to learn how we biblical scholars have been reading Mark's Gospel
for the past few centuries.

Others are welcome to use the bridge, too. Most reading of the Bible
takes place outside the boundaries of academic biblical or literary criticism—
in churches, Bible study groups, and private study and devotion. The modern
critical reading of the Bible came into being by striking a pose of critical
distance from such reverent reading, but the blessings of modern biblical
criticism have been mixed. Under one common scenario, the quest for greater
depth and subtlety in understanding drew reverent Bible readers to embrace
criticism, which indeed deepened and enriched their devotional reading of
the Bible, and reverent reading and critical reading lived happily together.
Under another common scenario, however, reverent readers and critical readers
of the Bible have come to a parting of the ways and heaped scorn and ridicule
upon each other. Perhaps the time has come to bridge the gulf between these
often estranged communities of Bible readers. I hope my work will in some
small way help to bring together reverent and critical readers of Mark's Gospel.

RHETORICAL STRATEGIES

Because this book is about learning to read with an ear attuned to the rhetoric
of Mark's Gospel, some comments about my own rhetoric are in order. My
major strategy in this book is to translate traditional philological-historical
comments about the Gospel of Mark into comments about the experience of
reading the Gospel of Mark. I also strive to persuade my reader to focus on
the discourse as opposed to the story of the Gospel narrative, on the temporal
experience of reading rather than the static structure of the text, and on the
omnipresent reception history of the Gospel rather than its lost production
history. These moves are conducted explicitly and aboveboard, my own version
of a rhetoric of direction.

I shall use less direct strategies as well. In the language game that I play
in this book, I shall be playing more than one role. Sometimes, while playing
the role of a reader, I shall be so bold as to offer a concretization of the text
based upon my own experience of reading the text. Implicitly, I invite my
reader to exercise some critical judgment over against my reading experience.
At other times, while playing the role of the critic, I shall point out rhetorical
strategies in Mark's text and the moves they seem to invite a reader to perform,
but then I shall step back and leave it to my own reader to make these

interpretive moves. That is, at times I shall slip into the role of a reader, implicitly inviting my reader to play the role of a critic, and at other times I shall slip into the role of a critic, implicitly inviting my reader to play the role of a reader. I shall orchestrate a dialogue between the act of reading and the criticism of the act of reading.

I shall not deal with the entire text of the Gospel the way a philological-historical commentary does. This book is therefore not a complete reading of Mark. Rather, it is a collection of hints, suggestions, and illustrations of how one might go about reading Mark. An entrée into the reading of Mark is offered rather than the last word on the subject.

Another way in which I shall gently nudge my reader into an active engagement with my text, as well as Mark's, is by leaving the gender of the reader of my text, as well as Mark's, an open question. That is, I have good reasons for my seemingly inconsistent use of masculine and feminine pronouns. I shall not force a bland but consistent "she or he" upon my reader at every turn. I refer to the reader of Mark as a "he" whenever that reader is either myself or the masculine implied reader that I suspect the masculine implied author of this Gospel has in mind. My suspicion that the implied author and the implied reader of the Gospel are both masculine is only a suspicion, however; only a native speaker would be able to discern confidently whether the Gospel is written in a masculine or feminine register of Koine Greek, and such native speakers have not lived for centuries. Women do read Mark's Gospel, so Mark's reader and my reader today may well be male or female, and will be so designated occasionally. For this and other good reasons, Who is the reader? should always remain an open question.

PART ONE

READER-
RESPONSE
CRITICISM

1

DISCOVERING THE READING
EXPERIENCE

Literary critics have until recently given slight attention to the reader and the reading experience. To cite one glaring example, Robert Scholes and Robert Kellogg, in *The Nature of Narrative,* describe narrative as "distinguished by two characteristics: the presence of a story and a storyteller. . . . For writing to be narrative no more and no less than a teller and a tale are required."[1] Someone to hear the story or, in the case of literature, someone to read it was apparently too obvious to mention. Yet why tell a story if no one is there to listen to it? Who writes a story not expecting it to be read? Even the storyteller who speaks or writes only to himself has himself as an audience. Hence, we must correct Scholes and Kellogg by saying that a narrative always has, minimally, a storyteller, a tale, and an audience or reader, if only an audience or readership of one. This common modern neglect of the role of the hearer or the reader in the narrative transaction is rapidly being remedied in current literary criticism,[2] and I shall strive to contribute to the remedy in the case of the criticism of the Gospel of Mark.

The neglect of the reader and the reading experience in modern literary criticism may strike us as odd because every reader knows intuitively that reading or hearing a story can be a powerful experience. The classic stories that we revere with the label *literature* are especially affecting, but so are the mundane stories that we hear every day, including jokes. We know that a well-told joke leads us down a path, only to have something unforeseen spring

1. Robert Scholes and Robert Kellogg, *The Nature of Narrative* (New York: Oxford University Press, 1966), 4.
2. "The Age of Criticism, which reached its zenith in the mid-decades of this century, has given way to the Age of Reading, and whereas the American new critics and European formalists of the Age of Criticism discovered the work-as-such, current literary theorists have discovered the reader-as-such" (M. H. Abrams, "How to Do Things with Texts," *PT* 46 [1979]: 566–88). Cf. Terry Eagleton, *Literary Theory: An Introduction* (Minneapolis: University of Minnesota Press, 1983), 74.

9

out at us. If a joke is told badly and the punch line hinted at, then the force of the story is diminished or destroyed altogether; if the storyteller can keep us in suspense, then we are drawn into the net that the story weaves around us. Even the reader who suspects that the following is a joke may not avoid being caught in the story's net.

> A man died and went to the nether regions. There the head devil told him he could take his pick of three rooms in which to spend eternity. The devil opened the first door, and revealed thousands of men standing on their heads on a brick floor. The man told the devil that he didn't want to spend eternity doing that. So the devil opened another door, and there were thousands of men standing on their heads on a wooden floor. Although the man thought that was better, he still wanted to see the third possibility. The devil opened a third door, and there were thousands of men standing up to their ankles in a foul substance. Each was drinking a cup of coffee.
> "That stuff they're standing in is horrible," the fellow said, "but I prefer this room to the other two."
> So he walked into the room and the door slammed behind him. Just then, an assistant devil hollered, "Okay, coffee break is over. All you guys go back to standing on your heads!"[3]

The referentially minded critic looks at this story and says that it is about the man in the story, who is ensnared by his own gullible presuppositions. The reader-oriented critic looks at this story and says that it is really about the reader of the story, who is ensnared by his or her own gullible presuppositions. The real victim of the story, in other words, is not its imaginary character but the real hearer or reader experiencing the story.

At the most superficial level, the aims of the joke and of the Gospel of Mark are similar: both seek to do something to the hearer or reader. In particular, both stories use covert means to induce an understanding or a belief in the reader or hearer. What they then do with the belief they have elicited differs immensely. The joke induces a belief to deceive the hearer only momentarily, until the deception is dropped and the belief exploded in an instant of comic revelation. The Gospel of Mark is also designed to elicit belief, but a belief that bids to have a profound and lasting significance for the reader's life and to persist long after the initial encounter with the story. In other words, both stories use the rhetorical resources of narrative to affect the reader, but the aim of Mark's Gospel is more difficult to achieve. The joke is designed to seduce us temporarily; the Gospel is designed to seduce us permanently.

THE EXPERIENCE OF READING MARK

I first became sensitive to the experience of reading Mark's Gospel in the course of writing *Loaves and Fishes: The Function of the Feeding Stories in*

---

3. Taken from *Reader's Digest* (February 1979), 127, which credits Ashley Cooper, in the Charleston, S.C., *News and Courier*.

the Gospel of Mark,[4] in which I examined a puzzling pair of episodes, the Feeding of the Five Thousand (Mark 6:30-44) and the Feeding of the Four Thousand (Mark 8:1-10). The puzzling thing about these episodes is that they are so similar. The standard scholarly explanation of the two stories has been that they are variants of a single traditional story that somehow got included twice in Mark's Gospel. After all, in the first of the two incidents, the disciples do not have the foggiest idea of how Jesus or anyone else might feed a hungry crowd of five thousand in the wilderness, but he nevertheless feeds the crowd, with the disciples' help; when the second feeding incident occurs, the disciples again reveal that they do not know what Jesus is capable of doing with a few loaves of bread. Such denseness, such stupidity, could not be part of the author's design, could it? Many modern critics have resisted a reading of these episodes that would find the disciples thoroughly obtuse or hardheaded, even though the storyteller gives clear hints that the episodes should be read that way (see, e.g., Mark 6:52 and 8:14-21). In the tandem feeding episodes, we encounter a masterful exercise of the storyteller's craft that includes, most importantly, the rhetorical use of irony. The author develops a strong ironic tension between the two feeding stories by having the disciples show their lack of understanding not once but twice. The irony is especially noteworthy when, in the midst of the second story, they look at the hungry crowd, consider the presence of just a few loaves and fishes, and say to Jesus, who has already fed one giant crowd in their presence and with their assistance, "How can one feed such a crowd here in the desert?" (8:4). Although the author does not comment on the stupidity of this statement, any reader is bound to observe it, ponder it, and try to understand why the disciples do not understand.

We are dealing here with what Wayne Booth calls the rhetoric of irony, an author's use of irony to communicate with the reader and get the reader to see certain things the author's way, by covert, indirect means.[5] Early in Booth's book on the rhetoric of irony, he specifically points out a famous moment of irony in the Gospel of Mark. In the crucifixion scene, bystanders mock Jesus as he hangs dying on the cross and say things such as, "He saved others; he cannot save himself. Let the Christ, the King of Israel, come down now from the cross, that we may see and believe" (15:31-32). Here the irony is double, operating at two levels. At one level the mockers are saying things ironically; they mockingly call Jesus the Christ, the King of Israel. The second level of irony is that, hidden from the characters in the story, their mocking words are true. The reader cannot mistake the storyteller's conviction that Jesus really is the Christ, the King of Israel.[6]

4. Robert M. Fowler, *Loaves and Fishes: The Function of the Feeding Stories in the Gospel of Mark,* SBLDS 54 (Chico, Calif.: Scholars Press, 1981).

5. Wayne C. Booth, *A Rhetoric of Irony* (Chicago: University of Chicago Press, 1974); Fowler, *Loaves and Fishes,* 91–99 and passim.

6. Booth, *Rhetoric of Irony,* 28–29.

Wayne Booth is particularly helpful to readers of Mark's Gospel when he points out further implications of the rhetorical strategy in this scene. He observes that the covertness of irony presents an interpretive challenge to the reader. If the reader is able to see through the double irony—to perceive the genuine convictions of the storyteller—the reader is liable to congratulate himself on his perceptiveness without realizing that the storyteller has induced him to see things from the storyteller's perspective. Moreover, all persons reading the Gospel, to the extent that they see through the irony, become a community—a community not bound together by ties of race, culture, or politics but by the common experience of reading and coming to terms with Mark's irony. By means of ironic narrative, Mark probably creates a more cohesive readership than he could have by means of plain, straightforward claims about Christ.

Booth's most significant accomplishment is his helpful discussion of the experience readers go through, first, to recognize the use of irony in literature and, second, to reconstruct what the author really intends to communicate by means of the irony. In my earlier work I discussed and made use of the four-step process of recognizing irony and reconstructing the meaning behind it that Booth suggests we all use intuitively:

> *Step one.* The reader is required to reject the literal meaning.
> *Step two.* Alternative interpretations or explanations are tried out.
> *Step three.* A decision must therefore be made about the author's knowledge or beliefs.
> *Step four.* Having made a decision about the knowledge or beliefs of the speaker, we can finally choose a new meaning or cluster of meanings with which we can rest secure.[7]

Especially important is step three, when the reader makes a decision about where the author really stands on the matter at hand. Booth supplies a shrewd discussion of the various "clues to irony" that enable the reader to detect when and how an author is using irony. Booth's explanations of the authorial use of clues to irony, together with his classic discussion of the authorial use of "reliable commentary" in *The Rhetoric of Fiction,* represent one of the best primers in reader-oriented criticism available today.[8]

For all of the usefulness of Booth's treatment of irony, however, it has its limitations, at least in its applicability to the Gospel of Mark. First of all, Booth is concerned primarily with verbal irony, whereby narrators of stories

---

7. Ibid., 100–12; Fowler, *Loaves and Fishes,* 94–96.

8. Booth, *Rhetoric of Irony,* 47–86; idem, *The Rhetoric of Fiction,* 2d ed. (Chicago and London: University of Chicago Press, 1983), 169–266; Fowler, *Loaves and Fishes,* 154–57. There is much truth in Frank Kermode's comment that Wayne Booth is the "rejected father" of contemporary reader-oriented criticism ("The Reader's Share," *TLS* [July 11, 1975]: 751–52).

or characters within stories speak ironically. He is not primarily concerned with the irony of situations or events, which often manifests itself in the theater and in literature as dramatic irony, whereby characters within the story speak or act in such a way that the audience alone perceives an ironic incongruity between the words or deeds of the characters and other elements of the story. That Booth talks about dramatic irony only briefly and in passing is unfortunate and a little surprising, because he does discuss some famous and powerful instances of dramatic irony, including the crucifixion scene in Mark and Mark Antony's speech in *Julius Caesar*.[9] Because these two examples of dramatic irony are coincidentally also instances of verbal irony (i.e., these both happen to be instances of double irony), Booth is able to pull such instances of dramatic irony into an orbit around his sun of verbal irony. Although he observes the importance of the two layers of irony in the rhetoric of Mark's crucifixion scene, he stops short of saying that this moment in the reading of Mark is powerful precisely because of its *dramatic* irony.

An additional limitation is that Booth restricts his attention, at least in the first two-thirds of the book, to verbal ironies that are "intended," "covert," "stable," and "finite." In other words, he spends most of his time dealing with those ironies for which we can come to a resolution of the ironic incongruity and "rest secure" on a "stable," "reconstructed" meaning. His careful and considered choice of the metaphor of reconstruction is noteworthy. He is concerned primarily with ironies from which meaning can be reconstructed that takes us above and beyond the ironic utterance with which we began. Most important, this reconstructed meaning is stable—it does not jump or shift around once reconstructed—and it is finite—its meaning is limited in scope.

Only late in his book does he deal with ironies that are not predominantly stable or finite. Although Booth allows for a spectrum of irony ranging from the stable and finite to the unstable and infinite, he concentrates so much on the former that his abrupt shift to the latter late in the book seems to imply a de facto dichotomy between the two extremes, and his discomfort with unstable or infinite ironies is ill disguised.

The examples of irony he cites do tend to get pushed to one end or the other of the spectrum. Some of his unstable and infinite ironies do not seem quite as unstable or infinite—and therefore not quite as vertiginous—as Booth suggests, and sometimes his examples of stable and finite ironies are not as stable or finite as he says. Good examples of the latter include many instances of dramatic irony that are relatively stable and limited in scope but nevertheless do not lend themselves to final resolution or reconstruction. Because dramatic irony involves the audience in perceiving incongruity that the characters in the story do not perceive, it always has a two-layered structure to it, a built-in dialectical relationship between what is not understood within the story

9. Booth, *Rhetoric of Irony*, 42, 63–67.

and what is understood in the audience's encounter with the story. Even when
the audience can establish rather securely what is happening in the story, the
incongruity between the story and the audience's experience of the story lingers
and never really dissipates. To be sure, a certain degree of resolution takes
place when the audience perceives an incongruity between elements of the
story, but Booth's language of reconstruction, which suggests that the resolution of the irony is complete and final, is much too strong for use here. In
visual metaphors, with dramatic irony we simultaneously see and see through
the ironic incongruity, which requires the exercise of a kind of double vision;
perhaps we can think of such irony as a kind of double exposure on a pho-
tographic plate.[10] An apt oral-aural metaphor is reverberation: After the audience comprehends the distance opened up between it and the undiscerning
character, the irony continues to reverberate in the gap between the story and
the audience. Dramatic irony is inherently reverberatory.[11]

In spite of these limitations in Booth's *A Rhetoric of Irony,* his book
remains the best discussion available of the rhetorical use of irony in literature
and our experience of irony as readers. Leonard Thompson, in *Introducing
Biblical Literature,* picks up and discusses Booth's remarks on the irony of
the crucifixion scene in Mark, but he uses the broader expression "rhetoric
of indirection" to describe Mark's strategy in this scene and elsewhere in the
Gospel.[12] His comments suggest another way in which Booth's work is too
limited for purposes of dealing with Mark's Gospel, which contains many
other forms of indirection besides irony. Thompson observes the major roles
metaphor and paradox play in Mark's rhetoric. Unfortunately, Thompson's
discussion of Mark's rhetoric of indirection is tantalizingly brief. Thus, in my
exploration of Mark's rhetoric of indirection, I am following a path blazed
by Booth and traveled by Thompson but not fully explored by either.

OBSERVING THE EXPERIENCE

Booth's discussion of the rhetorical use of irony in Mark's account of the
crucifixion provides important clues for the analysis of the rhetoric of the

10. All of these visual metaphors are used by D. C. Muecke, *Irony and the Ironic,* 2d ed.,
The Critical Idiom 13 (London and New York: Methuen, 1982), 45, 69.

11. "Reverberatory irony" is an expression used by David H. Richter ("The Reader as Ironic
Victim," *Novel* 14 [1981]:135–51), but I use the term differently (see chap. 7).

12. Leonard L. Thompson, *Introducing Biblical Literature: A More Fantastic Country* (En-
glewood Cliffs, N.J.: Prentice-Hall, 1978), 223–31. Thompson does not acknowledge his inspiration for the expression "rhetoric of indirection." It is strongly reminiscent of Søren Kierkegaard's theory of "indirect communication"; for a convenient collection of references to the
relevant passages in Kierkegaard's writings and in the critical literature on Kierkegaard, see *Søren
Kierkegaard's Journals and Papers,* ed. and trans. Howard J. Hong and Edna H. Hong (Bloomington: Indiana University Press, 1967–68) 2:596–97. Wayne Booth (*Rhetoric of Irony,* xii–xiii)
pays great respect to Kierkegaard's master's thesis, *The Concept of Irony, with Constant Reference
to Socrates,* trans. Lee M. Capel (Bloomington: Indiana University Press, 1965).

entire Gospel. He is by no means the first, however, to observe salient reading experiences the author of the Gospel puts the reader through. Virtually all modern interpreters of the Gospel have observed and commented perceptively upon the experience of reading Mark's Gospel, but we have not been very self-conscious about having made such comments because they have often been disguised as comments about other things.

Some time ago I fell into the habit of taking note of places in the scholarly literature on Mark where critics mention the reader or the reading experience. I soon found that marking with red pencil the comments about what "the reader knows," "the reader infers," "the reader questions," "the reader learns," "the reader recalls," and so on littered most articles and monographs. I found also that the critic's avowed methodological approach did not make much difference; a scholar dedicated to historical inquiry would offer the same kinds of observations regarding the experience of reading Mark as would a literary critic.[13] In spite of their differences, apparently their reading experiences are often similar. The text imposes powerful constraints upon the reading experience, constraints that to this point have been acknowledged only sporadically and unsystematically. Now is the time to make the text's impact on the reader an object of careful, critical scrutiny. In looking intentionally at the reader and the reading experience, I am trying to do consciously and carefully what critics of Mark's Gospel have always done unknowingly and haphazardly. I shall demonstrate that the scholarly literature on Mark is full of perceptive comments on the reading of Mark by looking at some noteworthy examples. In order to lay the groundwork for that discussion, I need first to discuss an important passage in Mark that we shall return to frequently and also to introduce in the process some helpful terminology.

In historical-critical scholarship, a common practice is to comment upon the differences between Mark's version of Jesus' baptism (Mark 1:9-11) and the parallel accounts in the other Gospels, which are thought to be dependent on Mark's version. Commentators suggest that Mark portrays the baptism, the rending of the heavens, the descent of the spirit, and the proclamation of the heavenly voice as a kind of private, revelatory experience that Jesus alone undergoes. After all, when the heavenly voice speaks, it addresses Jesus directly in the second person, and nothing in the story indicates that anyone else sees or hears anything. In Matthew, however, the voice speaks in the third person, not to Jesus but about Jesus (Matt. 3:17), in what seems to be more of a public acclamation than a private, direct address.

Commentators have been so pleased to have noticed the use of the second-person pronoun in Mark and the change to the third-person in Matthew—seemingly the difference between a private and a public statement—that they

---

13. See the reading observations I collected from the work of Howard Clark Kee (a historical critic) and Norman R. Petersen (a literary critic) in Fowler, *Loaves and Fishes,* 150–51.

have often neglected to observe someone else who hears the heavenly voice in Mark's account: the reader of the story. Indeed, both the storyteller and the recipient of the story are on the scene when Jesus hears the heavenly voice. To describe accurately what is going on here in Mark's narrative, we can use Seymour Chatman's distinction between the story and the discourse of a narrative.[14] *Story* refers to the what of a narrative—its settings, characters, happenings, and actions; *discourse* refers to the how of the narrative—how the narrative is told, employing the resources of narrative rhetoric. Roughly, *story* refers to the content of the narrative, and *discourse* refers to how the content is communicated. Using this terminology, we may say that in Mark, even though Jesus is the only character at the level of story to hear the heavenly voice, at the level of discourse the storyteller makes sure that the reader hears the voice, too. An awareness of what is or is not happening, both in the story and in the discourse, is crucial for understanding the workings of any narrative, especially the Gospel of Mark.

Concentration on the experience of reading not only leads to a greater awareness of what is transpiring on both the story and discourse levels but also helps us to be more aware of the ways in which acquaintance with one Gospel influences the reading of another Gospel. In discussions of Mark's baptism episode, for example, the spirit is usually said to descend "upon" Jesus. A more literal rendering of the Greek preposition *eis,* however, would have the spirit descend "into" Jesus. Each of the other evangelists uses *epi,* "upon," describing a more genteel resting of the spirit upon Jesus, and this understanding has usually been read into Mark, but inappropriately, because Mark is portraying for us a person being invaded and possessed by a spirit. In Mark, Jesus becomes spirit-possessed. See, for example, Mark 1:12, where the spirit within Jesus throws him out (*ekballō*) into the desert. Jesus has not so much acquired a spirit; rather, a spirit has acquired Jesus. In the baptism scene Mark is laying the basis for a debate that will arise later in the Gospel. Whether Jesus is spirit-possessed is not a question in Mark but rather whether the spirit in him is good or evil, from God or Satan (Mark 3:20-35). The storyteller nowhere clarifies explicitly the nature of Jesus' spirit possession but provides ample clues for the reader to figure out the puzzle.

I have already mentioned a puzzle or an ambiguity in Mark 1:10, 12 that has been clarified and thereby obscured by Matthew and Luke. Mark refers simply to "the spirit"; no adjective gives specificity to the noun or removes possible ambiguity. Although the reader has to infer that the spirit is "holy," doing so is easy because the spirit comes from heaven and a heavenly voice (itself ambiguous) accompanies it. By contrast, Matthew and Luke are careful to specify for the reader that the spirit is "of God" (Matt. 3:16) or "holy"

14. Seymour Chatman, *Story and Discourse: Narrative Structure in Fiction and Film* (Ithaca, N.Y., and London: Cornell University Press, 1978), 9 and passim.

(Luke 3:22), and forevermore Matthew and Luke's specificity is read back into Mark, where it is an intrusion, although perhaps an invited one; Mark's narrative seems to invite the kind of clarification or demystification so frequently provided by Matthew and Luke.[15] Unlike Matthew and Luke, Mark is comfortable with telling a story rich with ambiguity; he likes to offer puzzles for the reader to solve. In fact, the Gospels of Matthew and Luke may represent the earliest evidence we have of people who have responded to the challenge of the puzzles in Mark by retelling Mark's story with the ambiguities clarified and the ironies dissolved. They are the first known and still the most influential readers of Mark's Gospel.

READING WITH MORTON ENSLIN

Even without the distinction between story and discourse, interpreters have occasionally noticed how the discourse of 1:9-11 functions for the reader. One such interpreter is Morton Enslin, who, in his 1947 article, "The Artistry of Mark," defended the storytelling skills of the author of Mark's Gospel long before this stance became fashionable.[16]

One place where the narrative artistry of Mark is especially in evidence, Enslin says, is in the introductory verses of the Gospel (1:1-15), which he observes are aimed primarily at the reader of the Gospel.[17] Specifically with regard to the baptism scene, Enslin observes that

> here in this explicit reference to one individual, by name Jesus, who came to John, and the resultant spectacular revelation from heaven—represented as coming to Jesus alone but vividly before the eyes of the reader—we learn without being told in so many words that it is Jesus who is this "mightier one" and of his relationship to God. And this is essential as a prelude to the story of the tragic clash, the pathetic obtuseness, and the seeming defeat which is to follow.[18]

Curiously, however, even though Enslin emphasizes that Mark 1:1-15 is aimed primarily at the reader, by the time he gets to Jesus' proclamation of the Kingdom of God in 1:14-15, the reader has faded from his view. Enslin has shifted his attention away from the discourse of the narrative, aimed at the reader, to the story of the narrative, in which "Jesus is made to epitomize his message" in 1:14-15.[19] Enslin's attention might have been directed back

---

15. John's Gospel also offers an episode that serves to clarify the ambiguities in Mark's baptism episode. John's Gospel has *John the Baptist* report *his* witnessing of the spirit's descent upon Jesus, after what seems to have been *the Baptist's* own private audition of the heavenly voice (John 1:29-34).

16. Morton S. Enslin, "The Artistry of Mark," *JBL* 66 (1947): 385–99.

17. Ibid., 393–94.

18. Ibid., 395.

19. Ibid., 396.

to the level of discourse where he began if he had asked but one question here: By whom is Jesus "made to epitomize his message," and for whom does this epitome function? Enslin forfeited a chance to observe that the storyteller makes Jesus epitomize his message and that the recipient of the story alone is in a position to appreciate Mark 1:14-15 as an epitome. No less than 1:1-13, Mark 1:14-15 is aimed primarily at the reader and accentuates the discourse level.

Another way to frame the question of the narrative function of 1:1-15 is to consider what J. L. Austin called "uptake."[20] Who takes up 1:14-15 as an epitome of the entire narrative? Who is in a position to appreciate the force of this utterance? Only the reader. No one in the story, except Jesus, witnesses the descent of the spirit in 1:10 or hears the epitome of the narrative in 1:15. Uptake occurs only at the level of discourse, and none, except possibly for Jesus, occurs at the level of story.

What has happened in Enslin's reading experience is that, after having achieved some critical awareness of the experience of reading the first thirteen verses of Mark, in 1:14-15 he ceases to observe critically his own experience of reading and instead begins to read. Critical distance collapses, and the former critic of the reading experience submits to the spell of the narrative and becomes a reader. Whereas in his discussion of 1:1-13 he notes how a reader must draw inferences from a narrative that is frequently laconic and ambiguous, in his discussion of 1:14-15 he abandons himself to the act of inferring itself. The inferences he draws from 1:14-15—that Satan has met defeat, that Jesus' forty days in the desert are meant to parallel Israel's forty years of wilderness wandering, that Jesus' message in verse 15 is a victory proclamation—are all eminently defensible, but they are inferences never-theless. Making such inferences is one of the things we must do when we read, and Mark is so good at spurring us to do it that it is hard to step back from the act of reading in order to be a critic of the act of reading. The discourse of the narrative is so seductive that we tend to look past it and become caught up in the story of the narrative.

20. The *locus classicus* for "uptake" is in J. L. Austin's *How to Do Things with Words:* "I cannot be said to have warned an audience unless it hears what I say and takes what I say in a certain sense. An effect must be achieved on the audience if the illocutionary act is to be carried out. How should we best put it here? And how can we limit it? Generally the effect amounts to bringing about the understanding of the meaning and of the force of the locution. So the performance of an illocutionary act involves the securing of *uptake.*" (*How to Do Things with Words,* ed. J. O. Urmson and Marina Sbisà, 2d ed. [Cambridge: Harvard University Press, 1975], 117–18).

Or more concretely, in a reference by Stanley Fish to Shaw's *Major Barbara:* "Barbara does not need to accept the gift [of five thousand pounds to the Salvation Army] in order to complete the promise; it is complete as soon as it is understood to be one. The word for this understanding is 'uptake' ('Ah, so that's what he's doing') . . ." (Stanley Fish, *Is There a Text in This Class? The Authority of Interpretive Communities* [Cambridge: Harvard University Press, 1980], 224).

Even the critic who fails to observe that Mark 1:1-15 is designed to function primarily for the reader may at least comment on the unmistakable influence the first verse of the Gospel wields over the reader's perception of the entire Gospel. It functions for the reader as a descriptive title to the whole work, declaring, "The Beginning of the Gospel of Jesus Christ, the Son of God." In a way it tells the reader exactly what the author's main thesis is, and as a result any confusion, secrecy, or misunderstanding about Jesus in the story strikes the reader as ironic because the reader always perceives the incongruity between the confusion about who Jesus is in the story and the relative clarity about who Jesus is in the mind of the storyteller. A great deal of confusion, secrecy, and misunderstanding concerning Jesus takes place at the level of the story, and it has been a major topic in Markan scholarship—perhaps the major topic—since William Wrede's *The Messianic Secret in the Gospels*.[21] Scholars since Wrede have struggled to solve the puzzle of the Messianic Secret in Mark, which has usually been described in this way: in Mark, Jesus is Messiah, but that knowledge is hushed up in the story, or at least an attempt is made to do so. Even when the attempts at secrecy fail, as they frequently do, the resulting perceptions on the part of characters in the story are still garbled, confused, or insincere. In Mark's Gospel Jesus is undoubtedly the Messiah, but no one in the story seems capable of understanding that fact properly.

A few scholars have observed that the storyteller lays his trump card on the table in the first verse, so the Messianic Secret never really exists—as far as the reader is concerned. Nils Dahl once observed that "the Christ-mystery is a secret only for those persons who appear in the book. The readers know the point of the story from the very beginning: it is the Gospel of Jesus Christ."[22] Quentin Quesnell comments that "in 8:27ff. the disciples recognize Jesus as the Christ for the first time. The reader has known that he is the Christ since at least 1:1. The reader knows more about him—that he is the Son of God (1:1, 11)."[23] These scholars are saying that the secrecy and confusion about the identity of Jesus exist only at the story level. At the discourse level, the storyteller informs the reader of the identity of Jesus in the first verse. The problem of the Messianic Secret is that the reader's perceptions do not square with the characters' perceptions. The Messianic Secret is, in other words, a phenomenon in the experience of reading and a

21. William Wrede, *Das Messiasgeheimnis in den Evangelien: Zugleich ein Beitrag zum Verständnis des Markusevangeliums*, 3d ed. (1st ed. 1901) (Göttingen: Vandenhoeck & Ruprecht, 1963); Eng. trans.: *The Messianic Secret*, trans. J. C. G. Greig (Cambridge and London: James Clarke, 1971).

22. Nils A. Dahl, "The Purpose of Mark's Gospel," *Jesus in the Memory of the Early Church* (Minneapolis: Augsburg, 1976), 56.

23. Quentin Quesnell, *The Mind of Mark: Interpretation and Method Through the Exegesis of Mark 6:52*, AnBib 38 (Rome: Pontifical Biblical Institute, 1969), 132.

matter of the reader seeing and understanding, if not always what the characters do not understand, then at least that they do not understand.[24] Thanks to the narrator's discourse, the reader sees and understands many things that characters in the story do not.

Recognition of this incongruity between the discourse and the story occurs repeatedly in the reading experience. Insofar as modern biblical critics have focused on the story level of the narrative and the historical events or theological concepts that the narrative has been thought to point to, however, we have not been able to focus on the experience of reading the narrative, which has to do principally with the reader's encounter with the narrator's discourse. Quesnell, Dahl, Enslin, and others have made perceptive observations about the experience of reading the introduction to the Gospel of Mark, but they have lacked an adequate critical language with which to express their observations and to follow up on them with further reflection and inquiry. Distinguishing between story and discourse and then concentrating on the reader's uptake of the discourse illuminate us by allowing us to examine how a reader comes to apprehend the congruity or incongruity of what is known or understood on these respective levels. If a perennial puzzle such as the Messianic Secret is understood as the reader's encounter with a fundamental incongruity between story and discourse, then the interpretive puzzles frequently linked to the Messianic Secret (e.g., the failure of the disciples, the Markan parable theory, and the abrupt ending of the Gospel) are also most likely not puzzles in the story per se but puzzles encountered in the reading of the story.

READING WITH WALTER ERNEST BUNDY

In 1942 Walter Ernest Bundy published "Dogma and Drama in the Gospel of Mark."[25] Bundy's use of the word *drama* in connection with Mark is especially apt, not because the Gospel is modeled after ancient Greek drama, but because it is dramatic. It is an action-filled narrative played out with its audience always foremost in mind. The action of the story can often be imagined being enacted before our eyes, on a stage.

For example, Bundy recognizes, as have Enslin and others, that the baptism scene is directed toward the reader.[26] Mark 1:9-11 is only the first of three climactic acclamations of Jesus as Son of God in the Gospel, however. Besides the baptism scene, the heavenly voice also acclaims Jesus in the transfiguration episode (9:2-8), and at the death of Jesus a Roman centurion proclaims him Son of God (15:39). These latter two scenes, no less than the

24. On the Messianic Secret as a phenomenon in the experience of reading, see my article "Irony and the Messianic Secret in the Gospel of Mark," *PEGLMBS* 1 (1981): 26–36, ed. Phillip Sigal.

25. Walter Ernest Bundy, "Dogma and Drama in the Gospel of Mark," in *New Testament Studies*, ed. Edwin Prince Booth (Nashville: Abingdon Press, 1942), 70–94.

26. Ibid., 74.

baptism, function primarily for the reader: "In these scenes, Jesus, the three disciples, and the centurion are only the dramatic subjects. In each case the reader of Mark is the actual subject; it is he who sees and hears, in imagination, the unfolding drama, as a spectator might witness it enacted on a stage."[27]

In these and other episodes the characters on the stage with Jesus demonstrate no grasp of the action taking place before their eyes. What Bundy observes regarding one episode could easily apply to many in the Gospel: "What Mark depicts in 1:23-27 no contemporary eye ever saw; no contemporary ear ever heard. The scene is calculated solely for Mark's readers; it is they, not those assembled in the Capernaum synagogue, who are the real witnesses. This, of course, is familiar dramatic technique. The reader is again let in on a secret which the evident action of the story does not disclose. . . ."[28]

In other words, to combine Bundy's dramatic analogy with Austin's terminology, frequently in Mark the characters on the stage show no signs of uptake. Only the audience witnessing the drama is in a position to grasp what is happening on the stage; only among the audience is uptake occurring.

Bundy has even been able to observe that the three crystal-clear predictions of Jesus' death (8:31; 9:31; 10:32-34) secure no uptake within the story; if they have any function at all in the narrative, they function to alert the reader to what lies ahead:

> The same formula is solemnly intoned three times for dramatic effect. These predictions are not organic to the action of this section of Mark but appear rather as separate and independent units superimposed upon the traditional materials. Mark seeks to endow them with some life and color by adding editorial introductions and conclusions; but they still leave the impression of being detached monologues, dramatic asides, for the benefit of the reader. They have no bearing on the behavior or attitudes of the actors in the story when the catastrophe, here academically announced, actually strikes. They prepare the readers, not Jesus or the disciples, for what is to come.[29]

Bundy has seen what few have, that vast portions of the Gospel function for the reader *alone*. He has not exhausted the possibilities, however. To whom are the generalizing summary statements made in the narrative, if not to the reader? Are not the references to the future beyond the end of the story actually references to the present moment of reading? Are not the references to "gospel" within the story to be discerned by the reader as self-reflexive allusions to the "Gospel," the narrative being read? Who watches and prays with Jesus in Gethsemane, if not the reader? Who breaks the final silence of 16:8, if not the reader?

27. Ibid., 81.
28. Ibid., 84–85.
29. Ibid., 89–90.

READING WITH DONALD JUEL

Donald Juel has moved us a long way toward a thorough analysis of the experience of reading Mark's Gospel.[30] The scattered discussions of Mark in Juel's *An Introduction to New Testament Literature* represent a sensitive discussion of the reader-oriented nature of Mark's Gospel.

For example, Juel emphasizes that Mark's narrative functions on "two levels of meaning." "On the surface, the characters in the drama play out their roles as they understand them; beneath is the level at which only the reader understands the real meaning of the events."[31] Thus, not only has Juel seen two levels operating in the narrative but also he has seen a fundamental incongruity between what is known or understood on one level and what is known or understood on the other. Obviously, Juel is operating with another version of the distinction between story and discourse. Because Juel has clearly distinguished these two levels in Mark's narrative, he has stated even more sharply than Enslin or Bundy the disparity between story and discourse in the passages where Jesus is said to be Son of God:

> Only God himself and the demons know that Jesus is God's Son. To the characters in the story, Jesus' true identity is unknown and, according to Mark, that is what Jesus intends.
>
> Obviously, if the confessions of the demoniacs and the baptism and transfiguration have virtually no impact on the characters in the story, Mark must include them for the sake of the reader.[32]

What is hidden or misunderstood at one level, Juel says, is made known at the other level, and thus the Gospel of Mark is fraught with irony, ambiguity, mystery, and paradox. To illustrate, Juel observes the "irony" of the crucifixion scene, the "ambiguity" of the centurion's confession, and the "mystery" surrounding the abrupt conclusion of the Gospel—a mystery that can be solved only by the reader, who must supply a conclusion that moves beyond the end of the story.[33] Overall, the Gospel can be characterized by reference to the persistent "paradox" of "Mysterious Revelation": "revelation to the reader" as opposed to "mystery for the characters."[34]

That Juel has discerned the two levels operating in Mark and the radical incongruity that usually occurs between them is significant, but more significant still is his recognition that the storyteller is preoccupied with the discourse

---

30. Donald Juel, *Messiah and Temple: The Trial of Jesus in the Gospel of Mark*, SBLDS 31 (Missoula, Mont.: Scholars Press, 1977); idem, with James S. Ackerman and Thayer S. Warshaw, *An Introduction to New Testament Literature* (Nashville: Abingdon Press, 1978).

31. Ibid., 178–79.

32. Ibid., 188.

33. Ibid., 143, 146–47, 169–70.

34. Ibid., 182–96.

of the narrative and that the coherence of the narrative lies at the discourse
level.

> Mark's method of narrating . . . indicates his preoccupation with this second
> deeper level of meaning—to the exclusion of other considerations. . . .
>   There is no evidence that Mark has even tried to sketch a consistent picture—
> at least at one level of the story. Study of the trial, of the healings of the blind
> men, and of the confessions of the demons reinforces the opinion that the unity
> of the work lies at the deeper level of the story, the level that reads the "gospel
> of Jesus Christ, the Son of God." Mark makes sense only when one is constantly
> aware of the distance the writer has imposed between the reader and the characters
> and events of the story.[35]

Juel's comments are valuable, but he could benefit from a more precise
critical vocabulary. *Story* and *discourse* are preferable to Juel's *upper level*
and *lower level* because the former pair is less prejudicial. If, as Juel says,
Mark is preoccupied with what I would call the discourse level, and therefore
the coherence of the narrative is to be found at the discourse level, then the
story level is not at all aptly described as the "first level" or the "upper level."
The discourse, not the story, is the main concern of the author, so it should
be graced with the language of preeminence. Juel is here reflecting the bias
of modernity toward the referential function of language, whereby the content
of an utterance is regarded as its raison d'être. Such a view of language stands
over against the understanding of language common to the ancient world,
namely, that the chief function of language is pragmatic or rhetorical and
intended to persuade or somehow affect the hearer. More baldly, moderns
tend to be preoccupied with *what* is said (story), whereas the ancients were
preoccupied with *how* something was said and *how* it affected the hearer
(discourse). If the latter was the preeminent attitude toward language in antiquity, then we should not be surprised if a narrative such as Mark's reflects
this attitude.

What Enslin, Bundy, and Juel have all observed is that the Gospel of
Mark is an especially reader-oriented narrative. Its primary aim is to persuade
or somehow affect the reader. As a form of literary criticism that focuses on
the reader and the reading experience, reader-response criticism is well suited
to deal with a text that takes aim at the reader at every step. Reader-response

---

35. Ibid., 180. See also Alan Culpepper's observation that the coherence of the Gospel of
John similarly lies at the level of its powerful rhetorical effect (R. Alan Culpepper, *Anatomy of
the Fourth Gospel: A Study in Literary Design* [Philadelphia: Fortress Press, 1983], 234).
    The point that Juel, Culpepper, and others have made has been stated concisely by Inge
Crosman: "the purpose of a narrative is not necessarily to tell a story" ("Reference and the
Reader," *PT* 4 [1983]: 93).

criticism is actually a diverse assortment of methodological perspectives and practices, however, and setting forth the predominant characteristics of reader-response criticism will therefore be the task of the next two chapters. After that I shall put reader-response criticism to use in an effort to understand the experience of reading Mark's Gospel more fully.

2

THE READER AND THE READING EXPERIENCE

The spectrum of reader-response critics is so broad that whether they can all be categorized under that one heading is questionable. As an example of the breadth of the spectrum, Susan Suleiman and Inge Crosman divide reader-oriented criticism into six major categories: (1) rhetorical, (2) semiotic and structuralist, (3) phenomenological, (4) psychoanalytic and subjective, (5) sociological and historical, and (6) hermeneutic.[1] The range of this list is daunting, but most of these approaches share several major characteristics that cut across the boundaries delineated by Suleiman and Crosman. Most varieties of reader-response criticism share: (1) a preeminent concern for the reader and the reading experience and (2) a critical model of the reading experience, which itself has two major aspects: (a) an understanding of reading as a dynamic, concrete, temporal experience, instead of the abstract perception of a spatial form; and (b) an emphasis on meaning as event instead of meaning as content. In this chapter I shall examine the preeminent concern for the reader and the reading experience and, in the next, the critical model of reading.

Although in modern criticism the reader has often been slighted, nevertheless the reader has had advocates in the modern critical tradition. One well-known statement exalting the role of the reader is from Northrop Frye: "It has been said of Boehme that his books are like a picnic to which the author brings the words and the reader the meaning. The remark may have been intended as a sneer at Boehme, but it is an exact description of all works of literary art without exception."[2] This statement is hyperbole, but it is in line with the kinds of claims that are now being made on behalf of readers.

---

1. Susan R. Suleiman and Inge Crosman, eds., *The Reader in the Text: Essays on Audience and Interpretation* (Princeton: Princeton University Press, 1980).
2. Quoted by Wolfgang Iser, *The Act of Reading: A Theory of Aesthetic Response* (Baltimore and London: Johns Hopkins University Press, 1978), 27.

We hear now many varieties of the polemical slogan that "texts do not make meaning; readers make meaning." What is meant by meaning in this statement begs for clarification, but the critics who defend this slogan do have an important point to make. They are reminding us that once the author finishes the text and gives it to the world, she no longer has control over it; thereafter the text has a life of its own. Once out of the author's hands, the text is totally dependent on its readers. Such life as it continues to enjoy flows from them. Unless the text is read and comes to life in the reading experience, it is simply a lifeless assemblage of paper, binding, and dried ink. The text has no life or meaning unless life and meaning are conferred upon it by a reader.

Although perhaps indeed "readers make meaning," such slogans over-simplify. Saying that the reader is everything, the way some reader-response critics do, is misleading. Practically speaking, the text is important, the reader is important, and the interpretive community that provides the context in which text and reader interact is important. Nonetheless, readers and reading have been slighted, and the balance must be redressed. This slogan needs to be proclaimed, and it needs to be heard.

WHO IS THE READER?

Much perusal of reader-response criticism[3] suggests that the question at hand is seldom asked and answered carefully enough. This realization is especially surprising because reader-response critics do frequently ask, "Who is the reader?" and then proceed to offer an answer. "The reader" is variously labeled, however, as the ideal reader, the informed reader, the implied reader, the narratee, the authorial reader, the hypothetical reader, the optimal reader, the intended reader, the competent reader, the superreader, the composite reader, the average reader, the encoded reader, the actual reader, the flesh-and-blood reader, and so on. Although a critic often tries to clarify his particular version of "the reader," latent equivocations often persist. To these latent equivocations about "the reader" in reader-response criticism I now turn.

3. Reliable guides to reader-response criticism include the following: Jane Tompkins, ed., *Reader-Response Criticism: From Formalism to Post-Structuralism* (Baltimore and London: Johns Hopkins University Press, 1980); Suleiman and Crosman, *The Reader in the Text*; Steven Mailloux, "Reader-Response Criticism?" *Genre* 10 (1977): 413–31; idem, "Learning to Read: Interpretation and Reader-Response Criticism," *SLI* 12 (1979): 93–108; idem, *Interpretive Conventions: The Reader in the Study of American Fiction* (Ithaca, N.Y., and London: Cornell University Press, 1982), 19–65; Robert Holub, *Reception Theory: A Critical Introduction,* (London and New York: Methuen, 1984); Elizabeth Freund, *The Return of the Reader: Reader-Response Criticism* (London and New York: Methuen, 1987).

One may also consult issues of the journal *Reader: Essays in Reader-Oriented Theory, Criticism, and Pedagogy* (Department of Humanities, Michigan Technological University, Houghton, Michigan 49931, U.S.A.).

THE READER AND THE CRITIC

First, we need to distinguish between the reader and the critic.[4] Often a critic talks about being a reader of a text as if the critic were only a reader. The critic is clearly more than that, however, for being a critic means being part of a guild, or an "interpretive community," as Stanley Fish likes to say.[5] Such a guild has a history and its own special language, and it has rules and rituals for entrance into its ranks and for subsequent advancement, demotion, or excommunication. Therefore, even though a critic may sometimes speak in disarmingly simple terms about reading a text, in speaking as a critic he or she speaks to be heard by fellow critics, and thus the entire critical tradition of that particular interpretive community is evoked implicitly. When critics talk about reading, they usually mean reading critically, as their guild defines criticism. To be sure, reader-response criticism, more than other brands of literary criticism, is known for its willingness to grant value to all reading, whether expert or not, but it is still criticism, which is where equivocation begins to enter. The difference between being a critical reader and simply being a reader needs to be spelled out carefully.

One attempt to define this difference is a rich and subtle essay by George Steiner, " 'Critic'/'Reader.' "[6] Steiner poses an antithesis of critic versus reader. He is careful to note that this polarity is both fictional and heuristic; "in the ordinary run of things, 'criticism' and 'reading' interpenetrate and overlap."[7] Yet, confronting the opposing poles, even if they never exist in a pure state, is helpful in understanding the overlap.

Because Steiner repeats and develops his critic/reader antithesis in a variety of ways, summarizing the wealth of insights in his essay is difficult. Nevertheless, the foundational motif of his fugue seems to be that "the critic is judge and master of the text," whereas "the reader is servant to the text."[8] More specifically, we can observe two major ways in which the "judge and master" of the text contrasts with the "servant" of the text. First, the critic steps back from the text to strike a magisterial pose of critical, objectifying distance, whereas the reader tries to eliminate the distance between himself and the text to allow the merging of his being with that of the text. Because the critic stands over against the text, criticism is by nature "adversative," "competitive," and even "parasitic" in its relationship with the text.[9] The reader, by contrast, does not reify the text as an object but finds in it a "real

---

4. Sandra M. Schneiders has developed a similar distinction between the "believer" and the "scholar" in "Church and Biblical Scholarship in Dialogue," *TToday* 42 (1985): 353–58.

5. Stanley Fish, *Is There a Text in This Class? The Authority of Interpretive Communities* (Cambridge: Harvard University Press, 1980).

6. George Steiner, " 'Critic'/'Reader,' " *NLH* 10 (1979): 423–52.

7. Ibid., 451.

8. Ibid., 449.

9. Ibid., 433, 436, 437, 441.

presence" and often a locus of "inspiration" or "revelation." In "dynamic
passivity," a reader is read *by* the text;[10] distance collapses as the reader seeks
"to enter into the text and to be entered into by the text."[11]

A second major way of characterizing the antithesis is to say that a critic
makes judgments about the text and declares them, whereas a reader does
neither. Because the reader does not objectify and judge the text, the reader
tends not to talk about reading.[12] On the one hand, criticism requires the
exercise of rational choice, and "the critic must declare; this is his public and
legislative ordination." On the other hand, "the reader will often hold his
illumination mute."[13] After all, to the reader the text is " 'a real presence'
irreducible to analytic summation and resistant to judgment in the sense in
which the critic can and must judge."[14]

The legislative duty of criticism has as a central task the evaluation and
ranking of texts; part of the critic's job is to tell us what we should and should
not be reading. Steiner calls the set of texts prescribed by the critic a "syllabus."
The reader, too, has his selection of favored texts, which Steiner chooses to
call a "canon." The crucial difference is that the critic chooses her syllabus
by a conscious act of will, but the canon chooses the reader; a canon is
unsought and unwilled. Steiner's canon refers to those texts and text fragments
that capture our imaginations, sometimes against our will, and often without
our being conscious of it. "The canonic text enters into the reader, it takes
its place within him by a process of penetration, of luminous insinuation
whose occasion may have been entirely mundane and accidental. . . ." "The
occurrence is banal to anyone whose mind and body . . . have been seized
upon by a melody, by a tune, by a verbal cadence which he did not choose
by act of will, which has entered into him unawares." "The critic prescribes
a syllabus; the reader is answerable to and internalizes a canon." "A syllabus
is taught; a canon is lived."[15]

10. Ibid., 438–39.
11. Ibid., 443.
12. "It is easy to say something about criticism worth looking at and/or disagreeing with. It
is difficult to say anything useful about 'reading' in the sense in which this paper seeks to articulate
the term. Criticism is discursive and breeds discourse. 'Reading' yields no primary impulse
towards self-communication. The 'reader' who discourses is, in a certain manner, in breach of
privilege. . . . Reading is done rather than spoken about . . ." (439).
There are many versions of the anecdote about a reader who, when asked to tell what a story
is about, simply tells the story verbatim. Steiner refers to a variation involving the musician
Schumann, who, when asked for a critique of a musical composition, simply played the piece
in toto. A similar statement that the meaning of a story is the story itself comes from Flannery
O'Conner in *Mystery and Manners,* ed. Sally Fitzgerald and Robert Fitzgerald (New York: Farrar,
Strauss, and Giroux, 1961), 96.
13. Steiner, " 'Critic'/'Reader,' " 448.
14. Ibid., 440.
15. Ibid., 445–447. Steiner's use of the word *canon* could be confusing to "readers" and
"critics" of the Bible. If, by Steiner's definition, a canon is a set of texts or text fragments that

Much equivocation regarding the reader in reader-response criticism can be illuminated by reference to Steiner's critic/reader antithesis. When reader-response critics talk about readers and especially when they talk about themselves as readers, the reader being posited can be positioned somewhere along a wide spectrum running from Steiner's pure (but hypothetical) critic to Steiner's pure (but hypothetical) reader. We can briefly consider this spectrum here.[16]

At one end of the reader-response spectrum are critics who are very much aware of their position as critics within a critical tradition. Their acknowledgment of their critical tradition is particularly noticeable when they adopt one common strategy. Often a reader-response critic elucidates the history of the criticism of a particular text by observing what has happened in the reading experiences of various critics that has given rise to convergent or divergent critical assessments of the text. The critic presumes to use the text to explain the history of its reading. The goal here is to explicate not the text per se but previous readings of the text, and the critic intends to comprehend, encompass, and rise above a host of critical colleagues. This critical strategy is a powerful move that puts the critic in a position of standing not only over against the text but also over against his peers in an authoritative, magisterial pose. Steiner does not make much of this point, but to be a critic is to pose as judge and master, not only of the text but also of one's peers.

We could call the critic pole of Steiner's critic/reader spectrum the objectifying pole. What is objectified by the reader-oriented critic is not the traditional text object, however, but the experience of reading within a tradition of criticism. This pole could also be called the sociological or ideological pole, for we objectify our reading experience according to the critical presuppositions or ideology we share with our fellows in the guild.

The reader pole of Steiner's spectrum, by contrast, is the pole of subjectifying, the pole of the individual and the psychological. A reader-response critic positioned toward this end of the spectrum is less concerned about contributing to the development of a venerable critical tradition and more concerned about helping the individual reader find herself as the subject of

---

seizes our imaginations, then the canon of the Bible is not "canon," in Steiner's sense, for many in modernity. The canon of the Bible seizes few imaginations these days. Rather, it is recognized and accepted by an act of will. That is, the canon of the Bible is closer to being an example of Steiner's "syllabus" than it is to being an example of his "canon." We may even wonder if the canon of the Bible was ever "canon" in Steiner's sense, even in antiquity.

Among readers of the Bible, closer to Steiner's "canon" may be the familiar notion of the "canon within the canon"; both readers and critics of the Bible tend to prefer salient selections from the biblical literature.

16. The discussion that follows has many affinities with the schema of reader-response criticism worked out by Mailloux, *Interpretive Conventions*, 22.

her reading experience.[17] At this end of the spectrum we frequently find an unashamed acceptance of the nonexpert reader and a challenge to the implicit authoritarianism of the critical community. Subjective or psychological critics, such as David Bleich and Norman Holland,[18] eagerly welcome their students as peers and fellow readers with full reading privileges. Most empirical study of reading (the psychology of perception, developmental psychology, etc.) also tends to slide to this end of the spectrum.

Thus does Steiner give us one valuable measuring stick for sizing up the reader. According to this measuring stick, when reader-response critics talk about the reader, some are thinking primarily of Steiner's critic, others are thinking primarily of Steiner's reader, and most are probably somewhere in between. For me and for most other biblical scholars, Steiner's hypothetical antithesis is all too familiar. Historically and ontogenetically, reading the Bible (or rather being read by it) precedes biblical criticism. Many of us were readers of the Bible before we were critics of it, and we now struggle, in many cases, to reconcile the rational insights of criticism with the ecstasy of reading. We value and respect the ecstasy of reading, but many of us found another ecstasy in criticism because for the first time, with the achievement of critical distance, we could see features of the text that had hitherto read us, and we were enchanted and liberated by what we saw. Without criticism, we saw in retrospect, we could not see and know the text that had read us, not even know if it was the text we thought it was. Whoever serves the text with utter devotion cannot objectify and thereby know what text is actually being served. In the case of the Bible, many are read by and serve versions of the Bible that a critic in good conscience can only judge to be perversions. Only with critical distance can we see perversions, however; perversion is a concept of criticism. To the critic, the reader often appears to serve blindly texts he does not know and cannot understand; to the reader, the critic often assumes the arrogant role of master and judge over texts to which he is inferior. Must not some middle ground exist?

My duty, as Steiner puts it, is now to make my critical distance "explicit, responsible, and, therefore, open to argument."[19] I see myself striving to be both a reader and a critic of Mark's Gospel: a critical reader. Unless I specify otherwise, the reader I mention hereafter is just such a critical reader. To be

17. Marcel Proust, in *Remembrance of Things Past:* "In reality every reader is, while he is reading, the reader of his own self" (quoted by Gérard Genette, *Narrative Discourse: An Essay in Method,* trans. Jane E. Lewin, foreword Jonathan Culler [Ithaca, N.Y.: Cornell University Press, 1980], 261).

18. See David Bleich, *Readings and Feelings: An Introduction to Subjective Criticism* (Urbana, Ill.: National Council of Teachers of English, 1975); idem, *Subjective Criticism* (Baltimore and London: Johns Hopkins University Press, 1978); Norman N. Holland, *5 Readers Reading* (New Haven: Yale University Press, 1975); idem, *Laughing: A Psychology of Humor* (Ithaca, N.Y., and London: Cornell University Press, 1982).

19. Steiner, " 'Critic'/'Reader,' " 423.

a critical reader means for me: (1) to affirm the enduring power of the Bible in my culture and in my own life and yet (2) to remain open enough to dare to ask any question and to risk any critical judgment. Nothing less than both of these points, together, can suffice for me. I was a reader of the Bible before I was a critic of it, but I found becoming a critic to be liberating and satisfying, and therefore I judge criticism to be a high calling of inestimable value. Yet, I recognize the prior claim of the text and the preeminence of reading over criticism; accordingly, I seek and occasionally am apprehended by moments in which the text wields its indubitable power. The critic's ego says this could be a taste of the cherished postcritical naiveté; the reader's proper humility before the text says that a reader should not judge such things.

REAL READER, IMPLIED READER, NARRATEE

Having positioned myself as a critical reader, I need to introduce some terminology to facilitate critical discussion of the reading experience. Keeping in mind our question "Who is the reader?" we now expand that question: (1) Who is the reader? (2) How does the reader relate to the author by means of the text? and consequently, (3) Who is the author? Here I rely on Seymour Chatman's *Story and Discourse,* which distinguishes between real author, implied author, narrator, narratee, implied reader, and real reader.[20] Chatman illustrates the function of his critical entities by means of a diagram.[21]

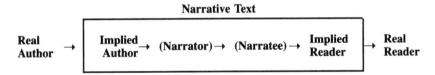

Narrative Text

Real Author → | Implied Author → (Narrator) → (Narratee) → Implied Reader | → Real Reader

The *real author* and *real reader* are easy enough to grasp. They are living, flesh-and-blood persons who actually produce the text and read it.[22] In the

---

20. Seymour Chatman, *Story and Discourse: Narrative Structure in Fiction and Film* (Ithaca, N.Y., and London: Cornell University Press, 1978) 146–51. Similar terminology is used by Wayne Booth (*The Rhetoric of Fiction,* 2d ed. [Chicago and London: University of Chicago Press, 1983], 428–31), Gerald Prince ("Introduction à l'étude du poétique narrataire," *Poétique* 14 [1973]: 178–96 [now translated and abbreviated as "Introduction to the Study of the Narratee," in *Reader-Response Criticism,* 7–25, ed. Jane Tompkins] and *Narratology: The Form and Function of Narrative* [Berlin, New York, and Amsterdam: Mouton, 1982]), and Peter Rabinowitz ("Truth in Fiction: A Reexamination of Audiences," *CI* 4 [1977]: 121–41), among others.

A model very similar to Chatman's has been applied to the Gospel of Mark by Hans-Josef Klauck, "Die Erzählerische Rolle der Jünger im Markusevangelium: Eine narrative Analyse," *NovT* 24 (1982): 1–26.

21. Chatman, *Story and Discourse,* 151.

22. Booth speaks of the "flesh-and-blood author, who tells many stories, before and after a given tale," and "the flesh-and-blood re-creator of many stories" (*Rhetoric of Fiction,* 428).

act of reading, however, we do not encounter a flesh-and-blood author but rather the author's second self, which was created for purposes of telling this tale. Similarly, we as readers are not wholly ourselves as we read but at least in part the reader the text invites us to be. The terms *implied author* and *implied reader,* therefore, have gained wide currency in recognition that a text implies a role or a persona for both the author and reader.[23] As Wayne Booth says, "the author creates, in short, an image of himself and another image of his reader; he makes his reader, as he makes his second self, and the most successful reading is one in which the created selves, author and reader, can find complete agreement."[24] Finally, *narrator* and *narratee* refer to the persons who are supposed to be telling and listening to the story.[25] Every story may be supposed to have a storyteller and a listener, but some stories have only oblique, covert evidence of either a narrator or a narratee; others may go so far as to have both the narrator and narratee overtly portrayed as characters in the narrative (e.g., in *The Thousand and One Nights,* where Scheherazade is the narrator and the sultan is the narratee).

Narrator and narratee are particularly useful terms when the narrator is explicitly characterized and the implied author clearly wants to distance herself from the narrator, because the narrator is unreliable. Such a case presents a corresponding pressure upon the implied reader to distance himself from the unreliable narrator's gullible narratee. That is, the distinctions between implied author and narrator or between implied reader and narratee are particularly valuable when these relationships are characterized by distance, incongruity, or ironic tension. A good example of a narrative with considerable distance between the implied author and the narrator—and therefore also between the implied reader and the narratee—is Mark Twain's *Huckleberry Finn.* The narrator in *Huckleberry Finn* is Huck himself, and the narratee must be imagined as a simple soul, someone rather like Huck, who would be inclined to listen credulously as Huck spins his yarn at length.[26] For all his worldliness,

---

Rabinowitz, who deals only with the audience side of the narrative act in the article mentioned above, uses the term "actual audience" ("Truth in Fiction," 126). Like Rabinowitz, once Gerald Prince gets beyond the narrator-narratee pair, he concentrates more on the audience side of the narrative than the authorial side; like Chatman, Prince uses the term "real reader" (*lecteur réel*) ("Introduction," 9).

23. Booth is currently using the terms "the implied author of this tale" and "the postulated reader" (*Rhetoric of Fiction,* 429). Rabinowitz speaks of (only on the audience side again) the "authorial audience" ("Truth in Fiction," 126). In a similar vein Prince uses the term "virtual reader" (*lecteur virtuel*) ("Introduction," 9).

24. Booth, *Rhetoric of Fiction,* 138.

25. Chatman credits Prince for the coinage of "narratee," the counterpart of the "narrator." Booth speaks of "the teller of this tale" and "the credulous listener" (*Rhetoric of Fiction,* 430). Rabinowitz uses the expression "narrative audience" ("Truth in Fiction," 127).

26. Booth is right when he says that the narratee is inherently a "credulous listener," someone inclined to listen to the narrator no matter what. The narratee that we must posit for *Huckleberry Finn* is a good illustration.

Huck is a young and naive narrator; clearly the implied author of *Huckleberry Finn* (whom we may distinguish from the real author, Samuel Langhorne Clemens) expects us to see through Huck's naiveté and thus to distance ourselves from the point of view of both Huck and his hypothetical narratee. The rhetorical strategy of *Huckleberry Finn* is to invite real readers to adopt the role of the implied reader of the narrative, at a considerable distance from the credulous and naive narratee the narrative requires us to imagine.

By contrast, with the Gospel of Mark the roles of the narrator and narratee are covert and effaced and therefore virtually identical with the roles of the implied author and implied reader, respectively; the distance involved in these relationships is absolutely minimal. That minimal distance implies a different rhetorical strategy on the part of the author.

Various critics have proposed their own versions of these basic concepts. Their refinements often complicate matters, however, by drawing in some of the considerations about the reader that are better considered separately.[27] The terminology offered here is minimal and serviceable and does not unnecessarily mix in important but tangential reading concerns.

By distinguishing between the narratee and implied reader, we discover that two major role models are often provided in the text for anyone reading it. The implied reader is the reader we must be willing to become, at least temporarily, in order to experience the narrative in the fullest measure.[28] The implied reader may relate to the narratee, in turn, in any number of ways, ranging from a close and intimate association to an ironic distancing, if the narratee appears to the implied reader to be gullible or otherwise deficient (e.g., in *Huckleberry Finn*). Chatman's terminology provides the vocabulary necessary to explore the myriad variations of distance that can exist between implied reader and narratee, between implied author and narrator, and between any of these four entities and the characters in the story.[29] Actually, the possibilities are reduced considerably because the implied author and implied reader, as well as the narrator and narratee, are mirror images of each other. For example, the cluster of authorial values and judgments that is the implied author is manifested in the implicit rendering of the text's reader, and vice

---

27. For example, both Rabinowitz and Prince also want to talk about "ideal readers": Rabinowitz, the "ideal narrative audience" ("Truth in Fiction," 134), and Prince, the "ideal reader" ("Introduction," 9). I want to reserve discussion of such ideal readers until later.

28. Readers sometimes discern implied readers that, for ethical reasons, they are unwilling to become. See Booth, *Rhetoric of Fiction*, 79–81, 138–39, and passim; idem, *Critical Understanding: The Powers and Limits of Pluralism* (Chicago and London: University of Chicago Press, 1979), 242 and passim; idem, *The Company We Keep: An Ethics of Fiction* (Berkeley: University of California Press, 1988); and Susan R. Suleiman, "Ideological Dissent from Works of Fiction: Toward a Rhetoric of the *roman à thèse*," *Neophil* 60 (1976): 162–77.

29. Chatman offers a sampling of the extensive range of possibilities that comes from varying the distances among just three entities, the narrator, narratee, and one character, in *Story and Discourse*, 259–60.

versa. Similarly, the diction of the narrator bounces back like a sonar wave off the outline of the supposed narratee; each reflects the presence of the other.[30] Therefore, another benefit of our adopted vocabulary is that it recognizes and provides a rudimentary way to talk about the dialectical processes that are built into the text and demanded by the reading experience.[31]

Granted the general usefulness of Chatman's terminology, one difficult remaining problem deserves some attention: the nature of the implied reader.[32] Chatman locates the implied reader wholly within the box labeled "narrative text," claiming it to be "immanent" to the text. Therefore, he makes a clean break between the reader in the text and the reader outside the text, a split that is problematic, to say the least. In fact, a recurring debate among reader-oriented critics concerns the relationship between the text and the reader. What is the relationship? Does one have precedence over the other? Can we fairly say that one controls the other? If so, which one? Concerning meaning, is its locus in the text or in the reader? Critics offer different answers to these questions. For example, Wayne Booth and Wolfgang Iser both talk about someone much like Chatman's implied reader, but the two of them mean something different when they talk about this entity. Booth's version of the implied reader, although it invites the assent of a real reader, is ultimately *in* the text and is the creation of an author.[33] Iser's implied reader,[34] however, is constructed by a real reader out of the material provided by the text, particularly its "spots of indeterminacy": "blanks," "gaps," and so forth.[35] Iser is careful to say that his implied reader is neither in the text nor outside it, but is the unique product of the "interaction" of a text and a reader.[36]

30. See Prince, *Narratology*, 7–25. He perceptively discusses how, linguistically, the "I" of a narrator intimates the corresponding narratee, and how the "you" identifying the narratee simultaneously identifies the narrator.

31. This points up a problem with Chatman's diagram: the arrows all point one way. Should they not point right and left, better to indicate the implicit dialogical quality of reading? We are dealing here with more than a deficiency in diagraming; implied here is the notion prominent in our culture that communication, for all our acknowledgment of the importance of "feedback," is basically a one-way street. Walter Ong speaks of a "conduit metaphor" that dominates our thinking about the function of language. According to this metaphor, the author-sender shoots a message-meaning through the chosen language-conduit to a waiting reader-receiver (*Rhetoric, Romance, and Technology* [Ithaca, N.Y., and London: Cornell University Press, 1971], 290).

32. The notion of the implied author has comparable problems associated with it, which I shall not address.

33. See again the quotation from Booth, *Rhetoric of Fiction*, 138 (the author "makes his reader, as he makes his second self"); cf. 422–23.

34. To Wolfgang Iser goes credit for popularizing the term "implied reader"; see *The Implied Reader: Patterns of Communication in Prose Fiction from Bunyan to Beckett* (Baltimore and London: Johns Hopkins University Press, 1974).

35. Iser, *Act of Reading*, passim.

36. Part of the difference between Booth and Iser is that the former tilts toward Steiner's reader whereas the latter tilts toward the critic. See, e.g., Booth, *Rhetoric of Fiction*, 422.

Other critics hold other points of view on the relationship between text and reader. Outdoing even Wayne Booth in respect for the rhetorical power of the text and outdoing even Wolfgang Iser in respect for the independence and creative activity of the reader are the early and later positions of Stanley Fish. In his early reader-oriented criticism, typified by *Self-Consuming Artifacts*,[37] Fish engages in brilliant word-by-word analyses of the way texts manipulate the developing response of the reader; no one could make a stronger case for thoroughgoing textual control over the reading experience. Fish even went so far as to argue that all readers are textually directed in the way he describes. Some of them have just not realized that direction, not having paid attention to the ways texts control them. In more recent work, Fish still affirms the immense value of this kind of close analysis of the reading experience, but he has now swung away from claiming textual control over the reader.[38] In fact, he has now swung over to the view that the text cannot really control reading in any objective sense, for the text itself is invented in the process of being read. The text and all its features are defined only by the exercise of the reader's interpretive strategies. Having essentially said earlier that the text controls the reader, Fish now says that the reader construes the text and its characteristics in the first place and thus controls it. From this later position, Fish's earlier position may be explained as a convenient and powerful critical fiction, adopted by the critic because of its potential for persuading a critical audience that already grants texts an objectivity and an authority to control the reader. Now, however, he wants to make clear that objectivity and authority are always, first, the reader's to grant.

Does Fish's new position now grant too much authority to the reader? In response to this question, Fish slips to the next station of his critical pilgrimage. The reader is not too powerful, he says, and the critical enterprise is not doomed to subjectivism or solipsism, because the critical presuppositions employed by the reader to objectify and analyze the text are derived from the "interpretive community" in which the reading takes place. Fish is now arguing for the preeminence of the social and political dimension in the critical practice of even the seemingly isolated, maverick critic.[39] In other words,

37. Stanley E. Fish, *Self-Consuming Artifacts: The Experience of Seventeenth-Century Literature* (Berkeley, Los Angeles, and London: University of California Press, 1972); see also his early programmatic essay, "Literature in the Reader: Affective Stylistics," *NLH* 2 (1970): 123–62; which was reprinted in *Self-Consuming Artifacts*, 383–427, and again in his collection of essays, *Is There a Text in This Class?*, 21–67.
38. See the latter essays in Fish, *Is There a Text in This Class?*
39. Of course, a prime example of such a maverick critic would be Stanley Fish himself. I would agree with a number of his reviewers that *Is There a Text in This Class?* only begins to explore the social and political dimensions of criticism. But see now Fish's *Doing What Comes Naturally: Change, Rhetoric, and the Practice of Theory in Literary and Legal Studies* (Durham, N.C., and London: Duke University Press, 1989).

readers may control texts, but anarchy does not result because interpretive communities control readers.

Fish has therefore bracketed Booth and Iser in his critical career; he attributed at one point more control to the text than Booth, then more control to the reader than Iser, and then located the source of all control in the presuppositions of the critic's interpretive community. In sliding from one extreme to the next, Fish has highlighted helpfully, if idiosyncratically, what must be simultaneous foci for a thoughtful and flexible reader-oriented criticism. The issue is neither a two-sided relationship between text and reader nor the overarching preeminence of interpretive communities, but rather a matter of text and reader meeting in the context of the critical community. Granted that the community defines what the text is and tells the reader how to go about reading it, at the same time the text molds its reader and constrains the critical gaze of the community, and at the same time the reader construes the text and contributes to the evolution of the critical community. That is, granted the undeniable importance of the interpretive community, within that social setting the text will always have a certain objectivity and the reader a certain subjectivity that are also undeniable. Moreover, the possibility always exists that the objectified text will wield such power, or the subjectified reader exert such genius, that the interpretive community will be re-formed in response.

In sum, the nature of the implied reader is the locus of a great deal of disagreement in reader-response criticism, but this disparity can only be expected because reading itself is a mysterious merger of text, reader, and context. Yet for all its ambiguity, implied reader is still a useful term. When I use it, I shall refer primarily to the reader implied in the text, but I shall take care to observe that different critical readers grasp that reader in the text differently, due largely to differences in the contexts of reading, which are governed by the critical presuppositions prevailing at the time and place of reading.

THE IDEAL READER

Yet another common family of reader terms is associated with the notion of the *ideal reader*. Mention is made of the ideal reader, the informed reader, the optimal reader, the superreader, the competent reader, the educated reader, and so on. What critics are grasping for here is an idealized reader that is intimately related to the implied reader discussed previously. Ideal reader adds a whole new dimension to implied reader, however, for it reveals the critical impulse not just to apprehend the reader implied in one text but also to apprehend the reader implied in many texts, so as to encompass and supersede them all.

A succinct description of the ideal reader is offered by Jonathan Culler: "The question is not what actual readers happen to do but what an ideal reader must know implicitly in order to read and interpret works in ways which we consider acceptable."[40] The ideal reader possesses not only "linguistic competence," a command of the language, but also "literary competence," an intimate acquaintance with Steiner's syllabus and a full grasp of the accepted critical techniques of working on it. The ideal reader would be Steiner's critic par excellence.

Another description of the ideal reader is Stanley Fish's description of the "informed reader":

> Who is *the* reader? Obviously, my reader is a construct, an ideal or idealized reader, somewhat like Wardhaugh's "mature reader" or Milton's "fit" reader, or to use a term of my own, *the* reader is the *informed* reader. The informed reader is someone who (1) is a competent speaker of the language out of which the text is built up; (2) is in full possession of "the semantic knowledge that a mature . . . listener brings to his task of comprehension," including the knowledge (that is, the experience, both as a producer and comprehender) of lexical sets, collocation probabilities, idioms, professional and other dialects, and so on; and (3) has *literary* competence. That is, he is sufficiently experienced as a reader to have internalized the properties of literary discourses, including everything from the most local of devices (figures of speech, and so on) to whole genres. . . .
>
> The reader of whose responses I speak, then, is this informed reader, neither an abstraction nor an actual living reader, but a hybrid—a real reader (me) who does everything within his power to make himself informed.[41]

Wolfgang Iser discusses several versions of the ideal reader and expresses dissatisfaction with all of them as too nebulous and lacking in theoretical rigor.[42] In their place he offers his own version of the implied reader, which does include some of the breadth and flexibility built into the notion of the ideal reader, inasmuch as Iser understands the implied reader to be "a textual structure anticipating the presence of a recipient without necessarily defining him."[43] Iser has sensed correctly that the implied reader lies at the core of all the talk about idealized readers, and so he says that having an implied reader is enough; going further to posit an ideal reader is unnecessary. Nevertheless, he loses the use of a valuable heuristic device by limiting himself to the reader implied by single text, which is what his version of the implied reader is, whereas an ideal reader is somehow a reader who can read well a multitude of texts.

Steven Mailloux, for example, has seen that the ideal reader is in a sense the implied reader writ large.

40. Jonathan Culler, *Structuralist Poetics: Structuralism, Linguistics, and the Study of Literature* (Ithaca, N.Y.: Cornell University Press, 1975), 123–24.
41. Fish, *Is There a Text in This Class?* 48–49.
42. Iser, *Act of Reading*, 27–38.
43. Ibid., 34.

> The "ideal reader" is merely an abstracted version of the "implied reader." He
> is not a reader of a specific text but one implied by all literary texts; or put
> another way, he is a hypothetical reader with the general ability to comprehend
> literature. . . . We have, then, a specific text's *implied reader,* which is really
> only a textual interpretation (or part of one) using a reader vocabulary. And we
> have an *ideal reader* who is also an interpretive construct, one that is abstracted
> from many specific instances of textual interpretation, one that defines the
> conditions of literary response.[44]

Mailloux's point is well taken, but it needs to be pushed further. The ideal
reader is not simply a hypothetical enhancement of the implied reader. The
ideal reader is a fictive role assumed by a critic in the process of presuming
to address the critical community. It is, in other words, a pose adopted by
the critic for rhetorical purposes. As Steiner observes, the fiction acted out
in the work of criticism is a pretense to supersedure: a critic strives to supersede
the text, the critical community and its history of reading, and even himself.
Surely no one is ever really the critic par excellence, but when playing the
game of criticism the critic cannot pretend to be anything less and still expect
to be taken seriously within the guild.

This analysis is hardly a revelation; numerous critics have admitted it
candidly. We can push still further to observe that the role of the ideal reader
can be played in two major ways. First is the pose of the individual ideal
reader per se, in which I adopt the stance of the supremely well-informed
and skilled reader-critic, possessing impeccable linguistic and literary competence. Second, I can construct a composite ideal reader out of the accumulated critical experience of my critical community. In practice, the construction of a composite ideal reader often goes hand in hand with striking a
pose as an individual ideal reader.[45] Rhetorically, these strategies support each
other. The individual and composite ideal readers represent the opposing poles
of another of those continua ranging from the individual to the social, but in
this case the continuum is narrow in its scope because we are dealing with
subjective and objective poles within a specialized sociological context: critics
in a particular critical guild.

The most pyrotechnic use of the individual and composite versions of
the ideal reader is found in the practical criticism of Stanley Fish. We have
already seen Fish's description of what he prefers to call the informed reader.
Tucked into the description is an admission that the informed reader is really
Stanley Fish: it is "a real reader (me) who does everything within his power
to make himself informed." After inserting himself into the picture modestly,

---

44. Mailloux, *Interpretive Conventions,* 203.
45. In the preface to a highly regarded piece of reader-oriented criticism, Stephen Booth lays
bare, in just a few lines, his use of both versions of the ideal reader (*An Essay on Shakespeare's
Sonnets* [New Haven and London: Yale University Press, 1969], x).

at first only within parentheses, Fish proceeds to say that of course he has the right to claim to be an informed reader, and, moreover, so does anyone in the guild: "Each of us, if we are sufficiently responsible and self-conscious, can, in the course of employing [Fish's critical] method, become the informed reader and therefore be a more reliable reporter of his [reading] experience."[46] In other words, the individual ideal reader is a rhetorical stance generally available to individual members in good standing of a particular critical guild. In Fish's criticism he makes masterful use of this rhetorical pose as the master of criticism.

Perhaps even more impressive is Fish's powerful use of the composite ideal reader. A frequent strategy in Fish's criticism is to examine an interpretive crux that has produced a diversity of critical judgments and then to seek a supposed common reading experience that lies unrecognized at the base of the disagreement. Fish asks, What reading experience have critics shared unconsciously that allows them to agree enough to disagree about this passage? Rather than trying to reconcile differences and thus form his composite ideal reader at the "surface level," Fish forms his composite ideal reader from a base of hitherto unrecognized agreement at a "deeper level," thereby encompassing and surpassing the history of criticism on the text under discussion. By descending to the "deeper level," he is able to transcend the critical disagreements altogether: "I perform the service of revealing to the participants what it is they were really telling us."[47] This use of the metaphor of levels is skillful rhetoric. Fish says that he is descending from the "surface level" in order to reveal the "deeper level," the common "base of agreement." We could just as easily argue that Fish is climbing to a higher level where he can stand alone above the entire critical debate. His skillful construction of an abstracted, composite ideal reader is a way of establishing his own professional credentials as an individual ideal reader.[48] What distinguishes Fish among critics is that he uses the rhetorical strategies of the individual and composite ideal reader so openly and so boldly. All critics, in one way or another, cast themselves in such roles; Stanley Fish and other reader-response critics are simply exposing this fiction to the light of day and exploiting it to the fullest.

Therefore, who is the reader in reader-response criticism? First, it is I, as a critical reader. It is also I, as a supposed ideal reader, a role I shall play both by demonstrating my own literary competence and by interrogating a composite ideal reader created out of what has been thought and said by my critical community. That ideal reader, individual or composite, is inevitably

---

46. Fish, *Is There a Text in This Class?* 49.

47. Ibid., 177–78.

48. Another version of the composite, communal reader is Michael Riffaterre's "superreader" ("Criteria for Style Analysis," *Word* 15 [1959]: 154–74; idem, "Describing Poetic Structure: Two Approaches to Baudelaire's 'Les Chats,'" *YFS* 36–37 [1966]: 200–42 [reprinted in *Reader-Response Criticism*, ed. Jane Tompkins, 26–40]).

a heuristic abstraction contrived from the countless readers implied by countless texts, chief among them in this book the Gospel of Mark. In short, the
critical reader of Mark has an individual persona (mine), a communal persona
(the abstracted total experience of my critical community), and a textual
persona (the reader implied in the text at hand). Yet, still more is involved
in talking about the reader and the reading experience.

3

A CRITICAL MODEL OF READING

What we need now is a heuristic model of the reading experience itself, one that respects the ecstatic experience of Steiner's reader and also provides a rational vocabulary for the critic to describe and discuss the act of reading. The model I propose is indeed heuristic: it provides a convenient vocabulary for talking about the reading experience from the perspective of the literary critic. It is not based on empirical laboratory research on real readers in the act of reading. Studies of that sort are certainly not ignored by reader-response critics, but such critics realize that empirical studies of reading do not provide a scientific refuge in which to find definitive answers to the perennial questions about what happens when we read. Researchers who study reading empirically have their differences of opinion, as do reader-response critics. My heuristic literary-critical model of reading is at least compatible with some respected empirical studies of reading,[1] but I and most reader-response critics remain primarily concerned with literary criticism and not with the empirical study of the psychology of perception, psycholinguistics, cognitive development, and the like.

The model proposed here is broad in outline. It is not exhaustive but is illustrative of major lines of agreement running through otherwise diverse brands of reader-oriented criticism. The model has two major components: (1) an emphasis on reading as a temporal experience and (2) a shift in the focus of criticism away from meaning as content to meaning as event.

---

1. Many reader-response critics would find congenial the widely respected empirical theory of reading presented by Kenneth S. Goodman. Goodman calls reading a "psycholinguistic guessing game" in which there are four main processes: sampling, predicting, confirming, and correcting. See the foreword to *Language and Literacy: The Selected Writings of Kenneth S. Goodman*, ed. Frederick V. Gollasch (Boston: Routledge and Kegan Paul, 1982) 1:xx. See also *Reader* 10 (Fall 1983), which is devoted to "Relationships Between Response Theories and Reading Research." Several of the articles in this issue praise Goodman's work.

THE TEMPORAL READING EXPERIENCE

The reading experience takes place through time; it is a temporal experience. Most of us have not been taught to monitor our reading experience as it occurs; rather, we have been encouraged to read in order to get to the end of a text and then to step back and comment on the final outcome of the reading. We tend therefore to view the text as a whole from the perspective of the end of the reading experience. The meandering path we have had to follow to get to the end of reading is regarded merely as prelude to the end product, that final distillate from the reading experience that we often call the content or the meaning of the text.

Reader-response critics promote a shift in critical consciousness by resolutely resisting the inclination to concentrate on the end product of reading. They argue for the appreciation of the entire reading experience, not just its end product. Reading a text is a rich and dynamic experience, but focusing on the end product of reading encourages a perception of the text as a static spatial form, like a painting, a sculpture, or a piece of architecture.[2] This argument may be putting things backwards, however; the spatial form of the printed text itself may encourage the desire to get to the last page of the book in order to reflect back upon the whole text from that vantage point. The physicality of writing tricks us into thinking of texts as objects existing in space rather than as experiences existing in time. As Stanley Fish puts it:

> Literature is a kinetic art, but the physical form it assumes prevents us from seeing its essential nature, even though we so experience it. The availability of a book to the hand, its presence on a shelf, its listing in a library catalogue— all of these encourage us to think of it as a stationary object. Somehow when we put a book down, we forget that while we were reading, *it* was moving (pages turning, lines receding into the past) and forget too that *we* were moving with it.[3]

Fish also provides one of the clearest descriptions of the critical focus required to shift attention away from the text as a physical object to the text as a temporal experience. The critical method he advocates is "an analysis of the developing responses of the reader in relation to the words as they succeed one another in time."[4] In his critical practice Fish devotes painstaking attention to the temporal flow of the reading experience: "in an utterance of

2. The distinction between the dynamism of reading and the perception of static art should not be pushed too far; art critics insist that even the perception of an obviously spatial form can be a dynamic, temporal experience. See E. H. Gombrich, *Art and Illusion: A Study in the Psychology of Pictorial Representation*, Bollingen Series 35, 5, 2d ed. (New York: Bollingen Foundation, 1961).

3. Stanley Fish, *Is There a Text in This Class? The Authority of Interpretive Communities* (Cambridge and London: Harvard University Press, 1980), 43.

4. Ibid., 26.

any length, there is a point at which the reader has taken in only the first word, and then the second, and then the third, and so on, and the report of what happens to the reader is always a report of what has happened *to that point.*"⁵ This method slows down the reading experience so that moments in the reading experience that usually pass in the blink of an eye are frozen in time and can be examined critically. "It is as if a slow motion camera with an automatic stop-action effect were recording our linguistic experiences and presenting them to us for viewing."⁶

Similarly, Wolfgang Iser has described not only the linear, temporal encounter with the words being read but also the psychological phenomena of anticipation and retrospection that accompany it. While we read, we are actively involved in reviewing what has preceded and speculating about what lies ahead. "Every moment of reading is a dialectic of protension and retention," Iser says.⁷ He likens the experience of reading a text to the author's original labor of creating it: "We look forward, we look back, we decide, we change our decisions, we form expectations, we are shocked by their nonfulfillment, we question, we muse, we accept, we reject; this is the dynamic process of recreation."⁸

This description represents a dramatic shift away from the formalism of the New Criticism, which exalted the text over both the author (to avoid the "intentional fallacy") and the reader (to avoid the "affective fallacy").⁹ Walter Ong gives us a broad, historical perspective from which to understand both the rise of formalism and subsequent attempts to move beyond it, especially the current movement to rehabilitate the reader and the reading experience. In numerous discussions of primary oral culture, manuscript culture, print culture, and our own culture of secondary orality,¹⁰ Ong has described how

5. Ibid., 27.

6. Ibid., 28.

7. Wolfgang Iser, *The Act of Reading: A Theory of Aesthetic Response* (Baltimore and London: Johns Hopkins University Press, 1978), 112.

8. Wolfgang Iser, "The Reading Process: A Phenomenological Approach," *NLH* 3 (1972): 293.

9. The classic exposition of these two "fallacies" is in articles by Monroe Beardsley and W. K. Wimsatt, Jr., published in the *Sewanee Review* in the 1940s. The two articles were reprinted as the first two chapters of W. K. Wimsatt, Jr., *The Verbal Icon: Studies in the Meaning of Poetry* (n.p.: University Press of Kentucky, 1954).

10. A "primary oral culture" is an oral culture that has not developed a technology of writing. "Secondary oral culture" refers to the current age of electronic technologies of the word. The current interest in primary oral cultures and the resurgence of reader-oriented/rhetorical/pragmatic criticism is encouraged by—indeed, made possible by—the cultural sensitivities of a postmodern, postliterate oral culture.

Although Ong is the more reliable scholarly resource, the expostulations of Marshall McLuhan on the Gutenberg Galaxy of print culture and the changes in culture and consciousness wrought by the electronic media are still rich with insight (*The Gutenberg Galaxy: The Making of Typographic Man* [Toronto: University of Toronto Press, 1962]; idem, *Understanding Media: The Extensions of Man* [New York: McGraw-Hill, 1964]).

the physicality of writing—especially print—lends itself to be taken as static spatial form and thereby promotes the objectification of the text and its distanciation from both the author and the reader. Inherent in the physicality of writing is an invitation to consider the text per se, divorced from author or reader; use of spatial or architectural metaphors to discuss the text per se follows naturally. Only literates, and probably only literates in a print culture, speak of the structure or form of an utterance, thanks to the reigning paradigm of spatially organized speech provided by the printed page. Furthermore, historically, once the strict uniformity of printed language becomes deeply interiorized in the consciousness of readers, the metaphor of language as a container or conduit, existing in space, which holds meaning within, is hard to avoid. Given this metaphor, the job of the reader or critic is to tap the container and drain off the contents—its meaning. Moreover, the metaphor promotes the idea that the container-text is a single entity and that the content-meaning is also a single entity, and therefore in theory we should all be able to agree on what the singular meaning of the singular text is. A major problem with the container metaphor is that it runs counter to how spoken language actually functions. From his study of language in many cultural settings, Ong has observed that the medium and message of an utterance are not clearly distinguishable.

> The message is neither content nor cargo nor projectile. Medium and message are interdependent in ways none of these carton and carrier metaphors express— indeed, in ways no metaphor can express. In the last analysis, the medium is not even a medium, something in between. Words destroy in-betweenness, put me in your consciousness and you in mine. There is no adequate analogue for verbalization. Verbalization is ultimately unique. True information is not "conveyed."[11]

Another problem with the container metaphor is that it does not easily accommodate the experience we have all had of disagreeing sharply with a fellow reader or critic over what a text says. In reifying the text as a static physical object, the container metaphor fails to take seriously enough the active role of the reader in construing the meaning of the text and even, in a profound sense, construing the text itself, with all its various characteristics.[12] After all, meanings differ because different readers construe them differently. Communication is a dialogue between two participants, even when the communication takes place by means of a written text, but we have neglected or

---

11. Walter J. Ong, *Rhetoric, Romance, and Technology: Studies in the Interaction of Expression and Culture* (Ithaca, N.Y., and London: Cornell University Press, 1971), 290.

12. A biblical scholar or anyone else who deals with the absolutely unique handwritten texts of a manuscript culture should know exactly what I mean. There is no singular text of the Gospel of Mark, except as constructed artificially out of the thousands of variant readings in the surviving manuscripts. *The* Gospel of Mark is a fiction, a creation of criticism.

minimized the reader's contribution to the communication that takes place via the written word.

Reader-response critics reject the container metaphor altogether. A text may be a spatial object, but the reading of a text is always an experience that takes place through time. The implications of this observation are quite significant, yet we have scarcely begun to explore them. In arguing for a temporal model of reading rather than a spatial one, we are adopting an understanding of language that has significant affinities with the language of oral culture. As Ong has observed, in an oral culture an utterance is never a static spatial artifact containing a univocal message or meaning. Rather, each utterance is a dynamic and unique temporal experience welding speaker, hearer, and context into community. Communication is then understood as "putting into communion" or "making common," not, as we so often think of communication, as "conveying the content of a message from sender to receiver by means of a language medium." Although the written word appears to be spatial and particularly in a print culture constitutes a literate-visual mode of consciousness, the spoken word is indubitably temporal, and it constitutes an oral-aural mode of consciousness.[13] Because a deeply oral culture persists prominently in the biblical texts, especially in the Gospel of Mark, the temporal model of reading employed by reader-response critics is especially well suited to the study of biblical texts in general and the Gospel of Mark in particular.

Reader-response critics make use of a number of striking metaphors to characterize the experience of reading. All of them are metaphors of action, movement, or some other dynamic process.

First, most reader-response critics make use of some version of the metaphor of "looking forward and looking backward." This metaphor acknowledges that as we read we are constantly looking back and re-visioning what we have already read, while at the same time looking forward in anticipation of what might lie ahead. We re-view and pre-view constantly to make as much sense of our experience as possible at each individual moment. This obviously visual metaphor invites us to consider how our view of the whole literary work changes ceaselessly, as we proceed step by step on our way through the reading experience. We could just as easily use an acoustic metaphor of hearing echoes of what has receded and the muffled rumblings of what is approaching.

A second metaphor, introduced by Stanley Fish, is the "self-consuming artifact." In his book by the same title, Fish discusses many instances of narratives that unravel themselves as fast as they knit their textual fabric together, sometimes leaving the reader in the end only with loose strands of yarn in his hands, plus the memory of the experience of having lived through the knitting and unraveling process. Besides imagining a self-knitting-and-unraveling textual fabric, I have imagined Fish's self-consuming artifact as a

13. Walter J. Ong, *Orality and Literacy: The Technologizing of the Word* (London and New York: Methuen, 1982), 31.

railroad locomotive with its crew tearing up the tracks behind it and re-laying the tracks in front of it, so that the locomotive can continue to roll forward. Regardless of its particular figurative manifestation, Fish's self-consuming artifact invites us to attend to the present moment of reading and to realize that once the present moment is past we may never be in this particular place, on this particular stretch of track, ever again. Indeed, subsequent reading experience may give us such insight and understanding that we may never be able to retrace our steps in exactly the same way again, even if we should happen to reread the text.

A third metaphor for the reading experience has been popularized by Wolfgang Iser, who speaks of the "gaps" encountered in reading that must be "filled" by the reader.[14] Perhaps the figure of speech is better put by saying that gaps are frequently encountered in reading and they must somehow be negotiated by readers, whether by being filled, bridged, bypassed, or leaped over. The gap metaphor helpfully reminds us that the job of reading requires us to make sense of what the text does not give us, as much as of what it does give us; we must wrestle with what the text does not say as much as with what it does say.

The fourth and last metaphor I want to mention is Wayne Booth's "reconstruction," which is how he characterizes the work required of a reader to make sense of irony.[15] The metaphor suggests that a reader's judgment that a linguistic construction is ironic is a judgment that the verbal edifice is unacceptable as it now stands and that it needs to be dismantled and reconstructed on a more stable and secure foundation of meaning. This metaphor is instructive for how we might go about making sense not only of irony but also of indirect uses of language of all kinds, but the end result of Booth's reconstruction metaphor is a stable new edifice of meaning that is a little too stable and complete for my taste. Much irony maintains a lingering incongruous tension: the foundation is unstable and the reconstruction job cannot be completed. Consequently, I have suggested that alternative metaphors for reading irony (and possibly other turns of indirection) might be the visual metaphor of double vision or the acoustic metaphor of incongruous reverberations.[16]

These are some of the metaphors reader-oriented critics use for the reading experience. They all serve to remind us of the dynamic temporal process that is reading, as we shall see.

14. Iser, *Act of Reading*.

15. Wayne C. Booth, *A Rhetoric of Irony* (Chicago: University of Chicago Press, 1974).

16. Still other alternatives would be Iser's images of the doubleness that is often encountered in reading, such as "figure and ground," "foreground and background," or "theme and horizon"; see Iser, *Act of Reading*.

MEANING AS EVENT

If we shift from focusing on the text as a static spatial form to concentrating on the dynamic temporal experience of reading, then we also need to become aware of the new understanding of meaning that is implied by such a shift. Largely because of the container metaphor, we have tended to think of the meaning of an utterance as its content. If our concern is no longer the text per se but the experience of reading the text, and if the reading experience is not static but dynamic and not spatial but temporal, then meaning can no longer be described in terms of content. We must speak not of the meaning of the text per se but of the meaning of the reading experience, and in dynamic, temporal terms. Thus reader-response critics discuss meaning in terms of event instead of content.

Many resources could be used to reconceptualize meaning as event. The three resources I have found to be most helpful are speech act theory, historical studies of orality and literacy, and critical compasses of the functions of language.

SPEECH ACT THEORY

One resource that has made a significant contribution to the reconceptualization of meaning within reader-response criticism is speech act theory, developed by J. L. Austin and John Searle.[17] Speech act theory is concerned about "performative language," language that does something. One of Austin's favorite examples is the "I do" of the wedding ceremony, which does not so much *say* something as much as it *does* something. In saying "I do," a person is not talking about marriage but committing marriage. Upon reflection, we can see that many other uses of language are also primarily performative: speech acts of promising, warning, threatening, and the like. Then again we could legitimately say that ultimately all utterances are performative: "to say something is to do something."[18] What an utterance does depends entirely upon the context in which it is uttered, including especially all the social conventions of language that are in force at that moment.

Speech act philosophers use three important technical terms. They talk about *locutions,* which refer to just the utterances themselves, that is, the particular sounds that are uttered. *Illocutions* are what a speaker intends to

---

17. J. L. Austin, *How to Do Things with Words* (Oxford: Oxford University Press, 1962); John R. Searle, *Speech Acts: An Essay in the Philosophy of Language* (Cambridge: Cambridge University Press, 1969). For applications of speech act theory to literary criticism, see Mary Louise Pratt, *Toward a Speech Act Theory of Literary Discourse* (Bloomington: Indiana University Press, 1977); Stanley Fish, "How to Do Things with Austin and Searle: Speech-Act Theory and Literary Criticism," *MLN* 91 (1976): 983–1025; now reprinted in *Is There a Text in This Class?* 197–245.

18. Austin, *How to Do Things with Words,* 12.

do by uttering a particular locution, and *perlocutions* are what the speaker actually accomplishes through uttering the locution. That is, these terms refer to what is uttered, what the speaker hopes to accomplish by the utterance, and what the utterance actually accomplishes. In a sense locution is trivial because it is merely the sound of utterance. Perlocutions may be laid aside for now also because they are ultimately beyond anyone's control; try as we might to achieve a purpose, we never know for sure what an utterance will actually accomplish. Speech act theory deals largely, then, with the illocution, which is where a speaker and a hearer, dealing with shared knowledge of the conventions of language, work toward an agreement about how an utterance is to be regarded, or toward "communication," in the sense suggested previously. For speech act theory the meaning of an utterance is not its supposed content but rather its "illocutionary force."[19]

The obverse of the illocutionary force set in motion by the speaker is the hearer's apprehension or uptake of that illocutionary force (see chap. 1). Both illocutionary force and its uptake are functions of the context of the utterance, which is to say that the meaning of an illocution in speech act theory has the nature of dynamic event rather than static content. Thus does speech act theory teach us not to seek meanings in locutions alone but in the exercise and uptake of the illocutionary force of utterances. In brief, an utterance means what it does, not what it says.

ORALITY AND LITERACY

A second resource for reconceptualizing meaning as event is historical studies of orality and literacy, what Ong would call the history of the "technologizing of the word."[20] This resource has had little influence on reader-response criticism, probably because most reader-response critics deal with modern texts, which reflect a congenial modern use of language.[21] By sticking largely to texts written in the modern era, a critic may escape having to face up to the radical changes in the way that language has been understood and used through millennia. The reader-response critic, especially one working with a text nineteen centuries old, should find particularly interesting that in antiquity virtually all "criticism" was reader oriented, because all literature was reader oriented. The thoroughgoing rhetorical or pragmatic orientation of ancient literature and criticism is made clear by M. H. Abrams in *The Mirror and the Lamp*. There he offers a simple categorization of literary theories based

19. Stanley Fish has found speech act theory an important influence on his own reader-oriented criticism. See his discussion of "illocutionary force" in *Is There a Text in This Class?* 284.

20. Ong, *Orality and Literacy.*

21. In classics and biblical studies, reader-response criticism is beginning to be applied to ancient texts; see *Semeia* 31 (1985) on "Reader Response Approaches to Biblical and Secular Texts," *Arethusa* 19,2 (Fall 1986) on "Audience-Oriented Criticism and the Classics," and *Semeia* 48 (1989) on "Reader Perspectives on the New Testament."

on their respective emphases. Abrams says a literary theory tends to concentrate on either the literary text itself (objective theories), the world reflected in the work (mimetic theories), the author of the work (expressive theories), or the audience of the work (pragmatic theories): "Although any reasonably adequate theory takes some account of all four elements, almost all theories . . . exhibit a discernible orientation toward one only."[22] According to this schema, reader-response criticism is a pragmatic approach to literary criticism.

In his discussion of pragmatic theories of language and literature, Abrams states that the pragmatic orientation predominated in Western culture from antiquity until the eighteenth century: "Measured either by its duration or the number of its adherents, therefore, the pragmatic view, broadly conceived, has been the principal aesthetic attitude of the Western world."[23] From this perspective, romanticism's quest to understand the mind of the author, historicism's inquiries into the world reflected in the text, and formalism's analysis of the text apart from its author or reflected world are all relatively recent departures from the norm that has dominated the history of literature and criticism in Western culture.

Jane P. Tompkins also helps us to view language, literature, and criticism in a broader than usual historical perspective. In "The Reader in History," she provides us with a perceptive historical summary of reader-oriented literature and criticism in Western culture.[24] One of her major concerns is that reader-response critics have not consistently reconceptualized the meaning of meaning as a result of their shift in focus away from the text and to the reading experience. She views the reconceptualization of meaning as so difficult for modern critics that forgoing the use of the word *meaning* altogether might be best. Instead of rehabilitating the word *meaning,* she prefers to avoid it in her own criticism. When she talks about the work of other critics, she may still use the word in the familiar sense of meaning as content, but she makes clear that it is an understanding of meaning that reader-response criticism ought to call into question.

Tompkins has a keen sensitivity to the historical gulf between antiquity and modernity, especially as regards changes in understandings of the nature of language. She points out that in the history of Western culture language and texts have usually been perceived differently than they are now and that the ancient world understood language primarily as a matter of pragmatics or rhetoric. The ancients did not view language as a way of conveying meaning; they looked upon language as power.[25] When we read what we might call

22. M. H. Abrams, *The Mirror and the Lamp: Romantic Theory and the Critical Tradition* (London, Oxford, and New York: Oxford University Press, 1953), 6.
23. Ibid., 20–21.
24. Jane P. Tompkins, ed. *Reader-Response Criticism: From Formalism to Post-Structuralism* (Baltimore and London: Johns Hopkins University Press), 201–32.
25. "A literary work is not so much an object, therefore, as a unit of force whose power is exerted upon the world in a particular direction"; ibid., 204.

ancient literary criticism, those critics do not do what a modern critic does; they do not tell us what a text means. Rather, they point out the rhetorical strategies employed in a text so that we may adopt and imitate those same techniques in our own future compositions. Criticism in antiquity was not a matter of finding the meaning of texts; it was a matter of observing how texts do what they do so that others could go and do likewise in their own speaking and writing. Tompkins cites the example of the critic Longinus and his *On the Sublime:*

> For Longinus, language is a form of power and the purpose of studying texts from the past is to acquire the skills that enable one to wield that power. It follows from Longinus's instrumental view of language that he should use Herodotus to illustrate the efficacy of direct address, ignoring what seem to us much deeper questions, because in his perspective the ultimate goal in studying literature is to become master of technique. Likewise, it is because of his unspoken assumptions about the nature of literary language that a contemporary reader-response critic would use the same passage as an occasion to discuss its meaning. All modern criticism—whether response-oriented, psychological, structuralist, mythopoeic, thematic, or formalist—takes meaning to be the object of critical investigation, for unlike the ancients we equate language not with action but with signification.[26]

Tompkins's insight is that in the ancient world—where the Gospel of Mark was written—language had to do primarily with action, not signification. Language was thought by the ancients to bear power, not meaning as content. An utterance or a text represented an active unit of force, not a passive object for analysis. Now reader-response critics such as Tompkins are rediscovering this ancient rhetorical understanding of language.

Confirming Abrams's and Tompkins's historical observations is the recent work of scholars, such as Eric Havelock and Walter Ong, who are exploring the shift from orality to literacy that took place in the ancient Mediterranean world.[27]

Havelock has advanced the provocative thesis that the development of Greek philosophy, especially in Plato, goes hand in hand with the reshaping of consciousness brought about by literacy. When Plato excluded the poets from his republic, he was engaging in a polemic against the oral culture and

---

26. Ibid., 203.
27. Eric A. Havelock, *Preface to Plato* (Cambridge: Harvard University Press, 1963); idem, *The Greek Concept of Justice: From Its Shadow in Homer to Its Substance in Plato* (Cambridge and London: Harvard University Press, 1978); idem, *The Literate Revolution in Greece and Its Cultural Consequences* (Princeton: Princeton University Press, 1982); Walter J. Ong, *The Presence of the Word* (New Haven and London: Yale University Press, 1967); idem, *Rhetoric, Romance, and Technology;* idem, *Interfaces of the Word: Studies in the Evolution of Consciousness and Culture* (Ithaca, N.Y., and London: Cornell University Press, 1977); idem, *Orality and Literacy.*

its habits of mind that he was trying to displace. Plato is the exemplar of a "literate revolution" in ancient Greece.

Following Havelock and others, Ong has documented the profound differences between an oral culture and a literate one. One important observation he makes is that language in an oral culture is inherently rhetorical. Without writing, a person speaks at a given moment, in a given place, and to a given audience for a purpose shaped by that time, place, and audience. The orator always speaks according to the immediate purpose because the language is ephemeral; words cannot be preserved by physical means. After an oral language event, only a memory of it remains, and we all know the tricks that memory plays. This lack of physical preservation is the reason that an oral culture must rely so heavily on the rhythmic and repeated formula to preserve traditional wisdom. As a culture becomes literate, it finds it not only can preserve its wisdom in writing but also can now launch out into genuinely original thought, facilitated by the powerful technology of writing. As a culture achieves literacy, orally produced and aurally comprehended language begins to take a back seat to language that is produced in writing and perceived through the eye. Because language can be preserved in texts, memory becomes less important for a literate culture; a literate culture preserves its memory in books. Because a text survives beyond the moment of its production, it becomes divorced from that moment, and perlocutions never dreamed of by the author begin to take effect. Only in a print-dominated culture do we find the distinctions between—and moreover the fragmentation of—Abrams's quartet of author, text, reader, and universe. The more literate the culture, the more easily they may be split, and their natural union becomes more and more difficult to perceive. In an oral-rhetorical setting, those entities are inseparable. The kind of text-oriented literary criticism that has characterized modern criticism is conceivable only in a print-dominated culture; it would be unimaginable in antiquity.

The shift from orality to literacy is often an uneven, ragged one that might take as little as a few years in the life of an individual or as many as several centuries in the life of a culture. Werner Kelber, in *The Oral and the Written Gospel*,[28] has argued persuasively that the Gospel of Mark represents a watershed in the shift from orality to literacy in the Christian tradition. Mark produces the first written narrative we have of the story of Jesus of Nazareth. Much of the material he uses in his narrative is derived from a rich oral tradition about the words and deeds of Jesus. Nevertheless, Mark writes not so much to preserve oral tradition he reveres as to bring the spoken word under written control, to domesticate it and replace it with his own written version of the *euangelion,* the good news of Jesus Christ. Kelber argues that

28. Werner H. Kelber, *The Oral and the Written Gospel: The Hermeneutics of Speaking and Writing in the Synoptic Tradition, Mark, Paul, and Q* (Philadelphia: Fortress Press, 1983).

Mark is not so much an early preservationist of the Christian oral tradition as he is its first great adversary. Mark's Gospel represents the crucial first step in the long transition from an oral to a written orientation in the narrative traditions about Jesus of Nazareth.

Yet Mark does, in the process of writing, preserve oral traditions, and oral tradition continued to exist alongside the written text of the Gospel. Even in trying to arrest the flow of the spoken word in his written text, the evangelist cannot help maintaining many of the same attitudes and techniques that characterized the predominantly oral-aural experience of language in his time. Because the oral-aural world that he was endeavoring to domesticate through writing was a world that reveled in rhetorical uses of language, he could hardly avoid being rhetorical himself. I am not necessarily thinking here of the classical rhetoric of oratory but rather of what Booth calls the rhetoric of fiction. Mark is a born storyteller, using the rhetorical resources of storytelling in order to bring under written control the oral traditions about Jesus in the early church.

Therefore, whereas most reader-response critics are consciously trying to correct the neglect of the reader in modern criticism, from an even broader historical perspective I see this as a sign of a reemergence of the pragmatic theories of language that have dominated most of Western literary history but have been eclipsed in the last two centuries. As a text from the ancient world— and one not far removed from a cultural situation of orality—we should expect the Gospel of Mark to manifest an understanding of language that befits its historical setting. Mark is an audience-oriented narrative, from an era in which audience-oriented language prevailed, and an audience-oriented approach to the narrative and its meaning is at least appropriate and perhaps unavoidable.

CRITICAL COMPASSES OF LANGUAGE

Another valuable resource in the reconceptualization of meaning is the attempt to lay out a model or a compass of the various functions of language. Recall first, however, that modern biblical scholarship has had either a historical or a theological bent to it. The text of Mark has been taken as evidence of the historical events to which it has been thought to refer, or evidence of the history of the tradition of which it is comprised, or evidence of the theological concepts held by its author or by a particular Christian community; that is, the language of the Gospel in modern times has been regarded as primarily referential in function. Invoking the common linguistic terminology of *syntactics* ("the relations holding among signs"), *semantics* ("the relations between signs and their referents"), and *pragmatics* ("the relations between signs and their human users"),[29] we would have to say that modern scholarship

29. This terminology derives from Charles Morris, who built upon the work of Charles Peirce; for a discussion that does justice to pragmatics, see Elizabeth Bates, "Pragmatics and Sociolinguistics in Child Language," in *Normal and Deficient Child Language*, ed. Donald M. Morehead and Ann E. Morehead (Baltimore, London, and Tokyo: University Park Press, 1976), 412; see also Colin Cherry, *On Human Communication: A Review, a Survey, and a Criticism*, 2d ed. (Cambridge, Mass.: M.I.T. Press, 1966), 219–57.

has approached the Bible with semantic concerns foremost. We have been in the habit of asking, "To what historical or theological referents does the text point?"

I claim that many scholars have unconsciously been impressed by the rhetorical or pragmatic function of the language of Mark, that is, the ways it is designed to affect the reader. In other words, the pragmatics of the Gospel has asserted itself in spite of critical approaches designed to bypass pragmatics in favor of semantics. The pragmatics of the Gospel apparently will not be denied, so we might as well explore the pragmatics of Mark's Gospel intentionally by means of audience-oriented criticism. To understand this proposed shift in orientation from the semantic and referential function of a text to its pragmatic and rhetorical function, we need help in mapping out the functions of language.

One model of the possible emphases of literary theory and therefore presumably of language itself is the one offered by Abrams.[30]

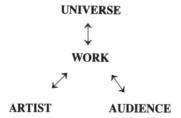

UNIVERSE

WORK

ARTIST   AUDIENCE

The literary work will always be the hub around which literary theory and criticism revolves, but unless we concentrate on the hub alone (and although this approach characterizes much twentieth-century criticism, historically "this point of view has been comparatively rare in literary criticism"[31]), we will tend to view the literary work as it is related to one of the other three foci. Thus mimetic theories examine the work-universe axis, expressive theories the work-artist axis, and pragmatic theories the work-audience axis.

Although this model is intended to be simple, it is probably too simple. For example, we can easily find fault with the unwieldy breadth of "universe." Abrams himself admits that his universe seems to include everything.[32] Similar models improve on Abrams's model by splitting his universe into the universe of language or code, out of which the text is formulated, and the universe of information or representation, to which the text points. One such improvement

30. Abrams, *The Mirror and the Lamp*, 6.
31. Ibid., 26.
32. Ibid., 6.

is the communications model of Roman Jakobson,[33] which views texts as communications, a matter of an "addresser" sending a "message" to an "addressee." Besides splitting Abrams's universe into code and context, Jakobson also clarifies Abrams's use of the notion of axis by employing intersecting vertical and horizontal axes. His model is twofold because he describes both the various factors involved in communication and the function associated with each factor. The factors he outlines as follows:[34]

CONTEXT

ADDRESSER   MESSAGE   ADDRESSEE
                     CONTACT
                      CODE

The functions parallel to the factors can be diagramed as follows:[35]

REFERENTIAL

EMOTIVE   POETIC   CONATIVE
                     PHATIC

METALINGUAL

To the extent that a text is oriented primarily toward expressing what is on the addresser's mind, it manifests an emotive function; to the extent that a text is oriented primarily toward its context (or referent), it stresses the referential (or denotative or cognitive) function of the verbal message; and so on. This model is an improvement over Abrams's. With it we can begin to sort out with some precision how different texts with different emphases serve different functions.

Yet another model, which pays respects both to Abrams and Jakobson, is the "Compass for Critics" laid out by Paul Hernadi.[36] It is the most

---

33. Roman Jakobson, "Closing Statement: Linguistics and Poetics," in *Style in Language,* ed. Thomas A. Sebeok (Cambridge: Technology Press, 1960), 350–77. See also the discussion of this model in the context of New Testament literary criticism by Norman Petersen, *Literary Criticism for New Testament Critics* (Philadelphia: Fortress Press, 1978). See also Wayne Booth's division of Abrams's "universe" into "mimetic" factors and "historical" factors in *Critical Understanding: The Powers and Limits of Pluralism* (Chicago and London: University of Chicago Press, 1979), 57.

34. The only factor that may require explanation is the "contact," which is "the physical channel and psychological connection between the addresser and the addressee"; Jakobson, "Closing Statement," 353; Norman Petersen, *Literary Criticism,* 34–35.

35. Jakobson, "Closing Statement," 357.

36. Paul Hernadi, "Literary Theory: A Compass for Critics," *CI* 3 (1976): 369–86.

illuminating use of the metaphor of axis so far. Hernadi picks up the two intersecting axes that are implicit in Jakobson's diagram, makes them much more explicit, and labels them clearly as the "rhetorical axis of communication" and the "mimetic axis of representation."

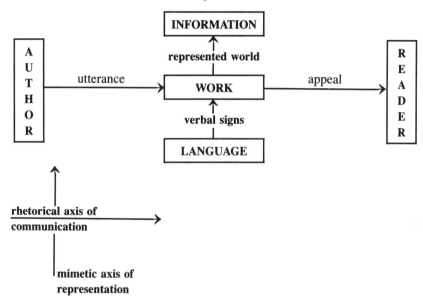

This diagram is only Map 1 in Hernadi's article. In the course of a stimulating discussion of major currents swirling through literary and linguistic theory today, he overlays Maps 2, 3, and 4 on top of this rudimentary one, thus adding great richness and complexity. For our purposes the map above is sufficiently complex because the main point I wish to make is the distinction between the rhetorical axis of communication and the mimetic axis of representation. Recalling again that most modern biblical scholarship has been either historical or theological in its orientation, we see then that it has centered its attention principally on Hernadi's mimetic axis. More precisely, it has focused on the pole of information at the north end of the mimetic axis.[37] Seen from this level of generalization many disparate and even seemingly incongruous stages in the history of Markan scholarship turned out to have much in common. The historicism of much nineteenth-century Markan scholarship, induced by the rediscovery that Mark's was the first Gospel written

37. Sociolinguists and psycholinguists have commented on this general tendency in modernity to concentrate on the vertical axis of reference, to the neglect of the horizontal axis of communication; see David R. Olson, "Some Social Aspects of Meaning in Oral and Written Language," in *The Social Foundations of Language and Thought: Essays in Honor of Jerome S. Bruner,* 90–108, ed. David R. Olson, foreword George A. Miller, afterword Jerome S. Bruner (New York and London: Norton, 1980), 90, 92.

(source criticism), took the earliest Gospel as a reliable historical report: the Gospel was supposed to point to real historical events. Early twentieth-century criticism exploded this historicism and suggested instead that the Gospel really represented evidence for the transmission and development of Christian tradition about Jesus (form criticism): the Gospel was supposed to point to the history of the traditional material of which it was comprised. Mid-twentieth-century criticism began to seek out, more consistently than had been done before, intentional theological significance in the Gospels (redaction criticism): the Gospel was now supposed to point to theological concepts. Each of these methodological approaches was perceived as a significant development beyond what had preceded it, but viewed from the broad perspective of the critical compasses of language they all share the conviction that biblical texts operate primarily along the mimetic axis, with a stress on the referential function.

No one has seen this more clearly than Norman Petersen. Petersen has chronicled the history of modern biblical scholarship from the vantage point of the genuine literary criticism to which it has given birth in recent years.[38] In an essay of crucial importance for biblical criticism, he describes the ascendency of the philological-historical paradigm in biblical scholarship, using the terminology of the Jakobson communications model. Petersen notes that the philological-historical paradigm stresses the referential function of language: the "world" pointed to or represented by language. In Petersen's estimation, however, biblical scholars have to realize the difference between the referential *function* of a narrative—its pointing to a world—and the referential *fallacy*—taking this narrative world naively as the real world, pure and simple.[39] In his analysis of Mark and Luke-Acts, Petersen proceeds to explore the worlds evoked in these narratives as imaginative narrative worlds instead of historical ones.[40] His literary critical analysis is masterful, but he, no less than his philological-historical predecessors, is still focusing on the mimetic axis and on the referential function of language. Moreover, because a significant amount of contemporary literary criticism continues to work along the mimetic axis, we should not be surprised if much of the emerging new literary criticism of the Bible also continues to stress the mimetic and the referential. For example, structuralist criticism, which was in vogue among adventuresome biblical critics in the 1970s and 1980s, concentrates on the same axis that philological-historical criticism favors, although structuralism accentuates the metalingual south pole of the mimetic axis, while philological-historical criticism accentuates the referential north pole of the same axis.

38. Besides Petersen's *Literary Criticism*, see his essay "Literary Criticism in Biblical Studies," in *Orientation by Disorientation: Studies in Literary Criticism and Biblical Literary Criticism. Presented in Honor of William A. Beardslee*, ed. Richard A. Spencer (Pittsburgh: Pickwick Press, 1980), 25–50.

39. Petersen, *Literary Criticism*, 40.

40. See Petersen's essays on Mark (49–80) and Luke-Acts (81–92) in *Literary Criticism;* and idem, " 'Point of View' in Mark's Narrative," *Semeia* 12 (1978): 97–121.

Structuralism is concerned with code more than context, language more than information, syntactics more than semantics. By occupying itself with the mimetic axis of representation, however, structuralism has much in common with the other theories that concentrate on the same axis, whether they be primarily philological-historical or literary-critical.

What would mark a departure from the modern critical preoccupation with mimesis, representation, and reference would be a shift in critical focus from the mimetic axis to the rhetorical axis. I suggest that the language of Mark's Gospel functions primarily along the rhetorical axis, with an emphasis on the pole of the reader and its associated pragmatic or conative function, and that we would do well to orient our criticism of Mark accordingly. The reason that so many scholars have commented perceptively on the experience of reading Mark's Gospel is that, in spite of their professed interest in its referential function, numerous passages in the Gospel do not function referentially. Rather, they function pragmatically, and a critic who wants to say anything at all at these junctures must abandon temporarily the professed critical focus on the referential in order to admit what the narrative is really doing—molding and shaping its implied reader. Biblical scholars have long been in the habit of seeking the story of Mark's narrative, but as often as not we end up responding to the discourse instead. We have sought the meaning of Mark's Gospel in terms of its informational content, but time and again we have found ourselves reflecting upon our experience of reading the Gospel. We could say that the Gospel is not so much designed to construct its own world as it is designed to construct its own reader; it is not designed so much to say something about its implied world as it is to do something to its implied reader; the narrative does not strive to convey meaning as referential content as much as it strives to achieve communion with its audience by means of a forceful event that takes place through time.

To be sure, any use of language touches upon at least a portion of every quadrant of Hernadi's compass. Mark's Gospel does imply a certain narrative world; it does imply the portrait of an implied author; it does manifest the linguistic codes out of which it is woven. Any usage of language tends to tip toward one pole or another of the compass, however, and Mark's Gospel tips toward the pole of the reader. The orientation of this text should be matched with a similarly oriented critical theory. Such a match is not as difficult if criticism is contemporary with—and therefore shares the same understanding of language as—the literature it examines, but Mark is a nineteen-hundred-year-old text; we should not be surprised that it reflects an understanding of language different from our own. Mark's Gospel is a written narrative that lies close to orality, and, as Ong has stated repeatedly, the language of oral culture is inherently rhetorical or pragmatic in function. On this basis alone we should expect Mark, and probably all other biblical books, to function primarily along the rhetorical axis. The fixation on referential meaning that

characterizes modern criticism is exactly that, a modern fixation, conceivable
only in the historical context of widespread acquaintance with printed texts,
that is, in the historical setting of Marshall McLuhan's Gutenberg Galaxy.[41]

In this chapter and the previous one I have proposed a version of reader-
response criticism that includes: (1) a focus on the reader and the reading
experience and (2) a critical model of reading that includes: (a) an emphasis
on the temporal experience of reading and (b) a focus on meaning as event.
I now want to apply this model of reader-response criticism to the Gospel of
Mark. One of my major concerns will be Mark's rhetoric of indirection: the
use of ambiguity, irony, paradox, and the like. Besides indirection, however,
the author also employs much direction. Stable, reliable guidance for the
reader is in good supply in Mark's Gospel. Thus both the direction and
indirection in Mark's rhetorical strategy invite exploration. Before proceeding
to direction and indirection, however, I want to make some more general
comments about Mark's narrative rhetoric.

41. Straws in the wind are today signaling a revival of interest in the rhetorical axis and the
pragmatic function of language. I see signs of discontent with the assumed preeminence of the
mimetic axis of language, and I hear suggestions that the rhetorical axis may be equally important,
or may even be itself the preeminent axis. See, for example:
  • In reader-response criticism: Stanley Fish, *Is There a Text in This Class?*
  • In speech act theory: Austin, *How to Do Things with Words*
  • In orality and literacy studies: Ong, *Orality and Literacy*
  • In rhetoric: Chaim Perelman and Lucie Olbrechts-Tyteca, *The New Rhetoric: A Treatise on
Argumentation,* trans. John Wilkinson and Purcell Weaver (Notre Dame, Ind., and London:
University of Notre Dame Press, 1969)
  • In anthropology: Michael Silverstein, "Shifters, Linguistic Categories, and Cultural De-
scription," in *Meaning in Anthropology,* ed. Keith H. Basso and Henry A. Selby (Albuquerque:
University of New Mexico Press, 1976), 11–55
  • In psycholinguistics: Elizabeth Bates, *Language and Context: The Acquisition of Pragmatics*
(New York, San Francisco, and London: Academic Press, 1976)
  • In sociolinguistics: Roger Fowler, *Literature as Social Discourse: The Practice of Linguistic
Criticism* (Bloomington: Indiana University Press, 1981).

PART TWO

THE
GOSPEL
OF MARK

4

THE STORYTELLER'S
CRAFT

My aim here is to clarify how the narrative rhetoric of Mark's Gospel functions in the experience of reading the Gospel. I shall explore the "rhetoric of fiction" in Mark's Gospel: the ways the Gospel writer "tries, consciously or unconsciously, to impose his fictional world upon the reader" and "the author's means of controlling his reader."[1] I am interested in how Mark's narrative affects the reader.

One of the chief ways the reliable narrator of the Gospel directs the reading experience is by providing "reliable commentary."[2] The notion of reliability is crucial here. Much of what Mark is doing—and much of what any implied author does—is to persuade the reader that he is reliable. Authors who wish to be read strive to present themselves as trustworthy and authoritative, especially if the narrator constructed to tell the story happens to be unreliable.

But in Mark we never have to deal with a narrator's unreliability. To the contrary, we have reliability and authority in spades; that *exousia* (authority) and *dynamis* (power) are recurring themes at the story level of the narrative is no accident. The implied author puts forth a reliable, authoritative narrator, who puts forth a reliable, authoritative protagonist named Jesus. If the rhetoric of the narrative is successful, then the *exousia* and *dynamis* attributed to Jesus by the narrator will implicitly garner *exousia* and *dynamis* for the narrator himself, and in turn for the implied author.

1. Wayne C. Booth, *The Rhetoric of Fiction,* 2d ed. (Chicago and London: University of Chicago Press, 1983), xiii. See also Norman Petersen: *"Mark's rhetoric is the rhetoric of fiction, and it provides the most compelling evidence that his Gospel is a bona fide literary composition"* (" 'Point of View' in Mark's Narrative," *Semeia* 12 [1978]: 114–15; Petersen's italics).

2. See Wayne Booth's chapter "The Uses of Reliable Commentary," in *Rhetoric of Fiction,* 169–209, and see my earlier discussion of reliable commentary in Mark in *Loaves and Fishes: The Function of the Feeding Stories in the Gospel of Mark,* SBLDS 54 (Chico, Calif.: Scholars Press, 1981), 149–79.

If this construction of homologous levels of authority in Mark's narrative seems to be done with mirrors, it is neither more nor less than what other written narratives do. A text is a fabric (*textus*), something produced by the act of weaving (*texere*). Unlike oral language, which is shared instantaneously by speaker and hearer, a text is an artifice that stands apart from its producer, its original recipient, and its original context. It can outlive them all. Therefore, even though a text may try to borrow authority from various outside sources (e.g., Mark's Gospel presupposes and tries to capitalize upon the authority of the Jewish scriptures), ultimately a text must create its own credibility. It must stand or fall on its own. A text must be self-authenticating, able to entangle the reader in its own network.

The claim to authority made implicitly by any text makes writing a bid for power, and texts do wield power, to varying degrees. Yet even the most powerful of texts is vulnerable to other texts. The vector of force represented by a text can be diminished or redirected by later texts; the power of the written word can be blunted by still other written words. One way to counter the effectiveness of a text-fabric is to weave yet another text-fabric that takes up and enfolds its predecessor. Matthew, Luke, and John can be seen as text-fabrics incorporating and thereby supplanting the text-fabric of Mark. How did Mark look before its fabric was thus assimilated? Alas, nineteen hundred years have passed since anyone has seen Mark's fabric not enfolded in the smothering embrace of its successors. In a Bible or in a Gospel Synopsis, we think we can see the warp and woof of Mark's fabric, positioned alongside its companion texts, but herein lies the secret of the rhetoric of Matthew, Luke, and John: by reweaving Mark's fabric into their own, they make the original fabric almost invisible, even when it seems to lie separate and distinct right before our eyes.

Contrasting Mark's narrative rhetoric with the rhetoric of the letters of Paul can give more insight into its self-authenticating nature. As Werner Kelber has observed, Paul places a very high premium on the spoken word; he represents a Christianity still deeply embedded in orality.[3] Recent studies of Paul's letters have found much evidence that Paul was conversant with the popular oratorical rhetoric of the Hellenistic age.[4] Like an orator, Paul appeals to his ethos or character[5] in his letters, appealing especially to his authority

3. Werner H. Kelber, *The Oral and the Written Gospel: The Hermeneutics of Speaking and Writing in the Synoptic Tradition, Mark, Paul, and Q* (Philadelphia: Fortress Press, 1983), 140–83.

4. See, e.g., Hans Dieter Betz, *Galatians*, Hermeneia Commentary Series (Philadelphia: Fortress Press, 1979); Robert Jewett, "Romans as an Ambassadorial Letter," *Int* 36 (1982): 5–20; George A. Kennedy, *New Testament Interpretation through Rhetorical Criticism* (Chapel Hill and London: University of North Carolina Press, 1984).

5. "Ethos means 'character' and may be defined as the credibility that the author or speaker is able to establish in his work. The audience is induced to trust what he says because they trust him, as a good man or an expert on the subject. In Aristotelian theory ethos is something entirely internal to a speech, but in practice the authority which the speaker brings to the occasion is an important factor, and this is especially true in the New Testament" (ibid., 15).

as an apostle of Jesus Christ. In each instance he presents an ethos predicated upon the apostolic authority established prior to the letter and presumed in it. Most of Paul's letters begin with some variation on the words "Paul, an apostle . . ." (*Paulos apostolos . . .*).

This presupposition is but the first of many upon which Paul builds his rhetoric. The presupposition of apostolic authority is evident, but many other presuppositions are less so; when reading Paul's letters we eavesdrop on a conversation and hear only one side of it. To make any sense at all of the conversation, we must endeavor to reconstruct the whole conversation. Construing the force of Paul's letters is quite impossible without some kind of hypothetical reconstruction of the ideologies and rhetorical strategies, both explicit and implicit, of both Paul and his dialogue partners. The letters of Paul are incomplete, fragmentary remains of concrete rhetorical situations. The letters themselves force us to go outside the letters to reconstruct the conversation.

The ethos or authority claimed by the author of the Gospel of Mark is of another sort altogether. No appeal is made to the personal authority of the author, as with Paul, nor are many appeals made to other authorities outside of the narrative itself. Not even the Jewish Scriptures authenticate the Gospel; the Gospel tells us how to read the Jewish Scriptures and thereby authorizes and authenticates them.

The Gospel is an anonymous work. The later attribution of apostolic authority to the Gospel by the Christian church is an attempt to grant it a kind of authority it does not claim for itself. The kind of authority to which it does lay claim is the kind of authority claimed implicitly by any well-told story. Mark's rhetoric is not, like Paul's, the rhetoric of oratory, with its logical arguments and emotive appeals. Rather, Mark's is the rhetoric of narrative. Its aim is "to make the whole package, story and discourse, including the narrator's performance, interesting, acceptable, self-consistent, and artful."[6] The author's aim in such a narrative is internally directed, to tell a story that is persuasive on its own terms. This inward orientation makes Mark an example of what Northrop Frye calls "centripetal" language. Paul's letters, by contrast, are "centrifugal,"[7] aimed outward and representing only a fleeting moment in an ongoing conversation that both predates the letter at hand and will continue to develop in the future, building upon the letter. Furthermore, Paul's rhetoric employs proofs and reasoned arguments; to an astonishing degree the Gospel of Mark eschews both. As George Kennedy has observed, Mark's Gospel features prominently "what may be called radical Christian rhetoric,

6. Seymour Chatman, *Story and Discourse: Narrative Structure in Fiction and Film* (Ithaca, N.Y., and London: Cornell University Press, 1978), 227.

7. Northrop Frye, *The Great Code: The Bible and Literature* (New York and London: Harcourt, Brace, Jovanovich, 1982), 57–58.

a form of 'sacred language' characterized by assertion and absolute claims of authoritative truth without evidence or logical argument."[8]

I am not saying that the events and characters of Mark's story bear no resemblance to the world outside it or that it was not originally aimed at real flesh-and-blood readers. Surely the Gospel does reflect certain events in first-century Palestinian history, and surely it does reflect the concerns of a genuine flesh-and-blood audience. My point is that the primary aim of the Gospel is neither to point to a real world nor to respond to a real audience. Rather, it evokes its own narrative world and shapes its own audience. To the extent that Mark is referential in function, its referentiality serves to further its rhetorical efficacy: "It is difficult to overstate the success of gospel textuality, its 'benign deceit' in seducing readers into taking fact-likeness for factuality. Indeed, so persuasive has the gospel's textuality been in drawing attention away from itself and toward what it has written, that it has until recently escaped inquiry into its own techniques and credentials."[9] My work is an inquiry into the "techniques and credentials" of Mark's narrative, an exploration of its narrative rhetoric.

THE NARRATOR'S STANCE

We must consider the stance of the narrator in the Gospel. The narrator of the Gospel is an omniscient, intrusive, third-person narrator. Rhoads and Michie have summarized the characteristics of this narrator.

> The salient features of Mark's narrator are these: the narrator does not figure in the events of the story; speaks in the third person; is not bound by time or space in the telling of the story; is an implied invisible presence in every scene, capable of being anywhere to "recount" the action; displays full omniscience by narrating the thoughts, feelings, or sensory experiences of many characters; often turns from the story to give direct "asides" to the reader, explaining a custom or translating a word or commenting on the story; and narrates the story from one over-arching ideological point of view.[10]

Rather than saying the narrator is omniscient or omnipresent ("not bound by time or space"), perhaps better terms would be *unlimited* or *unrestricted*.[11] This terminology is apt because, although such a narrator seems to know all, he never has the option to tell all, nor can he actually take us to all times and

8. Kennedy, *Rhetorical Criticism*, 104.

9. Kelber, *Oral and Written Gospel*, 116.

10. David Rhoads and Donald Michie, *Mark as Story: An Introduction to the Narrative of a Gospel* (Philadelphia: Fortress Press, 1982), 23. Rhoads and Michie are using Norman Petersen's ground-breaking essay on this subject, "Point of View."

11. See the recommendation for the word *unrestricted* by Gerald Prince, *Narratology: The Form and Function of Narrative* (Berlin, New York, and Amsterdam: Mouton, 1982), 51.

all places in the course of telling the story. He is merely unlimited or unrestricted in what he can choose to show or tell. Terms such as *omniscient* or *omnipresent* are revealing, however, for they indicate that the pose of an unlimited narrator makes an implicit claim to absolute authority and reliability. This kind of narrative stance has been called "godlike," and with justice.[12] The notion that the Gospels were dictated verbatim to his stenographers by God, although asserted nowhere in the Gospels themselves, is nevertheless a shrewd recognition of the degree of authority that the evangelists implicitly demand for themselves. Not even Jesus knows as much as our narrator; we may wonder whether God knows more.

Even more is involved in the omniscient third-person narrator's implicit claim to authority. Mark's is wholly a retrospective narrative; the narrator tells the story at a point in time after the events of the story have taken place. That this point needs to be noted is another indication of the rhetorical success of the narrative. Mark's narrator has masked his retrospective point of view in a manner that would be quite difficult to achieve were he a more limited narrator. A narrative told by a narrator who speaks in the first person (e.g., Huck in *Huckleberry Finn*), for example, is openly retrospective; storytelling in an autobiographical mode reminds the reader constantly that the "I" telling the story has lived to tell his own tale.[13] Mark's omniscient narrator, by contrast, hides his retrospective perspective, paradoxically, by being anywhere and everywhere, in a fashion that no first-person narrator can hope to emulate. By being omnipresent, the narrator of Mark's Gospel successfully creates the illusion of invisibility. He roams at will through time and space, knowing all and seeing all, even to the extent of moving freely in and out of the minds of his characters, Jesus included. With such freedom of movement he can put the reader in the very midst of the action, creating a narrative of tremendous vividness and immediacy. We get caught up in the story to such an extent that we tend to visualize the action taking place now, before our eyes, in a direct, unmediated way. Whereas a first-person narrative openly admits a retrospective view toward the story, a third-person narrative such as Mark's seems to take place in the here and now.

To illustrate, one of many stylistic features of the narrative that helps to create the illusion of presence and immediacy is the use of verbs in the historical present, present-tense verbs where the reader would expect verbs in a past

12. Gerald Prince refers to the "godlike vantage point" of the "unlimited" narrator (ibid., 51), a turn of phrase borrowed from Norman Friedman, "Point of View in Fiction: The Development of a Critical Concept," in *Approaches to the Novel: Materials for a Poetic*, ed. Robert Scholes (San Francisco: Chandler, 1961), 126.

13. On the various limitations inherent in the first-person narrative, see Chatman, *Story and Discourse*, 158; Gérard Genette, *Narrative Discourse: An Essay in Method*, trans. Jane E. Lewin, foreword Jonathan Culler (Ithaca, N.Y.: Cornell University Press, 1980), 168; Booth, *Rhetoric of Fiction*, 150.

tense. Mark is replete with phrases such as "So he says to the paralytic . . ." (2:10). This language is informal and colloquial, but vigorous and engaging as well. Along with stylistic characteristics that promote immediacy, the vividness of description in the Gospel is often stressed by critics. In weaving vivid scenes, the storyteller is not only engaging the reader but also making light of his discourse, the very act of weaving the tale. Mark's graphic showing of scene and action lulls us into forgetting that the whole performance is his telling.

POINT OF VIEW

The familiar literary critical language about narrative point of view can be useful here. The narrator is constantly trying to put us in the sandals of one character or another; we are made privy to what this character feels, what that one believes, what another one sees or hears. Are we not being given insight into the story world through these different points of view? Yes and no. The language about point of view is useful only if used with care. A helpful distinction can be made between point of view and voice.[14] If point of view is a matter of who sees in the narrative, then voice is a matter of who speaks. In other words, we may distinguish between the eyes that are seeing the action in the story and the voice that is describing what the eyes are seeing. Although the narrator shifts constantly from the visual perspective of one character to another, we always hear the narrator's reliable and authoritative voice. The apparent variety of visual perspectives or points of view in Mark is illusory because the only voice is the voice of the narrator, and it is always in control. This dominating narrative voice is especially present when we are supposed to be hearing Jesus speak. Jesus may speak, but never without the narrator's voice. The same is true for all other characters in the story.

Besides distinguishing between point of view and voice, we also need to distinguish between different kinds of point of view. Seymour Chatman suggests that we should distinguish among: (1) a perceptual point of view, that is, someone's sense perception from a real or imaginary physical location; (2) a conceptual point of view, that is, someone's ideological perspective, conceptual system, or Weltanschauung; and (3) an interest point of view, that is, what may be in someone's interest, or to her advantage, profit, or general well-being, perhaps without her even realizing it.[15] Using this language, we may say that in Mark we are given a variety of perceptual points of view— the sense perceptions of the various characters in the Gospel—but always from the consistent and dominating conceptual point of view of the omniscient narrator.

14. Here I rely on Genette, *Narrative Discourse*, 161–62, 185–86.
15. Chatman, *Story and Discourse*, 151–58.

Examples from the Gospel that illustrate this distinction are the episodes of the Stilling of the Storm (4:35-41) and the Walking on the Water (6:45-52). These stories function in the Gospel as a matched pair.[16] They are two of only three episodes in the Gospel that take place in a boat on the Sea of Galilee. Because of the small number of such sea stories in Mark and because of their clear similarities—both show Jesus' mastery over wind and wave—an attentive reader links the stories. Attention to point of view reveals some interesting narrative strategies in the telling of these stories.

In the first story, the Stilling of the Storm (4:35-41), Jesus is asleep in the stern as the boat is about to be swamped. We see his astonishing imperturbability from the perceptual point of view of the disciples. Because we see the slumbering Jesus through their eyes, we can readily sympathize with them in their fear; death by drowning seems near. We may next be surprised, however, to witness them awaken Jesus rudely, and chastise him for his lack of concern. Our perceptual point of view has now become distinct from that of the disciples. We are now in the position of an observer in the boat who is witnessing the developing confrontation between Jesus and the disciples. Next, we most likely are surprised by the harsh words Jesus levels at the Twelve: "Why are you cowards? Do you not yet[17] have faith?" (4:40; author's translation[18]). This double question is not answered in the story, but the reader can easily infer from Jesus' words that he thinks the disciples have behaved cowardly and do not yet have faith. The disciples' response to Jesus, in the form of another rhetorical question, tends to confirm Jesus' suspicion. They say: "Who then is this, that even wind and sea obey him?" (4:41). One-fourth of the Gospel has been narrated, and yet the disciples wonder who Jesus is! Having experienced earlier in the episode the perceptual point of view of the disciples, and especially having shared their fear, the reader probably retains a significant degree of sympathy for them. Because they are said to "not yet" have faith, we may hold forth some hope for the Twelve. We are inclined not to be too critical of them at this early stage in the Gospel, for perhaps they will yet arrive at understanding and faith.

In the Walking on the Water (6:45-52), the companion sea story two chapters later, some interesting moves occur in the course of the narration. In this episode we look first upon the action as rather neutral observers, watching Jesus send his disciples away in the boat, dismiss the crowd, and go to the mountain to pray. Next we are given Jesus' perceptual point of view: we see along with him the boaters struggling on the churning lake. We even seem to accompany him as he starts out walking across the lake toward the boat. "He wanted to pass by them," we are told, an enigmatic description of

---

16. Fowler, *Loaves and Fishes,* 100–05.

17. Reading *oupō* in v. 40, thus modifying the RSV.

18. Passages translated by the author will hereafter be designated "RMF."

68 THE GOSPEL OF MARK

a puzzling motivation, but nevertheless an inside view of Jesus' motivation given to us as readers. Therefore, when the perceptual point of view next shifts to that of the disciples, we cannot share with them their total ignorance as to who or what this apparition is that walks toward them, on the waves, through the wind. Rather than feeling empathy for the terror-stricken disciples, we cannot help judging them unfavorably. How could they not recognize who is coming to them? We, after all, know who it is; why do they not? Moreover, do they not remember, as we surely do, what happened in the previous sea incident back in Mark 4:35-41, when Jesus calmed both wind and wave in their presence? How could they be so obtuse as not to recognize who this must be, "that even wind and sea obey him"?

In fairness to the disciples, two things have happened in the narration of Mark 6:45-52 to thrust the reader into a position of privileged superiority over the disciples. Within the second sea story, the narrator has induced us to share his own lofty conceptual point of view by sharing with us the shifting of perceptual points of view. As a result of experiencing several different perceptual points of view, when the narrator finally offers us the disciples' perceptual point of view, we cannot accept it because we know too much already. In addition to what happens internally, within the water-walking episode itself, the narrator makes skillful use of the plotted design of the entire Gospel by using the two sea stories as a matched pair.[19] Because the reader is bound to remember the earlier sea episode, even if the disciples apparently do not, the narrator is able to build into the second episode covert ironies discernible only to the reader by using the first story as a backdrop for the second. In the midst of the second sea story, we are offered the disciples' defective perceptual point of view but are unable to accept it, in part because the shifting of perceptual points of view has made us captive to the narrator's superior conceptual point of view but in part also because we cannot help reading this story over against the backdrop of an earlier, similar episode. Curiously, as if he did not trust his own skill as a storyteller, the narrator ends the Walking on the Water episode with an explicit and ringing proclamation of the stupidity displayed by the disciples in this episode and in preceding ones: "And they were completely stunned within themselves, for they did not

19. Petersen emphasizes that the narrator's "ideological point of view" is communicated to the reader through the plotting of the actions in the story ("Point of View," 108). He borrows the notion "ideological point of view" from the rich, provocative work on point of view by Boris Uspensky, *A Poetics of Composition: The Structure of the Artistic Text and Typology of a Compositional Form,* trans. V. Zavarin and S. Wittig (Berkeley, Los Angeles, and London: University of California Press, 1973).

Uspensky is primarily concerned with the syntactics of point of view. Thus, Petersen, following Uspensky, deals only briefly with the pragmatics or rhetorical aspects of point of view, which I am suggesting should be the most important consideration when dealing with Mark or with any other text from the ancient world.

understand about the loaves. Instead, their minds were hardened" (6:51-52, R&M).

Similar manipulation of perceptual point of view occurs at least two other times in Mark. Both instances occur early in the Gospel, and both thrust the reader into a position of inability to accept the faulty perceptual point of view of the disciples. First is the episode of the woman with the flow of blood (5:24-34). There we are given first the perspective of the woman, who sur-reptitiously touches Jesus' garment in the midst of a crowd and feels herself healed of her malady (vv. 25-29). Then we are granted Jesus' perspective as he turns in the middle of the thronging crowd and asks who had touched him (v. 30). Thus far we have been made to know what the woman did in order to be healed, that she was indeed healed, and that Jesus knew that "power had gone forth from him" (v. 30). Then the reader is granted the perspective of the disciples, who say in a querulous tone, "You see the crowd pressing around you, and yet you say 'Who touched me?' " (v. 31), but we cannot join them in their lack of perception. We already know what they apparently do not know. The narrator has once again maneuvered us into being unable to accept the perceptual point of view of the disciples when he offers it to us.

Another instance is in the two episodes of a feeding of a multitude (6:30-44; 8:1-10). These episodes function as a matched pair, much like the two sea stories.[20] In the first feeding story, initially we see much of the action through the disciples' eyes. They come to Jesus, inform him of the late hour, point out the crowd's need for food, and suggest to him that he send the crowd away to find food for themselves (6:35-36). Jesus responds by trying to get the disciples to assume responsibility for the crowd (v. 37); when they fail to meet this challenge, he assumes responsibility and feeds five thousand men (*andres*) with five loaves and two fishes. Reading the first feeding story is thus an experience somewhat similar to the experience of reading the first sea story. In both cases we see much of the action through the eyes of the disciples, and when they falter we are inclined not to judge them too harshly. Perhaps they are just not yet aware of Jesus' mastery over wind and wave or over loaves and fishes, so we tend to be sympathetic. Reading the second feeding story is similar to the experience of reading the second sea story. In both episodes we see things initially from the perspective of Jesus, and when the perceptual point of view shifts to that of the disciples we cannot adopt their point of view. In the second feeding story, Jesus seizes the initiative at the start of the episode by summoning the disciples to himself, expressing his compassion for the vast crowd, and pointing out the crowd's hunger (8:1-3). In other words, he describes for the disciples a situation virtually identical to that of the first feeding story two chapters earlier. Jesus sets the stage for a

20. Fowler, *Loaves and Fishes,* 43–99.

repetition of that earlier feeding of a multitude, but the disciples do not pick up any of the hints. They respond with yet another querulous question: "How can one feed these men with bread here in the desert?" (8:4). The reader cannot join the disciples in asking this question, for the reader remembers, even if the disciples do not, the Feeding of the Five Thousand two chapters earlier, and therefore the reader knows without question that Jesus can feed multitudes in the desert with just a few loaves. As a result of having read the first sea story and the first feeding story, the reader cannot adopt the disciples' defective perceptual point of view when it is offered in a second sea or feeding story.

All of the preceding instances of the narrator's manipulation of perceptual point of view take place in the first half of the Gospel, and all are at the expense of the disciples. Consequently, these episodes provide some important clues regarding the vexed question of the role of the disciples in Mark's Gospel. The disciples of Jesus in the story are often suggested to be models for the reader outside the story; that is, the reader is supposed to "identify" with the Twelve. We have seen, however, that our identification with the disciples is far more complicated than it might at first appear. At several points early in the Gospel, we certainly do identify with the disciples, in the sense of seeing things through their eyes. We often hear and see along with them the words and deeds of Jesus. We experience along with them the shortest of distances between ourselves and Jesus. We are also often sympathetic when they fail to comprehend Jesus. Having seen astonishing or frightful things through their eyes, we are often inclined to forgive their lack of insight. When we are offered the opportunity to see things through their eyes and we cannot do so, however, because our knowledge and understanding is greater than theirs, in those moments the reader is closer to Jesus than are the disciples. The narrator has opened up distance between Jesus and his disciples and inserted the reader into the space between them. As this kind of reading experience is repeated, it has a cumulative effect. Maintaining sympathy for the stubbornly obtuse disciples becomes harder and harder, even when the narrative offers us the opportunity to identify and sympathize with the Twelve from time to time. Often we find ourselves on intimate terms with the Twelve, only to find ourselves far removed from them an instant later, wary of trusting them and their perceptual point of view. We learn to keep our distance from them even when the narrative seems to invite us to draw near to them. Thus, through the course of the narrative, as distance is opened up between Jesus and the disciples at the level of story, something analogous is happening at the same time between the reader and the disciples at the level of discourse. Distance grows throughout the narrative, unevenly but irreversibly, until at last at the level of story all of the disciples abandon Jesus, at which point the distance between Jesus and the Twelve has become total, which means that at the level of discourse the burden of discipleship now falls squarely upon the shoulders of the only remaining candidate for discipleship—the recipient of the narrator's discourse, the reader of the Gospel.

A pivotal development in the relationship between Jesus and the disciples—and therefore between the reader and the disciples—occurs in the Caesarea Philippi episode at the midpoint of the Gospel (8:27—9:1). We begin the episode by adopting with little difficulty the perceptual point of view of the Twelve as they offer to Jesus a variety of reports on who people say he is. Then Peter makes a potentially momentous assertion, perhaps on behalf of the Twelve, that Jesus is the Christ (8:29). The reader's hopes may be raised that at last the disciples have figured out what the reader has known about Jesus since the opening words of the Gospel (1:1). Any such hopes are soon dashed, however, as the episode quickly degenerates into the fiercest confrontation imaginable between a teacher and his pupils.

Peter says that Jesus is the Christ, but apparently he does not share Jesus' understanding of what that means; Jesus immediately silences Peter's seemingly correct assertion (v. 30) and proceeds to announce for the first time in the Gospel the impending rejection, suffering, and death of the "Son of man" (v. 31). Peter responds by rebuking Jesus, and Jesus responds in kind, going so far as to call Peter "Satan" and to say that Peter is "not on the side of God, but of men" (v. 33).

Through the course of these verses, the reader stands observing the scene, seeing things now from the perspective of the disciples, now from Jesus' perspective, and so on, back and forth. When we arrive at verse 33, however, no one can vacillate; the reader must choose. Will the reader side with Jesus and God or with Peter and humankind? Clearly the author wants the reader to choose the former.

In the story the disciples remain with Jesus until the final crisis in Jerusalem, and therefore we occasionally see things through their eyes right up to the end. The distance between Jesus and the Twelve is well established by the midpoint of the Gospel, however, and the gap continues to widen thereafter. Although earlier we often shared the disciples' perceptual point of view without giving it a second thought, no longer do we trust implicitly the disciples' perspective on the events of the story. More and more we find ourselves distrusting and rejecting their perceptual point of view the instant it is offered to us. Increasingly, we cannot maintain much sympathy for the disciples. The narrative requires that we journey with them to Jerusalem, but the narrative has taught us to keep our distance from them on the way. One more example may suffice.

Somewhat like the twin sea stories in Mark 4 and 6 and the feeding stories in Mark 6 and 8, twin episodes concerning the welcoming of children take place in Mark 9:33-37 and 10:13-16. As before, the reader is unable to accept the disciples' point of view when the second episode of the pair is narrated. With the twin sea and feeding stories, however, the reader is sympathetic with the disciples in the first episode; such is not the case here. In the first place, the first of the two child-welcoming episodes does not even offer the reader much of a perceptual point of view to adopt. The episode begins with the disciples in embarrassed silence (9:34), and we do not know why they are silent until the narrator explains the situation to us: on the road, while Jesus was predicting his impending suffering and death (9:30-32), the disciples were debating among themselves which of them was the greatest (9:34). This insensitivity to Jesus' fate, combined with crass egotism, is not a stance that the reader is likely to want to embrace, especially because we can anticipate that Jesus will probably respond by giving the Twelve a tongue-lashing over their glory-seeking. In this setting Jesus embraces a child as an object lesson for the self-seeking, self-glorifying disciples (9:33-35). Apparently the disciples need to hear Jesus' startling reversal of the normal human standard: "If anyone would be first, he must be last of all and servant of all" (9:35). According to this shocking new standard, embracing a child is like embracing God (9:37).

The narrator had alerted the reader with ample clues that a rebuke aimed at the disciples was forthcoming. The embracing of the child in 9:36-37 is preceded not only by Jesus' second passion prediction (9:31) but also by the narrator's clear comments that the disciples (1) did not understand the passion prediction (9:32), (2) were too afraid to ask for clarification (9:32), and (3) found themselves in embarrassed silence when Jesus brought to light their debate about their own greatness (9:34). Because the reader heard Jesus speak about dying in 9:31 and heard the narrator comment on the obtuseness of the disciples in 9:32 and 9:34, the reader cannot possibly sympathize with the self-aggrandizing disciples in 9:33-37.

If we cannot embrace the disciples' perspective at any point in 9:33-37, it is all the more so in 10:13-16. As if they never saw Jesus embrace the child in 9:36 or heard him say, "whoever receives one such child in my name receives me; and whoever receives me, receives not me but him who sent me" (9:37), when people bring children to Jesus, the disciples rudely rebuke them (*epitimaō*; 10:13). Jesus responds angrily to their callousness, and we are given little choice but to side with him against the Twelve. In these twin episodes we distance ourselves from the Twelve consistently, from beginning to end, instead of experiencing a turning point midway through the second of the two episodes. This change is a sign of the irreversible distance that is growing between Jesus and the Twelve at the level of story and therefore also between the reader and the Twelve at the level of discourse.

Often in episodes in the first half of the Gospel, the disciples clearly lacked perception (e.g., their not knowing that someone had touched Jesus, their inability to recognize an apparition walking on the lake, and their inability to comprehend a wondrous feeding of a multitude). Thus we found ourselves regularly distanced from their perceptual point of view. In the two child-welcoming episodes, however, the suspicion arises that the disciples may not only lack perception but also actually stand apart from Jesus conceptually as well as perceptually. Their distance from him now seems more conscious and willful. At this point in the Gospel we have now heard that Jesus called Peter "Satan" (8:33), that Peter was on the side of men and not of God (8:33), and that the disciples have repeatedly sought their own glory (see 9:34 followed by 9:38!). The disciples not only lack perception but also have defective conceptions. This insight should not be entirely new to us, however. Language about *perceptions* is an obvious way of speaking figuratively about *conceptions*. The language about the disciples' blindness and deafness (see 8:17-21) has all along really been more about the inadequacy of their conceptual point of view rather than about their perceptual point of view. In Mark seeing and hearing are recurring figures of speech for insight and understanding. In the first half of the Gospel, the figurative language lulls us into thinking of the disciples' problems chiefly in terms of flawed perception. From the midpoint of the Gospel onward, however, the narrator subtly begins to shift emphasis away from the disciples' perceptual point of view and to emphasize instead the inadequacy and even the danger (see 8:38) of their conceptual point of view. Concern for a flawed conceptual point of view, which the language about perception might have disguised previously, is now brought out into the open. Having taught us in the first half of the Gospel that we cannot trust the disciples' perceptions, the narrator is in a strong position to complete the job in the second half by undermining our faith in the disciples' conceptions.

THE PROTAGONIST'S AUTHORITY

Besides overseeing the shifting of perceptual points of view and thereby discreetly promoting or undermining various conceptual points of view, the narrator asserts his reliability and authority in a number of other ways, both explicit and implicit. One strategy looms so large that it is easy to overlook: in the Gospel Jesus speaks, but always with the narrator's voice. In other words, the narrator establishes his authority by establishing the authority of his main character, Jesus. The two become virtually indistinguishable; we could say that they share the same voice or that they share the same conceptual point of view. The narrator enhances his own authority by authorizing his protagonist in at least three major ways.

The first is the use of inside views, the narrator's comments concerning the perceptions, emotions, motivations, or thoughts of a character in the story, and one of the standard devices employed by an omniscient narrator. Several episodes in the Gospel hinge upon inside views, which is further evidence the whole Gospel is reader oriented, for no character within such an episode— except sometimes Jesus—possesses the penetrating insight that the narrator shares with the narratee. Only the narrator, the narratee, and perhaps Jesus fully realize what is happening in such stories. Jesus is the only character with whom the omniscient narrator shares this mind-reading power.

An excellent example is the Healing of the Paralytic (Mark 2:1-12). In verses 6-7 we are given the inside view that certain scribes question "in their hearts" why Jesus has presumed to "blaspheme" by pronouncing forgiveness of sins for the paralytic. We then are given the inside view that Jesus perceived "in his spirit that they thus questioned within themselves" (v. 8). The referential function of verse 8 is to inform us that Jesus knows what his opponents are thinking, but insofar as it is the revelation of privileged knowledge by the narrator to the narratee it functions primarily at the discourse level. Rhetorically, verse 8 reveals to the reader that Jesus knows something the reader already knows; if Jesus knows what the reader already knows, then what reader would not accept Jesus as a reliable, authoritative figure, worthy of the reader's trust? This response is predicated upon the reader first trusting the narrator to be reliable and authoritative, but trust is exactly what this kind of narrative demands of the reader from the start. If the reader is willing to presume the reliability of the unlimited third-person narrator, then the narrator may consolidate and enlarge that initially modest grant of authority, in this case by investing heavily in a thoroughly reliable protagonist. The protagonist serves as a reliable spokesperson for the reliable narrator.

A second way in which the narrator enhances the authority of Jesus—and thereby his own authority—is through the generous use of repetition at all levels of the discourse.[21] In numerous places the narrator shares a piece of information with the reader at the beginning of an episode (e.g., 8:1), and then a few lines later Jesus speaks, using the same words and showing that he too possesses this knowledge (e.g., 8:2). The semantically minded critic who looks for referential meaning is likely to pass over such repetition as mere redundancy in the story.[22] If our concern is the pragmatics of the discourse, however, then something interesting is taking place in such instances: the narrator and his chief spokesperson are, in echoing each other's words, confirming each other's reliability. We could say that the narrator is demonstrating his reliability by anticipating what Jesus will say or do or that Jesus shows himself to be reliable by echoing what the reliable narrator has already revealed to the reader.

---

21. See the exhaustive accounting by Frans Neirynck, *Duality in Mark: Contributions to the Study of the Markan Redaction,* BETL 31 (Leuven: Leuven University Press, 1972). The four broad categories in Neirynck's survey of Markan duality are (1) duality at the level of "grammatical usage," (2) "duplicate expressions and double statements," (3) "correspondence within one pericope," and (4) duality that is discernible generally in "the structuring of the gospel" (33–37).

22. But Mark is seldom genuinely redundant. Neirynck has demonstrated that at the level of double phrases the second phrase almost always adds something to the first; usually what we find is "a progressive two-step expression" (ibid., 46). In *Loaves and Fishes* I extended this observation to the level of entire episodes, which often work in pairs in the Gospel, and which often seem to offer a kind of two-step progression.

Sometimes the sequence is reversed and Jesus speaks first, for example, with a command: "Come after me" (1:17) or "Come out of him" (1:25). The narrator then provides a matching description of the fulfillment of the command: "and they followed him" (1:18) or "and [the spirit] came out of him" (1:26). A similar kind of parallelism between the speech of a character and of the narrator occurs when Jesus issues a prediction (e.g., 14:30) or some other statement about the future and the narrator later describes in similar terms the fulfillment of Jesus' words (e.g., 14:72). When Jesus speaks first and the narrator second, obviously we are hearing the narrator confirm Jesus' authority rather than the converse. The converse is also taking place, but surreptitiously; anything that bolsters the authority of the protagonist implicitly bolsters the authority of the storyteller.[23]

In my effort to discover what Mark does rhetorically to establish his authority, I have so far stressed that the narrator and Jesus are virtually identical. Among other things, they often exercise the same perceptual point of view, and they seem to speak with the same voice. Mark is trying to camouflage exactly this identity, however, by means of his narrative rhetoric. Giving an inside view into Jesus having an inside view into another character purports to establish Jesus as a discerning intelligence within the story and as one who has a perceptual point of view separate from that of the narrator. When the voice of Jesus and the narrator's voice seem to echo each other, the tendency is to regard them as distinct voices, in spite of their peculiar similarity. By encouraging us to imagine a separate perceptual point of view for Jesus, the narrator is trying to call attention away from his own dominating intelligence at the level of discourse by positing another intelligence of comparable perceptiveness at the level of the story. By means of the two echoing voices he distracts us into taking his voice for the voice of Jesus. Nevertheless, this separate intelligence with a distinct voice, which the narrator labels "Jesus," is illusory. In telling his story Mark is weaving an illusion of plural intelligences and plural voices, the most important of which are the one predominant intelligence and voice at the story level (Jesus) and the narrator's own intelligence and voice at the discourse level. Of these two, Mark always places the accent on the perceptive intelligence and authoritative voice of Jesus in the story. This emphasis distracts us from focusing upon the same perceptive intelligence and voice at the level of the discourse. Only by shifting our attention from story to discourse can we discover the intelligence and voice that is the narrator.

---

23. I have but touched lightly here the rhetorical use of repetition in Mark. The repetition involving the narrator and Jesus is only part, but the most crucial part, of the echoes between the speech of the narrator and that of all the characters in the story. We need only look at the third of Neirynck's major categories of repetition, "correspondence within one pericope," to see just how commonplace this kind of repetition is in Mark (*Duality*, 35–36, 112–31).

Once the narrator has established the authority of Jesus sufficiently, he can shift to Jesus some of the narrative responsibilities that are properly his prerogative as the narrator. For example, Mark's narrator makes extensive use of reliable commentary to shape the reader's understanding of the characters and events in the story, but the narrator avoids offering explicit "evaluative commentary" concerning the "norms" or the "beliefs"[24] he wants the reader to adopt. Instead of offering norms and standards of judgment openly, on his own authority, the narrator turns over to Jesus the work of articulating the major norms of the narrative. This strategy is the third way the authority of Jesus is promoted. Jesus stands in for the narrator as the predominant moral conscience and arbiter of norms in the narrative. Again Mark is weaving illusion. Having established Jesus as a supposedly separate intelligence through inside views and as a separate voice through repetition, the narrator now steps behind his protagonist and tries to disappear from view altogether. As any storyteller will, the narrator does offer us the norms by which he wishes the events and characters of his story to be judged, but he does so primarily by means of his stand-in, Jesus; that is, the predominant conceptual point of view of the entire Gospel is articulated most clearly not by the narrator directly but via the narrator's protagonist, Jesus. Thus we can say that the narrator and his protagonist share not only the same perceptual point of view and the same voice but also the same conceptual point of view.

When we realize that the teaching of Jesus in Mark's Gospel has little effect upon his hearers at the story level, we understand that his teaching serves primarily as evaluative and interpretive commentary for the reader. The words of Jesus in Mark do not contribute so much to the story as to the discourse. This efficacy at the level of discourse is generally true of the words of Jesus in Mark but especially true of the frequent "truly (amēn), I say to you . . ." phrases.[25] In such statements Jesus is interpreting the significance of events of the story from a position within the story.[26] They therefore function as pointed declarations originating from the hidden but ever present-narrator, aimed at the reader, and instructing the reader in the clearest of terms as to how to read the text. They are hermeneutical remarks aimed at shaping the reader's understanding of the narrative. Evaluative commentary is also found in all the universal pronouncements by Jesus beginning with "whoever. . . ."[27]

24. Booth, *Rhetoric of Fiction*, 177–82 and passim.

25. The "truly (amēn), I say to you . . ." passages in Mark are found in 3:28-29; 8:12; 9:1, 41; 10:15, 29-30; 11:23; 12:43; 13:30; 14:9, 18, 25, 30.

26. Noted frequently by Fernando Belo, *A Materialist Reading of the Gospel of Mark*, trans. Matthew J. O'Connell (Maryknoll, N.Y.: Orbis, 1981), 167, 200, 206, 222, 236 and passim.

27. Ibid., 118, 158. Many of the "whoever" statements employ *hos an* ("whoever . . ."; 3:29, 34-35; 8:35, 38; 9:37, 41, 42; 10:11, 15, 43-44; 11:23), but others simply *hos* ("he who . . ."; 4:9, 25; 9:39-40; 10:29-30), *oudeis* ("no one . . ."; 2:21, 22; 3:27; 9:39; 10:29-30), *tis* ("any one . . ."; 4:23; 8:34; 9:1, 35), *hostis* ("who, whoever"; 9:1), or *anthrōpos* ("a person . . ."; 8:36-37). John Donahue has moved cautiously toward seeing the *hos an* statements as functioning primarily for the reader ("A Neglected Factor in the Theology of Mark," *JBL* 101 [1982]: 584–85).

Significantly, *"amēn"* and "whoever" statements are frequently intertwined. Furthermore, all references in Mark to the authority, mission, or fate of the Son of man are evaluative or hermeneutical.[28] Nowhere in the story is any uptake on Jesus' use of "Son of man"; only the reader is enlightened by these hermeneutical remarks on the significance of crucial story elements.

The *"amēn,"* "whoever," and "Son of man" statements are the clearest expressions we have of the norms and standards of judgment of the narrator of Mark's Gospel. They are hard to see as the narrator's norms and standards because they are presented with such boldness as the norms and standards of Jesus and because we are accustomed to taking the Gospels referentially as expositions of the life and teachings of the historical Jesus. So consistently does the narrator shift over to Jesus the task of declaring the standards of judgment that he hopes the reader will embrace that he reinforces the illusion of Jesus as a separate intelligence and voice. Expressions such as *amēn, hos an,* and *ho huios tou anthrōpou* almost succeed in imputing an accent or a distinctive diction to the speech of Jesus in Mark's story. Although the narrator reserves *amēn, hos an,* and *ho huios tou anthrōpou* for Jesus' use only, nevertheless this unique vocabulary for the character Jesus is too limited and too stereotyped to succeed in creating a unique sound for his voice in the narrative. Other than a few such words reserved for Jesus, the diction of Jesus and of the narrator are identical. A few words reserved for Jesus' use represent the exceptions proving the rule that the narrator and his protagonist share the same perceptual point of view, speak with the same voice, and, most important, espouse the same conceptual point of view.

THE NARRATOR'S STRATEGY

We learn much about the rhetoric of the Gospel by examining the stance of the narrator, the heavy investment of authority in the protagonist, and the use of irony and other indirect moves to open up distance between Jesus (and the narrator and narratee) and other characters in the story, especially the disciples. What more can we say about the rhetorical strategy implicit in the narrator's stance?

Using the terminology of Chatman (see chap. 2), we may note that the unlimited third-person narrator of Mark's Gospel is virtually indistinguishable from the implied author of the Gospel. Any characterization of the narrator as a personage separate and distinct from the implied author is absolutely minimal. This becomes significant rhetorically when we remember that the implied reader mirrors the implied author and that the narratee reflects the narrator. In any reading experience, the real reader is beckoned to become the implied reader of the tale, at least while reading. If for all practical purposes

---

28. The Son of man (*ho huios tou anthrōpou*) passages in Mark are found in 2:9-11, 27-28; 8:31-32, 38; 9:9, 12, 31; 10:33-34, 45; 13:26; 14:21, 41, 61-64.

the implied author *is* the narrator, then for all practical purposes the implied reader *is* the narratee. The implicit invitation the narrative extends to the real reader is not only to play the role of the implied reader in the act of reading but also to go the slightest distance further and play the role of the narratee as well. The lack of distance between the implied author and the narrator exerts tremendous pressure upon the reader to allow the distance between implied reader and narratee to collapse. The significance of this for reading Mark becomes clear when we realize that a narratee is by nature credulous, whereas an implied reader possesses a modicum of critical consciousness. At the very least an implied reader is aware of being a reader, someone who is reading the product of an author. The narratee, however, is innocent of any such critical consciousness. The narratee "believes that it all really happened as reported by the teller [narrator]" and "accepts all its norms as permanent, unqualified by 'aesthetic distance' or by any sense of a possible return to a realer life; this *is* real life."[29] In short, the narratee of an unlimited third-person narrator is someone who is inclined to sit quietly at the feet of such a narrator, listen attentively, and believe the tale being told. The unlimited third-person narrator is a narrator predisposed to claim absolute authority; the corresponding narratee is someone predisposed to grant it. The absence of distance between the implied author and the narrator of Mark's Gospel, along with the narrator's unlimited third-person stance, is a rhetorical strategy calculated from the start to win over the reader to becoming not only the implied reader but also the credulous narratee of the omniscient narrator. To agree to read this narrative is to agree to play the part of someone who is won over by this narrative.

Simultaneously, another dynamic involving the narrator, narratee, and the characters of the story is taking place in the discourse of the narrative. The narrator and Jesus share the same conceptual point of view, often the same perceptual point of view, and always the same voice. The distance between the narrator and Jesus is minimal or nil. If the narrator is close to Jesus, then the credulous narratee is also close to Jesus. As the narrator and narratee draw closer and closer to Jesus, they become increasingly distant from all other characters in the story, inasmuch as the characters in the story all but universally distance themselves from Jesus. Jesus is misunderstood, rejected, or failed by almost everyone in the story, even by God, seemingly. As Mark's Gospel is narrated, a chasm widens, separating the narrator and the protagonist on one side from the other characters of the story on the other side. If the rhetoric of the narrative is successful, then the real reader, as implied reader and as narratee, sides with the narrator and the narrator's Jesus.

Still, the bleak generalization that all characters fail Jesus has some happy exceptions in the story. We may not think of them first, but in a Gospel that

29. Booth, *Rhetoric of Fiction*, 430.

proclaims that "the last shall be first" perhaps they should be given the highest rank: the so-called little people of the Gospel.[30] These often anonymous characters appear in a scene, have their dealings with Jesus, often show remarkable faith or persistence, and then disappear forever in the story. As the author understood so well, "wherever the gospel is preached [or read!] in the whole world, what she has done will be told in memory of her" (14:9). Their roles within the story may be small, but their examples of faithfulness shall live as long as the Gospel of Mark is read.

The exception most often suggested to the gloomy portrait we have painted is the Twelve, the closest associates of Jesus. Despite their total failure within the story as each and every one of them forsakes Jesus, readers commonly argue that the last scene of the Gospel holds forth hope for some kind of future reconciliation or restoration (16:7; cf. 14:28). I am convinced, however, that to read the ending of Mark in this fashion is to read it through the overlays of Matthew, Luke, and John. Each of those other Gospels has an unmistakable reconciliation with the risen Lord in the final scenes, and familiarity with these clearer and more direct Gospel endings makes Mark's haunting and enigmatic ending difficult to appreciate.

Few would deny that the author of Mark places a severe strain upon the relationship between Jesus and his disciples. Sometimes the disciples are close to Jesus, but early on they begin to grow more distant, and this distancing becomes more frequent and more pronounced as the story progresses. At the end the distance is total. To fret about this distance, however, and especially to play the game of trying to guess the rest of the disciples' story beyond Mark 16:8 is to fixate on the story level to the neglect of the discourse. The future of the disciples beyond Mark 16:8 is quite irrelevant to the chief aim of the Gospel. The Gospel is designed not to say something about the disciples or even to say something about Jesus, but to do something to the reader.

Nonetheless, we need to grasp the reason that understanding the role of the disciples—not so much in the story as in the discourse—is so central to an understanding of the reading experience. Just as the narrator speaks to the narratee in the course of telling the story, so within the story Jesus speaks to his primary listeners, the disciples.[31] Because the narrator and Jesus are so close to each other as to be virtually indistinguishable, the supposition naturally arises that the narratee is supposed to be close to or identify with the disciples. Often this process is exactly what happens in the reading experience. Through much of the Stilling of the Storm episode, for example, we share the disciples' perceptual point of view and therefore readily sympathize with their fear.

30. On the "little people" in Mark, see Rhoads and Michie, *Mark as Story,* 129–36. See also Donahue, "Neglected Factor," 583.

31. Or as Genette would say, there is the *extradiegetic* narrator and narratee outside the story, and frequently an *intradiegetic* narrator and his assembled narratees within the story, the latter being Jesus and (usually) the Twelve (*Narrative Discourse,* 228–31.)

Frequently, however, an ironic distance opens up between the narratee and the characters in the story, especially Jesus' disciples. This ironic distance develops, as in the Walking on the Water episode, because of the covert knowledge and overarching conceptual point of view the omniscient narrator shares with us. We are put in a position of knowing more than the disciples do. Then when the narrative offers us the opportunity to identify with the disciples we find that we cannot do so because we know things that preclude us from accepting the invitation. Of all the characters in the story, only Jesus is included consistently within the circle of intimacy occupied by narrator and narratee. The ironies and other indirect moves shared by the narrator and the narratee operate at the expense of virtually all characters in the story except Jesus and put distance between us and them. At the same time, the intimate experience of sharing and understanding irony drives the narrator and narratee closer together. Already inclined by nature to believe whatever the omniscient narrator has to say, in the course of the narrative the narratee draws still closer to the narrator—and closer to the narrator's Jesus. Surprisingly, Jesus' own narratees within the story—the disciples—are progressively excluded from this circle of intimacy. Many readers are so scandalized by this exclusion that they refuse to accept it.

To put all the pieces together, we may say, first, that the absence of a significant distinction between the implied author and the narrator encourages a similar identification of the implied reader with the narratee. Second, the sharing of voice and point of view by the narrator and Jesus puts the shortest of distance between these two entities. Third, the ironic distance created between the narrator and narratee, on the one hand, and all major characters of the story except Jesus, on the other hand, brings an already close narrator and narratee still closer together. We can readily see what these pieces add up to: in the course of reading the Gospel, a real reader is invited to play the role of the implied reader and also the role of the narratee, and from that position the reader is encouraged to move as close as possible to the narrator and the narrator's Jesus and to adopt their conceptual point of view. To say that in the experience of reading the Gospel the reader is invited to become aligned with its version of Jesus sounds banal until we realize that much confusion still exists among critical readers about the degree to which the reader of Mark's Gospel is supposed to identify with Jesus or, alternatively, with the disciples. As we continue to explore Mark's rhetoric, we shall see further evidence that the author is so eager to secure the reader's adherence to the Jesus of his story that he is willing to sacrifice the disciples of his story. Lest we become nervous about what Mark may be thereby asserting about the twelve apostles, the historical pillars of the early Christian church, let us recall that this narrative does not claim to be history. It is not even referentially oriented. Rather, it is pragmatically or rhetorically oriented. It is not "about" its characters; it is "about" its reader. The Gospel writer's chief concern is not the fate of either Jesus or the Twelve in the story but the fate of the reader outside the story.

5

EXPLICIT COMMENTARY
BY THE NARRATOR

For Mark's rhetorical use of irony, paradox, and ambiguity to work effectively, the narrator constantly constructs a stable backdrop of *direction* for the reader, over against which he can perform rhetorical moves of *indirection*. Here we shall examine the construction of this reliable backdrop for Mark's rhetoric of indirection. Then we shall be in a position to explore the sometimes unsettling challenge to the reader to work through puzzles, incongruities, and secrets. For now, however, we are still on the relatively secure footing, offered to the reader now and again, that makes navigation through Mark's indirection possible.

My major concern here is the narrator's use of "reliable commentary."[1] Seymour Chatman provides the most convenient categorization of the varieties of commentary.

> Commentary is either implicit (that is, ironic) or explicit. The latter includes interpretation, judgment, generalization, and "self-conscious" narration. Among explicit comments, the first three are upon the story. "Interpretation" (in this special sense) is the open explanation of the gist, relevance, or significance of a story element. "Judgment" expresses moral or other value opinions. "Generalization" makes reference outward from the fictional to the real world, either to "universal truths" or actual historical facts. "Self-conscious" narration is a term recently coined to describe comments on the discourse rather than the story, whether serious or facetious.[2]

---

1. The expression "reliable commentary" comes from Wayne C. Booth, *The Rhetoric of Fiction*, 2d ed. (Chicago and London: University of Chicago Press, 1983), 169–209. I began to explore the reliable commentary in Mark already in *Loaves and Fishes: The Function of the Feeding Stories in the Gospel of Mark*, SBLDS 54 (Chico, Calif.: Scholars Press, 1981), 157–79.

2. Seymour Chatman, *Story and Discourse: Narrative Structure in Fiction and Film* (Ithaca, N.Y., and London: Cornell University Press, 1978), 228.

Chatman is shrewd to observe that storytellers sometimes comment implicitly on the story, but his discussion of implicit commentary is much too narrow in scope. He restricts his attention to examples in literature and film in which the narrator shares ironies with the narratee at the expense of a character in the story or the implied author shares ironies with the implied reader at the expense of the narrator. Implicit commentary includes much more than just irony, however, and irony can be used for many purposes besides commentary. Mark contains much irony, but the narrator of Mark does not use verbal irony (saying something other than what he means) as much as he uses dramatic irony (the irony of incongruous speech, actions, or circumstances involving characters in the tale but fathomed only by the audience); the narrator of our Gospel does not himself speak ironically as much as he conducts his characters and weaves his plot ironically. Covertly ironic speech of a narrator would provide implicit commentary for the reader, but in Mark's Gospel implicit commentary typically takes on other forms.[3] What I would call implicit commentary in Mark is any guidance provided by the narrator in the course of telling the story that helps to direct the reading experience without explicitly invoking the narrator's voice. I see this happening in two ways in Mark. First, statements supposedly uttered by characters within the story provide much trustworthy guidance for the reader. Jesus is the most prominent source of such implicit commentary. The other way that implicit direction is given is through the arrangement of the episodes in the story, in the plotting of the story itself. Implicit commentary lies somewhere between explicit commentary and strategies of indirection, so my order for examining these moves is, first, various kinds of explicit commentary, then implicit commentary, and finally strategies of indirection. Under the heading of explicit commentary, we shall examine what Chatman calls "comments on the discourse" and "interpretation of a story element."

COMMENTARY ON THE DISCOURSE

THE LITTLE APOCALYPSE

We begin our discussion of Mark's explicit commentary with a look at the clearest example in the Gospel of a comment by the narrator on the discourse: "But when you see the desolating sacrilege set up where it ought not to be

3. Perhaps because Chatman is so brief in his discussion of implicit commentary, I have taken this term quite differently than R. Alan Culpepper has in "Implicit Commentary" in *Anatomy of the Fourth Gospel: A Study in Literary Design* (Philadelphia: Fortress Press, 1983), 151–202. Under the rubric of implicit commentary, Culpepper discusses the Johannine use of misunderstanding, irony, and symbolism in the rhetoric of the Fourth Gospel. However, none of these seems to me to warrant the label "commentary"; I would prefer to call them rhetorical strategies in the service of a Johannine rhetoric of indirection. I have tried to distinguish between the narrator's commentary, both explicit and implicit, and the indirect rhetorical strategies that presuppose knowledge of the narrator's commentary. Culpepper collapses together what I would call "implicit commentary" and "indirection" and then calls it all "implicit commentary."

(let the reader understand),[4] then let those who are in Judea flee to the mountains; . . ." (13:14). This parenthetical comment by the narrator to the reader, which occurs abruptly in the midst of words supposedly uttered by Jesus, lays bare the narrative situation obtaining throughout the entire Gospel. Besides revealing the presence of the narrator in the present instant, the realization is forced upon us that not just here does the narrator address the reader—the rest of the Gospel is equally from the narrator and offered for "the reader" to "understand."

Once alerted to the presence of the ubiquitous narrator, we can more easily see that 13:14 is far from unique. What distinguishes it from other commentary by the narrator is the word *reader*. It is the only place in the Gospel that the storyteller calls the recipient of the story by name. The word *reader* makes the parenthetical remark impossible as a statement by Jesus at the story level because characters within the story do not address "the reader" outside the story, at least not in ancient literature. Furthermore, "the reader" is referred to in the singular, but Jesus is speaking to his disciples using the second-person plural. The parenthesis makes no sense at all as a statement by Jesus.

Regardless, little would be required to turn the parenthesis in 13:14 into the kind of comment that could be an utterance by Jesus in the story. If we were to eliminate specific mention of "the reader" in 13:14, or if we were to substitute for the whole parenthesis any one of several other phrases often attributed to Jesus in Mark (e.g., "Listen!" [4:3]; "He who has ears to hear, let him hear" [4:9]; or "Hear me, all of you, and understand" [7:14]), then we would indeed seem to have just one more comment by Jesus, urging his story-level listeners to attend to his words. Then again, even if Jesus were clearly to speak in this way to his intranarrative audience, we would still have one of those many places in the Gospel where Jesus speaks, but with the narrator's voice and in such a way as to be heard most attentively by the narratee. The carefully cultivated equivocation between the narrator and Jesus in Mark encourages us not to distinguish whether Jesus is speaking to his audience or the narrator is speaking to his. As a rule, we do not notice; the distinction between the narrator and Jesus is a distinction we are not supposed to make. The parenthesis in Mark 13:14 is unusual because it forces upon us the distinction between the narrator and his protagonist.

Is "the reader" of 13:14 identified satisfactorily as the reader of the Gospel? Complications here suggest that we shall never fully understand who "the reader" of 13:14 is, or for that matter exactly what the reader is to understand. Someone who is probably not in the mind of the author here is the modern image of a solitary, individual reader of the Gospel, reading silently

---

4. Here, and frequently hereafter, I have added emphasis to the clauses in scripture quotations to which I am paying special attention.

in private. First of all, the practice in antiquity was to do all reading, whether private or public, aloud. Writing was the act of preserving the memory of sounds by means of marks on a surface, and reading was the act of giving utterance again to those sounds. Also, the common practice among both Greeks and Romans was to publish (*publicare*) literature by means of public recitation, performed either by the author himself or by a professional reader or actor.[5] Furthermore, Christianity inherited from Judaism its own tradition of the public reading of scripture, and we have evidence in the New Testament of the public reading of early Christian literature (e.g., Col. 4:16; 1 Thess. 5:27; 1 Tim. 4:13; Rev. 1:3). Therefore, the Gospel of Mark was probably written to be read aloud to an assembled audience,[6] and one possibility for identifying "the reader" of 13:14 would be to take the parenthesis as a kind of wink or stage direction to an *anagnostes,* a professional reader reciting the Gospel of Mark before an assembled audience.[7] What would such an aside signify? It is too nebulous to be a stage direction in the manner of modern scripts, in which hints are directed toward actors regarding proper gestures or movements, tone of voice, or facial expression.

Another possibility is that the parenthesis is an interpretive clue, intimating strongly that "the reader" is supposed to perceive that contemporary events (e.g., the Jewish-Roman War of 66–73 C.E. and the destruction of Jerusalem in 70 C.E.) have fulfilled Scripture (e.g., Dan. 11:31; 12:11).[8] In particular, the reference to the "desolating sacrilege" in 13:14 is often thought to echo the use of the same phrase in Daniel. If "the reader" in 13:14 means "the astute reader of Daniel, who can see how that book sheds light on contemporary events," however, then this "reader of Daniel" could be either the *anagnostes* reciting Mark's Gospel, someone in the audience, or even a solitary, private reader of the Gospel.

The possibilities multiply, and we are not able to discern whether "the reader" in 13:14 is (1) an isolated, individual reader of Mark's Gospel, reading the Gospel aloud to himself in private; (2) an *anagnostes* reading the Gospel aloud to an assembly; or (3) an individual student of the Jewish Scriptures, who should be able to recognize and comprehend an allusion to Daniel and who could be (a) an isolated, individual reader of the Gospel; (b) an *anagnostes*

5. Moses Hadas, *Ancilla to Classical Reading* (Morningside Heights, N.Y.: Columbia University Press, 1954), 50–64.

6. Given ancient reading and publication practices, one may assume that this would have been the case for most, if not all, of the books of the Bible; so George Kennedy, *New Testament Interpretation Through Rhetorical Criticism* (Chapel Hill, N.C. and London: University of North Carolina Press, 1984), 5–6.

7. *The Oxford Classical Dictionary* (Oxford: Clarendon Press, 1949), s.v. *anagnostes* and *recitatio*. The editors of the *Greek-English Lexicon of the New Testament* suggest that Mark 13:14 may refer to the act of public reading; BAGD, s.v. *anaginōskō*.

8. Rudolf Bultmann suggests that the "reader" of 13:14 is "whosoever reads the apocalypse in question—Daniel?" (*TDNT* 1:343, s.v. *anaginōskō, anagnōsis*).

reading the Gospel publicly; or (c) a member of the *anagnostes'* assembled audience.[9]

We can discern some other things, however, if we look beyond 13:14 to the entire chapter in which it appears. For example, we can note that the entire apocalyptic discourse is directed not so much to Jesus' intranarrative audience (Peter, James, John, and Andrew; 13:3) as to Mark's extranarrative audience. Imagining the scene as drama is helpful. Mark 13 begins with Jesus and the four disciples walking onto a stage set as the Mountain of Olives, strategically "opposite the temple." Jesus has just said that the stones of the temple will all be torn down. The disciples ask when this destruction will occur and what sign will point to this calamity. Jesus then delivers the chapter-long discourse, full of the veiled, figurative language of apocalyptic. Although the disciples remain on the stage throughout the apocalyptic discourse, we in the audience tend to forget their presence because the entire discourse is spoken over their heads and directly at us.

One linguistic signal of the dramatic nature of Mark 13 is the profusion of second-person plural pronouns in the discourse. In a highly inflected language such as Greek, the use of pronouns, at least in the nominative case, is semantically redundant. Therefore, the use of such superfluous pronouns serves as a way of adding unusual emphasis to an utterance. Mark 13 contains a number of such emphatic second-person plural pronouns (e.g., "Now you look out for yourselves" [13:9; R&M]). Ostensibly these pronouns engage the four disciples on the stage, but they are too emphatic to do only that. Rather, they raise the intensity of Jesus' language to such a pitch that the story level is all but transcended. Jesus' words in the story function primarily at the discourse level, and the second-person plural pronouns point primarily at Mark's, not Jesus', audience. If this intent were not clear enough in the midst of the chapter, the last verse of the chapter spells out explicitly at whom the whole speech is really aimed: "And what I say to you I say to all: Watch" (13:37). What Jesus says to "you"—ostensibly the four disciples—is really aimed at "all"—the audience of the Gospel drama. This statement is about as close as an ancient author can come to direct address by a character within the story to the audience outside the story.

9. Throughout this book I have had little choice but to equivocate between the words *narratee* and *reader*. The first recipients of Mark's narrative were probably genuine narratees; they probably *heard* the narrative, as it was read aloud to them. We now, however, *read* Mark's Gospel, often in silence, and even if we read it aloud, or hear it read aloud to us, it is not the same experience as in antiquity. In oral performances of Mark's Gospel today, we usually have a literate person, reciting to an audience of literate persons, who know, or think they know, the story already. After centuries of widespread literacy and familiarity with print culture, to say nothing of centuries of acquaintance with the Gospel narratives, we cannot hope to retrieve anything like a first-century oral delivery and reception of this story. However, reader-response criticism, with its focus on the temporal experience of narrative, helps us to come closer than we might otherwise.

Another sign that all of Mark 13 functions as a discourse aimed primarily at Mark's audience is the framing of the entire chapter as a discourse about the future. Ostensibly, again, Jesus is describing the future of the disciples, but clear reference to their own personal roles in this future is oddly absent, if the apocalyptic discourse is intended for them. Rather, the future referred to in Mark 13 concerns primarily the time of the Gospel's implied audience. The future that the story level of Mark seems to be concerned about is actually the present for the reader, indeed, the present moment of the reading experience.

Because Jesus talks about the future with some frequency in the Gospel, we should notice that all of Jesus' other references to the future within the Gospel function similarly at the discourse level as commentary or direction for the reader in the present moment of reading. These references include several of the most arresting statements made by Jesus in the Gospel: 8:38—9:1; 9:9; 13:26; 14:28; 14:62; 16:7. Especially noteworthy is Mark 9:9, the verse following the Transfiguration episode and a verse infamous as the linchpin of William Wrede's theory of the Messianic Secret: "And as they were coming down the mountain, he charged them to tell no one what they had seen, until the Son of man should have risen from the dead." Wrede took this verse as a dogmatic rationalization on the part of the evangelist as to why the disciples historically did not comprehend the messiahship of Jesus until after his resurrection. Only in the light of the Easter experience could people grasp who Jesus was; stories such as the Transfiguration would only make sense when told in a post-Easter setting, in the light of Jesus' crucifixion and resurrection. So Wrede took 9:9 as a retrospective, dogmatic rationalization of the disciples' befuddlement before their eventual post-Easter enlightenment.[10] In contrast, I take 9:9 as a specimen of rhetoric, not as a specimen of dogmatized history; that is, I take it not as a statement of Jesus to his disciples in the past about their future but as a statement by the narrator to the reader in the present moment of reading. After all, what is Mark's story of the Transfiguration (9:2-8) but the very "telling of what they saw" that Mark has Jesus postpone at the story level until after the resurrection of the Son of man? The narrative that has been postponed at the story level has at the discourse level just been told! Even though at 9:9 we have not yet read a narrative from Mark about Jesus' resurrection, nevertheless we have read 9:2-8, which 9:9 tells us is to be narrated only after the resurrection. Therefore, readers must realize, consciously or unconsciously, that they are reading at a time after the resurrection. From this point on the reader's mind is forced to work using the datum provided by the narrator that, as of the present moment of reading, the Son of man has been raised from the dead. This example

10. William Wrede, *The Messianic Secret,* trans. J. C. G. Grieg (Cambridge and London: James Clarke, 1971), 67–68, 211–36.

shows how a narrative can be constructed so that anyone who wishes to play the role of its reader must play along according to the presuppositions and norms it dictates.[11]

In view of all of the dramatic features of Mark 13, I imagine this whole chapter to be directed primarily to the extranarrative audience of the Gospel, a group of assembled narratees rather like the audience viewing a drama on a stage. This still does not provide definitive clarification for the identity of "the reader" of 13:14, but I am inclined to read the parenthetical comment as the narrator's comment on his own discourse to the individual narratee, who is presumed by the implied author to be a part of a larger, assembled narrative audience. This individual narratee is alerted, in a brief, obscure fashion, to remember what he has previously read (probably alluding to Daniel) and to perceive how it is relevant to first-century historical events alluded to in Jesus' apocalyptic discourse. Modern scholarship has long taken Mark 13 to be a murky reflection of what was happening historically at the time of the composition of the Gospel, perhaps around 70 C.E. I see no reason to dispute this supposition about the referential meaning of the cryptic allusions in Mark 13. Far more interesting to me, however, is the function of Mark 13 as the discourse of the narrator. The historical events to which Mark 13 may allude remain dim to us, but we can still appreciate the contribution of Mark 13 to the construction of Mark's narrative world and its effect on the reader of the story even today.

Where else in Mark, besides 13:14, do we have explicit commentary by the narrator upon his discourse? We might argue for various instances scattered throughout the Gospel, but one other major occurrence is clearly in the opening verses of the Gospel, which provide so much direction for the reader before the main action of the story ever gets under way. As Morton Enslin has noted,[12] the entire introduction to the Gospel functions as a kind of prelude, aimed primarily at the reader. In particular, the storyteller gives us a title (1:1), an epigraph (1:2-3), and an epitome (1:14-15) in the opening verses of the Gospel.

THE TITLE AND EPIGRAPH

The first verse of the Gospel functions as a kind of descriptive title for the entire work. It tells the reader who Jesus is and offers an important evaluative description of the narrative about him: it is *euangelion*—"good news" or "gospel."

Immediately following the title is an epigraph drawn from the Septuagint. The first significant aspect of it is that the narrator provides the first quotation

---

11. The other instances of clarion statements by Jesus ostensibly about the future of the world in the story would be equally interesting to explore. Several of these statements about the future are also "Son of man" statements (8:38; 9:9; 13:26; 14:62), which never receive uptake at the story level.

12. See chap. 1.

from the Jewish Scriptures to be found in the Gospel, and, moreover, that he provides it so early. Second, the epigraph serves to alert the reader that the entire narrative that follows is anchored in the Jewish Scriptures. The reader is supposed to be able to recognize the allusions to and quotations from it made frequently in the narrative.

Third, the abundance of scriptural echoes in Mark is evidence of the phenomenon that contemporary literary theorists have labeled *intertextuality*. Intertextuality is the recognition that no text is ever truly autonomous; no text is ever produced or read apart from other texts. A text always implicates other texts in its weave. In the case of the Gospel of Mark, the implied author announces already in 1:2-3 the interweaving of his text and the Jewish Scriptures. Mark offers his own text as the proper reading grid through which not only the Jewish Scriptures are to be read but also all of history. Mark's story is about the "filling full" of scripture (14:49b) and of time itself (1:15). This describes the story level of the narrative, however, which is always in service to the discourse level in Mark. If the Gospel is not so much about the characters and events it describes as it is about the reader and the reading experience, then "fulfillment" is perhaps better understood as something that is supposed to happen in the experience of reading, as much or more than it is something that happens in Mark's story. For the reader, in reading Mark's Gospel itself scripture is "filled full"; the reading of the Gospel is itself the fulfillment of time.

The looseness and fluidity of the interweaving of Mark and the Jewish Scriptures is puzzling for modern, print-oriented scholars. We can observe the effort made in critical editions of the Greek text of the New Testament or in translations of the New Testament to pin down quotations from and allusions to the Jewish Scriptures. We use italics, quotation marks, indentation, and elaborate cross-reference systems to set off scriptural echoes from the rest of the text, thereby revealing our "anxiety of influence." Only literate-visualist moderns worry so about giving proper credit to antecedent texts; only we strive so to achieve originality and to avoid plagiarism. As Walter Ong has observed, the modern rediscovery of the inevitability of intertextuality has come as a shock; ancient authors, on the contrary, took intertextuality for granted.[13]

Echoes of the Septuagint are diffused throughout Mark, and for this reason alone we cannot describe a definitive experience of reading Mark's Gospel. Scriptural echoes are always discerned differently by different ears. Mark's Gospel does not even pretend to be a closed text, structured by a neat outline. Mark's openness to the Jewish Scriptures is alone sufficient to render the

---

13. Walter Ong, *Orality and Literacy: The Technologizing of the Word* (London and New York: Methuen, 1982), 133–34.

experience of reading Mark inexhaustible, for Mark's gridwork offers innumerable openings into the experience of reading the various texts of Jewish Scripture.

Fourth, because the first evocation of the Jewish Scriptures comes from the narrator, in the form of an epigraph, we should be alert henceforth to notice how other scriptural quotations and allusions may function implicitly, if not explicitly, as commentary from the narrator.[14] Sometimes a quotation from scripture offered in the story by Jesus serves as direction for the reader at the level of discourse. Consider the quotation from Zechariah in 14:27, which secures absolutely no uptake within the story—the characters in the story act as if Jesus had not uttered it—but of course the reader takes note and understands. Then, too, there are the hermeneutical comments by Jesus about the "fulfillment" of scripture or about how this thing or that "is written" in scripture (9:12-13; 14:21; 14:49). Such intranarrative commentary upon the experience of reading scripture has little or no impact within the story; it is meant principally for the extranarrative reader.

Finally, just as the opening verses of the Gospel provide much clear direction for the reader, we also already begin to find in the epigraph the indirection that will so characterize Mark's narrative. A familiar problem associated with 1:2-3 is the question of exactly what scriptural passage(s) is being quoted. Mark says he is quoting Isaiah, but he actually offers a pastiche of phrases drawn from Malachi, Exodus, and Isaiah. The perceived problem may be of our own making, a symptom of our own anxiety of influence. When the author says he is quoting Isaiah, who are we to say that he must quote only Isaiah and then only with rigorous precision? That problem aside, however, other ambiguities remain in the epigraph. Just what is the epigraph saying? To whom does it refer? It says: "Behold, I send my messenger before thy face, who shall prepare thy way." This statement prompts several questions: (1) Who is supposed to be speaking? (2) Who is the messenger (*ton angelon*)? (3) For whom does the messenger prepare the way? Reading Mark through the eyes of Matthew, Luke, and John, as well as through nineteen centuries of the history of reading, we have trouble seeing that these implicit questions are never answered explicitly anywhere within the Gospel. By the time we have read through 1:9-11, we will be able to infer that the answers are "God," "John," and "Jesus," respectively, but infer we must. That is a portent of the many inferences that lie ahead in the experience of reading Mark's Gospel. The act of inferring is difficult to objectify, however. We are so used to supplying unthinkingly the answers to the questions implicitly asked by this narrative—and puzzling through the other indirect moves it pursues—that we have difficulty achieving a critical distance from the covert question-and-answer process in which it ensnares us.

---

14. Noted also by Willem S. Vorster, "The Function of the Use of the Old Testament in Mark," *Neot* 14 (1981): 62–72.

THE EPITOME

Morton Enslin calls Mark 1:14-15 the epitome of the preaching of Jesus *in* the Gospel of Mark, but it is also the epitome *of* the Gospel of Mark.[15] While Jesus speaks, epitomizing his story-level message, the narrator is also speaking, epitomizing his discourse. No one in particular at the story level is said to have heard the proclamation of 1:14-15. It has no genuine setting at the story level; it functions only for the narratee, at the discourse level.

At the level of story, Mark's narrative is about Jesus' proclamation of the *euangelion* (1:14); at the level of discourse the narrative is also *euangelion* (1:1). The narrative mirrors itself, discourse reflecting story, which is not surprising; any reader-oriented narrative is similarly reflexive. A reader-oriented narrative is in a sense always "about" itself or, better, always "about" the reader's experience of reading it. The referential function of a reader-oriented narrative is largely a matter of self-reference, and the standard description of the experience of reading such a text is always that "reading this text is the experience of learning how to read this text." Strikingly, Mark's Gospel celebrates its reflexivity boldly by making the term *euangelion* the preeminent characterization of both the discourse level and the story level. Wherever Jesus refers to "the gospel" or, even more pointedly, wherever Jesus says that something is done "for my sake and for the sake of the gospel,"[16] the reader may take the phrase as a token of the narrator hidden behind Jesus, a masked but unmistakable invitation from the narrator to recall that "gospel" is how he has entitled his entire narrative (1:1). In such places the narrative gestures toward itself, story commenting upon discourse.

Once we recognize the reflexivity of the Gospel narrative, additional insights into the reading experience follow. To say that the Gospel is largely self-referential is to say that the Gospel is not primarily referential at all but rather is primarily pragmatic or rhetorical in orientation. What we may now observe in the experience of reading 1:14-15 is that as much as Jesus may be epitomizing the events transpiring within the story (referential function) the narrator is all the more epitomizing the events transpiring in the reading experience (rhetorical function). These verses refer, to be sure, but the reference is in service to the rhetoric and not vice versa. In other words, 1:14-15 is an admission by the narrator of what he wants to happen to the reader in the course of the reading experience. After all, the reader encounters the delivering up of John the Baptist and the preaching of Jesus by reading Mark's Gospel. The reader hears Jesus' proclamation of the gospel by reading or hearing Mark's story about that preaching. For the reader, the time is filled full and the kingdom of God draws nigh in the experience of reading Mark's

15. See chap. 1.

16. "The gospel" (13:10; 14:9); "for my sake and for the sake of the gospel" (8:35; 10:29). Cf. "me and my words" (8:38); "my words" (13:31).

Gospel. Finally, if the rhetoric of the Gospel is successful, then the readers will be converted, will repent, and will change their minds because they believe in the Gospel that has been read. Mark really could not have offered a clearer statement of the rhetorical goal he wishes to accomplish and the design he has upon the reader. It is open but hidden because it is couched as the rhetorical goal sought by Jesus, whose eye is seemingly on prospective converts within the story.

Furthermore, within such a thoroughly rhetorical and reflexive narrative, hardly an episode of importance is not an episode about reading. The reading of this narrative constantly evokes attention to its reading. Because the Gospel so steadily points to itself, moreover, it demands a return to itself upon the completion of reading; that is, it demands a rereading. If its rhetoric is successful, then each successive reading should deepen the reader's commitment to the act of reading this narrative and strengthen the hold the weave of the textual fabric has upon the reader. The flaw in this strategy is that a written text is vulnerable to the rhetorical strategies of successor texts, which can supplant the antecedent text. This fate befell Mark's Gospel at the hands of the competing weavers we know as Matthew, Luke, and John.

COMMENTARY ON THE STORY

We have now examined "comments on the discourse" in Mark 13:14, 1:1, 1:2-3, and 1:14-15. Much of what Chatman calls "judgment" and "generalization" is in the Gospel, but it is largely left up to Jesus to deliver (e.g., see chap. 4), so these two kinds of commentary are properly classified as implicit commentary and will be dealt with later. The narrator restricts himself to a few self-conscious comments upon the discourse itself and numerous instances of what Chatman calls "interpretation": "any relatively value-free attempt to account for something in terms of the story itself, without going outside it (as do judgment and generalization)."[17] The rest of this chapter is devoted to an examination of "interpretation," commentary on the story by the narrator.

Many of the narrator's interpretations are offered smoothly and unobtrusively in the course of his narration; they contribute inconspicuously to the narrator's exposition of the action in the story. Others are noticeable, however, because they disrupt the flow of the story. Such a disruption can be conducted with a degree of gracefulness, in which case we call it a "parenthesis," or it can be ungrammatical and awkward, in which case we call it an "anacoluthon."[18] *Parenthesis* and *anacoluthon* are appropriate terms to use, as long

---

17. Chatman, *Story and Discourse,* 237–38.
18. See BDF, sections 458, 465(2). The parenthetical comment has long been recognized as a typical characteristic of Mark's Gospel; see C. H. Turner, "Marcan Usage: Notes, Critical and Exegetical, on the Second Gospel," *JTS* 26 (1924–25): 145–56; Max Zerwick, *Untersuchungen zum Markus-Stil: Ein Beitrag zur stilistischen Durcharbeitung des Neuen Testament* (Rome: Pontifical Biblical Institute, 1937), 130–38.

as we keep certain things in mind. First, we should remember that the true parenthesis is a typographical convention apprehended visually; Mark's parentheses were meant to be heard, not seen. The same holds for Mark's use of ruptured syntax. Such liberties taken with syntax are inexcusable in a polished, literate text, but they can be effective and therefore acceptable in an oral presentation. The abundance of anacolutha is yet another characteristic of Mark's narrative that suggests that it was intended for oral performance. Mark's Gospel is not far removed historically from a situation of predominant orality, and it retains a strong oral flavor. A literate-visualist modern can scarcely appreciate the original oral-aural apprehension of Mark's parenthetical comments and, of course, of his entire narrative. Reader-response criticism can help us, however, because it attunes our ears to the narrator's discourse and dissuades us from submitting freely to the lure of his story.

The discussion of Mark's "interpretations" that follows is divided into three sections. The first examines the use of relatively clear linguistic signals to introduce an interpretive comment (i.e., parenthesis), the second examines comments that are distinguished by their awkward or disrupted syntax (i.e., anacoluthon), and the third examines comments introduced by weaker signals, such as *kai* ("and"), *de* ("and, but"), and apposition. After that we can profitably examine one way in which commentary is repeatedly used in Mark, the use of inside views.

PARENTHETICAL COMMENTS

The kinds of linguistic signals that may introduce a parenthesis are many and varied. Various signals introduce statements of cause or reason, statements of purpose, and statements of result, and various other parts of speech (e.g., relative pronouns, adverbs, and participles) can also signal a parenthesis.

Statements of Cause or Reason

Three linguistic signals commonly introduce a parenthetical statement about cause or reason: *gar* ("for"), *hoti* ("because"), and *dia* ("because of").

***Gar* ("for").** Mark frequently uses *gar* to offer explanatory, parenthetical remarks on the story.[19] Critics often note Mark's peculiar usage of *gar* clauses, which almost always take on the appearance of an awkward afterthought;[20] that is, the *gar* parenthesis almost always follows an element of the narrator's

19. The salient examples of *gar* parentheses are found in: 1:16, 22; 3:21; 3:34-35; 5:7-8, 27-28, 42; 6:14-20, 51-52; 7:2-5; 9:5-6, 33-34; 10:21-22, 45; 11:13, 18; 12:12; 14:70; 15:9-10; 16:3-4, 8. Not to be overlooked is the presence of *gar* parentheses and interpretive comments of other kinds in the direct discourse attributed to characters in the story. Mark's characters always speak with the diction of the narrator.

20. See my discussion of the Markan *gar* clauses, as well as references to the relevant secondary literature, in *Loaves and Fishes*, 77–78, 162–64, 207.

exposition that it should logically precede. Although the inherent nature of the use of *gar* in Greek is largely to blame, Mark's *gar* clauses are often abnormally tardy and awkward, for example, ". . . he saw Simon and Andrew the brother of Simon casting a net in the sea; *for they were fishermen*" (1:16), or "immediately the little girl rose and began walking *(for she was twelve-years-old)*" (5:42, R&M). An even more tardy and awkward use is "And they were saying to themselves, 'Who will roll away for us the stone from the door of the grave?' And looking up they observed that the stone had been rolled away. *For it was very large*" (16:3-4, R&M).

The narrator is so fond of the *gar* clause that he sometimes uses one after another, the second *gar* clause explaining the first, as in 9:6: "And Peter said to Jesus, 'Master, it is well that we are here; let us make three booths, one for you and one for Moses and one for Elijah.' *For he did not know what to say, for they were exceedingly afraid.*" Similarly, Mark 11:18 reads: "And the high priests and the legal experts heard and began seeking how they might destroy him. *For they were afraid of him. For the whole crowd was astonished at his teaching*" (R&M). Another kind of construction using two *gar* clauses in rapid succession occurs in the last verse of the Gospel (16:8): "And they went out and fled from the tomb; *for trembling and astonishment had come upon them;* and they said nothing to any one, *for they were afraid.*" The most concentrated collection of *gar* clauses in Mark occurs in the opening verses of the story of Herod's Banquet (6:14-29); no less than four *gar* clauses (6:14, 17, 18, 20), one *dia* clause, and one *hoti* clause make the whole first half of that episode a dense web of commentary by the narrator.

Interpreters have often commented upon the awkwardness of the *gar* clauses in Mark's Gospel, but laying aside our prejudice in favor of logical and especially chronological sequence in narrative may enable us to see what the narrator's afterthoughts do to the reader in the reading experience. After all, the violation of logical sequence may have interesting effects on the reading experience, and authors use it far more than we realize.[21] When a *gar* clause in Mark provides a piece of information that has hitherto been missing, the reader is being informed implicitly of a gap in his knowledge. The existence of the gap is revealed in the moment of its being filled.

Another way to describe what happens is to say that the proffered *gar* clause is rather like an answer provided to a question that has not yet been asked. Just as asking a question creates a desire for an answer,[22] offering an answer prompts the hearer to supply the question. The unstated question that the *gar* clause answers is often simply a variation of the question, Why?

21. For a discussion of the rhetorical effects of violations of logical sequence in narrative and a demonstration that they are far more common in narrative than we might suspect, see Gérard Genette's discussion of "anachronies," violations of chronological sequence, in *Narrative Discourse: An Essay in Method,* trans. Jane E. Lewin, foreword Jonathon Culler (Ithaca, N.Y.: Cornell University Press, 1980), 33–85.

22. On the rhetorical use of questions, see below; also Fowler, *Loaves and Fishes,* 167–68.

He saw Simon and Andrew the brother of Simon casting a net in the sea; [Why were they casting a net?] *for they were fishermen* (1:16).

And they were astonished at his teaching, [Why were they astonished?] *for he taught them as one who had authority, and not as the scribes* (1:22).

And when his family heard, they came out to seize him, [Why did they come to seize him?] *for they were saying "He's out of his mind"* (3:21, R&M).

More significant perhaps than the answer supplied or the question implied is the rapport that is being developed between narrator and narratee. If the narrator can get the narratee to supply answers to his questions and questions to his answers, then cooperation and communication, which are ultimately more important to the narrator than any single question or answer, are being achieved.

Therefore, one of the chief rhetorical effects of the *gar* clause is reinforcing the reader's dependence upon the narrator. In referential terms, the *gar* clause might be considered merely an awkward afterthought. In terms of the syntax of narrative it is, as Gérard Genette would say, an "analepsis": a jump backward in the narrative, narrative element A following what it logically should have preceded, narrative element B—B/*gar*/A, to describe it with a formula.[23] In rhetorical or pragmatic terms, however, what the B/*gar*/A sequence does is to take the reader forward one step and then backward two steps. The *gar* clause simultaneously reveals and fills a gap in the reader's knowledge, but probably more important it teaches the reader to follow the narrator, even in momentary retreat.

For all the reputed awkwardness of Mark's *gar* clauses, they are often employed to great effect. One common use to which the *gar* clause is put is offering inside views to the reader, and frequently the reader's grasp of a whole episode hinges upon such an inside view. For understanding the experience of reading the story of the woman with the flow of blood (5:24b-34), for example, we must recognize that the narrator privileges the reader with the unspoken thoughts and feelings of both the woman and Jesus. The thronging crowd, including the disciples, have not the slightest idea of what is happening in their midst, but we understand completely. In the episode the narrator delays telling us the woman's thinking until after she has actually touched Jesus: "She had heard the reports about Jesus, and came up behind him in the crowd and touched his garment. *For she said, 'If I touch even his*

---

23. Genette, *Narrative Discourse*, 40. The *gar* clause is akin to Mark's favorite two-step progression, in which A is followed and further explained by A'; see Frans Neirynck, *Duality in Mark: Contributions to the Study of Markan Redaction*, BETL 31 (Leuven: Leuven University Press, 1972). In the A/A' two-step progression, the second, explanatory element occurs in its "proper" chronological sequence, whereas in the B/*gar*/A arrangement, the chronological sequence is violated. In both cases, however, the reader is required to depend upon the narrator for crucial explanatory comments.

garments, I shall be made well' " (5:27-28). In this way we learn what she is hoping for in the instant that her hopes are fulfilled.

No *gar* parenthesis bears a greater burden for guiding reading than the inside view in 12:12. This comment comes at the end of the parable of the vineyard (12:1-12), which Jesus tells during his confrontations with the authorities in the Jerusalem temple. This context by itself might be sufficient to allow the reader to infer that the wicked tenants in Jesus' parable represent "the chief priests and the scribes and the elders" who were mentioned back in 11:27, just prior to the vineyard parable. Such an inference is eminently reasonable. However, this inference is turned into an absolute certainty for the reader in a skillfully offhand manner. The narrator ends the episode: "And they tried to arrest him, but feared the multitude, *for they perceived that he had told the parable against them;* so they left him and went away" (12:12).

Initially, we can perceive some ambiguity here. The "they" that tried to arrest him and that feared the multitude can be only the authorities specified in 11:27, but the "they" of the "for . . ." clause could be the multitude, which Jesus has perhaps stirred up against the Jewish authorities by telling his inflammatory story. This reading would give us a *gar* clause with a gist something like this: "for *the multitude* perceived that he had told the parable against *the authorities.*" However, because *gar* clauses in Mark are usually logically antecedent to the statements they follow, we should probably take all third-person plural forms in 12:12 as pointing consistently to the Jerusalem authorities.

Once the ambiguity is cleared up, we can observe how effectively the parenthetical comment functions. Everything here seems to be operating nicely at the story level: the *authorities* realized that *Jesus* had aimed his story at *them.* In this seemingly intramural contest, the narrator's commentary indicates that both sides know the score. Both Jesus and his opponents know full well the condemnation of the opponents that is implied by the veiled, figurative language of the story. Nevertheless, this parenthesis functions also at the discourse level to provide the reader with the single interpretive key needed to unlock all of the figurative language of the parable. This discourse-level revelation to the reader is skillfully disguised as a perception within the story by one set of characters about the motivation of another character. Once the reader figures out—thanks to the narrator—that the villains in Jesus' parable stand for the authorities that Jesus faces in the temple, only a little imagination is necessary to determine who the "beloved son" is (Jesus), who the "owner of the vineyard" is (God), what the "vineyard" itself is (Israel), and perhaps who the "servants" are (the prophets), at least the one who is specifically said to receive a head wound (the fate of John the Baptist in 6:16). In reading this episode we encounter a typical example of Mark's mixture of direction and indirection. We are given a puzzle to solve and the key to unlock it, but the unlocking is left up to us. He leaves the work for us to do but provides the necessary tools.

Besides offering inside views, the *gar* clause also lends itself to the strategic withholding of information from the reader until the propitious moment for its revelation. This strategic delaying action is what is actually happening in the narrator's discourse in a number of places where he has been criticized for inserting clumsy afterthoughts. Some are clumsy, but they are still often effective rhetorically.

For example, we are told that Jesus is hungry. He sees a fig tree in the distance and approaches it to see if it bears fruit. He comes to it, and finds only leaves, *"for it was not the season for figs"* (11:13)! Why would he even look for figs if it was not the season for them? we may ask. The narrator holds back the most crucial piece of information, and then, when he offers it, we realize instantly that the search for fruit out of season was futile from the start. Even more, it was ludicrous. When Jesus then curses the tree for being barren, we are shocked. How manifestly unfair and wanton! Small wonder that Matthew deletes the troublesome *gar* clause from his version of the story and turns the undeserved curse into a seemingly deserved one. Luke and John just omit the story altogether.

From the vantage point of reader-oriented criticism, what is interesting about the story is not the wantonness of the curse per se but the reaction of readers to the curse. The dismay and shock felt by readers of this story— which seems to begin already with Matthew, Luke, and John—can be matched within Mark's Gospel only by the depth of dismay and shock felt by Jesus when he discovered that businessmen and currency exchangers had turned a house of prayer into a den of robbers (11:15-20). Of course, I am alluding to the interpretive strategy by means of which modern readers have softened the offense they have felt at the cursing of the fig tree. We can observe that the fig tree episode is split in two by the narrator (11:12-14, 20-25) and that the episode of the temple "cleansing" (or better, "disqualification"[24]) is sandwiched between the two halves of the fig tree story, giving every indication that the fig tree is meant to be taken figuratively; that is, the fig tree story is a metaphoric explanation of Jesus' violent suspension of the temple activities, and thus it functions primarily at the discourse level. For those who have eyes to see and ears to hear, Jesus' action against the temple is like his action against the fig tree. The fate of the fig tree is a figure for the fate of the temple, which itself is only pre-figured in the penultimate cessation of temple activities in 11:15-19. The ultimate fate of the temple is made clear in 13:2: it will be destroyed. Readers of Mark, especially the first flesh-and-blood readers, always grasp this with poignancy because readers of Mark have always already been aware that the temple was actually destroyed by the Romans in 70 C.E.

If the cursing of the fig tree is unpalatable to the reader, the way lies open to take it figuratively. Even so, the troubling vividness and realism of

---

24. Werner H. Kelber, *Mark's Story of Jesus* (Philadelphia: Fortress Press, 1979), 59.

the narrator's description of the curse and the withered tree remains. The symbolic significance of the act at the discourse level does not make the act itself any less shocking. As a narrator, perhaps Mark has stumbled here, having made a parabolic episode too lifelike in its violence. What interpretive options remain open to us? We can adulterate the fig tree story, as Matthew did. We can choose to ignore it altogether, as did Luke and John. We can blunt the edge of Jesus' curse and soften the impact of the narrator's *gar* clause by concentrating upon the figurative significance of the entire episode, as countless modern interpreters have done. Or perhaps we can acknowledge and contemplate our own shock and distress at the tree's undeserved and violent fate. If the story of the tree does function primarily at the discourse level, then we might say that the tree has been cursed specifically for us, so that if we turn our heads away from the scene in disgust we may miss something we were meant to see and contemplate.

If we can bear to face up to the experience of reading this episode, it cannot help giving rise to thought. The tree is surely intended to have some metaphorical relationship to the temple, which has a fate of its own in store for it (see Mark 13:2). Also to be contemplated, however, are the intimations in the Gospel that the fate of the temple and the fate of Jesus are also somehow intertwined (14:58; 15:29-30; 15:37-38). In Mark's story a fig tree is cursed and withers, Jesus is crucified, and the doom of the temple assured. How might the three—tree, Jesus, temple—be related? Is the fate of the temple or of Jesus any more deserved than the fate of the fruit-barren tree? Will a reader who is embarrassed by and quickly explains away dismay at the undeserved and violent fate of a tree be able to respond with appropriate emotion to the undeserved and violent fate of either a beloved son or a cherished institution? Or will the reader there, too, quickly deny the shock, the hurt, and the anger she genuinely feels? The practice of reader-response criticism encourages us to be honest about what we have actually felt or experienced in reading. By denying embarrassing reading experiences, we have often forfeited experiences that authors have labored mightily to offer us. An indignant reader who denies he is indignant at the cursing of the fig tree not only has denied his own experience of reading the fig tree's story but also runs the risk of impoverishing his reading of the rest of the Gospel, in which other curses are uttered and other limbs wither.

Gar clauses that offer strategically withheld information may occur at the very end of an episode. We have already seen one example in 12:12, which provides the interpretive key for the vineyard parable in the last verse of the episode. Another example is 6:52, the concluding verse of the Walking on the Water (6:45-52): "And they were completely stunned within themselves, *for they did not understand about the loaves. Instead, their minds were hardened*" (R&M).[25] This commentary is particularly noteworthy because it

---

25. All together, Mark 6:51-52 is a triple inside view into the fear and obtuseness of the disciples.

not only sheds light on the immediately preceding water-walking episode but also accentuates the disciples' obtuseness in the incident preceding the sea story, the Feeding of the Five Thousand (6:30-44). We are told that the dullness of the disciples in one scene is linked to the dullness they displayed in the preceding scene. Mark's commentary on the benighted condition of the disciples, which is direction for the thinking of the reader, could hardly be clearer.

The last and perhaps best example of a strategically delayed *gar* clause is 10:22b.[26] That the story usually bears the title of "The Rich Man" is unfortunate because not until we reach the very last line in the episode is the reader told that the man in the story is rich. The story begins with a man coming to Jesus to ask what he needs to do to obtain eternal life. In response, Jesus quizzes him about the commandments of the Decalogue, and the man responds by saying that he has faithfully kept them all. The episode then moves rapidly toward its denouement: "And Jesus looking upon him loved him, and said to him, 'You lack one thing; go, sell what you have, and give to the poor, and you will have treasure in heaven; and come, follow me' " (10:21). Jesus acts as if he has found the man's weak spot, and the man responds as if that were so: "At that saying his countenance fell, and he went away sorrowful; . . ." (10:22a). Only at the end does the reader learn the truth: ". . . *for he had great possessions*" (10:22b). By delaying the most critical piece of information until the end, the reader's interest in the outcome of the story is sustained. Initially the man is portrayed positively as a sincere seeker of eternal life. Who would not want him to succeed? By withholding the crucial information until the end, the narrator induces an experience of surprise and disappointment in the reader that corresponds to the surprise and disappointment the man himself experiences in the story. The needs of the discourse dictate the shape of the story.

Hoti ("because"). The clauses introduced by *hoti* (when used as a causal conjunction) offer explanations of cause or reason and are therefore similar in function to the *gar* clauses.[27] The first example of a *hoti* clause in the Gospel comes strategically at the end of a healing clinic held by Jesus. We are told that "he would not permit the demons to speak, *because they knew him*" (1:34). Verses such as this one have been discussed endlessly by twentieth-century scholars under the rubric of the Messianic Secret in Mark. Why does Jesus the Messiah (see 1:1) try to keep his identity a secret? Why should he not wish to be revealed as who the demons say he is, "the Son of God" (3:11; 5:7; cf. 1:1)? The scholarly debate over these questions has been long, complicated, and frustrating.[28] We can shed some light on the problem if we

26. For this example I am indebted to James L. Resseguie, "Reader-Response Criticism and the Synoptic Gospels," *JAAR* 52 (1984): 307–24; esp. 312–13.

27. The salient examples of *hoti* parentheses are found in 1:34; 3:29-30; 5:9; 6:17; 9:41; 14:21, 27.

28. The Messianic Secret in Mark is treated at greater length in a later chapter.

shift our focus away from the story and toward the encounter with the narrator's discourse in the reading experience. By the time we read 1:34, Jesus himself has already come into possession of a spirit from on high (1:10), and consequently we might expect that the inhabitants of the spirit world would be able to recognize one invested with power within their realm. Mark 1:34 is one of several places where the narrator tells us directly that the perceptions of the demons concerning Jesus' identity and power are in fact accurate. If Jesus silences demons *because* they knew him, then the implication is minimally *that* they knew him. The *because* of 1:34 really tells us little of a causal nature; we are not told explicitly why Jesus had reason to fear the demons' knowledge of him. The *because*, however, masks a *that* that is crucial, not within the story, but within the discourse. The reader may still be puzzled here and elsewhere in the Gospel about the secrecy and confusion surrounding Jesus' identity within the story but only because the reader knows and understands things about Jesus that characters in the story do not.

As is the case with the *gar* clauses, besides the *hoti* clauses used explicitly in the discourse of the narrator, several are in the direct speech attributed to characters. These clauses are worth noting, even though they are not strictly the narrator's commentary. Some *hoti* statements are supposedly the speech of Jesus within the story, but they might just as well be taken instead as comments by the narrator to the reader for all the impact they have on story characters. For example, in 14:21 a woe is pronounced by Jesus on the betrayer of the Son of man. Like all other Son of man sayings in Mark, it secures no uptake within the story. Then a few verses later, in another *hoti* statement, Jesus quotes scripture to the disciples who are about to abandon him: "And Jesus said to them, 'You will all stumble, *because it is written, "I will strike the shepherd, and the sheep will be scattered."* However, after I'm raised, I'll go ahead of you to Galilee' " (14:27-28; R&M). Peter responds immediately, but his response is curiously restricted to Jesus' words about their stumbling (14:27a). Peter is silent about the scriptural quotation in 14:27b and about the haunting and enigmatic utterance in 14:28, as if he had heard neither. Mark 14:27b and 28 are guides for reading, aimed principally at extranarrative rather than intranarrative narratees.

The *hoti* clauses of 14:21 and 14:27 are supposedly the words of Jesus, but who is supposed to be speaking the *hoti* clause in 9:41 is not immediately clear. The clause is undoubtedly parenthetical, tucked into a collection of "whoever" and "*amēn*" sayings by Jesus: "For whoever gives you a cup of water for a name's sake"—*because you are of Christ*—"truly, I say to you that he certainly will not lose his reward" (RMF). Granted, my translation and especially my punctuation are slanted toward the way I read this *hoti* clause. The second-person plural form of the verb *este* ("you are") allows us to read the parenthesis either as a comment by Jesus to his intranarrative audience or as a comment by the narrator to his extranarrative audience (cf.

Mark 13). The aspect of the parenthetical comment that makes it problematic as a statement of Jesus at the story level is the use of the term "Christ." Nowhere else in Mark does Jesus so casually use so weighty a title to refer to himself. Here we are probably hearing the narrator speaking, interjecting his own parenthetical comment into a speech otherwise supposedly by Jesus. Then again, for me to speak this way implies that I have fallen under the narrator's spell, which would have me believe that whenever "Jesus" speaks in this story, it is indeed Jesus who speaks and not the narrator. The *hoti* clause in 9:41 is in this regard similar to the parenthetical comment to "the reader" in 13:14. Both parentheses reveal suddenly the presence of the narrator in the midst of a discourse supposedly from Jesus, but these parentheses do not reveal a narrator who has hitherto been absent from the telling of the story. Rather, parentheses such as those in 13:14 and 9:41 focus our attention for a moment upon the omnipresent narrator. The voice that has been telling us the story all along is heard, if only for an instant, for what it genuinely is—the voice of the narrator. Prodded by this realization, we are then in a position to observe that the "whoever" and "*amēn*" statements that surround the "because you are of Christ" parenthesis in 9:41 are also every bit as much statements by the narrator at the discourse level as is the little parenthesis in their midst. If the *hoti* clause in 9:41 is foreign or awkward at all, it is so only at the story level, for it is not something the "Jesus" of this story would say. If the whole passage is grasped at the level of the narrator's discourse, however, then the *hoti* clause makes perfect sense. This statement bears repeating: If we consider 9:38-50 at the level of story, then 9:41 stands out as an awkward disruption in the speech of a story character; if we consider 9:38-50 at the level of discourse, then the entire passage is told with a steady and consistent narrative voice.

One last observation on Mark's use of *hoti*: Although *hoti* often introduces explanatory comments by the narrator and therefore is often translated "because" or "for," it is a versatile conjunction with other uses. One of Mark's favorite uses for *hoti* is to introduce the direct discourse of characters in the story, the so-called *hoti* recitative.[29] When used in this way, *hoti* is sometimes translated as "that," omitted altogether from the translation, or replaced by the usual typographical signal for the beginning of quotation: a colon followed by the first of two quotation marks. Would that we had a first-century Greek speaker's grasp of the nuances of the different uses of *hoti* and the other linguistic signals of the narrator's commentary! Nevertheless, a modern critic might notice things no native speaker would. A modern critical reader of Koine Greek can discern, for example, that sometimes *hoti* introduces a parenthetical comment explicitly from the narrator and at other times it is used to introduce direct, verbatim quotations attributed to characters in the

29. On *hoti* recitative, see Fowler, *Loaves and Fishes,* 203.

story. These equivocal uses of the vocable *hoti* encourage laziness on the part of the hearer in distinguishing between narrator and character. The reader is supposed to relax and overlook that often the narrator is his characters, and they are he.[30]

Statements of Purpose (Hina)

Hina is a conjunction that introduces clauses that for our purposes are often weak and uninteresting. The few salient examples of its use with commentary involve *hina* used in a "final sense to denote purpose, aim, or goal."[31] In such usage it is usually translated "in order that" or "that."

Several times the narrator uses *hina* clauses to inform the reader of ulterior motives on the part of Jesus' opponents.

> And they watched him, to see whether he would heal him on the sabbath, *so that they might accuse him* (3:2).
> And they sent to him some of the Pharisees and some of the Herodians, *to entrap him in his talk* (12:13).
> Then Judas Iscariot, who was one of the twelve, went to the chief priests *in order to betray him to them* (14:10).

These comments come at the beginning of their respective episodes (or in an interlude between episodes, in the case of 14:10), and they provide crucial information for the reader. Everything that follows will be read and apprehended by the reader with these pieces of information foremost in mind. After both 3:2 and 12:13, Jesus demonstrates quickly that he, too, perceives the aim of his adversaries; that the reader and Jesus share insight into the opponents' designs is thus revealed to the reader. In a way, the information provided puts the reader in a position alongside Jesus vis-à-vis the opponents, but the reader cannot predict how Jesus will handle the situation and can only stand off to one side and observe how the episode unfolds. In 3:2 and 12:13 the disciples are not present and, accordingly, we cannot look to them as role models, even if we wanted to. We also have no positive model for discipleship in 14:10. There we are informed that one of Jesus' handpicked disciples, Judas Iscariot, has chosen to join the opposition and will participate in the plot against Jesus' life that was already foreshadowed back in 3:6 and 3:19.

---

30. One other way of introducing statements of cause or reason is by use of the preposition *dia*, which is translated as "because of" or "for the sake of" when it is used with the accusative case (e.g., 5:4; 6:6, 17; 15:10). The two most interesting examples are the inside views of Jesus in 6:6 ("And he marveled *because of their unbelief*") and of Pilate in 15:10 ("For he knew that *it was because of envy that the high priests had handed him over*" [RMF]). As with *hoti*, the *because* of these comments usually is less important for the reader than the *that* implied in them.

31. BAGD, s.v. *hina*. The salient examples of *hina* parentheses are found in: 2:9-11; 3:2; 4:11-12; 12:13; 14:10, 49.

At other times the author uses *hina* in places where the distinction between the narrator and Jesus is cloudy. The least debated of these *hina* clauses is the infamous quotation of Isa. 6:9-10 in the aftermath of the parable of the sower in Mark 4:12: "And he said to them, 'To you has been given the secret of the kingdom of God, but for those outside everything is in riddles, *so that in seeing, they may see and not perceive, and in hearing, they may hear and not understand, lest they should turn and be forgiven'* " (4:11-12; RMF).

Readers have never taken this *hina* clause as anything other than a statement by Jesus, albeit a disturbing one, because he seems to be saying that his parables are riddles designed to provoke a blind and deaf response and are not supposed to encourage repentance and make possible forgiveness. Because, if taken directly at face value, this statement is exactly opposite to what we would expect Jesus to say (cf. 1:14-15), we would be wise *not* to take it directly at face value, but rather as a move of indirection, at least by the narrator and maybe by Jesus, too.[32] Are not Jesus, the narrator, or both likely to be speaking ironically here? That we should read 4:12 ironically seems to be confirmed when we move on to verse 13, in which we learn that Jesus' story-level narratees, the privileged inner circle of followers, do not understand the riddle of the sower and thereby may miss out completely on understanding all the parables of Jesus. The insiders in the story reveal themselves (to the reader) really to be outsiders, a revelation that turns the natural outsider of the story (the reader) into an insider.[33] Notice that Mark 4:12 receives no uptake at the story level. No one within the story is described as seeing or hearing the statement about seeing and hearing. Therefore, the only one in a position to perceive or understand this statement is the reader of the Gospel. Moreover, verse 12 is an unannounced but nevertheless fairly clear allusion to the Jewish Scriptures, and the offering of such reading directions is already established in 1:2-3 as the prerogative of the narrator. Therefore, this verse, like so many others in Mark, is probably supposed to be taken at first blush as a statement by Jesus at the story level, but because it receives no uptake there it ends up functioning exclusively at the discourse level as a piece of ironic commentary by the narrator.

Another *hina* that is usually credited to Jesus but should be credited to the narrator is the parenthetical comment in 2:10: " 'Which is easier, to say to the paralytic, "Your sins are forgiven," or to say, "Arise, take your bed,

32. Robert M. Fowler, "The Rhetoric of Direction and Indirection in the Gospel of Mark," *Semeia* 48 (1989): 115–34.

33. Interpreters of Mark 4, the parable chapter, are beginning to catch on to the primacy of the narrator's discourse over his story and the rhetorical strategies of indirection employed here. See Werner H. Kelber, *The Oral and the Written Gospel: The Hermeneutics of Speaking and Writing in the Synoptic Tradition, Mark, Paul, and Q* (Philadelphia: Fortress Press, 1983), 117–29; Vernon Robbins, *Jesus the Teacher: A Socio-Rhetorical Interpretation of Mark* (Philadelphia: Fortress Press, 1984), 137–38; and Perry V. Kea, "Perceiving the Mystery: Encountering the Reticence of Mark's Gospel," in *PEGLMBS* 4 (1984), 181–94.

and walk"?'—*but so that you may know that the Son of man has authority to forgive sins on earth—he says to the paralytic:* 'I say to you, arise, take your bed, and go to your home' " (2:9-11, RMF). The adversative *de* ("but") with which the parenthesis begins helps to set it apart from the preceding words of Jesus but perhaps not enough to indicate unambiguously that the narrator is now speaking for himself. The second-person plural verb form ("you may know"; *eidēte*) is ambiguous, possibly referring either to Jesus' intranarrative or to the narrator's extranarrative narratees. The decisive evidence is the last three words of verse 10, the narrator's introduction to the words of Jesus in verse 11: "he says to the paralytic" (*legei tō paralytikō*). Here unmistakably the narrator and no one else is speaking. These words by the narrator refer to Jesus in the third person, but the preceding words in verse 10a likewise referred to the Son of man in the third person. Consequently, all of verse 10 makes excellent sense as a parenthetical comment by the narrator to the narratee. Admittedly, the narrator's shift from verse 10a to verse 10b is abrupt, but the shift is even more abrupt if verse 10a is taken as a parenthetical statement by Jesus to his intranarrative audience and verse 10b is taken as a parenthetical comment by the narrator to his extranarrative audience. The "forgiveness of sins" mentioned in 2:10a is a theme in the larger episode (2:1-12), but the fact remains that 2:10a receives no uptake at the level of story. So why not take all of 2:10 as a parenthetical comment by the narrator to the reader? Once again, regardless of whether verse 10a is attributed officially to the narrator or to Jesus, the parenthesis has little to do with the story level and everything to do with the discourse level. No matter who we suppose is speaking it, it is taken up only by the reader.

Statements of Result (Hōste)

Now we turn to commentary about results or consequences deriving from occurrences in the story. Several noteworthy statements of result are introduced by *hōste*.[34] Most of the *hōste* clauses in Mark are dependent clauses of actual result. In these clauses *hōste* is often translated "so that." In two places in Mark, however, *hōste* introduces an independent clause, and there the appropriate translation options would be "for this reason, therefore, so."

One of the independent clauses is the well-known Son of man statement in 2:28: "And he said to them, 'The sabbath was made for humankind, not humankind for the sabbath'; *so the Son of man is lord even of the sabbath*" (2:27-28; RMF). The placement of quotation marks in the RSV and in most other translations reflects the translators' belief that verse 28 is a continuation of Jesus' utterance in verse 27. This supposition is dubious for several reasons. For one thing, as an independent clause, 2:28 stands apart from the preceding verse, and therefore it could just as well be the narrator's explanatory comment

---

34. The salient examples of *hōste* parentheses are found in 1:27; 2:12, 27-28; 15:5.

to the reader about the preceding words of Jesus. Moreover, verse 28 comes at the very end of the episode, where it could easily be the narrator's concluding comment on the whole episode, a practice we examined several times previously. Besides, no Son of man statement ever receives any uptake in the story, and 2:28 is no exception. Far from accepting or rejecting the statement in 2:28, no one in the story even seems to hear it. Consequently, I argue that 2:28 is a comment by the narrator. Yet, from the perspective of the reader, this point is really moot. Once more, the narrator himself would probably prefer us not to concern ourselves about distinguishing between him and Jesus; he would just as soon disguise his own commentary and interpretation as words of Jesus. He cares little who gets credit for his words, as long as they sink into the reader.

Hōste introduces several noteworthy dependent clauses. The one I shall examine offers a rich inside view: "And they were all amazed, *so that they questioned among themselves, saying, 'What is this? A new teaching with authority?*[35] *He commands even the unclean spirits, and they obey him'*" (1:27). This inside view is twofold: we are told of the amazement of the audience in the synagogue; then we are told about their private questioning about Jesus' evident authority. The *hōste* clause in 1:27 also echoes another inside view that was offered to the reader earlier in the same episode in 1:22. There we had the narrator's initial indication in this episode—and indeed in the entire Gospel—that people respond to Jesus with amazement. That inside view in 1:22 was then followed by a *gar* clause in which the narrator explained that people were amazed because Jesus taught "as one who had authority," a discreet way for the narrator to broach the authority issue for the reader for the first time in the Gospel. Thus, in 1:21-28 the narrator himself first raises the authority issue in 1:22. As a result, when characters wonder at the authority of Jesus in 1:27, behind their thoughts we can recognize the already familiar conceptual point of view of the narrator. Amazed onlookers are useful devices in telling the story, but we may look behind them to see that ultimately the storyteller is the one who is claiming that Jesus possesses authority and provokes amazement.

Relative Pronouns

Another kind of clear linguistic signal of the narrator's commentary is the use of relative pronouns such as *hos* ("who") and *hostis* ("whoever"). Many important declarations in the Gospel are introduced with *hos* ("he who . . .") or *hos an* ("whoever . . ."), but the most notable are judgments or generalizations placed on the lips of Jesus, which disqualifies them as instances of explicit commentary offered by the narrator. Nevertheless, we can examine

---

35. Recognizing that Mark likes to use double questions, I am using the translation of the RSV but changing its punctuation.

here some significant instances of the use of a relative pronoun to introduce explicit commentary from the narrator.

Hos ("who, which, what, that"). The use of the relative pronoun *hos* to introduce a comment by the narrator is often not striking. By its nature the relative pronoun tends to introduce supplementary information about persons (e.g., 5:3-4; 15:40-41, 43), places (e.g., 14:32), or things (e.g., 15:46) we have already encountered. I shall examine two noteworthy instances of *hos* used to introduce the narrator's commentary[36] and then a highly stereotyped use of *hos* in the expression *ho estin* ("that is . . ."), which is often used in Mark to offer explanations of foreign words and customs.

One occurrence of a *hos* comment is in 3:19: ". . . and Judas Iscariot, *who delivered him up*" (RMF). The *hos* clause here is short, simple, and direct, but it is also ominous; it comes at the end of the roster of Jesus' handpicked group of twelve disciples (3:13-19), and it tells us at an early point in the Gospel that one of his chosen followers "delivered him up."[37] This insight is a crucial one for the reader to receive so early in the narrative. Already we know the identity of the one—a disciple!—who will later deliver up Jesus. We should take care to observe that the verb in 3:19 is not in the future tense; the aorist indicative tense of the verb describes Judas' delivering up of Jesus not as an event that is forthcoming in the world of the story but as an event that lies in the past of the narrator's world and our own. This verse reminds us, when we stop to think about it, that the entire narrative is told from a retrospective point of view. As we read, almost everything mentioned in the story has already come to pass,[38] presumably just the way the narrator describes it.

For all we know, the first Christian storyteller to cast Judas in the role of traitor was the author of Mark's Gospel.[39] The statement about Judas in 3:19 is one of those fixed and incontrovertible points in Mark's narrative that every reader must accept. Mark fixes this point so firmly that subsequent authors (Matthew, Luke, and John) can only enlarge upon it or embroider around it. We have become so accustomed to the portrayal of Judas' treachery in the other Gospels that we have lost the ability to feel the shock such treachery would have produced in the first readers to encounter Mark's story. The modern

36. The salient examples of *hos* parentheses are found in 2:26; 3:19; 5:2-3; 14:32; 15:40-41, 43, 46.

37. "To deliver up" or "to hand over" are more literal renderings of the verb *paradidōmi* than "to betray." For a discussion of the virtue of translating *paradidōmi* consistently in this literal manner, avoiding the tendentious rendering of "to betray" in the special case of Judas, see Fowler, *Loaves and Fishes,* 136–38.

38. The one grand event mentioned so often in the story that has not come to pass by the time of the telling of the story is the coming of the Son of man, on the clouds of heaven, i.e., the parousia.

39. Fowler, *Loaves and Fishes,* 136, 224.

reader of the canonical Gospels takes for granted Judas' treachery, but the reader implied in Mark's Gospel is supposed to be shocked by Jesus being "delivered up" by one of his intimates.

Another piece of commentary introduced by *hos* is found in 2:26: " '[David] ate the bread of the Presence' (*which it is not lawful for any but the priests to eat*) . . ." (RMF). Observe how 2:26 functions for the reader. First, Jesus is addressing Pharisees who hardly need to be informed that the bread of the Presence can be eaten only by priests because Pharisees as well as most other Jews would have known this law. The reader of Mark may not know it, however, and so the comment offers an explanation of a "foreign" custom to the implied, uninformed reader. This verse is yet another parenthetical comment that makes more sense as a comment by the narrator (cf. Mark 9:41 or 13:14) than by Jesus.[40]

The function of verse 26 at the level of discourse goes far beyond merely providing needed information to the reader, however. In the episode including verse 26 (2:23-28), Jesus defends the practice of plucking and eating grain on the sabbath. He appeals to what (soon-to-be-king) David did "when he was in need and was hungry." What David did was to usurp a priestly prerogative, the eating of the bread of the Presence. The function of verse 26 for the reader is to show Jesus defending himself and his disciples by appealing to the paradigm of Israelite royalty par excellence, King David, in an episode in which David took to himself the prerogatives of priesthood. To be sure, nowhere in the Markan episode is an explicit claim made either to royalty or to priesthood on Jesus' behalf, but strong implicit claims begin to take shape from here on. The claims become stronger as the narrative progresses, but they are never explicit. Jesus indeed is acclaimed "Son of David" later in the Gospel, but what this title might mean—or even whether it is appropriate for Jesus—remains ambiguous to the end. He is also called "Christ" and "King of the Jews," but these acclamations turn out to be either insincere (e.g., Mark 15:2, 12, 18, 32) or shallow (8:29). Jesus is not acclaimed a high priest in the Jerusalem temple in Mark's Gospel, but he has confrontations with the priestly establishment of the Jerusalem temple, due in large part to his enforced cessation of temple operations (11:12-25). In so doing he displays an authority far exceeding that of priests or kings, the authority to seal the doom of the temple. Yet the temple's doom goes hand in hand with Jesus' own doom; they are somehow connected (13:1-37; 14:57; 15:29; 15:37-38). A certain kind of royalty and a certain kind of authority over the priestly domain are granted to Jesus in this narrative, but these privileges are fraught with ambiguity, irony, and paradox to the end.

The *hos* clause in 2:26 has a companion piece of commentary in 2:28 ("so the Son of man is lord even of the sabbath"). Both 2:26 and 2:28 are usually

---

40. Turner offers a tentative conclusion that 2:26 does indeed contain a parenthetical comment by the narrator ("Marcan Usage," 147–48).

taken as statements by Jesus, and both would be better understood as statements by the narrator. Yet in both who utters them matters little; they both function primarily for the reader. Still, two such parenthetical comments in such close proximity to each other helps us hear the narrator's voice in both.

Hos also appears a number of times in the Gospel in a stereotyped phrase that employs the neuter singular form of the pronoun to introduce a translation of a foreign term or an explanation of a foreign custom. The expression *ho estin* . . . ("that is . . .") appears nine times in the Gospel; a variation of it, *tout' estin* . . . ," appears once.[41] Six times *ho estin* is used to render in Greek an Aramaic or Hebrew expression.[42] These explanations perhaps indicate that the implied author of the Gospel is Jewish and the implied reader is not, but clearer evidence on this score would be helpful. Twice the phrase introduces an explanation of a religious custom, once a currency exchange rate is stated, and once a clarification is offered regarding the stage scenery that the reader is to imagine for the story.[43]

In every case the *ho estin* phrase is indubitably the commentary of the narrator. Several times the phrase occurs in the midst of the exposition of an episode by the narrator, and other times it follows a short statement by Jesus in direct discourse; in either circumstance, however, that the *ho estin* comment comes from the narrator is never in doubt. The only instance in Mark in which the narrator's *ho estin* comment is embedded in a relatively lengthy speech by Jesus is 7:11:

> And he said to them, "How well you nullify the ordinance of God in order to establish your tradition! For Moses said, 'Honor your father and your mother' and 'The one who pronounces misfortune upon father or mother must certainly die.' But *you* say that if a man says to his father or his mother 'whatever from me might be a benefit to you is *Corban'* "—*that is, a gift consecrated to God*— "no longer do you allow him to do anything at all for his father or his mother, thereby invalidating the word of God by your tradition which you have handed on. And you do many such things like this." (7:9-13; R&M)

The parenthetical comment makes sense only as a comment by the narrator; Jesus would hardly need to pause for the benefit of his Pharisaic audience to translate the Hebrew word for "gift" (*qorban*) into Greek (*dōron*). Translations such as *ho estin dōron* are crucial to the reader; they give us information

---

41. The salient examples of *ho estin* parentheses are found in: 3:17; 5:41; [7:2, *tout' estin*]; 7:11, 34; 12:42; 15:16, 22, 34, 42.

42. Aramaic or Hebrew expressions: 3:17; 5:41; 7:11, 34; 15:22, 34.

43. Religious customs: 7:2; 15:42; currency exchange rate: 12:42; stage scenery: 15:16. The *ho estin* comments in 12:42 and 15:16 both employ Latin loanwords in their explanatory comments—*kodrantēs* in 12:42 and *praitōrion* in 15:16. These terms have led some critics to suggest that Mark's Gospel was written in a Latin setting, maybe even in Rome. At the remove of nineteen centuries, we are unlikely to have sufficient knowledge to infer with accuracy the possible Jewish, non-Jewish, or Roman associations of Mark's Gospel.

that characters in the story already possess. Sometimes they even provide information that characters in the story do not possess.

Consider the entire collection of *ho estin* comments that offer translations of Aramaic or Hebrew words. I have noted that such parenthetical comments serve the purpose of informing the reader of the meanings of words that would presumably already be familiar to characters in the story. This observation is true enough as far as it goes, but it is a banal observation oriented along language's referential axis. What other function might these comments have along the rhetorical axis? First, the Aramaic or Hebrew words stand out in a narrative written in Hellenistic Greek. They lend an exotic flavor to the narrative, especially in the two episodes in which Jesus utters Aramaic words in the manner of magical spells, once to effect the resuscitation of a dead girl (5:41) and once to heal a deaf-mute (7:34). In this Greek narrative, the Palestinian Aramaic once familiar to Jesus and his disciples has become a mysterious and sometimes magical foreign tongue. The offering of Aramaic or Hebrew words accompanied by a Greek translation allows the narratee both to experience the exotic strangeness of the words and to go beyond the strangeness into understanding.

We should not be too hasty to say that in a translation introduced by *ho estin* the reader is given knowledge that the characters in the story already have. The Gospel of Mark is, after all, told entirely in Greek. Even the quotations of Jewish Scripture in the Gospel are derived not from the Hebrew Bible or from its Aramaic paraphrases but from the Septuagint, the Greek translation of the Hebrew Bible. Consequently, unless we actually observe uptake of the meaning of the Semitic words that Jesus uses, we should not merely assume that characters in the story understand these words. The Jews of Mark's Gospel are all Greek-speaking Jews; no one in this story habitually speaks Aramaic or Hebrew. Therefore, the narrator's translation of an isolated Aramaic or Hebrew expression may provide the reader with an insight that no one in the story has. At the very least, because the translations are offered to the reader alone, the effect of receiving a clarifying translation is experienced by the reader alone.[44]

The best example is the *ho estin* comment in 15:34: "And at the ninth hour Jesus cried with a loud voice, 'Eloi, Eloi, lama sabach-thani?' *which means, 'My God, my God, why hast thou forsaken me?' "* In his anguish Jesus cries out, quoting words that anyone knowing Hebrew or Aramaic would probably recognize as the opening words of Psalm 22, yet no one demonstrates such recognition in the story. For the Greek-speaking reader outside the story,

44. Thanks to modern historical research, we may be more sensitive than Mark's original audience to the fact that the historical Jesus and his audiences probably spoke Aramaic, not Greek. Conversely, we probably appreciate too little that we have only Greek-speaking versions of Jesus represented in our canonical Gospels.

who would probably not recognize or understand the Aramaic[45] words, the narrator provides the necessary translation. We hear Jesus' cry in the foreign tongue, and we learn instantly what this foreign utterance means. That no one in the story understands his cry is revealed to us, not directly in a comment from the narrator, but indirectly, by what characters in the story say and do immediately thereafter: "And some of the bystanders hearing it said, 'Behold, he is calling Elijah.' And one ran and, filling a sponge full of vinegar, put it on a reed and gave it to him to drink, saying, 'Wait, let us see whether Elijah will come to take him down.' And Jesus uttered a loud cry, and breathed his last" (15:36-37). The cry to God (*Elōi*) is misheard as a cry to Elijah (*Elias*), the prophet of old who folklore said was the rescuer of those in distress.[46] Thus, this *ho estin* translation is quite distinctive in the Gospel in that the reader is made to understand exactly what the strange Aramaic words signify, while the characters in the story demonstrate clearly that they thoroughly misunderstand the very same words. No one but the reader understands Jesus' dying words! In a profound sense, the only genuine witness to the crucifixion in Mark is the reader. This stark incongruity between understanding at the discourse level and misunderstanding at the story level produces a deeply ironic experience for the reader. Indeed, this scene has great dramatic power. Oddly enough, too few readers have appreciated Mark's skillful manipulation of story versus discourse here. This oversight is a tribute to the success of Mark's rhetoric of indirection. Careful rhetorical criticism is required to lay bare such indirect strategies and to bring awareness of their effects to critical consciousness.

Hostis ("who, whoever").   The narrator uses the indefinite relative pronoun *hostis* twice to insert an explanatory comment into his narration. The first occurrence is in 12:18: "And Sadducees came to him, *who say that there is no resurrection;* and they asked him a question. . . ." This parenthetical comment explains who the Sadducees were, at least for the purposes of this particular episode, which pivots around the question of the resurrection. The narrator gives us the one piece of information on which everything in this episode hinges. In the episode the Sadducees propose the hypothetical example of a woman who had married each of seven brothers, all of whom die. When they finally arrive at their question ("In the resurrection whose wife will she be? For the seven had her as wife" [12:23]), we know that they do not pose the question sincerely. Having first been told that Sadducees say there is no resurrection, a question they submit that presupposes the reality of the res- urrection cannot be taken as a sincere inquiry. The reader has been placed in

<hr/>

45. Most scholars agree that the quotation in Mark 15:34 renders the first verse of Psalm 22 in Aramaic, instead of the original Hebrew; Vincent Taylor, *The Gospel According to St. Mark,* 2d ed. (New York: St. Martin's Press, 1966), 593.

46. Ibid., 594.

a position to see through the Sadducees' ploy, just as at the story level Jesus himself immediately sees through their hypocrisy (12:24).

The other instance of a parenthetical comment introduced by *hostis* is in 15:7: "And among the rebels in prison, *who had committed murder in the insurrection,* there was a man called Barabbas." This parenthesis is intriguing in that it seems to allude to portions of Mark's story that have been submerged or suppressed. After encountering 15:7 we may well ask, What rebels? What insurrection? This verse lends support to readers, such as Fernando Belo, who see in Mark's discourse an "erased" narrative about Zealotic insurgency against Rome. Jesus' disciples often advocate the Zealot point of view, Belo says, while Jesus distances himself from this perspective but perhaps not enough to avoid being crucified as a Zealot.[47] Mark, the master of indirection, may tantalize us with traces of submerged or erased narratives.

Adverbs

***Hote* ("when").**   Adverbial forms such as *hote* ("when")[48] introduce several parenthetical comments by the narrator. Usually *hote* clauses give the narratee an awareness of when things in the story happened. *Hote* lends itself to use in the familiar and nearly ubiquitous Markan two-step progression.[49] One example is 1:32: "When it grew late, *when the sun had set,* they brought to him all who were sick or possessed by demons" (RMF). Unlike the rhetorical function of the *gar* clause, which simultaneously reveals and fills a previously unknown gap in the reader's knowledge, the Markan two-step progression is accretive, the second clause adding specificity to the first. The two halves of a Markan two-step progression are often so similar that scholars have tried to see in them the awkward conflation of pre-Gospel sources by the Gospel writer. With Neirynck's demonstration that the two-step progression so pervades the Gospel that it must be regarded as a characteristic of Mark's own writing style, such appeals to redundant pre-Markan tradition will henceforth be difficult to defend. As unlike the *gar* clause as it first appears, the *hote* clause also promotes the narratee's reliance upon the narrator. In the *gar* clause the narratee takes a step backward with the narrator; in the *hote* clause the narratee takes a small step forward with the narrator.

The *hote* clause can do more than clarify a preceding clause; in 14:12 it offers the reader what amounts to an explanation of a foreign custom: "And on the first day of Unleavened Bread, *when they sacrificed the passover lamb . . ."* (14:12). Once more, the foreign custom that is explained is a

47. Fernando Belo, *A Materialist Reading of the Gospel of Mark,* trans. Matthew J. O'Connell (Maryknoll, N.Y.: Orbis, 1981), 157, 224.

48. Labeled an "adverb of time" and a "temporal conjunction" in BDF (sections 105, 455[1]), and a "temporal particle" in BAGD (s.v. *hote*).

49. Neirynck, *Duality.*

matter of Jewish practice, in this case the sacrifice of the passover lamb. Once more, the implied reader is apparently not familiar with such a basic Jewish practice.

In 15:41 *hote* appears in a dependent clause introduced by a form of the relative pronoun *hos,* which introduces an interesting analepsis: "There were also women looking on from afar, among whom were Mary Magdalene, and Mary the mother of James the younger and of Joses, and Salome, *who, when he was in Galilee, followed him, and ministered to him;* and also many other women who came up with him to Jerusalem" (15:40-41). Here the positioning of the *hote* clause as the second member of a two-step progression is ambiguous: does it mean all of the women who were watching the crucifixion from afar (v. 40a), or does it mean specifically the three women mentioned in verse 40b? In any case the *hote* clause is an analepsis; it refers back to the earlier days of Jesus' ministry in Galilee and says that these women had followed him back then. Because Mark has thus far refrained from introducing these women into the story, they must be introduced now; the disciples have abandoned Jesus (14:50), and these women are the central characters in the rest of the story. I cannot help thinking that Mark, whose parenthetical comments are often abrupt, is more abrupt than usual here. Viewing Mark's narrative retrospectively from the vantage point of 15:40-41, finding the places in the narrative where these characters were supposed to have been present is difficult. Consequently, I suspect that Mark has simply neglected to introduce these actors before the moment comes when they assume center stage. This abrupt parenthesis may simply represent careless storytelling. Or is it more Markan indirection?

Kathōs ("as, just as").   Another adverb used to introduce commentary by the narrator is *kathōs* ("as, just as"). The narrator explicitly uses it only once in a parenthesis, but this instance is of major importance:

> The beginning of the Gospel of Jesus Christ, the Son of God—*as it is written in Isaiah the prophet: "Behold, I send my messenger before your face, who will prepare your way; a voice of one crying in the desert: 'Prepare the way of the lord; make his paths straight' "*—John the baptizer was in the desert and preaching a baptism of repentance for the forgiveness of sins. (1:1-4, RMF)

The narrator is so partial to parentheses that he inserts his first in the second and third verses of the Gospel![50] This quotation of scripture functions in a manner similar to most other scripture quotations in Mark: it is a hermeneutical guide to reading at the level of discourse.

---

50. Mark 1:2-3 is also regarded as a parenthesis by Turner, "Marcan Usage," 146; Zerwick, *Markus-Stil,* 133; and Frans Neirynck, with Theo Hansen and Frans Van Segbroeck, *The Minor Agreements of Matthew and Luke Against Mark with a Cumulative List,* BETL 37 (Leuven: Leuven University Press, 1974), 220.

The only other place where *kathōs* may possibly introduce a comment by the narrator is in 9:11-13, a passage that is convoluted and notoriously difficult to understand. We cannot render the passage transparent, but taking the most troublesome phrases as the narrator's commentary can at least help us to appreciate their rhetorical force for the reader:

> And they asked him, saying: "Why do the scribes say that Elijah must come first?" And he said to them: "Elijah does come first to restore all things"— *and how is it written of the Son of man, that he should suffer much and be treated with contempt?*—"but I tell you that Elijah has come, and they did to him whatever they wished"—*as [kathōs] it is written of him.* (9:11-13, RMF)

This typographical presentation of 9:11-13 endeavors to distinguish sharply between Jesus' direct discourse in the story and the narrator's own commentary on the story at the discourse level. We are thereby resisting the narrator's invitation to concentrate on the story and to forget that we are responding to his discourse. Distinguishing sharply between story and discourse is a heuristic critical move designed to give us a fighting chance to hear the discourse as discourse. Only the reader recognizes and understands that the fate of "Elijah" (the reader infers "John the Baptist") is similar to and even intertwined with the fate of the "Son of man" (the reader infers "Jesus"). Also prominently on display in this passage is the self-referential nature of the Gospel. What writing concerning the Son of man is referred to in verse 12 and what writing concerning Elijah verse 13 refers to may not be clear, but at the very least, the reader knows that the Son of man and Elijah go to their respective but intertwined fates "as it is written" *in Mark 9:11-13.*

Participles

Sometimes a parenthetical comment is introduced with a present tense participle.[51] Twice, for example, the brief participial phrase *peirazontes auton* ("testing him") is used to give an inside view into the motivations of Jesus' opponents (8:11; 10:2). In both instances the parenthesis comes near the beginning of an episode and provides the reader with decisive information to judge everything that follows.

AWKWARDNESS IN SYNTAX (ANACOLUTHON)

At this point we leave behind commentary by the narrator that is introduced by clear and usually grammatical linguistic signals. Here we shall consider commentary signaled by awkward or ruptured syntax.[52] Many of Mark's

---

51. The salient examples of participial parentheses are found in 7:18-19; 8:11; 10:2; 13:14.
52. The salient examples of commentary introduced by anacoluthon are found in: 1:2-3; 2:10-11, 22; 3:30; 7:2-5, 19; 11:31-32; 14:49.

"interpretations" are indicated by both a clear linguistic signal and ruptured syntax.

In a narrative that is not far removed from orality and probably written to be read aloud to an assembled audience, awkward or ruptured syntax is not necessarily a deficiency because it can be an effective communicative device. Disruptions of syntax punctuate the spoken word in much the same way that typographical punctuation marks regulate the reader's progress through the printed page. Of course, this views things backwards because punctuation was invented by literates to represent visually the originally oral disruption of syntax. Even hopelessly literate people, who regard a breakdown of syntax in formal, written communication as an inexcusable fault, punctuate their own informal, oral utterances with numerous ruptures in syntax. The spoken word readily forgives and perhaps even favors anacoluthon. If Mark's Gospel is deeply implicated in orality, we visually oriented literates ought to *hear* the awkward spots in Mark's grammar as instances of a speaker pausing for commentary rather than insisting on *seeing* the awkward spots in the Gospel as blemishes in a printed text.

We must recognize, however, that modern textual critics and translators have to represent anacoluthon visually, on the printed page, in a logical and consistent way. Perhaps the most common method is to use a dash wherever syntax breaks down. The dashes in the United Bible Societies' Greek text of Mark represent almost all major examples of disrupted syntax that occur in conjunction with a comment by the narrator.[53] I would add to the list only the elliptical *hina* comment in 14:49. Note, however, that although these dashes are the chief instances of anacoluthon in Mark, the UBS editors could easily have used many more dashes. I have used dashes liberally in my own translations of Mark in this book. Mark's writing style is paratactic and rough, and the modern textual critic or translator has little choice but to use dashes, ellipses, and other strategies to represent visually Mark's wrenching syntax.

The first example of an interpretive comment signaled by anacoluthon is also signaled by a participle: the narrator's comment in 7:19, in the midst of Jesus' speech about the clean and the unclean:

And he said to them: "Do *you* lack understanding like this too? Don't you comprehend that everything that enters into the man from outside isn't able to defile him, because it doesn't enter into his mind but into his stomach and goes out into the toilet?"—*thereby pronouncing all foods clean.*

[And] he said, "What comes out from the man, *that* defiles the man. (7:18-20, R&M; my emphasis added in v. 19 only)

The comment disrupts the syntax of Jesus' speech (the participle with which it begins cannot be made to fit grammatically into Jesus' speech) and

53. Commentary is marked by dashes in the UBS text of Mark 1:2-3; 2:10, 22; 3:30; 7:2-5, 19; 11:32; cf. 9:23.

thus is indicated in both the UBS text and the Rhoads and Michie translation by a dash. Immediately following the narrator's comment in verse 19, as a way of reintroducing Jesus' speech, is the expression *elegen de . . .* ("and he said . . ."). It marks the end of the narrator's brief interpretive comment and the resumption of direct discourse by Jesus in the story.

This point is worth exploring further. Mark is widely recognized to habitually introduce direct discourse by Jesus with *legei* ("he says"; i.e., the historical present tense of the verb *legō*) or *elegen* ("he said"; imperfect tense). This usage is so typical of Mark, in fact, that it has been labeled one of Mark's distinguishing "redactional" characteristics; that is, it is one of Mark's favorite ways of stitching together disparate traditional sayings of Jesus, sometimes one right after another.[54] Notwithstanding its possible significance as evidence of Markan redaction, *legei* or *elegen* at least occasionally marks a shift in the narrative from a comment by the narrator to the direct discourse of Jesus. The narrator uses the *legei/elegen* formula sometimes to reestablish the voice of Jesus after he has broken off Jesus' words in order to offer a piece of his own commentary. This process is obviously what is happening in 7:20, but we can observe the same phenomenon elsewhere in Mark, both in places where the narrator has without doubt offered a parenthetical comment and in other places where who is supposed to have been speaking is less clear.

For example, in Mark 3:5 we are granted a double inside view (we are told of Jesus' anger when he perceives the "hardening" of the minds of his opponents) that comes to an end when the narrator introduces direct discourse by Jesus: "he says to the man [*legei tō anthrōpō*], 'Stretch forth the hand . . .' " (RMF). Similarly, the inside view in 5:36 (here we are told something that Jesus hears) comes to an end when the narrator introduces another direct quotation by Jesus: "he says to the synagogue head [*legei tō archisynagōgō*], 'Do not fear—only have faith' " (RMF). Less obvious than these instances, perhaps, but probably also an example of the same phenomenon is the infamous Son of man saying in 2:10: ". . .—but so that [*hina*] you may know that the Son of man has authority to forgive sins on earth—he says to the paralytic [*legei tō paralytikō . . .*], 'I say to you, arise . . .' " (RMF). This verse is not only an example of the use of the *legei/elegen* formula to introduce the speech of Jesus after a parenthesis but also a major example of parenthesis signaled by anacoluthon, indicated here by the dashes. The degree of syntactic awkwardness perceived in 2:10 depends largely, however, upon who the speaker of the Son of man saying is supposed to be. If Jesus is speaking in 2:10, then the *legei* phrase that follows is awkward indeed, the narrator's needless interruption in what would otherwise be a coherent speech by Jesus in 2:8-11. If, however, we take all of verse 10 as

54. Fowler, *Loaves and Fishes*, 50, 199 n.20.

a comment by the narrator, then the *legei* phrase makes a great deal of sense as a way of reintroducing Jesus as the main speaker at the level of story.

This use of the *legei/elegen* formula to reintroduce Jesus as the chief speaker in the narrative possibly occurs more frequently than we have realized because we have not been sufficiently aware of the narrator's interruptions in Jesus' discourse. Another instance where *legei* might have the function of reintroducing speech by Jesus is in 4:13:

> And he said to them [*kai elegen autois*]: "To you has been given the secret of the Kingdom of God, but to those outside everything is in riddles." (So that [*hina*] in seeing, they may see and not perceive, and in hearing, they may hear and not understand, lest they should turn and be forgiven.) And he says to them [*kai legei autois*]: "Do you not know this riddle? And how will you understand all the riddles?" (4:11-13, RMF)

When we observe that the parenthesis in 4:12 begins with a *hina*, ends with a *legei* formula reintroducing the words of Jesus, and is an allusion to the Hebrew Bible, then we have abundant evidence that 4:12 is indeed a comment by the narrator to the narratee, who is perhaps expected to recognize it as an allusion to Isa. 6:9-10. Mark apparently expects his narratees to recognize such unheralded allusions to Jewish Scripture. What we tend not to recognize is the degree to which such comments by the narrator are subtly interwoven with the words of Jesus in the story.

So far we have noted anacolutha in 7:19 and 2:10.[55] The other anacoluthon I want to examine is in 11:32, which occurs in the midst of a debate over Jesus' authority (11:29-33). This verse is a textbook example of anacoluthon; the rupture in syntax is complete. Some editors and translators mark it with a dash; some with ellipsis; Rhoads and Michie use both: "And they began discussing among themselves, saying, 'If we say "From heaven," he'll say, "Then why didn't you put faith in him?" But, if we say, "From men . . ." '— *they were afraid of the crowd, for everyone held that John really was a prophet*" (11:31-32, R&M). In verse 32 the narrator breaks off abruptly from the words of the temple authorities in order to offer an inside view ("they were afraid . . ."), which itself is then explained by a *gar* parenthesis ("for everyone held that John really was a prophet"). The shift from the speech of characters to that of the narrator is illusory, however, because the words of the authorities beginning in verse 31 are already offered to the reader as an inside view: "they began discussing among themselves. . . ." In 11:32 one inside view is interrupted by another.

Moreover, the larger episode of which this verse is a piece is constructed masterfully by the author to manipulate the perceptions of the reader. The

---

55. Already discussed previously were several examples of anacoluthon that occur along with a clear linguistic signal (cf. 1:2-3 [s.v. *kathōs*], 3:30 [s.v. *hoti*], and 14:49 [s.v. *hina*]).

issue under debate in the episode is the source of Jesus' authority. The temple
authorities ask Jesus by what authority he does what he does. Instead of
replying directly to the question, Jesus responds by asking a counter-question:
"The baptism of John—was it of heaven or of men? Answer me!" (RMF).
In response to this challenge, the temple authorities huddle together and discuss
the options for their response, which the narrator conveniently arranges for
the reader to overhear. If they say John's baptism was of heavenly origin,
then Jesus can ask them why they did not believe in John, but if they say his
baptism was of human origin. . . . At this point the narrator forgoes any
further pretense of offering the internal speech of the authorities and explains
in his own voice that choosing the second position would earn the authorities
the enmity of the crowd, which held John to be a true prophet. Seeing no
viable option, the authorities refuse to answer Jesus' question, which leads
him to refuse to answer theirs. Referentially, the episode is disappointing:
important questions have been raised but none answered explicitly. Pragmatically, however, where is the reader who cannot supply answers for herself,
based on reading this episode and the entire Gospel? This episode exemplifies
Mark's confidence in the strategy of offering the reader vital questions and
the reading experience with which to answer them and then leaving the work
of formulating explicit answers up to the reader. As much direction as the
narrator's commentary provides in 11:31-32, just as much evidence exists for
Mark's rhetoric of indirection—requiring the reader to draw conclusions from
the clues provided.

WEAKER SIGNALS

Often clear and grammatical linguistic signals or ruptured syntax introduces
commentary, but sometimes the narrator's commentary is introduced by relatively weak signals: *de* ("and, but"), *kai* ("and"), and apposition.

De ("and, but")

Students of Greek know that *de* is a weak particle, often not even worth
translating. Furthermore, because Mark's writing style is characterized by the
ubiquitous *kai* parataxis ("and this . . . and that . . . and this"), *de* is employed infrequently in the Gospel. Because of its infrequency, *de* is sometimes
a relatively strong particle in Mark, particularly when used in an adversative
fashion, setting one phrase sharply against another.[56] Several times in the
Gospel a *de* signals a piece of commentary by the narrator.[57] One is in 7:26:
"But immediately a woman, who had a daughter with an unclean spirit, heard

56. Fowler, *Loaves and Fishes,* 81–82, 208 n.96.

57. The salient examples of *de* parentheses are found in 2:10, 2:22, and 7:26. The adversative
de in 2:10 ("*but* that you may know that the Son of man . . .") lends additional support to my
suggestion that 2:10 as a whole is a comment by the narrator. Besides employing *de,* in both
2:10 and 2:22 the parenthesis is also signaled by anacoluthon.

about him, came, and fell at his feet. (*And the woman was a Greek, a Syrophoenician by birth.*) And she asked him to cast out the demon from her daughter" (7:25-26, RMF). At first this parenthetical comment seems relatively innocuous; it tells us about the ethnic identity of the woman. Nevertheless, this information proves to be essential to the reader's understanding of the exchange that follows between the woman and Jesus. Jesus responds to the woman's request for an exorcism by saying: "Let the children first be fed, for it is not good to take the children's bread and throw it to the dogs" (v. 27). The woman responds: "Lord, even the dogs under the table eat the children's crumbs." The woman takes up the figures of speech Jesus uses and turns them against him. In this instance he who lives by the metaphor dies by the metaphor. Bested in this contest of wits and words, Jesus relents from his initial reluctance to help the woman and pronounces her daughter free of the demon.

The reader who is to make sense of the elliptical dialogue concerning children, bread, and dogs must make use of that seemingly innocuous parenthesis in 7:26. If Jesus is reluctant to grant the woman's request—to give bread to dogs—his reluctance must have something to do with her Syrophoenician Greek (that is, non-Jewish) heritage. The reader can infer that *dogs* represents Gentiles, *children* represents Jews, and *bread* represents whatever Jesus is able to do for people. All of this information must be inferred, however, because it is not explicitly stated in the text.[58]

Kai ("and")

As previously noted, *kai* parataxis is ubiquitous in Mark's Gospel. Anyone reading Mark's Gospel in Greek encounters a steady, almost hypnotizing flow of *kais*. Remembering that ancient Greek had no punctuation system, we might suggest that *kai* serves as the most common form of punctuation in the Gospel. Because of its ubiquity, it is a weak signal when used to introduce a parenthetical comment by the narrator.[59] *Kai* and apposition are the most unobtrusive methods that this narrator uses to introduce his commentary; they are the methods least likely to call attention to the narrator's parentheses.

Several scholars have recognized and discussed the *kai* parenthesis in 13:10: "And the gospel must first be preached to all the nations" (RMF).[60]

---

58. It is instructive to see what Matthew does to this episode (Matt. 15:21-28). Matthew takes up the ethnic rivalry that is implicit in Mark and makes it explicit, thus leaving his reader comparatively little inferential work to do in this passage.

In a way Matthew is doing to Mark's story what any reader must do: he produces a concretization of Mark's narrative in the act of reading. However, by sharing his reading of Mark with us in the form of his own Gospel narrative, he has made it extraordinarily difficult for anyone to read Mark in an other-than-Matthean fashion.

59. The salient examples of *kai* parentheses are found in 3:22; 8:31-32; 13:9-10; 14:61-64.

60. Turner, "Marcan Usage," 152; Neirynck, *Agreements,* 220. In a work as heavily freighted with Jewish concerns as is Mark's, the word translated "nations" (*ethnē*) might just as well be translated "Gentiles."

Although the *kai* hardly distinguishes this verse from surrounding *kai* phrases, the content of this statement makes it stand out quite prominently. The verses preceding the parenthesis and the verses following it all have to do with followers of Jesus being delivered up to rulers and kings, all of which is disrupted sharply by verse 10. If the verse were deleted from its present location, we would never miss it at the story level. Hence, it is a parenthetical comment, and we should take care to recognize it as a narrator's comment at the discourse level that interrupts the speech of Jesus in the story.[61] In this instance, although verses 9 and 11 supposedly refer to future events in the story world, verse 10 drops this pretense of speaking about the future altogether in order to address explicitly the present moment of the implied reader's reading experience, which is a moment that anticipates the imminent "preaching of the gospel to all the nations." Moreover, the reflexive term *gospel* is used. A reader of this narrative cannot help associating somehow "the gospel preached to the nations" with the very story he or she is reading. Is not 13:10 fulfilled as it is read? When a reader, especially a non-Jewish one, reads Mark 13, the Gospel/gospel is being promulgated "to the nations."

Having seen an unmistakable example of the narrator's commentary introduced mildly by *kai*, we are in a better position to appreciate another example of a *kai* parenthesis that is not widely recognized as such, although some critics have suggested that this verse is a wink at the reader.[62]

> Again the high priest asked him and said to him, "Are you the Christ, the Son of the Blessed?"
>
> And Jesus said, "I am."
>
> (*And you will see the Son of man seated at the right hand of Power and coming with the clouds of heaven.*)
>
> And the high priest, tearing his garments, said, "Why do we still need witnesses? You have heard the blasphemy. How does it appear to you?" And they all condemned him as worthy of death. (14:61-64, RMF)

Because most interpreters take 14:62 not as a statement by the narrator but as the continuation of Jesus' confession of his identity, I need to defend my suggestion that we have here a parenthetical comment by the narrator.

First, the absence here of anacoluthon or some other clear linguistic signal does not rule out a parenthesis, for interpretive comments may be introduced with *kai, de,* or apposition as well.

Second, the high priest's response in verses 63 and 64 makes good sense as a response to the two words that Jesus undoubtedly utters: *egō eimi* ("I

---

61. The comment in 13:10 is another indication that Mark 13 is aimed principally at the reader.

62. See Norman Perrin, "The High Priest's Question and Jesus' Answer (Mark 14:61-62)," in *The Passion in Mark: Studies on Mark 14–16,* ed. Werner H. Kelber (Philadelphia: Fortress Press, 1976), 92; and Fowler, *Loaves and Fishes,* 162.

am"), the formula of self-revelation commonly used by Greek-speaking gods and goddesses in the Mediterranean world, including the God of Israel in the Septuagint; that is, it could be solely in response to Jesus' *egō eimi* statement that the high priest asserts that blasphemy has been uttered. To be fair, we must recognize that what the high priest is responding to in Jesus' speech is ambiguous, perhaps intentionally so. The high priest could be responding to the *egō eimi* statement, the Son of man statement, or both. Nevertheless, at least a possibility exists that the high priest is responding only to the *egō eimi* statement. I suggest that he does not even hear the Son of man statement because it transcends the level of story and functions only on the level of the discourse.

Third, the parenthesis is a Son of man statement, indeed, the last Son of man statement in the Gospel. Like all other such statements in this Gospel, it receives no clear and unmistakable uptake at the story level. That the high priest is responding to the Son of man statement is by no means certain. Because the reader is always in a position to take up a Son of man statement and surely does so here, we can reasonably suggest that the Son of man statement of 14:62 is offered only to the reader.

Fourth, 14:62 employs the second-person plural, which in this case is better suited for addressing Mark's extranarrative audience than for addressing Jesus' single interlocutor in the story, the high priest.

Fifth, the parenthesis is a scripture quotation, and, as we have seen, scripture quotations in Mark operate primarily at the discourse level to provide interpretive guidance for the reader. In this parenthesis the author assumes that the implied reader will recognize and comprehend allusions to Dan. 7:13 and Ps. 110:1.

Sixth, the narrator is not concerned whether he or Jesus gets credit for the words within the parentheses. The important thing is that the implied reader does take up the words and connects them with scripture passages and with similar words already offered in the Gospel in 8:38—9:1 and 13:26. By this point in the narrative Jesus has been invested with such reliability and authority that the implied reader is inclined to heed and trust these words, whether they come from the character Jesus or are spoken about him by the narrator.

Besides observing the reliable commentary provided by 14:62, we can also observe Mark's rhetoric of indirection in this passage. When the high priest calls Jesus' words, whatever they may be, "blasphemy," we discern that he has, ironically, misjudged Jesus. If anyone has committed blasphemy, it is he and those who join him in condemning to death the "Christ, the Son of the Blessed." Mark does not tell us directly that the high priest and his colleagues erred; we are allowed to arrive at that conclusion for ourselves.

Apposition

The least obtrusive method of inserting a comment is by means of an appositive comment.[63] Just as in the case of the *ho estin* ("that is . . .") comments, appositives in Mark frequently clarify an expression or translate a foreign term (e.g., 10:46; 14:36). Explanations, if not direct translations, of terms of foreign origin are found in 9:43 (*Geenna*), 14:61 (*Christos*), and 15:32 (*Christos*). All of these are instances of direct speech by characters in the story, but nevertheless the explanations that are offered for these terms function principally for the reader.[64]

The narrator uses many appositive comments to describe characters in the story. Many of these identifications are prosaic, but some are noteworthy. Mark 1:1, for example, with its clear identification of Jesus as Christ and Son of God, offers the reader vital information. Other identifications are surprising, even shocking: At one point Jesus is identified, not by reference to his father, as would be the usual practice in a patriarchal culture, but by reference to his mother; he is the "son of Mary" (6:3). Elsewhere, Herodias, the wife of Herod Antipas, is identified as "the wife of Philip, his [Herod's] brother" (6:17). Emphasis is placed on the fact that the one who hands Jesus over to the authorities, Judas Iscariot, is one of Jesus' own followers; he is "the one of the twelve" (14:10).[65] Mary, the mother of Jesus, is identified late in the Gospel not as the mother of Jesus but as "the mother of James the lesser and of Joses" (15:40). This peculiar way of referring to Jesus' mother implies that the estrangement between Jesus and his mother remains so great that it is not appropriate to call her the mother of Jesus, but the mother of his brothers.[66] Even the simplest of appositive comments is sometimes not so simple or innocent.

INSIDE VIEWS

Because the narrator of Mark's Gospel is an omniscient third-person narrator, inside views are ubiquitous in the Gospel; providing inside views is one of the chief prerogatives of such a narrator. Many of the explanatory comments

63. The salient examples of commentary introduced by apposition are found in 1:1; 6:3, 17; 9:43; 10:46; 14:10, 36, 61; 15:32, 40.

64. In all of the appositives mentioned thus far we have explanatory comments for terms of Jewish origin, words either from Aramaic (*Abba, Bartimaios*), from Hebrew (*Geenna*), or a Greek translation of Hebrew (*Christos* for the Hebrew *Mashiach;* "anointed one"). The implied reader must be someone who requires such clarification of Jewish terminology.

65. This is the literal translation of R&M. Regarding Judas, cf. 3:19 and 14:43.

66. The identification of "Mary, the mother of James and of Joses" as Mary, the mother of Jesus, is based upon Mark 6:3, where Mark says that Jesus had a mother named Mary and brothers named James and Joses. That Jesus is estranged from his family in Mark is clear from Mark 3:21, 31-35 and 6:4. See Kelber, *Oral and Written Gospel,* 102–4.

we examined above (e.g., many *gar* clauses) were inside views. Here I want to describe briefly the varieties of inside views in Mark.[67]

Thomas Boomershine has proposed a useful categorization of inside views in Mark.[68] He divides inside views into "perceptions," "emotions," "inner knowledge/motivation," and "inner statements." Although he examines only briefly the inside views in the Passion narrative in Mark, his categories hold up well when applied to the whole Gospel. Therefore, I shall follow Boomershine's schema, with my own refinements added.

PERCEPTIONS

As Boomershine notes, the narrator often gives us insight into what a character sees or hears; seeing and hearing seem to cover adequately the range of inside views into the sense perceptions of the characters of this narrative.[69] However, what constitutes seeing or hearing is often difficult to determine. Sometimes we are told that a character visually apprehended an object or aurally apprehended a sound, but frequently seeing and hearing are figures of speech connoting "understanding" and "grasping and heeding a verbal expression," respectively. For example, in 2:5 Jesus "sees" the "faith" of four litter bearers; sight is used as a figure of speech for the shrewd inference that is based upon observed behavior. In 5:15 the crowd "sees" the former demoniac "clothed and in his right mind"; that the man is clothed is surely visually apprehended, but that the man is in his right mind is an inference based on what was visually apprehended. Again, a scribe strikes up a conversation with Jesus after he has "seen" how well Jesus responded to some Sadducees (12:28), and at the end of their conversation Jesus "sees" how well the scribe himself has responded to Jesus' words (12:34); sight here is used as a figure of speech for insight. Yet again, this time with regard to hearing, the scene often labeled The Cursing of the Fig Tree comes to an end with the words *kai ēkouon hoi mathētai autou* ("and his disciples heard"; 11:14); these words do not mean merely that they heard Jesus curse the fig tree but imply as well that the words penetrated them. For the reader, the connotations here go beyond the fact of mere audition. The reader is being signaled that he or she will hear still more

---

67. I first gave attention to inside views in *Loaves and Fishes*, 166–67. See also Norman Petersen, " 'Point of View' in Mark's Narrative," *Semeia* 12 (1978): 116–18; and David Rhoads and Donald Michie, *Mark as Story: An Introduction to the Narrative of a Gospel* (Philadelphia: Fortress Press, 1982), 37–38.

68. Thomas E. Boomershine, "Mark, the Storyteller: A Rhetorical-Critical Investigation of Mark's Passion and Resurrection Narrative" (Ph.D. dissertation, Union Theological Seminary, New York, 1974), 273–75.

69. *Seeing:* 1:10, 19; 2:5, 14, 16; 3:5, 34; 5:6, 15, 22, 32, 38; 6:33, 34, 48, 49, 50; 7:2; 8:24-25, 33; 9:4, 8, 14, 15, 20, 25, 38; 10:14, 21, 23, 27; 11:11, 13, 20; 12:28, 34, 41; 14:67, 69; 15:39, 40, 47; 16:4, 5. *Hearing:* 2:17; 3:8, 21; 5:27; 6:2, 14, 16, 20, 29; 7:25; 10:41, 47; 11:14, 18; 12:28, 37; 14:11; 15:35.

about the curse later (that it will have a devastating result). As much as the sound of the curse sinks into the disciples in the story, it sinks all the more into the memory of the reader.

Inside views in general are designed to serve rhetorical purposes. Even though they are offered to us as inside views into the perceptions, emotions, knowledge, or interior speech of story characters and therefore might be regarded referentially as evidence of character development, they are always offered to the narratee, by the narrator, and only because they suit the narrator's purposes. Although they seem to be revealing characters at the level of story, inside views are more helpfully understood as narrative commentary at the level of discourse. Perhaps the most cautionary observation of all is that in a narrative so invested in ambiguity, irony, and paradox we learn in the course of reading that we often cannot trust the narrator's inside views into characters, not because the narrator is unreliable but because the characters are unreliable. The characters in this story see and hear many things, but as often as not they neither see nor hear aright. For instance, as Jesus dies, he cries out to God in anguish (15:34). Then we are told that "certain ones standing by *heard* and said, *'See!* He is calling Elijah!' " (15:35, RMF). They "hear" the words and "see" that Jesus is calling Elijah, but they neither hear nor see correctly. Only the reader, who has been given in a parenthetical comment the true meaning of the cry ("My God, My God, why have you forsaken me?"), truly hears and sees what happens. Those in the story do not really see or hear; they are really outsiders. We who are outside the story, separated from the scene by time and space, do see and hear and are made insiders by virtue of the insight that is given to us by the narrator. Thus even inside views into warped or misguided perceptions (such as in 15:35) serve the narrator's rhetorical strategies.

This reversal of roles between unperceptive story characters and the perceptive reader should not surprise us because an analogous reversal of roles takes place frequently within the story itself. People in the story who think they see and hear (e.g., the disciples?) turn out not to, and those who do not see or hear (e.g., the physically blind and deaf) do receive sight and hearing, thanks to the narrator's representative, Jesus. As we have seen before, Mark's narrative is reflexive; what happens in the story figures directly or indirectly the reading experience, where the reader is encountering the narrator's discourse.

EMOTIONS

The two emotions Mark invokes most frequently are widely recognized to be amazement and fear.[70] I take the predominance of these emotions in the story

70. *Amazement:* 1:22, 27; 2:12; 5:20, 42; 6:2, 6, 51; 7:37; 9:15; 10:24, 26, 32; 11:18; 12:17; 14:33; 15:5, 44; 16:5, 8. *Fear:* 4:41; 5:5, 33; 6:20, 50; 9:6, 32; 10:32; 11:18, 32; 12:12; 16:8.

as a token of what the narrator hopes to achieve through his discourse. If these emotions are regularly elicited *in* the story, most likely the narrator feels that they would be appropriate responses by the reader *to* the story. If this reaction is one of the major goals of inside views of emotion, we may question whether the narrator's strategy is successful. Can the narrator really hope to elicit amazement and fear in the narratee by asserting the prevalence of these emotions in the story's characters? Is this strategy not naive? Yet we should remember that we now look at Mark's narrative through the overlay of nineteen centuries of the history of reading. In particular, familiar as we are with the modern, introspective, psychological novel, will not Mark's use of inside views of emotion inevitably seem feeble to us? Mark's narrative would surely affect a first-century reader differently than it affects us. We will always read Mark as twentieth-century readers and never as first-century readers.

The two emotions invoked next in order of frequency are anger and then sadness or grief. Anger and sadness suggest a narrative full of pathos, as indeed most interpreters have found Mark's Gospel to be. Following amazement, fear, anger, and sadness, in order of frequency, are joy, pity, courage or daring, cunning or deceit, envy, being offended or scandalized, love, hunger, being pleased, holding a grudge, weariness, distress, and perplexity.[71]

KNOWLEDGE AND MOTIVATION

Telling us what the characters know (or think they know) and what their motivations are is also the omniscient narrator's privilege.[72] This category can also include inside views into the memories of characters.[73]

A consideration of the inside views into characters' knowledge or understanding helps us recognize the ideological alignment of the narrator with his protagonist Jesus. Of all the characters in the story, the narrator shares his mind-reading powers with Jesus alone. Several times Mark gives us an inside view into Jesus having an inside view into other characters in the story (see esp. 2:8 and 12:15). This rhetorical strategy is designed to help us understand things the way the narrator and his Jesus understand them. In such places in the narrative, if we entrust ourselves to the insight of the narrator, then we must entrust ourselves to the insight of his Jesus.

---

71. *Anger:* 3:5; 10:14, 41; 14:4, 5. *Sadness or Grief:* 3:5; 6:26; 10:22; 14:19, 34. *Joy:* 6:20; 12:37; 14:11. *Pity:* 1:41; 6:34. *Courage or Daring:* 12:34; 15:43. *Cunning or Deceit:* 14:1. *Envy:* 15:10. *Being Offended or Scandalized:* 6:3. *Love:* 10:21. *Hunger:* 11:12. *Being Pleased:* 6:22. *Holding a Grudge:* 6:19. *Weariness:* 14:40. *Distress:* 14:33. *Perplexity:* 6:20.

72. *Knowledge or Understanding:* 1:34; 2:8; 3:5; 5:29, 30, 33; 6:20, 49, 52, 54; 8:17-21; 9:6, 32; 12:12, 15; 14:40; 15:10, 45. *Motivations or Intentions:* 3:2, 6, 21; 5:27; 6:19, 20, 26, 48; 7:24; 8:11, 14; 9:30; 10:2, 13; 11:18; 12:12, 13; 14:1, 10, 11, 55, 56, 57; 15:10, 15, 43; 16:1. We are dealing here with what Chatman would label comments about the "cognition" of characters (*Story and Discourse*, 181).

73. *Memories:* 11:21; 14:72.

Just as the narrator gives us access to the characters' deficient perceptions, often inside views of knowledge or understanding reveal false knowledge or inadequate understanding. For example, either through fear or embarrassment the disciples are sometimes said not to know how to answer or respond to Jesus (see 9:6; 14:40). Once we are told that a statement by Jesus, clear to any reader, was not understood by the disciples (9:32). Once we are told bluntly that the disciples did not understand statements or actions in the story because their "hearts were hardened," their minds clouded (6:52; cf. 8:17-21; 3:5). Often, that is, inside views of knowledge inform us that characters in the story (usually the disciples) do not know something. In keeping with Mark's rhetoric of indirection, moreover, when the narrator tells us that the disciples did not understand something, he refrains from telling us exactly what they did not understand. We are then in a position of ignorance not unlike that of the uncomprehending disciples, with the difference that often they do not realize that they do not understand whereas usually we do. We may not know much, but we usually know more than they do.

Characters' knowledge or understanding may be false or inadequate, but inside views into characters' motivations and intentions are usually straight-forward and reliable; we therefore receive them as trustworthy insight into what is motivating the characters. Inside views of motivation usually come to us with clear linguistic signals. The character's motivation may be expressed with an infinitive, often with an auxiliary verb such as *zēteō* ("to seek to . . ."), *thelō* ("to wish, desire, want to . . ."), or *boulomai* ("to want, desire, wish to . . ."). Frequently, statements of motivation or intention are *hina* ("in order that") statements of purpose.

Inside views of motivation give us insight into the strategies of characters. For example, the narrator alerts the reader to the existence of plots to ensnare Jesus in controversy or even to take his life, beginning early in the narrative and recurring frequently thereafter (3:2, 6; cf. 3:19; 8:11; 12:13; 14:1, 10-11). Yet, as reliable as such inside views of motivation are, the reader learns not to place too much weight on them, just as the reader learns not to trust too much the perceptions and understandings of story characters. The per-ceptions of characters can be garbled, their knowledge may be warped or lacking, and their best or worst intentions can go awry. For example, Herod wants to protect John the Baptist (6:20) but ends up having him executed. Jesus wishes (*thelō*) to walk past the disciples on the lake (6:48), but he is diverted to their boat. A while later he wants (*thelō*) to remain incognito in the region of Tyre (7:24) but is unable to do so. Later, when the opponents of Jesus are about to bring their death plot to a successful conclusion, the wheels of their machinery temporarily grind to a halt: they seek (*zēteō*) tes-timony against Jesus to secure a trumped-up death sentence, but they are unsuccessful because they cannot get the perjurers to agree on their false testimony (14:55-57)! In the last scene of the Gospel, women bring aromatic oils to a tomb to anoint a dead body (16:2), but their intention goes unfulfilled because no body is there to anoint.

Inside views often supply clear, direct, and indisputable guidance for the reader, but we learn not to trust inside views without reservation. Seeing and hearing can be blindness and deafness. Knowledge can turn out to be a delusion. Motivations and intentions have a way of not being fulfilled.

INTERIOR OR PRIVATE SPEECH

The narrator sometimes goes so far as to let us hear what characters are saying to themselves, either silently in their own minds, out loud but only to themselves, or in whispers among a group of comrades.[74] Inside views into interior or private speech are thus a literary counterpart to the stage whisper in the theater. The audience alone is supposed to hear the musings of an individual or the privileged discussions of a group on the stage.

Inside views into interior or private speech tell us reliably what is on the minds of characters in the story. Not infrequently an entire episode hinges for the reader (or the audience) on the reported interior speech (or the stage whisper). In some episodes in the Gospel, so much depends upon the inside view of interior speech that the reader is the only one in a position to understand the episode and to learn from it. Here the narrative is working primarily at the level of discourse; the genuine progress of the story level is in these instances thwarted or broken off altogether. Although the narratee receives a stream of privileged insight, characters within the story are generally bereft of such insight. (Jesus is the one great exception.) We walk in the light, they in the dark, all in the course of the same narrative. Nevertheless, the narrator's discourse engages us so successfully that we seldom grow weary or wary of asking why the characters in the story do not share the insight we possess.

Noteworthy instances of episodes hinging for the narratee on inside views into interior or private speech include the following: in 2:6-7 certain scribes question "in their hearts" the reason that Jesus commits "blasphemy" by daring to pronounce forgiveness of sins, and thereby usurping divine prerogative. The next verse gives an inside view of Jesus having an inside view of the scribes' internal questioning. In this instance Jesus makes the gist of his own inside view known within the story by confronting the scribes openly with their thoughts.

More typically no one in the story realizes or experiences fully what the narratee realizes or experiences. For instance, in 5:27-30 we read a series of inside views, some into a woman with a flow of blood, who comes to Jesus for healing, and some into Jesus, who feels a drain of healing power when the woman touches him surreptitiously. Although the woman does eventually

74. *Interior or Private Speech:* 1:27; 2:6-7; 3:21; 4:41; 5:28; 6:16; 8:16; 9:10, 34; 10:26; 11:31-32; 14:2, 4; 16:3; cf. 12:7.

tell Jesus what she has done, thus making public her secret intention and action, only the narratee experiences firsthand both her hopefulness in reaching out to touch Jesus' garment and Jesus' realization that power has gone forth from him. In this episode the narrator makes the narratee more knowledgeable than either the woman or Jesus. The insight granted us is extraordinary: not even Jesus is privileged to share with us our inside views into the woman's motivation (5:27), interior speech (5:28), and knowledge (5:29).

Other instances of interior or private speech move away from direction toward indirection. Take the inner debate by the high priests, scribes, and elders in 11:31-32. Jesus has adroitly skewered them with the question of whether John the Baptist's baptism was of heavenly or human origin, so the authorities decide not to answer Jesus. Accordingly, he decides not to answer their question about his authority (11:28). The episode is full of unanswered questions: the authorities' initial question aimed at Jesus, then Jesus' counter-question aimed at the authorities, and then the truncated, final, hypothetical question that the authorities are shrewd enough to guess that Jesus would ask if they answered him in a particular way. This latter inside view does not so much grant the narratee an insight as it confronts the narratee with the challenge of an unanswered question.

In the same fashion, inside views into other interior or private speech in the Gospel offer us not the direction of declarations, but the indirection of unanswered questions:

"What is this? A new teaching with authority?" (1:27; R&M)
"Why does this man speak thus? It is blasphemy! Who can forgive sins but God alone?" (2:7)
"Who then is this, that even wind and sea obey him?" (4:41)
"Why was the ointment thus wasted?" (14:4)
"Who will roll away the stone for us from the door of the tomb?" (16:3)

What better way to channel our thinking than to challenge us with un-answered questions?

6

IMPLICIT COMMENTARY
BY THE NARRATOR

In Mark some commentary comes explicitly from the narrator; other commentary comes implicitly from the narrator. I want to broaden Seymour Chatman's term *implicit commentary* (under which heading he considers only ironic commentary by the narrator) to include all commentary on the story that derives from the narrator covertly. Mark's Gospel offers implicit commentary in at least two major ways. One is by means of the statements of characters in the story, especially the narrator's protagonist, Jesus. The other is by means of the emplotment of the narrative, that is, how the story is organized or structured.

BY MEANS OF CHARACTERS

The reliable, omniscient, third-person narrator of Mark's Gospel invests heavily in the reliability and authority of his protagonist, Jesus (see chap. 4). Then, once the reliability and authority of Jesus is established, the narrator can shift over to him much of the work of offering commentary to the reader.[1] Such commentary is implicit because it is not overtly the word of the narrator aimed at the narratee but instead is ostensibly the word of a character in the story that is addressed to other characters.

JESUS

We are so accustomed to attending to the words of Jesus in the story as the words of Jesus that we have to make a special effort to take them as the words

---

1. I do not think it coincidental that most of the implicit commentary that comes to us via Jesus occurs in the second half of the Gospel, i.e., after his reliability and authority has been well established. If we designate Mark 8:27 as the midpoint of the Gospel, then the following statistics may be noted: of thirteen "truly, I say to you" sayings, eleven occur in the second half of the Gospel; of twenty-six "whoever" sayings, eighteen occur in the second half; and of thirteen "Son of man" sayings, eleven occur in the second half of the Gospel.

of the narrator. If we are able to attune our ears to hear the narrator's discourse whenever the character Jesus speaks, however, then we will discover perhaps the richest source of guidance for the reader in the Gospel. Upon further reflection, we could hardly expect it to be otherwise. At the story level Jesus tells and interprets his own stories (cf. 4:33-34), an intranarrative narrator speaking to intranarrative narratees. He frequently provides, ostensibly for his intranarrative narratees, commentary on the very narrative in which he and his narratees are the chief actors and thereby functions as an intranarrative spokesperson for our extranarrative narrator.

Here we will look briefly at three obviously stylized forms of sayings that are often found on the lips of Jesus in Mark: the "truly (*amēn*), I say to you" sayings, the "whoever" sayings, and the "Son of man" sayings (see chap. 4). In these utterances by Jesus, the narrator is usually offering us the kinds of commentary that Chatman calls "judgment" or "generalization." Sometimes Jesus is also the vehicle for providing us with what Chatman calls "interpretation," a form of commentary more typically exercised explicitly by the narrator. For instance, the "truly (*amēn*), I say to you" saying can be used to communicate either an interpretation, a judgment, or a generalization to the reader. By using *amēn,* the traditional Jewish conclusion to prayer, at the beginning rather than the end of the utterance, these sayings function as a striking form of solemn asseveration. Although the distinction between judgment and generalization is frequently difficult to make, an example of an *amēn* judgment expressing a "moral or value opinion" might be 3:28-29: "Truly, I say to you, all sins will be forgiven the sons of men, and whatever blasphemies they utter; but whoever blasphemes against the Holy Spirit never has forgiveness, but is guilty of an eternal sin." An example of an *amēn* generalization expressing a "universal truth" might be 11:23: "Truly, I say to you, whoever says to this mountain, 'Be taken up and cast into the sea,' and does not doubt in his heart, but believes that what he says will come to pass, it will be done for him." Instances of *amēn* interpretations of "the gist, relevance, or significance of story elements" on the lips of Jesus would include:

"Truly, I say to you, no sign shall be given to this generation" (8:12).
"Truly, I say to you, there are some standing here who will not taste death before they see that the kingdom of God has come with power" (9:1).
"Truly, I say to you, this generation will not pass away before all these things take place" (13:30).

Although accepting as implicit commentary from the narrator the judgments and generalizations uttered by Jesus is not too difficult, more difficult is grasping the *amēn* sayings just quoted not just as sayings in the story by Jesus but also as interpretations of the story offered by the narrator to the narratee; that is, whereas in the story Jesus is speaking to his contemporaries when he says "this generation" and "some standing here," at the discourse level the narrator is also speaking to his contemporaries, his extranarrative audience.[2] In fact, these *amēn* comments may be far more a matter of the narrator and his discourse than a matter of story-level commentary on story-level events. Again, imagining the Gospel being performed on the stage can be helpful. As the actor playing Jesus says "this generation" or "some standing here," he gestures not only toward his listeners on the stage but also to the audience in the seats. If we are right to think that Mark's Gospel was first read around 70 C.E., about forty years after Jesus' crucifixion, then in verses such as 8:12, 9:1, and 13:30, we do not have the historical Jesus saying that his generation is the last in history but rather Mark saying that his generation is the last.

Another stylized form of statement frequently used by Jesus in the Gospel is the "whoever" statement. "Whoever" statements function as judgment and generalization par excellence. They are clarion statements of norms of judgment or general principles.[3] More than anywhere else, here the narrator offers us the norms of judgment that he would have us adopt while reading and if possible remain committed to after reading has ceased. Some of the norms of judgment that this Gospel invites us to embrace are: whoever blasphemes against the Holy Spirit is guilty of an eternal sin (3:29); whoever does the will of God is Jesus' brother, sister, or mother (3:34-35); whoever loses his life, for Jesus and the gospel, saves it (8:35); whoever gives a drink of water or embraces a child in the name of Jesus will not lose his reward (9:37 and 41); whoever divorces his wife and marries another commits adultery (10:11); and whoever would be great must be a servant, a slave of all (10:43-44). Obviously, a major rhetorical goal of Mark is to persuade us to embrace such judgments and generalizations as our own. This rhetoric is at once both explicit and implicit: explicitly it is the rhetorical appeal of Jesus in the story; implicitly it is the appeal of the narrator through the discourse.

The last stylized form of speech used by Jesus that I shall examine is the "Son of man" sayings. The "Son of man" sayings evoke mystery, unlike the clarity of the "truly, I say to you" or the "whoever" sayings. Ambiguity lingers in all of the Son of man sayings because no one explicitly says who the Son of man is in either the story or the discourse. Readers must come to understand the riddle of the Son of man on their own. To be sure, the first two Son of man sayings in the Gospel—the only two in the first half of the Gospel (2:10, 28)—occur in contexts that make inescapable the inference that Jesus is the Son of man. Infer we must, however, because Jesus always speaks

2. In the *amēn* pronouncements, the second-person pronoun "you" is in the plural form, suitable both for Jesus' intranarrative audience and for the narrator's assembled extranarrative audience.

3. "Whoever" statements are often intertwined with "truly, I say to you" sayings (e.g., 3:29 and 11:23).

of the Son of man in the third person and because a distinction seems to be drawn between Jesus and the Son of man in places such as 8:38: "For whoever is ashamed *of me and my words* in this adulterous and sinful generation, of him will *the Son of man also* be ashamed, when *he* comes in the glory of *his* Father with the holy angels." "Son of man" is a cipher, a not-so-secret code or epithet for Jesus. If any doubt remains in the reader's mind as to the identity of the Son of man, one oblique comment by the narrator renders the identi- fication certain: "And taking the twelve again, *he began to tell them what was to happen to him,* saying, 'Behold, we are going up to Jerusalem; *and the Son of man will be delivered to the chief priests and the scribes . . .'*" (10:32-33).

Although the reader may pierce the cloud of mystery that surrounds the Son of man in Mark, it never fully dissipates. The mystery of the Son of man persists to the end of the Gospel and beyond, and Jesus remains—throughout the Gospel and beyond—a mysterious, reticent, and paradoxical figure. "Son of man," like all epithets attached to Jesus in Mark's Gospel, is a correct but ultimately inadequate description of who he is.[4] He is "Son of man," just as he is "Son of God" and "Christ," but to apply these terms to Jesus is not necessarily to apply them correctly; even the best understandings of these terms remain deficient.

Because the reader has little difficulty in determining that when Jesus speaks of the Son of man he is really talking about himself, the reader recognizes that the Son of man statements are commentary Jesus offers in the story about his own role in the story. When we observe further that no one in the story ever demonstrates uptake of Jesus' Son of man sayings, however, we understand that these sayings function primarily at the discourse level, as implicit commentary by the narrator about the central character in the story. Indeed, the first two occurrences of "Son of man" in Mark (2:10, 28) and the last one (14:62) are not even statements by Jesus but pieces of explicit commentary directly from the narrator.[5] Regardless of whether these verses are explicitly credited to the narrator, the fact remains that no one in the story ever demonstrates uptake of the Son of man sayings; effectively they function only for the reader.

---

4. I agree with Jack Dean Kingsbury that the titles given to Jesus in Mark are generally "correct" but "insufficient" (*The Christology of Mark's Gospel* [Philadelphia: Fortress Press, 1983], 108, 149 and passim). However, I fail to see how "Son of man" is different from all of the other titles. Although it might be fair to say, with Kingsbury, that "Son of man" is the title Jesus habitually uses for himself "in public," Kingsbury fails to take seriously that there is no evidence of uptake of this title by other characters in the story. As a result, he does not observe that it is only the reader of the Gospel who hears these seemingly public statements by Jesus, and therefore that the Son of man statements are far more effective at the discourse level than at the story level.

5. We might note as well that the third and fifth occurrences of the expression "Son of man" in Mark (8:31-32; 9:9) employ indirect discourse, not direct discourse, to report Jesus' speech, and therefore their wording is the narrator's.

Therefore, by means of Son of man sayings the narrator tells us clearly but covertly some important things about Jesus and his role in the story. First, we are told that the Son of man has authority to forgive sins on earth (2:9-11), and he is also lord of the sabbath (2:27-28); both sayings seem to attribute divine prerogatives to him. This Son of man must also be handed over to the authorities, suffer, be killed, and rise after three days (8:31-32; 9:9, 12, 31; 10:33-34; 14:21, 41), because the Son of man came "not to be served but to serve, and to give his life as a ransom for many" (10:45). When the Kingdom of God comes in power, the Son of man will come on the clouds, with the holy angels, in power and glory (8:38; 13:26; 14:62). All of these sayings are interpretive comments on elements of the story, most of them anticipating future events within the story (e.g., the suffering and death of the Son of man on the cross) and some of them anticipating future events just beyond the end of the story (e.g., the parousia of the Son of man on the clouds of heaven). The experience of reading Mark's Gospel depends heavily upon this commentary. If the reader is willing to accept the bold assertions Jesus makes about the Son of man, then to a large extent Mark's rhetoric of direction has succeeded. If the reader cannot accept these bold claims, however, Mark's rhetorical strategy fails. In the end, the believability of Mark's Gospel depends upon the believability of Mark's version of Jesus; if the reader is not persuaded by the "Son of man" sayings, alongside the "truly, I say to you" and "whoever" sayings, then Mark's whole narrative effort runs aground.

OTHER CHARACTERS

No other character in Mark's Gospel approaches the central role of Jesus in providing reliable but implicit commentary for the reader. However, Jesus is not the only character who functions as a channel for conveying reliable commentary. Twice a voice from heaven proclaims Jesus to be "my son" (1:11; 9:7); the narrator enlists God himself (although discreetly, in that the owner of the voice is never explicitly identified) as a vehicle for communicating to the reader who Jesus is. Confirming the statements by the heavenly voice are the utterances by other denizens of transcendent realms, the demons. Repeatedly the demons cry out that Jesus is the son of God (1:24, 34; 3:11-12; 5:7), which confirms what the heavenly voice tells us, as well as what the narrator himself tells us about Jesus in the first verse of the Gospel. Reliable commentary is where you find it; God and demons both are useful to our narrator's rhetorical aims.[6]

Besides those places in the story where entities shout out the identity of the protagonist, all characters in the story provide implicit commentary for

---

6. The centurian's acclamation of Jesus as "son of God" (15:39) is also usually thought to be a reliable comment for the reader, but for reasons I shall indicate later, it is too ambiguous and too ironic to be regarded as reliable.

the reader in one ubiquitous way: the questions they ask, questions that may be answered or unanswered in the story.[7]

Most of the questions uttered by the characters in the Gospel do in fact remain unanswered and therefore are sometimes called "rhetorical questions." Often in common parlance a rhetorical question is understood to be a question for which no response is expected. The unanswered questions in Mark should not be understood that way. Rather, they are rhetorical in the sense that, by remaining unanswered at the level of story, they implicitly solicit a response by the reader at the level of discourse. They prod the reader to think about the question and to compose an answer of her own, or at least to begin to work toward that end. Even if the reader makes no significant progress toward an answer, the rhetorical question may still leave its mark by insinuating an idea or a presupposition that may be implicit in the question. In a variety of ways, posing questions sows seeds of thought.

Questions are employed masterfully in the narration of Mark's Gospel. The number of questions, both answered and unanswered, that the narrator weaves into his telling of the tale is astonishing.[8] They comprise a network in the narrative like the nervous system of the human body. The experience of reading Mark is the experience of being inundated by these questions. That they seemingly come from story characters encourages us not to think of them as questions deriving ultimately from the narrator, and they are successful as rhetorical questions because we tend not to think of them as part of a rhetorical strategy. We think of them as elements of a story instead of manifestations of a narrator's discourse. Furthermore, that so many of the questions are left unanswered suggests that in this narrative questions are sometimes more important than answers. In another respect, however, the narrator is manifesting confidence in the reader's ability to work toward answers or to figure out implications on her own, in the light of the wealth of direction the narrator provides in his rhetoric. He hands us questions to try to answer on our own but also plenty of resources with which to work.

We may look briefly at several examples. The first three questions that appear in the Gospel are typical. Each remains unanswered in the story. The first is uttered by a demoniac, the second by onlookers in a synagogue, and the third by scribes opposing Jesus:

> "What have you to do with us, Jesus of Nazareth? Have you come to destroy us?" (1:24).

7. Discussed briefly in Robert M. Fowler, *Loaves and Fishes: The Function of the Feeding Stories in the Gospel of Mark*, SBLDS 54 (Chico, Calif.: Scholars Press, 1981), 167–68, and see here chap. 5. See also David Rhoads and Donald Michie, *Mark as Story: Introduction to the Narrative of a Gospel* (Philadelphia: Fortress, 1982), 49–51. For a superb discussion of the variety of indirect speech acts that can be accomplished by means of questions, see Esther N. Goody, "Towards a Theory of Questions," in *Questions and Politeness: Strategies in Social Interaction*, 17–43, ed. E. N. Goody (Cambridge: Cambridge University Press, 1978).

8. By my count there are 114 questions in Mark's Gospel, 77 of them unanswered.

"What is this? A new teaching with authority?" (1:27, R&M).
"Why does this man speak thus? It is blasphemy! Who can forgive sins but God alone?" (2:7).

Each of these questions is in fact a double question, a common stylistic trait in Mark, as Neirynck has observed.[9] While we are still absorbing the first question, a second question is offered that develops the first or sharpens it. Double questions contribute to training the reader to follow the lead of the narrator as he takes incremental steps in his discourse. Observe the magnitude of the implicit ideas that just the first three questions in the Gospel lead us to contemplate: Jesus has a mission to destroy demonic powers; his teaching is new, astonishing, and authoritative; and he assumes the divine prerogative to forgive sins. All of this is insinuated in just three rhetorical questions!

Elsewhere in the Gospel, some episodes are constructed around the questions posed by the characters in them. My favorite example is the Stilling of the Storm episode (4:35-41). Apart from Jesus' initial command to the disciples to make the boat trip (4:35) and his command silencing the wind and the waves (4:39), the words spoken in the episode are entirely in the form of unanswered questions:

"Teacher, do you not care if we perish?" (4:38).
"Why are you cowards? Do you not yet have faith?" (4:40, RMF).
"Who then is this, that even wind and sea obey him?" (4:41).

The inferences we are led to draw from these questions are of great importance: the disciples do not trust Jesus, he thinks they are cowards and that they have no faith, and they do not know who he is. As important as all three inferences are for understanding what is happening in the story, the implication of the last question in the episode (4:41) is of overwhelming importance as a piece of disguised, implicit commentary from the narrator. It implies that people who think they know Jesus, even people who become his disciples, may find themselves realizing that they really do not know who he is. "Who then is this?" is in a way the question that energizes the whole Gospel, story and discourse alike. As often as this question is answered clearly and correctly in the story (e.g., by the heavenly voice or the demons), even these answers are never completely adequate. Something always seems to be lacking. "Who then is this?" is a question that remains open for the reader and the disciples alike in the course of the telling of the story (e.g., at 4:41), and it may still be open at story's end. Mark's Gospel is designed to ask and to keep open this one all-important question; it resists the temptation to answer the question once and for all. The Gospel seems to be designed to present

9. Frans Neirynck, *Duality in Mark: Contributions to the Study of the Markan Redaction*, BETL 31 (Leuven: Leuven Unviversity Press, 1972), 54–63, 125–26.

Jesus with question marks rather than with periods or exclamation marks. Mark wants to acquaint us with a Jesus who defies familiarity; that is, Mark "defamiliarizes" Jesus for us.[10]

BY MEANS OF PLOTTING

Besides providing implicit commentary by means of characters' utterances in the story, another major source of implicit commentary is the plotting of the narrative, that is, the way the narrator orders and structures the story. Although plotting has not been discussed in terms of implicit commentary, critics have long recognized that the narrator of the Gospel provides much direction for the reader in the way the story is organized. As Norman Petersen has observed:

> It is, I think, only in the plotting of the episodes and the motivations imputed to the actions of the characters that the full extent of Mark's ideological point of view can be seen. For in the plotting of incidents we can detect the formal manner in which the narrator successively discloses information to his reader, and sequentially relates items of information to one another, creating thereby a world of values as well as of events.[11]

We can approach the implicit commentary provided by the plotting of Mark's Gospel in several useful ways. First, I shall consider Mark's pervasive paratactic and episodic style of writing, which exerts a tremendous influence over the way he shapes the narrative. Such a writing style, which was common in antiquity,[12] is full of gaps and places of indeterminacy and thus offers the reader many empty spots to fill in while at the same time it invites the reader to hold seemingly disparate pieces of the narrative together through constant prospection and retrospection. Second, as Neirynck has observed, Mark has a penchant for repetition or "duality" in his narrative. However, to observe Mark's duality is not necessarily to understand how it works because it has a variety of rhetorical functions. Finally, I want to comment on the efforts to discern the outline of the Gospel of Mark, that is, "the figure in the [Markan] carpet."

PARATACTIC-EPISODIC NARRATION

Mark shows a striking consistency of style, from the level of phrases and sentences to the level of the arrangement of episodes. At the level of phrases

---

10. On the function of art to "defamiliarize" the familiar, see the classic article by Victor Shklovsky, "Art as Technique," in *Russian Formalist Criticism*, ed. L. T. Lemon and M. J. Reis (Lincoln: University of Nebraska Press, 1965), 3–24.

11. Norman Petersen, " 'Point of View' in Mark's Narrative," *Semeia* 12 (1978): 108.

12. Walter J. Ong, *Orality and Literacy: The Technologizing of the Word* (London and New York: Methuen, 1982), 143–44.

and sentences, Mark consistently employs *kai* parataxis and eschews what is usually regarded as the more polished and literate periodic style of Greek.[13] One sentence is juxtaposed to another, often with wrenching shifts of direction in the action or with unannounced changes in the subjects of the sentences. Analogously, at the level of episodes, the structuring of incidents in the story is episodic, one episode juxtaposed to another, often with little or no explicit linkage between them. As a result of the paratactic-episodic style of the narrative, the Gospel is full of what Wolfgang Iser would call "gaps," "blanks" (Iser uses both English words to translate the German *Leerstellen*), and "places of indeterminacy" (*Unbestimmtheitsstellen*).[14] The experience of reading Mark's Gospel is regularly the experience of being enticed to fill in the gaps and places of indeterminacy that the narrative presents to us.

The discussion of the gaps in Mark has a long history. The seminal critical discussion is Karl Ludwig Schmidt's, which, along with William Wrede's, tolled the death knell of the historicist critical reading of Mark's Gospel.[15] As Schmidt observes, biblical scholars in the nineteenth century had come to a correct literary-historical conclusion (that Mark was the first of the canonical Gospels to be written), but they proceeded to draw an incorrect inference (that Mark's Gospel therefore must be a reliable historical account of the life of Jesus).[16] Schmidt demonstrated that Mark's narrative reads poorly as history; it lacks the concrete geographical settings and the coherent chronology expected of historical narrative.[17] The Gospel manifests no genuine historical outline (*Aufriß*), only an artificial framework (*Rahmenwerk*), the product of an editorial process in which one episode or pericope was juxtaposed to another with only the flimsiest of framing material constructed by the evangelist to surround the juxtaposed pericopes.[18] Consequently, Mark's narrative is full of "joints" (*Fugen*), "seams" (*Nähte*), and "gaps" (*Lücken*).[19]

13. BDF 458; Aristotle, *Rhetoric* III:9/1409a:24ff.
14. Wolfgang Iser, *Der Akt des Lesens: Theorie ästhetischer Wirkung* (München: Wilhelm Fink Verlag, 1976); idem, *The Act of Reading: A Theory of Aesthetic Response* (Baltimore and London: Johns Hopkins University Press, 1978).
15. Karl Ludwig Schmidt, *Der Rahmen der Geschichte Jesu: Literarkritische Untersuchungen zur ältesten Jesusüberlieferung* (Berlin: Trowitzsch & Sohn, 1919; reprinted: Darmstadt: Wissenschaftliche Buchgesellschaft, 1969); William Wrede, *Das Messiasgeheimnis in den Evangelien* (Göttingen: Vandenhoeck & Ruprecht, 1901; Eng. trans.: *The Messianic Secret*, trans. J. C. G. Greig [Cambridge and London: James Clarke, 1971]). Wrede had undermined faith in the historicity of Mark (and the other Gospels) by arguing that the Gospels are primarily narrative expressions of theological ideas. Schmidt further contributed to the dismantling of the notion of the Gospels as history by exposing the structure of the Gospels as arbitrary, artificial, literary constructs. Thus the historicist reading of Mark was thoroughly discredited, at least among "critics" (Steiner). It probably remains the predominant approach to Mark among "readers."
16. Schmidt, *Rahmen*, 17.
17. Ibid., v and passim.
18. Ibid., 317 and passim.
19. Ibid., 306 and passim.

Even Schmidt himself perceived his scholarly achievement in negative terms; he had demonstrated that Mark was not constructed as a historical work. Constructed by juxtaposing pericopes "side by side" (*nebeneinander*) and therefore littered with joints, seams, and gaps, Mark's Gospel was judged to be rough and unpolished at best, defective at worst. Unfortunately, Schmidt and his generation were not in a position to appreciate sufficiently the qualities of Mark's narrative and the extent of his literary achievement. From our vantage point we can see that Schmidt and his generation reflect a modern bias against primitive narrative. As Tzvetan Todorov observes, however, to speak of "primitive narrative" is live out of a modern myth that a well-formed narrative must be psychologically consistent and believable, stylistically unified, serious in tone, noncontradictory, nonrepetitious, and free of long digressions, and expecting an author from antiquity to adhere to modern literary standards of taste is unfair.[20] The literature of antiquity is no less complex and rich than modern literature. That it is different does not make it inferior. In an age often called "postmodern," we have disentangled ourselves sufficiently from "modern" narrative conventions to allow "primitive" narratives, such as the *Odyssey* or Mark's Gospel, the freedom to exercise their own conventions.

Like lace, which is characterized as much by its open spaces as by the tangible threads that outline them, Mark's fabric is so full of gaps that we could look almost anywhere for salient examples. Perhaps the most obvious place to look would be the junctures between episodes, and an easy procedure would be to observe how an early reader of Mark, the author of Matthew's Gospel, sought to fill such gaps. In a number of instances Matthew has filled gaps in Mark in exactly the way every reader must in order to make sense of Mark. For instance, Mark 3:19-35 finds Jesus teaching in a house, but then abruptly "he began to teach by the sea" (Mark 4:1). Matthew fills in the gap by explicitly moving Jesus out of the house before placing him by the sea (Matt. 13:1). A gap-filling move such as this one is fairly banal. It clarifies and rationalizes the physical movements of the actors on the stage.

More interesting are Matthew's gap-fillings that articulate the characters' motivations. For example, in Mark 3:1-6 Jesus heals a man in a synagogue on the sabbath, which somehow (a spot of indeterminacy that Matthew does not clarify) induces the Pharisees and Herodians to plot against Jesus' life (Mark 3:6). Then in Mark 3:7 Jesus withdraws to the Sea of Galilee, where he heals many people (Mark 3:7-12). Mark has a gap between the narrator's revelation of the plot against Jesus in 3:6 and the withdrawal to the sea in

20. Tzvetan Todorov, *The Poetics of Prose*, trans. R. Howard (Ithaca, N.Y.: Cornell University Press, 1977), 54–55. Todorov deals primarily with Homer's *Odyssey* in this essay: "Few contemporary works reveal such an accumulation of 'perversities,' so many methods and devices which make this work anything but a simple narrative" (53). He could just as easily have referred to much biblical narrative.

3:7. Are readers to supply a missing connection here? Matthew supplies one. After the mention of the plot in Matt. 12:14 (//Mark 3:6), Matthew tells us that "Jesus, aware [gnous] of this, withdrew from there" (Matt. 12:15//Mark 3:7). In Matthew's telling of the story, a single word, the participle *gnous,* tells us that Jesus knew of the plot against him and for that reason withdrew.

Similarly, a participle such as *akousas* ("having heard") can deftly bridge a gap. For instance, in Mark 1:14, a gap occurs in midsentence: "Now after John was arrested, Jesus came into Galilee. . . ." Juxtaposed as the two phrases are, we are all but compelled to believe that a connection must exist between them, but the narrator does not tell us what it is. That Jesus went into Galilee after John's arrest might just be coincidence, but in the magical world of narrative, who believes in sheer coincidence? In a logical, rational world, *post hoc, ergo propter hoc* ("after this, therefore because of this") is a logical fallacy, but in the world of narrative, *post hoc, ergo propter hoc* is the reigning presupposition, unless we are told otherwise.[21] The yawning gap in Mark 1:14 gives us much room in which to speculate about the relationship between two characters whose lives have already been intertwined for us in the brief introductory verses of the Gospel (Mark 1:1-13). Matthew does not fill Mark's gap completely, but he does at least throw a rope across the gap: "Now when he heard (*akousas*) that John had been arrested, he withdrew into Galilee . . ." (Matt. 4:12). What was in Mark only *post hoc* ("after John was arrested . . .") becomes in Matthew *propter hoc* ("having heard that John had been arrested . . .").

Mark's paratactic-episodic style involves another dynamic that provides an important countervailing force to the effects of gaps and places of indeterminacy upon the reading experience. At the same time that the narrator is weaving a narrative that is full of holes, he is telling us a story with powerful impulses toward prospection (looking ahead) and retrospection (looking back). In the act of reading we are constantly re-visioning what has already transpired and envisioning what lies ahead, which helps us keep the narrative tied together, more by spanning the gaps than by filling them. That reading is a ceaseless dance between prospection and retrospection is nowhere more evident than in our critical distinction between the narrative's story and its discourse. The discourse of Mark's Gospel is thoroughly retrospective; as we read we are always looking back on the story of Jesus from a vantage point after the time when the story events are supposed to have taken place. Yet Mark's retrospective discourse offers us a story that is unremittingly prospective; the story rushes us forward, breathlessly, to a seemingly preordained conclusion. Indeed, in ancient literature we often encounter a "plot of

21. Gerald Prince quotes Roland Barthes to the effect that narrative involves "a systematic application of the logical fallacy denounced by scholasticism under the name of *post hoc ergo propter hoc" (Narratology: The Form and Function of Narrative* [Berlin, New York, and Amsterdam: Mouton, 1982], 40).

predestination"[22] in which the reader knows for certain what will happen in the story before it happens, often both because the story is already well known to its audience and because of clear predictions uttered within the story itself. Such plots give us valuable insight into how an ancient author can feel comfortable with episodic narrative, a style of narration that moderns often find uncomfortable. Episodic narrative can work successfully when the narrator and narratee share a conviction that the causal connections between episodes are not as important as the *telos,* the predestined outcome of the story. Even if some gaps go unfilled or unbridged, the episodes can still be held together by the prospect of the inevitable *telos.*

Actually, saying that Mark's story has a plot of predestination is only partially correct. The plot of Mark's story is in fact composite, consisting of at least two major plot lines in tension with each other. One plot line is indeed one of predestination, a plot line of divine necessity wherein things must necessarily take place: "And he began to teach them that the Son of man must [*dei*] suffer many things, and be rejected by the elders and the chief priests and the scribes, and be killed, and after three days rise again. And he said this plainly" (8:31-32). Add to this passage the prediction of the parousia of the Son of man, and we have a clear indication of the *telos* to which Mark's plot of predestination rushes.

The other major plot line is one of contingency and freedom, wherein "certain events occur because of preceding events," as Gerald Prince would say; in Todorov's terms, it is a "plot of causality."[23] In the plot of predestination, Jesus goes to his death because it is foreordained in an inscrutable divine script; in the plot of causality, however, he goes to his death because he freely chooses to, or at least because he does not try hard enough to avoid it. In the plot of predestination, Judas is a pawn fated to fulfill the role of the traitor, but in the plot of causality he freely elects to hand Jesus over to the authorities. And so it goes. The intertwining of incongruent (paradoxical?) plot lines in

22. This expression, applied by Todorov to the *Odyssey,* applies just as well to Mark's Gospel (*Poetics of Prose,* 64–65); see also Gérard Genette, *Narrative Discourse: An Essay in Method,* trans. Jane E. Lewin, foreword Jonathan Culler (Ithaca, N.Y.: Cornell University Press, 1980), 67. Instead of "plot of predestination," Gerald Prince speaks of narratives that are "teleologically determined" (*Narratology,* 157).

23. Although the similar language used by Fernando Belo tends to confuse literary, historical, and theological concerns, he must be congratulated for teasing apart the strands of these two incongruent but intertwined plot lines in Mark's story. Belo calls the plot of contingency or causality the "prepaschal [i.e., pre-Easter] story"; the plot of predestination he calls the "postpaschal story"; see *A Materialist Reading of the Gospel of Mark,* trans. Matthew J. O'Connell (Maryknoll, N.Y.: Orbis, 1981), 156, 210, 238, and passim. The prepaschal story is the story told as if its outcome is unknown and everything appears contingent or in doubt. The postpaschal story is the story told in hindsight from a vantage point after the *telos* (which Belo places at Easter), from which everything appears to have been predestined.

Mark gives the story great dramatic power, but it has puzzled modern interpreters, who, following Aristotle, presume that good plots must be "complete
and whole," although Mark's is neither.[24]

For a moment, let us consider some verbal signals by the narrator that
invite us to think back and think ahead. Gérard Genette calls such comments
"analepses" and "prolepses" (my "retrospections" and "prospections").[25]
Examples of analepses that function as implicit commentary include references
to memory, relatively few of which appear in Mark's predominantly prospective story. Only twice does someone remember something in the story
(11:21; 14:72), and once the disciples are chided for not understanding something they had remembered (8:19-20). At the level of discourse, such analepses
remind the reader to remember earlier portions of the narrative. In the case
of 14:72, what Peter remembers is a prediction by Jesus that has come to
pass in the story, which points up another way in which we receive implicit
prolepses and analepses in Mark, that is, through the dynamic of prediction
and fulfillment. As the narrator's reliable spokesperson, Jesus is able to predict
the future. Virtually everything he predicts, with the clear exception of the
parousia,[26] comes to pass within the bounds of the story. Once the reader
catches on to this inevitability, Jesus' predictions will be perceived as reliable
prolepses that will be matched sooner or later by an analepsis (explicit or
implicit) at the point in the story when the prediction is fulfilled. Jesus'
predictions always seem to be explicit in the story, although they usually
receive no uptake there, but their fulfillment is rarely noted explicitly in the
story, which all goes to show for whose benefit the predicting and fulfilling
take place—the narratee and no one else.

Finally, the Gospel contains numerous uses of *euthys* and *palin. Euthys*
is an adverb usually translated as "immediately" or "at once." *Palin,* also
an adverb, is usually translated as "back," "again," "once more," or "anew."
Both are used so frequently in the Gospel that they are widely recognized as
favored words in Mark's vocabulary.[27]

Euthys serves the pragmatic function of promoting the rapid forward
progress of the narrative. It typifies a narrative that wants to catch us up and

24. Besides not being "complete and whole" (Aristotle, *Poetics* 7/1450b:24), the plotting of
Mark's Gospel also contains submerged or erased plot lines. See Belo, *Materialist Reading,* 157,
208, 358, and passim; and Norman Petersen, "The Reader in the Gospel," *Neot* 18 (1984): 48.

25. Genette, *Narrative Discourse,* 48–79.

26. I do not think that Jesus "predicts" a postresurrection meeting with his disciples (my
reading of 14:28 and 16:7). But I am unsure how to read 10:39. If this is part of Mark's plot of
contingency, then by story's end James and John have failed to live up to the ideal of dying for
one's commitments, making this one prediction by Jesus that is not fulfilled in the story, because
of human obtuseness. If, however, this is part of Mark's plot of predestination, then Jesus'
prediction must yet come to pass beyond the bounds of the narrated story. In other words, Jesus'
predictions are usually in the service of the plot of predestination, but 10:39 may instead be part
of the plot of contingency, and thus may not be destined for fulfillment.

27. Fowler, *Loaves and Fishes,* 49, 52, 67–68, 199, 200.

hurry us forward to an appointed destiny. *Euthys* has more of the phatic function of a nudge forward than it has the referential function of conveying information. It propels the plot of predestination toward an appointed *telos,* and at the same time it lends credence to the plot of causality by implying subtly that one thing does freely and logically lead to another.

Palin is the Janus face opposite that of *euthys: euthys* hurries us forward, whereas *palin* is used with some care as a signal with a specific backward reference. It is usually iterative, serving to indicate that something that has happened before in the story is happening again and thus "again" is usually the best translation for *palin* in Mark. For example, the *palin* at the beginning of the second feeding of a multitude (8:1) alerts the narratee that the prior feeding episode (6:30-44) is about to be reenacted. Without difficulty, we can work through all the occurrences of *palin* in Mark, as Neirynck has done, to find the antecedent circumstances or events to which they allude.[28] The twenty-eight occurrences of *palin* in Mark's Gospel are a significant source of implicit commentary for the reader that signal quite clearly that a connection needs to be drawn retrospectively.[29]

DUALITY

Intimately related to the paratactic-episodic style of Mark's narrative is its pervasive repetition or "duality" (Neirynck). It, too, is a means by which the narrator offers us reliable but implicit commentary through the structuring and ordering of episodes in the story. Here I shall comment only briefly on some of the ways that repetition functions rhetorically in Mark.[30]

The most obvious rhetorical use of repetition is to drive home a point by a succession of hammer blows. Redundancy breeds familiarity in the reader and therefore, often, acceptance. Things that are repeated demand attention, and so the narrator may stress the importance of something by repeating what he wants to highlight. This fairly obvious use of repetition does not take us very far, but the use of repetition for purposes of emphasis is the starting point for observing what narrators say to us implicitly by means of repetition.

In the standard discussion of Markan duality, Frans Neirynck observes that Mark has very little genuine redundancy. Typical of the narrator's discourse is the "progressive double-step expression," in which expression, statement,

28. Frans Neirynck, with Theo Hansen and Frans Van Segbroeck, *The Minor Agreements of Matthew and Luke Against Mark with a Cumulative List,* BETL 37 (Leuven: Leuven University Press, 1974), 276–77.

29. *Euthys* and *palin* provide reliable direction for the reader, but are they not explicit, instead of implicit, commentary? They are both found only in the narrator's speech, and this would make them explicit commentary. *Euthys* and *palin* are both reliable signposts for the reader, but neither is very explicit about how the reader is to go about prospecting or retrospecting, so I have treated these here as implicit commentary.

30. See further Fowler, *Loaves and Fishes.*

or question *a* is extended or made more specific by expression, statement, or question *a'*.[31] The two-step progression is also in evidence in larger narrative structures in Mark, such as those pairs of episodes that have been called "doublets"[32] because they so closely resemble each other (e.g., 4:35-41 and 6:45-52; 6:30-44 and 8:1-10; 7:31-37 and 8:22-26). Whether at the level of expressions, statements, and questions or at the level of entire episodes, the double-step action combines the familiarity created by redundancy with the novelty of genuine progression. Such redundancy as there is in the second of the two steps reinforces the first step, but the second step usually does proceed beyond the first, sometimes by the smallest of incremental steps. This kind of duality is comfortably progressive. Incremental progression is therefore another rhetorical function of repetition.

When repetition or duality is found at the level of episodes, however, another dynamic comes to the fore. Here I need to express strong reservations about the term "doublet," which has been used to justify the practice of discounting these pairs of episodes as variants of oral tradition instead of treating them as discrete episodes in a thoughtfully constructed narrative. The apparent repetitiveness of the doublets at the level of story has led scholars to neglect the function of the repetition at the level of discourse. Too much attention has been paid to the apparent semantic redundancy of the doublets, and not enough to the pragmatic functions of repetition.

A better term than "doublet" for a number of these episodes would be "matched pair" because these pairs of episodes work in tandem with each other.[33] Several of these matched pairs cross over the elusive boundary line separating implicit direction from indirection by serving to weave some exquisite dramatic irony into the narrator's discourse. That the disciples do not understand or perhaps are not even conscious of the miraculous feeding of a multitude may not surprise us the first time it happens (6:30-44; cf. 6:52). However, when a second miraculous feeding occurs and they still do not grasp what Jesus is capable of doing, we cannot help being surprised by their obtuseness (see 8:1-10, esp. 8:4). The repetition that easily serves to emphasize for us, at the level of discourse, the power that Jesus wields in the story is not matched by a comparable growth of insight by characters in the story. The reader is aware of not only events in the story but also their apparent repetition, whereas characters in the story apparently grasp nothing! Consequently, our respect for the disciples is eroded by the repetition of experiences

31. See chap. 5.
32. Fowler, *Loaves and Fishes*; see also Rhoads and Michie, *Mark as Story*, 47–49.
33. The use of the term "doublet" indicates that scholars have experienced the rhetorical strategy of matched pairs, but have lacked the critical vocabulary with which to describe this reading experience. Rather than discussing the matched pairs in terms of one's own reading experience, the term "doublet" has been used to explain (away) the phenomenon historically as the fortuitous preservation of variant traditions.

in which they should have grown in insight but have not. The two feeding incidents offer us a wonderfully rich dramatic irony, and a similarly provocative incongruity manifests itself in the reading of several other matched pairs of episodes in Mark. Overall, the repetition in Mark may serve not only to emphasize, reinforce, or further the progress of the story but also to contribute to a tensive, negative, or erosive reading experience.

Another common function of repetition in the structuring of the narrative is its function as reliable framing material. The framing function of repetition manifests itself at many levels, from small parenthetical constructions or inclusions, to the intercalation or sandwiching of episodes, to the use of some nonironic matched pairs of episodes to frame intervening material.

As we have seen, the narrator of this Gospel makes numerous parenthetical comments. Many such parenthetical comments are framed by repetitious statements. For example, in Mark 7:5, after the long parenthesis in 7:3-4 in which Jewish table practice is explained, the narrator reintroduces the Pharisees, who had already been introduced in 7:1-2. Such a frame around a parenthetical comment is a way of reestablishing the flow of the story after a brief pause for a comment by the narrator. In Mark 7:1-2 and 7:5 the narrator echoes himself, tying the story together for the reader in the dance of prospection and retrospection. The repeated elements are verbal brackets, signaling to the reader that the bracketed material is worthy of note. By the same token we need to read around the bracketed material in order to follow the flow of the narrative. A reader must both read a parenthesis and read around it.

In other instances repeated phrases function to bolster the reliability and authority of the narrator and his alter ego, Jesus. In some instances the narrator makes a comment (e.g., 2:6) that is echoed a few verses later in words he attributes to Jesus (e.g., 2:8b). Similarly, Jesus may ask a question or issue a command (e.g., 6:31b) whose response or fulfillment is narrated by the narrator in similar language (e.g., 6:32). In such instances the narrator and his protagonist appear to echo each other, which is especially useful for lending credence to the reliability and authority of both.[34]

Small-scale uses of repetition serve to keep the story tied together for the narratee or to reinforce reciprocally the reliability of the narrator and his protagonist. At this level, therefore, interplay between the framework and the material framed seldom yields further implicit commentary. By contrast, the larger the framing device, the more that can be offered in the way of implicit commentary, because the frame and the framed have more interplay. The

34. This narrative strategy was discussed in chapter 4. I made note there of the exhaustive accounting of the instances of these kinds of repetitions by Neirynck, *Duality*, 35–36, 112–33. See also John Donahue's discussion of what he calls the Markan "insertion technique" (*Are You the Christ? The Trial Narrative in the Gospel of Mark*, SBLDS 10 [Missoula, Mont.: Scholars Press, 1973], 77–84, 241–43); and see Fowler, *Loaves and Fishes*, 47–49, 69–71, 164–65.

paradigmatic large-scale framing device in Mark is the intercalation or sandwich arrangement, wherein one episode is split in two and another episode tucked between the split halves. This technique is universally recognized as a favorite of Mark's, a technique that the other Gospel writers tend to subvert or undo when they get their hands on Mark's narrative.[35]

At least seven intercalations are generally recognized in the Gospel:[36]

- The Beelzebul controversy, within the confrontation between Jesus and his family (3:20-21, 22-30, 31-35)
- The healing of the woman with the hemorrhage, within the raising of Jairus's daughter (5:21-24, 25-34, 35-43)
- Herod's banquet (and the death of John the Baptist), within the sending out of the Twelve, their return, and Jesus' banquet (6:7-13, 14-29, 30-44)
- The purging of the temple, within the fig tree incident (11:12-14, 15-19, 20-25)
- Jesus' anointing by the anonymous woman, within the plot against Jesus' life (14:1-2, 3-9, 10-11)
- The trial of Jesus before the Sanhedrin, within the denial of Peter (14:53-54, 55-65, 66-72)
- The mock coronation of Jesus as king, within the trial and execution of Jesus by the Romans as the "king of the Jews" (15:6-15, 16-20, 21-32)

These constructions produce provocative moments in the experience of reading the Gospel. None of the intercalations (with the possible exception of the third[37]) has been found to be especially puzzling. What I want to highlight here are the implications that must be drawn in the act of reading these intercalations. Despite the commentary implied in these strategically arranged episodes, the reader is left to make what he will of the implicit commentary within the constraints of what the text and the critical community allow.

The intercalations exhibit a hermeneutical function for duality. The intercalated episodes are sharply opposed to each other, but at the same time they frequently contain so many verbal echoes of each other that the reader can scarcely fail to take up the implicit invitation to read the framed episode in the light of the frame episode and vice versa. The frame episode and the framed episode are thus placed on a par with each other, with neither having priority, either logically or chronologically. Intercalation is narrative sleight

35. E.g., see the steps Matthew and Luke take to dismantle the intercalation of the temple incident into the fig tree story in Mark 11:12-14, 15-19, 20-25 (Matt. 21:10-22; Luke 19:45-48).

36. Neirynck, *Duality*, 133; Fowler, *Loaves and Fishes*, 165.

37. Fowler, *Loaves and Fishes*, 114–32.

of hand, a crafty manipulation of the discourse level that creates the illusion that two episodes are taking place simultaneously. In an intercalation neither episode has begun until both have begun, and neither is concluded until both are concluded. In Mark this simultaneity is clearest in the sixth intercalation, where we are invited to understand that at the same time that Jesus is on trial for his life before the Sanhedrin, Peter is also "on trial" for his "life" down in the courtyard below. At the same time that Jesus is confessing who he is, Peter is denying who he is by refusing to confess that he knows who Jesus is.

Thus the commentary offered by intercalation is the implicit direction from the narrator to read this episode specifically in light of that one, and that one in light of this one. This narrative strategy can appropriately be linked with the discussion of Mark's episodic narrative style. By his use of intercalation, the narrator reveals his own awareness of the dynamic of creating and filling gaps, which is exactly what the narrator himself is doing in the act of intercalating: he is simultaneously creating and filling a gap in his own story. Thus, the narrator is not only issuing an implicit challenge to read two episodes simultaneously, each in the light of the other, but also implicitly training the reader in the general practice of perceiving and filling gaps in narrative. Observing how the narrator practices intercalation encourages the reader to discover and fill other gaps and to associate other pairs of episodes in imitation of the narrator's own practice. The practice of intercalation by the narrator in telling the story gives the reader the license to go and do likewise in reading the story.

Besides intercalation, the other large-scale use of repetition for framing purposes is the use of certain matched pairs of episodes to bracket the intervening narrative. As we have observed, some matched pairs of episodes have an ironic tension between them, but others the narrator uses effectively to complement each other and at the same time to bracket the episodes in between. Probably the most widely recognized example of framing by means of a matched pair of episodes is the two stories of the healing of blind men (8:22-26; 10:46-52) that frame chapters 8–10, in which Jesus repeatedly teaches his disciples about the path of service and suffering as they travel the path to Jerusalem. In these chapters Jesus is trying to bring sight to his disciples, analogous to his effort to bring sight to the blind men in the frame episodes. Opinions differ as to how successful Jesus is with the disciples, but the consensus seems to be that, unlike his success with the blind men, the disciples do not gain much sight as the story progresses. The ironic tension is not between the two frame episodes themselves but between the sight achieved by the blind men in the frame stories and the stubborn, persistent blindness of the disciples in the chapters in between.

Such a reading of the frame episodes and the episodes framed in Mark 8–10 is not novel because the reader has perhaps already made a similar judgment about frame and framed in Mark 7–8. The healing of the blind man in Mark 8:22-26 is not just the opening and thus the prospective episode of the entire Mark 8–10 complex. It is also the concluding and therefore retrospective episode in a smaller complex in Mark 7–8. In Mark 7–8, the frame episodes are the healing of a deaf-mute, by means of Jesus' double touch (7:31-37), and the healing of the blind man (8:22-26), which also involves two healing touches.[38] Between the two frame episodes, we find a summary passage in which the narrator pulls together various narrative threads of several preceding episodes, ranging all the way back to the beginning of the Gospel. In particular, in 8:14-21 we find Jesus and his disciples together in the boat, on the Sea of Galilee, for the third and last time in the Gospel. On the two previous boat journeys Jesus has calmed wind and waves in the presence of his disciples (4:35-41) and walked on the waves, through the wind, to their boat (6:45-52). Should we expect now a third storm, during which Jesus again will conquer wind and wave? We might say that a storm does take place in 8:14-21, but it is inside the boat! In the boat together for the third time, the disciples fret over a lack of bread, which happens to be the third time that their meager provisions have been mentioned in the Gospel. The first such episode in which the inadequacy of the disciples' food supply was mentioned was when Jesus fed five thousand men with five loaves and two fishes (6:30-44). The second time the lack of food was mentioned, Jesus fed four thousand with seven loaves and a few fishes (8:1-10, just prior to 8:14-21). Therefore, when we arrive at 8:14-21, we find ourselves in the third and final sea incident and bread shortage. Yet in the boat the disciples mutter about their lack of bread. They have learned nothing from their past experience with boats and bread. Consequently, Jesus levels a bitter rebuke at the Twelve in the form of a devastating series of rhetorical questions:

"Why do you discuss the fact that you have no bread?
"Do you not yet perceive or understand?
"Are your hearts hardened?
"Having eyes do you not see, and having ears do you not hear?
"And do you not remember?
"When I broke the five loaves for the five thousand, how many baskets full of broken pieces did you take up?" They said to him, "Twelve."
"And the seven for the four thousand, how many baskets full of broken pieces did you take up?" And they said to him, "Seven."
And he said to them, "Do you not yet understand?" (8:17b-21)

Among other things, the rhetorical questions suggest that the disciples say the wrong things, for they neither see nor hear correctly. When we read

38. For a discussion of the double-step progression within these two healing stories and within a number of other episodes in Mark, see ibid., 100–14.

on to 8:22-26, the episode of the healing of the blind man, 8:14-21 assumes a new poignancy. Now we realize in retrospect that with two touches Jesus could make a deaf-mute speak and hear properly (7:31-37) and with two touches he could make a blind man see clearly (8:22-26), but after two sea miracles and two feeding miracles, the disciples still do not see, hear, or speak properly (8:14-21). Jesus seems to be least successful with those who are closest to him. Those who are supposed to be the closest turn out to be the furthest away. While this is happening at the level of story, at the level of discourse just the opposite is happening. We may not understand fully what the disciples do not understand about Jesus, but at least we understand that they do not understand. At this point in the story, we may not know a great deal more than they do, but we do know more, and we are therefore necessarily closer to Jesus than they are. The story level of the narrative shows us insiders revealing themselves to be outsiders; the discourse level of the narrative thereby makes us outsiders into insiders.

In the framing constructions in Mark 7–8 and 8–10, the frame episodes cohere and together provide an implicit metaphorical (and ironic) commentary upon the intervening episodes. Deafness, muteness, and blindness are physical handicaps that are overcome in the frame episodes and are offered implicitly to the reader as metaphors for the incorrigible spiritual and intellectual handicaps of the disciples in the framed episodes (e.g., 8:14-21). The frame episodes provide metaphorical illumination for the framed episodes.

Implicit metaphorical commentary is also present in the intercalations, and the metaphorical illumination is more reciprocal there. Because an intercalation places two episodes on a par with each other and essentially narrates them simultaneously, each episode in an intercalation serves as an implicit metaphor of the other. The metaphorical illumination works in both directions, from frame to framed and from framed to frame. I am reminded of the etymology of the Greek word *parabolē,* from which our English words *parable* and *parabola* derive. A *parabolē* is literally something "thrown alongside of" something else. A parable is thus a narrative that stands over against something else and beckons us to dare to "carry over" (*metapherō* in Greek) an insight from one thing to another. Parables are thus metaphorical; they induce us to "carry over" insight. In the case of Mark's intercalations, a parabolic, metaphorical relationship is set up between two narratives by embedding one within the other. Each then becomes a parable or metaphor of the other. By the nature of the intercalation strategy, neither narrative has precedence over the other. To the extent that the narratives exercise a referential function, they each refer to the other. At the story level of Mark's Gospel, Jesus is an inveterate parabler; he tells stories and propounds figures of speech to illuminate—in a dark and mysterious way—the Kingdom of God. The discourse of the narrative is patently parabolic whenever Jesus is telling parables at the story level. In addition, the discourse is often parabolic when the story does not purport to be, for instance, in many instances of duality in the discourse, especially in the use of matched-pair episodes and in intercalation. The Markan narrative is, as we have seen, inherently reflexive; it turns back upon itself, again and again, in a variety of ways. Repetition in the discourse is only one among many ways that this narrative turns upon itself to provide parabolic and metaphorical illumination of itself.

Thus Mark's duality often gives us, implicitly, turns of metaphor in narrative form. We have also seen how duality can create ironic tension, especially in those matched pairs of episodes in which the same set of actors, usually the disciples, seem not to be able to learn from their repeated experience. The reader sees and sees through such narrative turns of dramatic irony. Of course, metaphor and irony often go together; a metaphor can be ironic, and irony can be metaphorical. We have also observed duality employed for the sake of reinforcement and progression, especially in double-step expressions, statements, and questions. I am tempted to label this a metonymous use of repetition because the repetition is often contiguous, the second step of the sequence representing a juxtaposed expansion or development of, and thereby a substitution for, the first step. Perhaps Mark also uses synecdoche-like[39] duality. If so, we would have discovered metaphor, irony, metonymy, and synecdoche (Kenneth Burke's four "master tropes"[40]) functioning implicitly in Markan duality. I do not intend to conduct here a full-scale tropological survey of Markan duality. I have not discovered an example of what I would regard as synecdoche by means of duality in the Gospel, and I think that "metonymy" is a weak description for how double-step expressions work in the Gospel of Mark, but I do believe that paired episodes in the Gospel often function as metaphor, often as irony, and sometimes as both.

That we find ourselves talking about the tropes of metaphor and irony indicates that we are rapidly approaching a discussion of Mark's rhetoric of indirection. Implicit direction by means of various kinds of repetition does frequently stray over the boundary line into what might be better called a rhetoric of indirection, which will be the topic of discussion in the next chapter. Before turning to Mark's rhetoric of indirection, however, a few last remarks need to be made about the organization and structuring of the Gospel.

"THE FIGURE IN THE CARPET"

The first-person narrator of Henry James's short story "The Figure in the Carpet" is a critic who takes as a professional challenge the discovery of the

---

39. J. Lee Magness takes up the suggestion by Frank Kermode that the empty tomb scene at the end of the Gospel (16:1–8) might be taken as a synecdoche for the ending of the narrative that is withheld from us (*Sense and Absence: Structure and Suspension in the Ending of Mark's Gospel*, SBLSS [Atlanta: Scholars Press, 1986], 113–17).

40. Kenneth Burke, "Four Master Tropes," *A Grammar of Motives* (New York: Prentice-Hall, 1945), 503–17.

hidden meaning that he feels necessarily must lie at the heart of the latest
novel of the writer Vereker.[41] The critic publishes a review of Vereker's novel
in which he is confident he has solved the puzzle of the work and has laid
bare its hidden meaning. Then the critic's smugness is shattered when Vereker
rebukes him to his face and calls the critic's proposed solution the "usual
twaddle."[42] The critic redoubles his efforts to uncover the hidden meaning of
the novel. His quest becomes obsessive when his friend Corvick seems to
discover the secret while he remains in the dark. To make matters worse,
before the critic can get him to divulge the secret, Corvick dies in an accident.
The critic then hounds Corvick's widow and, after she dies, her second
husband, in hopes of learning the secret, but all to no avail. The story ends
with the secret still undiscovered by the narrator and therefore never made
known to the narratee either. In the end we are as much in the dark as the
narrator of the story.

Wolfgang Iser reads James's story as a symptom of the (post)modern
decline of meaning as reference, which is what the critic obsessively pursues,
and as a portent of the emerging shift to "meaning as effect,"[43] which is what
Vereker, Corvick, and the implied author of the short story seem to espouse.
A key moment in the story, and the source of James's title, is a conversation
between the critic and Vereker in which the critic tries to ferret out Vereker's
narrative secret: "For himself [Vereker], beyond doubt, the thing we were all
so blank about was vividly there. It was something, I guessed, in the primal
plan, something like a complex figure in a Persian carpet. He highly approved
of this image when I used it, and he used another himself, 'It's the very string,'
he said, 'that my pearls are strung on!' "[44]

The more intently the "figure in the carpet" is sought, the more elusive
it becomes. Our critic-narrator wants to find a meaning clearly delineated in
the lines of the printed text, but the closer he looks, the more blanks and
opacities he finds. The implied reader of the story is bound to be frustrated
by the narrator's failure to find the figure in the carpet, which leads the implied
reader to distance himself from the story's increasingly tiresome narrator. As
we read, we ourselves experience the futility of the narrator's enterprise. As
we distance ourselves from the narrator, and therefore from being the kind
of narratee who would relish such a display of critical obtuseness and ob-
session, we increasingly suspect that his quest is not successful because it is
wrong-headed. At the very least, should he not accept and work with what
he does find in the novel (i.e., blanks and opacities)? Ill-disposed to embrace

41. Henry James, "The Figure in the Carpet," in The Complete Tales of Henry James, ed.
with an intro. by Leon Edel (Philadelphia and New York: J. B. Lippincott, 1964) 9:273–315.

42. Ibid., 278.

43. ". . . it therefore follows that meaning is no longer an object to be defined, but is an
effect to be experienced" (Iser, Act of Reading, 10).

44. "Figure in the Carpet," 289.

such openness and ambiguity in the text, he prolongs the quest to a bitter and desiccated end. He never discovers blanks and opacities as invitations to make his own contribution to the text. He is blind to the clues that point to the possibility that "the figure" is to be found, not in the text, but perhaps in the encounter with the text, or maybe even in love, in art, or simply life itself. Obsessively seeking the meaning in the text, he never learns to appreciate his own encounter with the text, to say nothing of his failure to build a meaningful life for himself—like his friend Corvick—outside of the text.

A biblical scholar may read James's story with a gulp and a hard swallow. As Iser observes, the critic-narrator of the story is a paragon of nineteenth-century philological-historical criticism, someone who employs "the tools of referential analysis" to excavate the referential meaning thought to lie buried in texts.[45] Such is the intellectual heritage of modern biblical scholarship as well as modern literary criticism, and so the critic in James's story could just as easily be a critic of biblical narrative as a critic of novels. The possibility that philological-historical criticism might not solve our interpretive puzzles— or, worse, that our philological-historical puzzles are phantoms born out of our own obsessions—is an unsettling notion. Perhaps particularly unsettling for Markan scholars are those images James uses, "the figure in the carpet" and the "pearls on a string," for these images have been used with great seriousness in the quest to find the referential meaning of the Gospel of Mark. Karl Ludwig Schmidt long ago likened the construction of the Gospels to the stringing of pearls on a string.[46] Sherman Johnson has compared Mark to an oriental rug with overlapping patterns.[47] The pattern in Mark's carpet has often been thought to be a theological concept (or, as James says, a "general intention") such as "the Messianic Secret" or a "theology of the cross." Much effort has also been expended to discover the compositional outline of the episodes in the Gospel. Many have sought this kind of figure in Mark's carpet and ignored thoughtful protests, such as Johnson's, that such a figure in the carpet should not be pursued in a manner of "mathematical exactitude."[48] In different ways, many have sought the figure of Mark's carpet, and no one has ever failed to find it. That no two versions of the figure are ever identical

45. Iser, *Act of Reading*, 5–7.

46. Schmidt said that the episodes in the Gospels are "pearls, which are loosely strung together" ("Die Stellung der Evangelien in der allgemeinen Literaturgeschichte," in *EUCHARISTERION: Herman Gunkel zum 60. Geburtstag*, 2 vols., ed. H. Schmidt, FRLANT 19 (Göttingen: Vandenhoeck & Ruprecht, 1923) 2:127.

47. Sherman F. Johnson, *A Commentary on the Gospel According to St. Mark* (London: Black, 1960), 24. Johnson is quoted with approval by Joanna Dewey, *Markan Public Debate: Literary Technique, Concentric Structure, and Theology in Mark 2:1—3:6*, SBLDS 48 (Chico, Calif.: Scholars Press, 1980), 38; idem, "Mark's Structure: Discrete Segments or Interwoven Tapestry?" unpublished paper read at the August 1985 meeting of the Catholic Biblical Association, San Francisco.

48. Johnson, *St. Mark*, 24.

simply makes critics try harder. Unlike the critic in James's story, who could consult the living author and be chastised by him for chasing down the wrong paths, biblical critics live under the blessing and the curse of not having a living biblical author to contend with. Not having Mark around to consult is a curse because we will never know for sure whether we have discovered his figure or not, but not having him around is also a blessing because we can propound solutions ad infinitum. We are a guild of Jamesian critics, proposing one version of the figure after another with no end to this critical game in sight.

In fairness to generations of biblical critics, we need to understand the siren that lures critics to seek the figure, however it may be conceived, in the Markan carpet. The image of pearls on a string reflects the fact that the Gospel is indeed episodic in arrangement. The narrative can be easily segmented into discrete episodes. As Norman Petersen has observed, almost universal scholarly agreement exists as to the delineation of the discrete episodes or "minimal composition units" in the Gospel, and at the same time little agreement exists as to how these "minimal compositional units" fit together into larger patterns.[49] What the guild needs to recognize is that the reader deals with the seemingly fragmented, pearls-on-a-string narrative by processes of gap filling, of prospection and retrospection, and of continuous encounters with many kinds of repetition or duality. In episodic narrative the discrete episodes are connected, held together in fluid and ever-changing association, and thus receive their coherence only in the act of reading. The narrative invites us to tie together its disparate pieces ourselves. At the end of the reading experience, the critic within us may return to the text in search of an innate outline or structure, but the structure, the unity, the general intention, the figure in the Markan carpet, is something we ourselves have already created in the temporal experience of reading the text. Although the story may be episodic and disjointed, in our experience of the narrator's discourse we organize the episodic story by construing associations between its discrete pieces. Such unity and coherence as the Gospel of Mark has must be discerned at the level of discourse and not at the level of story; it is actually construed by the reader in the experience of reading the story and is not found ready-made in the story.

Understanding the figure in the carpet of this narrative is impossible without understanding our own contribution to the definition of the figure. At that point we will realize and perhaps even learn to accept that the number

49. ". . . the single most important result of previous research is the widespread and long-term agreement among critics of diverse methods and interests on the boundaries of the minimal units in Mark's narrative. This agreement is matched in importance only by the conspicuous lack of agreement among these same critics about the boundaries of larger units comprised of two or more minimal units" (Norman Petersen, "The Composition of Mark 4:1—8:26," *HTR* 73 (1980): 186–87.

of figures in the carpet equals the number of readers and reading experiences. This multiplicity is a sign of the narrative's wealth, not a sign of our criticism's poverty.

I am not saying that every critic's figure in the carpet is as good as any other's, nor that the Gospel does not have some clear and compelling patterns in its arrangement of episodes, ones that are widely agreed upon by critical readers of the Gospel. For instance, the use of matched pairs of episodes, intercalations, and other framing devices represent modest and indisputable patterns in the Gospel. What we as readers are to make of these relatively clear patterns is another matter, however. For example, I want to keep an open mind about the use of chiasm (arrangements with the form ABCB'A' and the like) or concentric arrangements of narrative in Mark's Gospel and in ancient literature generally. Joanna Dewey, for instance, has made a convincing case for the chiastic structure of Mark 2:1—3:6.[50] She summarizes the careful concentric arrangement of episodes found in these five controversy stories as follows: "Thus the five controversy stories of Mark 2:1—3:6 form a tightly constructed literary unit which has a quite elegant symmetrical pattern: the first two stories have to do with sin; the last two with the sabbath law; the first and last stories describe resurrection-type healings; the second, third and fourth in some way concern eating; the disciples play a role in the middle three controversies but not in the first or last one."[51] Her discussion is clear and persuasive enough, but when she tries to discover similar structures elsewhere in Mark's Gospel her argument is less persuasive.[52] Chiastic or concentric structures may be regarded as yet another form of Markan repetition or duality, but we hardly have here the predominant, recurring motif of the figure in Mark's carpet.[53]

Chiasm is also often argued to be the predominant organizing principle of virtually every ancient corpus of literature.[54] What are we to make of this current critical zeal for chiasm? Is it as ubiquitous in ancient literature and therefore as important as some claim? Note that these concentric patterns are

---

50.

A.	2:1-12	The healing of the paralytic
B.	2:13-17	The call of Levi/eating with sinners
C.	2:18-22	The sayings on fasting and on the old and the new
B'.	2:23-27	Plucking grain on the sabbath
A'.	3:1-6	The healing on the sabbath

Dewey, *Markan Public Debate*, 110; idem, "The Literary Structure of the Controversy Stories in Mark 2:1—3:6," *JBL* 92 (1973): 394–401.

51. Dewey, *Markan Public Debate*, 115–16.

52. See my review of Dewey's book in *JR* 64 (1984): 246–47.

53. As seems to be argued by Benoît Standaert, O.S.B., in *L'évangile selon Marc: Composition et genre littéraire* (Brugge: Sint-Andriesabdij, 1978) and in *L'évangile selon Marc: Commentaire*, Lire la Bible 61 (Paris: Cerf, 1983).

54. See the references to the critical literature cited by Dewey, *Markan Public Debate*, 31–39, 206–9.

geometrical in form and are typically explicated by means of a diagram or chart. They are thus set forth only by modern critics and as strikingly visual or architectural patterns. They are, therefore, more typical of the discourse of the visual-literate modern critic than of the oral-aural ancient reader or listener. In short, I suspect that only a modern critic, with all the resources of typography at her disposal, is able to objectify such a thoroughly spatial, visual pattern.[55] My suspicions about chiasm are strengthened by the observation that nowhere in the ancient handbooks on rhetoric or poetics is chiasm as such ever discussed.[56] Is this absence mere coincidence? I suspect that an ancient would not recognize a chiasm if he saw one diagrammed on the wall, but he might recognize it if he heard it performed orally. If so, what would he hear? Chiasms, I suspect, were for the ancient experiences of the ear rather than of the eye. If chiasm, in Mark at least, is yet another narrative strategy of duality, then we may want to inquire as to the pragmatic and rhetorical functions of such repetitive arrangements at the level of discourse and not just at the level of story. Modern critics have tended to define chiasm more in terms of story content and less in terms of narrative strategy or discourse. If attention can be shifted from neat diagrams and architectural symmetry, visually apprehended, to the progressive, temporal encounter that every hearer and reader of the Gospel experiences, then we may better understand not what chiastic structures are visually but how they function temporally. Only Steiner's "critic" can see a chiasm; a "reader" always experiences one episode after another in temporal sequence, with the readerly work of prospection and retrospection enabling her to tie discrete and sometimes distantly removed episodes together. Critics' perceptions of chiasms may be better described as the critical recognition of repetition in the discourse that is sufficiently dense to encourage the reader to engage in a concentrated moment of prospection and retrospection. Indeed, Dewey's analysis of Mark 2:1—3:6 is strongest when she is discussing what she calls the "linear development" of the episodes. The critical description of particular compositional arrangements of episodes in a narrative will always be debatable. What is undebatable, however, is that readers, following the various clues and invitations issued by the narrator, will associate one episode with another in the temporal experience of reading through a process of prospection and retrospection—the continuing dance.

Besides observing the typically modern inclination to uncover a figure hidden in the Markan carpet, we also need to recognize a reluctance to perceive and to appreciate the inherent openness of Mark's narrative. That Mark is not closed but open may be discerned in a variety of ways.

55. In a comment on Dewey's work, Werner H. Kelber seems to share my suspicion; (*The Oral and the Written Gospel: The Hermeneutics of Speaking and Writing in the Synoptic Tradition, Mark, Paul, and Q* [Philadelphia: Fortress, 1983], 134 n. 48.

56. George Kennedy, *New Testament Interpretation Through Rhetorical Criticism* (Chapel Hill and London: University of North Carolina Press, 1984), 28–29.

Mark's Gospel exploits the rhetorical possibilities of a variety of kinds of gaps and places of indeterminacy, all of which help to make it open and indeterminate. The first kind of gap I explored in this book was the gap, or at least the ironic tension, that ebbs and flows between story and discourse in Mark's Gospel. Furthermore, the paratactic-episodic style in which the story is told presents gaps and moments of indeterminacy at every turn. More like lace than carpet, actually, many patterns in the narrative consist of outlined but empty space. Even when the narrative is made relatively coherent and connected by the reader in the dance of prospection and retrospection, we discover nonetheless that the plot of the story is not unified and consistent. The plot has at least two major, incongruent strands—one of predestination and one of causality—and an additional tension, if not a gap, persists between these intertwined but conflicting plot lines. The tension is not easily resolved, and the plot of the story remains incomplete, dissonant, and ultimately unresolved.

The narrative is open and unresolved in other ways as well. The narrative begins in medias res and thus is open-ended from the outset. Is an indeterminate beginning really a beginning at all? In a sense, a beginning in medias res is no beginning. That the first word of Mark's nonbeginning is *archē* ("beginning") gives us our first taste of our author's irony. Scholars cannot agree on how to interpret this word, and the lack of agreement is telling. If Mark 1:1 is taken as a comment by the narrator on the story, then it is ambiguous. In that case, the "beginning of the good news of Jesus Christ, Son of God" could be (1) the ancient prophecy of Isaiah (and others) quoted in 1:2-3, (2) the preaching of John the Baptist narrated in 1:4-8, or (3) the baptism of Jesus in 1:9-13. If it is taken as the narrator's comment on his own discourse, then the verse is still unclear: (1) Is the narrator simply saying, "Here begins my discourse; I'm starting to weave my tale now"? (2) Is he daring to claim that his entire narrative effort is somehow itself the beginning of the good news and to entitle his narrative, with no small degree of presumption, *The Beginning of the Gospel?* (3) Is *archē* a comment on both the story and the discourse simultaneously? Whether we take *archē* as part of the story, as part of the discourse, or as both simultaneously, it remains ambiguous and open. If this narrative has a beginning at all, it has many beginnings.

The ending of the narrative is also open. The empty tomb episode (16:1-8) is a masterpiece of indirection, especially in its use of ambiguity and irony. A mysterious young man, dressed in white and sitting in the empty and open tomb, is a kind of deus ex machina ending,[57] but an ambiguous and ironic one. The young man "sitting on the right side"—for what or for whom does he stand? Overall, the empty tomb episode leaves a host of story elements

57. Augustine Stock, *Call to Discipleship: A Literary Study of Mark's Gospel,* GNS 1 (Wilmington, Del.: Michael Glazier, 1982), 51–52.

unresolved (the episode ends in fear and silence), which is another way of saying that the discourse leaves the narratee dangling. If the narrative is to be brought to closure, the narratee has to close it, a highly appropriate way to end a narrative that places so much responsibility upon the shoulders of the narratee. Only the reader can write the ending of this narrative. The empty and open tomb is a narrative gap par excellence. The emptiness of the tomb is a story-level figure for the emptiness the narratee encounters in the discourse of this episode. The empty tomb is indeed empty: it becomes meaning-full only when the reader fills it with meaning. The empty tomb awaits the fulfillment that only the reader can supply.

Between the open beginning and the open end, the narrative is open in a variety of other ways. Besides the openness of the gaps produced by parataxis and episodic arrangement, the openness of metaphoric and ironic structures of duality, or the openness of the intertwined but incongruent plot lines, we might recall also that the numerous scriptural quotations and allusions in the Gospel open up countless paths of access into the Jewish Scriptures. The echoes of the Jewish Scriptures that thereby invade and pervade the experience of reading of Mark's Gospel would be sufficient by themselves to make the Gospel a narrative deeply implicated in intertextuality and thus perpetually open to the influence of the echoes from these precursor texts.

Therefore, regardless of the direction Mark's narrative provides us, both explicit and implicit, the narrator leaves enough open for us to give us a narrative that is open at the beginning, open at the end, and open in between. If we are looking for a neat and determinate Aristotelian beginning, middle, and end, we will not find it in Mark's Gospel. That most readers find much in the Gospel that is clear, determinate, and direct is obvious, but much of the Gospel is not clear, determinate, or direct. Indeed, as we move from explicit commentary to implicit commentary, we move ever closer to what gives the narrative its distinctiveness and great power as a work of literature: its rhetoric of indirection. Only a fine line separates implicit direction from indirection. The time has come to step across that fine line, wherever it is, into the realm of indirection.

7

THE RHETORIC OF INDIRECTION

As direct as the Gospel's discourse can be, the key to Mark's success as a narrative is its masterful rhetoric of indirection. In Mark direction and indirection work in a dialectical relationship with each other. On the one hand, indirection plays off against direction; it is indirect to the degree that it swerves from the path of direction. On the other hand, direction serves to make the experience of indirection intelligible or at least tolerable. Direction guides the reader down a relatively clear pathway; indirection beckons the reader to step off of the clear pathway, to ponder puzzles. Direction, although sometimes subtle or implicit, is largely determinate. Indirection is more indeterminate and open-ended; some indirection can be puzzled over and resolved, but much remains permanently obscure or uncertain.

All readers of the Gospel, critics especially, must deal with its indirection. For example, the quest for the solution to the puzzle of the Messianic Secret has produced many perceptive comments on Mark's rhetoric of indirection,[1] but few scholars have been aware that in their comments on the Messianic Secret they were responding to Mark's narrative rhetoric, which they had encountered in the act of reading. For many, the Messianic Secret has been conceptualized as a puzzle embedded in the text of Mark that should be solvable by scrutiny of the text. In practice, however, no solution has won critical acclaim. The harder we look, the more elusive the solution, because

---

1. The literature on the Messianic Secret is voluminous. See William Wrede, *Das Messiasgeheimnis in den Evangelien* (Göttingen: Vandenhoeck & Ruprecht, 1901; Eng. trans.: *The Messianic Secret*, trans. J. C. G. Greig [Cambridge and London: James Clarke, 1971]); G. Minette de Tillesse, *Le secret messianique dans l'évangile de Marc*, LD 47 (Paris: Cerf, 1968); Heikki Räisänen, *Das "Messiasgeheimnis" im Markusevangelium: Ein redaktionskritischer Versuch*, Schriften der Finnischen Exegetischen Gesellschaft 28 (Helsinki: Finnish Exegetical Society, 1976); Jack Dean Kingsbury, *The Christology of Mark's Gospel* (Philadelphia: Fortress Press, 1983); Christopher Tuckett, ed., *The Messianic Secret*, Issues in Religion and Theology 1 (Philadelphia: Fortress Press; London: SPCK, 1983).

the Messianic Secret is not in the text itself but in the experience of reading the text. The Messianic Secret is best understood as a variety of closely related experiences that occur when the reader of Mark's Gospel encounters the indirect rhetorical strategies of the narrator's discourse. Because all readers experience Mark's rhetorical strategies, many critics have commented shrewdly on their own reading experience. They were unaware that they were doing so, however, for they lacked a critical tradition and vocabulary with which to approach and talk about their own reading experience.

In this and the next chapter I shall describe the indirect rhetorical strategies in Mark that readers have always encountered but seldom self-consciously. I shall begin with a discussion of the crucifixion scene, the irony of which Wayne Booth has so helpfully discussed. Not only does this scene display a masterful use of irony but also it employs other moves of indirection, which will serve to introduce us to the range of indirect moves Mark employs.

MARK'S CRUCIFIXION SCENE

We have no better place to begin a discussion of indirection in Mark than the crucifixion scene:

> And those passing by blasphemed him, shaking their heads and saying, "Aha, the one who would tear down the temple and build it in three days, save yourself, and come down from the cross!" Likewise, the high priests also mocked him to one another, with the scribes, saying, "Others he saved; himself he cannot save. Let the Christ, the King of Israel, come down now from the cross, that we may see and believe!" And those who were crucified with him insulted him. (15:29-32, RMF)

The double irony of 15:32 is unmistakable. The high priests, with the scribes, "mock" (*empaizō*) Jesus as "the Christ, the King of Israel," and thus they speak ironically, mouthing a title for Jesus that they believe to be false. Ironically, however, in Mark's Gospel this title describes exactly who Jesus is. The verbal ironies spoken insincerely at the story level are recognized by the narrator and narratee as—ironically—true statements, and thus two levels of irony are at work simultaneously here, one level cutting against the grain of the other. One attractive feature of indirection for a storyteller is the capability it affords to go (indirectly, of course) in more than one direction at the same time. Indirection by a character in the story can simultaneously be indirection by the narrator, but not necessarily the same indirection.

The narrator hardly needs to tell us that the authorities are mocking Jesus, but by so doing he makes quite explicit or overt that the characters in the story are employing *verbal irony*. The second layer of irony, namely, that at the discourse level the insincere acclamation can be recognized as a true one, is unannounced as ironic by the narrator and therefore is covert, *dramatic irony.* Thus, sometimes the narrator announces his use of irony, for example, when he alerts us that his characters are speaking ironically, but usually he does not announce his own covert use of dramatic irony. In 15:29-32 Mark both does and does not announce his use of irony.

Other overt signals of verbal irony occur in this same episode. Other passersby are said to "blaspheme" (*blasphēmeō;* 15:29) Jesus, and even his two crucified companions "insult" (*oneidizō;* 15:32) him. Because the narrator is careful to tell us that the various bystanders are verbally abusing Jesus, we cannot take at face value the titles of honor for Jesus that come from their lips. Thanks to the narrator's commentary, we cannot help seeing through what they are saying. Yet in announcing the verbal ironies uttered by characters at the level of story, the narrator cleverly encourages us not to contemplate the second level of dramatic irony, which is perceived and experienced only by the narrator and the narratee.

Even earlier in the Passion narrative, the narrator had already given the narratee explicit signals of verbal irony by characters in the story. For example, before they crucify him, the Roman soldiers conduct a mock coronation for Jesus (15:16-20). Only in the last verse of this episode does the narrator explicitly tell us that they were mocking (*empaizō;* 15:20) Jesus, at such a late point in the episode that the narratee hardly needs this kind of assistance anymore. Already when the soldiers begin the scene on a seemingly positive note, by cloaking Jesus in purple, we must suspect that they are up to no good; the narrator has already told us that Pontius Pilate has turned Jesus over to them for scourging and crucifixion. With a cross already looming on the horizon, an investiture and coronation by the appointed execution squad is easy to comprehend. Indeed, after bestowing the purple upon Jesus, in the next instant we learn indirectly and yet precisely what their game is when we are told that the soldiers plait and bestow on Jesus a crown of thorns, which is a superb ironic twist in Mark's story.[2] The oxymoronic crown of thorns is an implicit but unmistakable foretaste of the further ironies (and outright paradoxes) that will follow in the crucifixion narrative. In the mock coronation scene, much ironic action by the soldiers precedes a little ironic speech. When at last the soldiers issue their own version of verbal irony—"Hail, King of the Jews"—it is easily seen and seen through for what it is.

Another place in the Passion narrative where the narrator offers the narratee an unmistakable clue to the presence of verbal irony is in the trial of Jesus before the Sanhedrin: there the narrator says twice that witnesses came forward to "testify falsely" (*pseudomartyreō*) against Jesus. The first such statement by the narrator is the wry, almost ironic comment that "many

---

2. I suspect that it is Mark who invented the irony of the crown of thorns, as well as Judas' patently ironic betrayal by means of a kiss. At the very least we can say that Mark's Gospel is the oldest piece of Christian literature in which both of these superb touches of irony are employed.

witnessed falsely against him and [yet] their testimonies were not consistent"
(14:56, RMF). This comment is a surprising turn in the narrative. The reader
does not expect the evidence against the accused in a kangaroo court to be
inconsistent and therefore ineffectual. If they have gone to the bother of bribing
Judas so that they could capture Jesus, we would think that they would rehearse
the perjurers enough to get their stories straight.

The second reference to false testimony in the same episode occurs in
14:57-58: "And some stood up and bore false witness against him, saying,
'We heard him say, "I will destroy this temple that is made with hands, and
in three days I will build another, not made with hands."' Yet not even so
did their testimony agree" (14:57-59). Although he has told us twice that the
testimony against Jesus was false, when the narrator finally quotes the false
testimony in 14:58 we find ourselves at a loss. With the narrator's clear signals
in hand, we think we should be able to see through the liars' words, but
wherein lies the lie is not at all clear. The narrator tells us they are untrustworthy
witnesses, but where exactly is the falsehood in what they are saying? Because
Jesus has not spoken words to this effect anywhere in the Gospel, one possibility is that the witnesses have concocted a wildly inflammatory statement
and falsely attributed the whole thing to Jesus. Even though Jesus has never
spoken exactly these words in the Gospel, however, these words do resemble
a garbled version of words he has spoken. He has predicted that the Jerusalem
Temple will be destroyed (13:2), and he has several times predicted his
resurrection after three days, if indeed that is what "in three days I will build
another temple, not made with hands" alludes to. Moreover, the reader recalls
the perplexing episode of the cursing of the fig tree, which was sandwiched
within Jesus' (symbolic? prophetic?) demonstration in the temple. In other
words, another possibility is that the testimony is false because the witnesses
misunderstood and therefore misreported either words or deeds for which
Jesus really is responsible in the story we have read. As a third possibility,
maybe they are quoting accurately words that Jesus is supposed to have uttered
offstage, but he meant them figuratively and they mistakenly took them
literally. In brief, according to our reliable narrator, their testimony is clearly
false, but in what way it is false is entirely ambiguous.[3] The reader who has
to decide in what way the false testimony is false may not be able to arrive
at a comfortable, incontrovertible decision.

Ambiguity also makes itself felt in that other explicit signal of verbal
irony in the crucifixion narrative, the narrator's reference to the "blasphemy"
that takes place at the foot of the cross (15:29). This comment by the narrator
alerts us that the words that follow are cruel words of abuse hurled at the

---

3. Augustine Stock points out that it is "ambiguous" how the charge is false (*Call to Discipleship: A Literary Study of Mark's Gospel*, GNS 1 [Wilmington, Del.: Michael Glazier, 1982],
199).

dying Jesus, even if they are couched in the form of honorific acclamation. "Blasphemy" here may thus carry the ordinary connotation of "verbal abuse" or "ridicule." Nevertheless, it could also entail much more. Blasphemy par excellence is an offense against God. Should not the reader discern that both senses of the word are simultaneously appropriate here? Does not the narrator want us to discern that in knowingly blaspheming this dying man, they are unknowingly committing a far more serious blasphemy? Although the narrator is utterly explicit in labeling the blasphemy a blasphemy, he thereby offers an ambiguous invitation to the reader to discern alternative, implicit ways of grasping the blasphemy.

The narrator's explicit but ambiguous comments on both false testimony and blasphemy are good examples of how ambiguity in the narrator's rhetoric can provoke and broaden the thinking of the reader by introducing the reader to a range of possibilities for consideration. In itself, therefore, ambiguity can be a useful narrative strategy to induce the reader to consider a range of options and perhaps (but perhaps not) make a choice among them. It can also be useful in an auxiliary mode, assisting the functioning of other rhetorical moves. For instance, the appearance of something ambiguous in the story— its ambiguity notwithstanding—may more than adequately prepare the narratee for the approach of yet another move of indirection. As we have seen, even an ambiguous clue can be clue enough to equip the narratee to deal with an irony. One move of indirection may serve another. More often than not, however, *ambiguity* is in and of itself a useful strategy of indirection, and it should be included alongside irony in Mark's repertoire of storytelling strategies.

Explicit signals from the narrator that alert us to the presence of verbal irony are relatively rare. Almost all of the statements by characters in the Passion narrative are ironic, ambiguous, or otherwise oblique, but few are accompanied by explicit interpretive signals from the narrator. For example, note some of the many unheralded verbal ironies in the Passion narrative:

- Judas calls Jesus "rabbi" and kisses him, thereby handing him over to death (14:45).
- Jesus is beaten and told to "prophesy!" just after his prophecy that he would be betrayed has been fulfilled in the story and just before his prophecy of Peter's denial will be fulfilled (14:65).
- Peter, "the Rock," the first in tenure and rank among Jesus' disciples, says of Jesus: "I do not know this man of whom you speak" (14:71).
- Pilate asks Jesus if he is "the King of the Jews," and Jesus' reply is consummate ambiguity: "*You* are saying so" (15:2, R&M).
- Pilate turns to the crowd and asks (deadpan?): "Do you want me to release for you the King of the Jews?" (15:9).

In sum, hardly a word is spoken by any character in the Passion narrative that the reader can take up in a straightforward fashion. That characters speak thus at the level of story means that the discourse also proceeds obliquely, and yet most readers can follow its meanderings, thanks in part to a steady supply of the narrator's reliable commentary but thanks also to the accumulated experience of having read the Gospel up to this point.

So far I have noted rhetorical moves of irony and ambiguity in the Passion narrative. Several other strategies of indirection remain to be discovered here. In light of the "false testimony" about Jesus' threatened destruction of "this temple" (14:58), the echo of this charge against Jesus at the foot of the cross (15:29), plus several other incidents in which "temple" features prominently (e.g., 11:12-25), we should add the use of *metaphor*. Mark's whole Gospel is rich with metaphors, which often are riddlelike.[4] How to understand the metaphors in Mark is not always obvious, and so they are frequently figures of speech that the reader needs to figure out. At the level of story Jesus is the undisputed master of metaphor. Jesus employs both the classic verbal metaphor (e.g., physician [2:17], bridegroom [2:19], patched garment [2:21], wineskin [2:22]), as well as the extended metaphorical discourse that both the narrator (at the level of discourse, e.g., 4:2) and Jesus (at the level of story, e.g. 4:10-12) like to call "parable." To say that the Jesus of this Gospel habitually speaks in parables is to say that he speaks metaphorically, in riddle style, which is to say that the narrator's discourse is habitually parabolic and metaphorical. After all, if Jesus speaks parabolically, he does so only because the narrator speaks parabolically, and the narrator often speaks parabolically when he is not attributing words to Jesus.

So, what of Mark's temple metaphor, if that is what we have in 14:58 and 15:29? The temple metaphor turns out to be a complex and multifaceted riddle, and critics have toiled to find a solution.[5] The shorter version of the metaphorical statement is in 15:29. Here Jesus is accused of claiming that he would destroy "the temple" and "build" it [again?] "in three days." Figuring out the riddle is hard enough if it is taken as something that Jesus really said, but because Jesus himself never says exactly these words anywhere in the Gospel, how can we hope to solve this riddle? The riddle of the temple metaphor is itself wrapped in the riddle of whether Jesus uttered the temple riddle or not. This indirection is masterful. Many have taken the temple statement in 15:29 as a version, however muddled, of something that we may suppose that Jesus did utter; many have confidently identified the "three days" as the key to unlocking the riddle. "Three days" is usually taken as an allusion to Jesus' resurrection; if the "three days" alludes to the resurrection, then the rebuilt "temple" could be the resurrected body of Jesus, or, less literally and

4. That metaphors often have the quality of a riddle about them was observed long ago by Aristotle, *Rhetoric* III.2/1405b.

5. For a good discussion of the temple references in Mark's Passion narrative, see Donald Juel, *Messiah and Temple: The Trial of Jesus in the Gospel of Mark*, SBLDS 31 (Missoula, Mont.: Scholars Press, 1977).

more figuratively, it could be the renewed fellowship of Jesus' followers in the post-Easter setting. In the view of many, therefore, the "three days" points to Jesus' resurrection, and the rebuilt "temple" points to the birth of the post-Easter Christian church. Such a solution to the riddle of the temple is eminently logical and defensible. I wish only to observe that such a solution is nowhere explicitly authorized by the narrator. This metaphor-riddle is one of many in the Gospel that are left up to us to solve, given the resources that the narrator supplies by means of his discourse. In this case, Jesus' cursing of a fig tree, which is intertwined with his obstruction of temple operations, plus his prediction of the temple's fall and his prediction that the Son of man will die and rise after three days—all encourage us to take the temple references of 14:58 and 15:29 as riddles worth serious consideration. Because the narrator gives no clear solution to the temple riddle, perhaps we can fairly say that the challenge represented by the riddle is more important to the narrator than a definitive solution.

Two verses beyond the temple metaphor of 15:29 we encounter *paradox,* another form of indirection: "Others he saved; himself he cannot save" (15:31). Paradox is a contradiction that nevertheless describes the truth. Curiously, in this paradoxical statement everyone—whether characters in the story or the narratee—will see some truth. Depending on who we are, however, we will grasp that paradoxical truth differently. Here again is a move of indirection that can cut in different directions simultaneously. The mockers in the story know that the contradictory statement they utter is true, and therefore they mock Jesus as a failure. The reader knows the contradictory statement is true and says to herself, in so many words, "Yes, this is exactly what has come to pass in the story, and, if I can believe the narrator, it had to be so; this fulfills a divine destiny." If the narrator has told his story well to this point, we will be inclined to embrace the paradox but reject the mocking tone in which it is uttered at the story level. Instead of joining in the mocking, we will respond to the crucifixion with at least a degree of reverence and respect for the dying man. The verbal paradox on the lips of the mockers offers us, surprisingly and therefore ironically, a reliable plot summary of the plot of predestination. Small wonder that when critics reach for an expression to sum up what this Gospel is about, they reach for paradoxical or oxymoronic expressions such as "the Crucified Messiah" or "the Suffering Son of Man." The verbal paradox uttered by disbelievers in 15:31 sums up neatly a reading experience that has been characterized throughout by encounters with incongruity and contradiction in the midst of which, nevertheless, truth is perceived: the will of God is fulfilled in the midst of ambiguity, irony, and paradox.

One major strategy of indirection remains to be identified—*opacity.* A clear instance of opacity may be found at the moment of Jesus' death cry in 15:34. As already noted, when Jesus cries out to God, the narrator immediately supplies a translation of the Aramaic utterance. The bystanders mistake the cry as addressed to Elijah, but we see through their mistake immediately and without thinking about having done so. In this scene a veil seems to surround Jesus on the cross, preventing onlookers from perceiving or understanding (i.e., seeing or hearing) what is happening right before their eyes.[6] The veil of opacity does not exist, at least not in this scene, however, for the narratee of the narrative. In 15:34 the narrator's clear and explicit commentary puts the narratee in a privileged position of insight and understanding before revealing to us that the characters in the story hear Jesus' cry in a twisted, garbled form.

Such opacity pervades not only the crucifixion scene, and but also much of Mark's Gospel. Characters in Mark's story demonstrate regularly that they cannot "see" Jesus for who he really is. Even the disciples, those closest and most committed to him, fail repeatedly to understand him, and by the end of the Gospel they have abandoned, betrayed, and denied him. By contrast, in the course of the narration the narratee learns more and more about who Jesus is, and therefore the narratee is frequently in a position to see through the blindness, deafness, and stupidity of the characters in the story. Opacity is what makes the double irony of the mockery at the cross the effective rhetorical strategy that it is. The mockers know they are speaking ironically, but they are blind and deaf to the deeper knowledge of which the narrator has made us the possessors, namely, that their ironic mockery is, ironically, true: Jesus is indeed the Christ, the King of Israel.

Blindness, deafness, and other metaphors for the lack of insight and understanding are inevitably featured prominently in narratives deeply involved in dramatic irony. We need only think of Oedipus's blindness to the truth that the audience of *Oedipus Rex* knows from the beginning of the play, or of the divine incognito of Dionysus in *The Bacchae,* whereby characters in the play struggle to perceive the identity of the stranger in their midst, an identity again that everyone in the audience knows. That veils of opacity blind and deafen the characters in the Gospel of Mark as frequently as they do goes hand in hand with the pervasive use of dramatic irony. Where Mark differs from *Oedipus Rex, The Bacchae,* and another Christian masterpiece of indirection, the Gospel of John, is in the frequent use of opacity (and ambiguity) to put not only characters but also the audience in the dark. Sometimes in Mark the roles of the blind characters and the knowing audience members are reversed. Sometimes I, the reader of the Gospel of Mark, stare blankly at a veil of opacity that keeps me from seeing or hearing correctly what characters in the story apparently do see or hear. Reading Mark's Gospel gives the reader the opportunity to experience both sides of the veil of opacity from time to time. This is a major reason why the experience of reading Mark's

6. "Opacity" has limitations as a visual metaphor; in 15:34 the veil of opacity that shrouds Jesus is both visual and aural.

Gospel does not result in the resolution and clarity that we frequently achieve even in works deeply committed to indirection.

FAMILY RESEMBLANCES

I have identified irony, metaphor, paradox, ambiguity, and opacity as the chief rhetorical strategies of indirection in the crucifixion scene specifically but also in the Gospel of Mark generally. As different as these indirect moves are, they nonetheless share some common characteristics.[7] This family of indirect moves is well known; what I have called "indirection" is called by others "figurative," "tropical," or "tensive" language. In semantic terms these uses of language involve double meanings or "dual semantic structures." I prefer to speak of them as rhetorical strategies of indirection, however, meandering storytelling strategies that readers follow as best they can. In rhetorical or pragmatic terms, a dual semantic structure is an utterance that a listener may take in one way or another (or in both ways, in neither way, first in one way and then a little in another way, etc.). The language is figurative, that is, it needs to be figured out. It is not straightforward or direct; it resists being taken at face value. "Trope," that which gives language a turn and thereby turns the users of language along with it, nicely reminds us of the dynamism of indirect language. To the rhetorically minded critic, talking about dual semantic structures is a futile attempt to distill a static essence from what is a dynamic temporal experience of following the turn of a word, a phrase, or a longer utterance. Nevertheless, the observations and comments of semantically minded critics may be useful. An important move of reader-oriented criticism is the translation of statements oriented toward referential, semantic considerations into language oriented toward the pragmatics of the temporal reading experience out of which the semantic statement was abstracted. We translate from the language of semantics into the language of pragmatics.

Especially noteworthy here are observations about double-meaning utterances. Each of Mark's indirect moves can be said to have a double meaning, but each handles double meaning differently. For instance, Paul Werth compares ambiguity, irony, and metaphor as uses of language that require of the speaker and listener alike a capability for "double-vision" (and "double-hearing," presumably).[8] Werth's differentiations between ambiguity, irony, and metaphor are too neat, but that each is a kind of "dual semantic structure" is clear enough. Fredric Bogel offers a helpful suggestion that the family of double-meaning devices is not a group of discrete linguistic devices but is

---

7. I do not intend to discuss irony, metaphor, paradox, ambiguity, and opacity in general terms, only how they are used as *rhetorical* strategies *in Mark's Gospel*. I shall cite later some of the critical literature that has sensitized me to these reading experiences, but I do not pretend to do justice to the vast critical literature that exists on each of these tropical uses of language.

8. See, e.g., Paul Werth, "The Linguistics of Double-Vision," *JLS* 6 (1977): 3–28, esp. 25.

rather a continuous spectrum: "For 'irony' is really the label we give to a particular sort of self-contradictory text that occupies a place on a spectrum including the self-contradiction of mere ineptness, unironic metaphor (which we often denature by taking as compressed simile), *and other forms of doubleness.*"[9] Building on this insight, I shall later venture to describe the spectrum of indirect devices used in Mark's Gospel.

Thus *doubleness* is the first and most prominent characteristic of the indirect language in Mark; it is shared in some fashion by all of the indirect devices in Mark that I have identified above. Bogel also alerts us to another characteristic that the devices in Mark share, but instead of his "self-contradiction" I prefer the term *incongruity.*[10] Not only are the devices under consideration dual but also the two aspects of the duality are incongruous with each other. Although incongruity is present in some form in all of the indirect moves, it is particularly strong in irony and paradox. Irony may often be described as the experience of seeing and seeing through an incongruity, whereas paradox heightens the incongruity to the point of bold contradiction. Thus, paradox in Mark tends to the self-contradictory or oxymoronic. Metaphor, ambiguity, and opacity also have their own special kinds of incongruity.

Two other common characteristics of Markan indirection are exemplified in the distinction between verbal and dramatic irony. Verbal irony in Mark is typically found only in the speech of characters; the narrator himself rarely speaks ironically. He does regularly use dramatic irony, which occurs when the reader perceives an incongruity between what is happening in the story and what is happening in the reader's understanding of the story, thanks to the reader's experience of the narrator's discourse. Dramatic irony occurs in the narratee's experience of an incongruity between story and discourse.

The verbal ironies in Mark's story (e.g., throughout the crucifixion scene) are relatively easily seen and seen through by the reader. To use Wayne Booth's metaphor, to "reconstruct" the intention that lies behind the ironic utterances of characters in Mark's story is not too difficult. Dramatic irony, however, is a different matter. Unlike verbal irony, which often arises in an instant and is fathomed an instant later, dramatic ironies are often construed gradually by the reader. To be sure, some of Mark's most vivid dramatic ironies are precipitated in an instant by a statement made by a character and sometimes even by a verbally ironic statement made by a character, but even so the dramatic irony that results can be seen to have been in preparation for some

9. Fredric V. Bogel, "Irony, Inference, and Critical Uncertainty," *YR* 69 (1980): 513; my italics added. It is common to find critics exploring the similarities and dissimilarities of irony and metaphor; see Neil Schaeffer, "Irony," *CR* 19 (1975): 178–86. Wayne Booth tries to differentiate sharply between the rhetorical effects of irony and metaphor, but that he feels the need to do so dignifies the case for some kind of family resemblance (*A Rhetoric of Irony* [Chicago: University of Chicago Press, 1974], 22).

10. "Tension" would be another possibility.

time and it usually continues to "reverberate"[11] in the mind of the reader for some time to come. Unlike verbal irony, dramatic irony is frequently not resolved or diminished by being recognized. To the contrary, dramatic irony is often so broad in scope—spanning perhaps the farthest reaches of the narrative in which it occurs, and sometimes even into intertextual realms beyond the present narrative—that the incongruity between story and discourse may seem to widen instead of being dissipated or resolved by virtue of its discovery. Dramatic irony tends to persist, to reverberate, and to engage the reader in an ongoing experience of dialectical incongruity.[12] Booth's metaphor of reconstruction, with its connotations of resolution and clarity, is therefore not apt for describing the reader's encounter with the dramatic irony in Mark's Gospel.

Dramatic irony is thus open and uncertain, both with regard to the range and scope of the ironic tension and with regard to the nagging doubt that we may not be able to shake off completely as to whether the irony is really ironic or not. Students of irony often note that the most haunting irony leaves us less than one hundred percent certain that "irony" is the best label for what we are experiencing.[13] Dramatic irony (and sometimes verbal irony, too) makes the most of its inherent uncertainty[14] by encouraging us to continue to ask the question, Is it really ironic? even as we proceed to answer the question, Assuming it is ironic, just how far and in what direction(s) does the ironic tension lead us?

These observations concerning verbal and dramatic irony have their analogies with the other major indirect moves Mark employs. As with irony, so also with the other indirect moves: limited, local, verbal versions of these turns occur at the level of story, as well as broader, extended, dramatic versions of these moves that manifest themselves only to the reader in the course of

11. "Reverberatory irony" is a term coined by David H. Richter, "The Reader as Ironic Victim," *Novel* 14 (1981): 135–51. However, he uses the term differently than I do. For him, reverberatory irony is "double-bind irony," irony that not only makes victims of characters in the story but also turns upon the reader to make of her or him a victim as well. I use the term more broadly as a way of acknowledging the fundamental irresolvability of dramatic irony. In a certain sense, Mark's indirection often makes a victim out of the reader, but primarily by means of ambiguity and opacity. Mark tends not to victimize the reader by means of irony.

12. Paul Werth suggests that the perception of irony requires a kind of "double vision," an ability to see two things at once, and Fredric Bogel comments that irony involves a kind of "rhetorical double exposure." Both of these figures, double vision and double exposure, are also used by D. C. Muecke, *Irony and the Ironic*, 2d ed., The Critical Idiom 13 (London and New York: Methuen, 1982), 45, 69. Also, see chap. 1.

13. On the inherent uncertainty of irony, see Muecke, *Irony*, 8, 31, 45; and Bogel, "Irony," 518: ". . . the very nature of irony is to resist certainty, to undermine it, to reserve a margin—however small—of uncertainty."

14. As I am using "uncertainty" it is even broader than "ambiguity," for one can even be uncertain as to the existence or the scope of an ambiguity.

the temporal experience of reading.[15] Similar to the lingering uncertainty in the most intriguing of ironic moves, uncertainty is also a common element in the rest of Mark's indirection. To say that Mark employs a rhetoric of indirection is to say, among other things, that he employs uncertainty rhetorically. So, two more characteristics of Mark's indirection are that these strategies of indirection are used in both *verbal and dramatic forms* and that they all make strategic use of *uncertainty*.

We can note one final characteristic of Mark's indirection. In highlighting indirection in the crucifixion scene, we encountered all of Mark's major moves in a brief section of narrative, an indication that Mark's indirect moves frequently work closely together. We saw indirect moves that possessed qualities of more than one trope simultaneously, for example, a (doubly) ironic statement uttered by a character and phrased in the form of a verbal paradox. We encountered one indirect move that paved the way for another, such as an ambiguous statement by a character that prepares the reader for an ironic turn later on. If we had examined Mark's narration over a wider expanse, we would have discovered other ways that Mark's tropical discourse turns upon itself. The tropical language in Mark's Gospel turns with and within itself when different indirect moves occur simultaneously, it turns over against and on itself when one indirect move gives way to or prepares the way for another, and it also turns from one move into another when a single move takes on new shape and complexion in retrospect as the reading experience progresses. Indirection is protean; just when we think we have it figured out, it transfigures itself. What Kenneth Burke says in general about the *changeability* of the four "master tropes" (metaphor, irony, metonymy, synecdoche) applies in particular to Mark's indirect turns: "Not only does the dividing line between the figurative and literal usages shift, but also the four tropes shade over into one another. Give a man but one of them, tell him to exploit its possibilities, and if he is thorough in doing so, he will come upon the other three."[16] In Mark, one turn leads to, or turns into, another.

The major characteristics of Markan indirection are thus doubleness, incongruity, verbal and dramatic forms, uncertainty, and changeability. We

---

15. My distinction between verbal and dramatic occurrences of irony, paradox, and the rest is a fairly common one, if we allow a rough equivalence between what is often called "situational" and "dramatic" versions of irony, paradox, and so forth. On the distinction between the verbal and situational (and/or dramatic) turns, see for irony, D. C. Muecke, *The Compass of Irony*, (London: Methuen, 1969), 42–52; for paradox, Cleanth Brooks, "The Language of Paradox," *The Well Wrought Urn: Studies in the Structure of Poetry* (New York: Reynal & Hitchcock, 1947), 3–20; for metaphor, John Dominic Crossan, *In Parables: The Challenge of the Historical Jesus* (New York: Harper & Row, 1973), 10–22; for ambiguity, Donald N. Levine, *The Flight from Ambiguity: Essays in Social and Cultural Theory* (Chicago and London: University of Chicago Press, 1985), 8. Regarding this characteristic alone, opacity stands apart from the rest of the family; it is inescapably dramatic.

16. Kenneth Burke, *A Grammar of Motives* (New York: Prentice-Hall, 1945), 503.

need to say more about how opacity and ambiguity play heavily on uncertainty, how paradox emphasizes incongruity, and how irony and metaphor involve both uncertainty and incongruity but in different ways. Eventually, I shall hazard a sketch of the spectrum of Markan indirection to indicate pictorially how Mark's indirect moves relate to each other. Then I shall be able to discuss the effects of Mark's rhetoric of indirection upon the reading experience. First, I shall examine briefly each of Mark's major moves of indirection: irony, metaphor, and paradox in this chapter, and ambiguity and opacity in the next.

MARK'S INDIRECT MOVES

IRONY

The Passion narrative, as I have observed, is the source of the greatest concentration of verbal irony in the Gospel, but other instances of verbal irony are scattered elsewhere in the Gospel. As with all of Mark's indirect moves, learning to handle the verbal turns of indirection is good training for handling the more subtle, extended, dramatic turns. Developing sensitivity to the variety of indirection in Mark is valuable because readers and critics alike still have difficulty grasping that a book found in the Bible can be anything other than straightforward and direct.

That Jesus, at least in Mark's Gospel, can speak ironically if he wishes is significant. For example, who can mistake the ironic tone of Jesus' hearty congratulations in Mark 7:9? "Well do you set aside the commandment of God, in order to keep your tradition!" Because this comment comes after a series of preparatory clues, we can hardly fail to catch the covert, ironic thrust of Jesus' words. A brief catalogue of the clues that prepare us to handle this verbal irony includes:

1. Mark 7:2-5 introduces the topic of this episode—ritual washing before meals—in an extensive, awkward parenthetical construction. Jesus and his disciples are being opposed by Pharisees and certain scribes from Jerusalem on the issue of the ritual purity of the dinner table. The antagonism between the two sides of the debate is made clear in 7:2-5, which leads one to expect no positive word from Jesus about his adversaries. On this basis alone the reader could see through any utterance of Jesus that seems on the surface to be congratulations extended to his opponents.

2. Once in the narrator's commentary (7:3) and once again in the direct discourse of the adversaries (7:5), the Pharisaic practice of handwashing is described as "the tradition of the elders." In 7:8, in direct discourse by Jesus, this expression is transformed into the expression "the tradition of men," which is contrasted sharply with "the commandment of God." Thus the two sides in the argument are not simply scribes and Pharisees

versus Jesus and his disciples, but veritably the human versus the divine. The rift between the two sides in this debate is so great that no compromise is thinkable. It is not a breach to be healed but a summons to choose one side or the other. No reader can doubt which side he or she is being invited to join.

3. Preceding the ironic use of "well" (*kalōs*) in Jesus' statement in 7:9 is a nonironic, deadly serious use of the same word in Jesus' speech beginning in 7:6: "Well did Isaiah prophesy of you hypocrites, as it is written, 'This people honors me with their lips, but their heart is far from me; in vain do they worship me, teaching as doctrines the precepts of men.' " Having called them hypocrites in the "well" statement in 7:6, the statement that begins with the word "well" in 7:9 is not likely to sing the praises of the scribes and Pharisees.

Thus does the narrator equip us with so much insight into the sharp confrontation between Jesus and his foes that we are never in doubt as to how to grasp the spirit in which Jesus' statement in 7:9 is offered. With this clear and uncontroversial example of verbal irony in mind, recall an episode early in the Gospel in which verbal irony occurs less obviously. Mark 4:10-13 are the transitional verses between the parable of the sower (4:1-9) and the allegorical interpretation Jesus gives to it (4:14-20). In modern discussions 4:10-13 has been the focus of much debate. These verses have been taken as an important clue for discerning how the author of the Gospel understood the function of the parables in the teaching of Jesus. Most discussions have therefore concentrated on the story level of the Gospel narrative. I focus instead on the neglected discourse of the narrator and the moves of indirection therein, especially the use of verbal irony.

"To you has been given the secret [*mysterion*] of the Kingdom of God, but for those outside everything is in riddles [*parabolais*] . . ." (4:11, RMF)— a great many suggestions have been made as to what the "secret" of the Kingdom of God is and when this secret might have been "given" to Jesus' disciples in the story. What has not been grasped is that here is a moment of opacity in the discourse. It is the first time in the Gospel that any mention has been made of the giving of the secret of the Kingdom of God. Typically critics have flipped back through the early pages of the Gospel to seek when and where this might have taken place in the story. The thought has not occurred to such critics that the secret of the Kingdom of God might be intended to be a secret that excludes them. The notion that this episode is an intentionally opaque moment in the narrative has been unthinkable to many. Narrative, especially biblical narrative, is supposed to be clear and illuminating, is it not? Because this presupposition seems common among readers and critics alike, I must make the point here that the secret of the Kingdom of God is *perhaps* given to characters in the story but is definitely *not* given to the narratee through the discourse. For the reader of the Gospel, the giving of this secret lies behind an opaque veil. We are not privy to it. Until 4:11 we did not even know that the secret existed. Mark 4:11 confronts us with our own blindness as readers, a blindness to which most critics have been blind.

We can better understand the strategy of intentional opacity if we attend to the language of 4:11. The disciples are said to have been given privileged access to the secret (*mysterion*) of the Kingdom of God. For outsiders (*tois exō*), however, everything (*ta panta*) is in riddles (*parabolais*). On the one hand, the disciples are said to be insiders, supposedly able to see through Jesus' puzzling *parabolai*. On the other hand, an outsider is anyone who has not obtained access to the secret of the Kingdom of God and therefore cannot understand Jesus' parables. This contrast raises problems for the reader. Most troubling perhaps is the clear indication that the disciples themselves do not in fact understand the parables, which is implied by their call for a clarification in 4:10. Only slightly less troubling is the realization that must come to every reader at this juncture, if only unconsciously, that because the reader does not possess this touted "secret of the Kingdom of God," the reader must therefore be an outsider.

The reader who despairs because she has been excluded from insight and understanding should continue reading. As I have already suggested, 4:12 is implicit commentary from the narrator, and we should read it as verbally ironic. Neither the story nor the discourse of Mark's Gospel is intended to promote blindness and lack of understanding in order to throw roadblocks in the way of repentance and forgiveness! Nevertheless, blindness and lack of understanding do indeed occur, both in the story and at the level of the discourse, and both story and discourse involve surprising turnabouts, whereby those who should see and understand do not, and those whom one would least expect to turn around and be forgiven do turn around and are forgiven.

That language is turning on itself and is turning us with it in 4:12 is confirmed when we read 4:13. For the first time Jesus seems to awaken to his disciples' lack of understanding of the parables, which was what led them to question him in the first place back in 4:10. I read 4:13 as a double question: "Don't you know this riddle? And how will you learn all the riddles?" (R&M). We can perhaps hear in these unanswered questions an ironic tone. Is he chiding the disciples sarcastically? Rather than concluding that Jesus is only now awakening to the obtuseness of his disciples in this episode, maybe only now are we learning (at the discourse level) that Jesus has all along understood his disciples' lack of understanding. In retrospect, the verses immediately preceding 4:13 begin to take on a new tone. Jesus may now appear to have been toying with the disciples all along, playing a cat-and-mouse game with them, or perhaps more to the point, the narrator has been playing with us. Although 4:11 might not have sounded ironic when we first heard it, having now encountered the ironic quotation of Isaiah in 4:12 and the irony-tinged double question of 4:13, the earlier comment about insiders and outsiders either knowing the secret or not knowing it now takes on a dramatic ironic twist that was not there before. Mark 4:11 becomes dramatically ironic when re-visioned from the vantage point of 4:13, which makes clear to the reader that Jesus' disciples, the insiders par excellence in this Gospel, not only do not understand the riddle of the sower but also stand in danger of failing to understand all of Jesus' riddles[17] and perhaps his whole ministry. For outsiders, everything (*ta panta*) is in riddles, and that state seems to describe the plight of the disciples. Far from being the privileged recipients of the secret of the Kingdom that 4:11 first led us to suppose, 4:13 reveals them to be outsiders for whom all of the parables are riddles that must be explained. By contrast, the reader who was subjected to a moment of opacity in 4:11 and was thereby forced into the position of the unknowing outsider is now in 4:13 ushered forcibly into the position of knowing, if not the content of "the secret of the Kingdom," then at least that the disciples do not understand the secret. Mark 4:13 reveals to the reader that the insiders of 4:11 are in fact outsiders, a revelation that turns the outsider of 4:11, the reader, into an insider. Moreover, at the heart of the indirect path meandering through 4:10-13 is 4:12, the verbally ironic signal that the path we are following through this section of the Gospel—and maybe throughout Mark—is intentionally indirect. "Seeing, they see and yet do not perceive . . ." is a hint for us to proceed with caution through this stretch of narrative and through the rest of the Gospel as well. A gesture is made here, ironic and oblique, to what is happening in the story, but all the more so to what is happening in the discourse. Moreover, what is happening in the story and in the discourse are frequently in ironic tension with each other. One cuts against the grain of the other. Seeing in the story may mean opacity in the discourse; seeing in the discourse may mean perceiving the blindness in the story.

I turn now from verbal irony to a brief discussion of dramatic irony in Mark. Because incongruity between story and discourse takes time for the narrator to develop and time for the narratee to discern and appreciate fully, and because dramatic ironies in Mark remain unannounced or covert, critical readers have ample room for argument as to whether one episode or another involves dramatic irony. I remember well a criticism of my claim that the unanswered question by the disciples in Mark 8:4 gives the reader an experience of irony.[18] In 8:4, for the second time in the story, Jesus and the Twelve

17. See John Dominic Crossan's claim that the parable of the sower was used by the historical Jesus of Nazareth as a "metaparable," a "parable about parables of the Kingdom" (*Cliffs of Fall: Paradox and Polyvalence in the Parables of Jesus* [New York: Seabury, 1980], 49). Whether or not the historical Jesus so used the parable, I am convinced that it has this kind of paradigmatic function in Mark's Gospel. Mark 4:1-20 is paradigmatic of the rhetoric of indirection employed both at the story level, by Jesus, and at the discourse level, by the narrator.

18. See Robert M. Fowler, *Loaves and Fishes: The Function of the Feeding Stories in the Gospel of Mark*, SBLDS 54 (Chico, Calif.: Scholars Press, 1981), 93 and passim.

face a large, hungry crowd in the desert, with only a few loaves of bread on hand, and the disciples ask Jesus, "How can one feed these men with bread here in the desert?" Apparently they ask this question innocently and sincerely. This question shows no sign of verbal irony. Dramatic irony is, however, precipitated by the disciples' question. Even if the disciples do not remember and comprehend the earlier feeding of a multitude (6:30-44), the reader does remember and comprehend. Indeed, the reader remembers that the disciples themselves pointed out the hungry crowd and the desert location (6:35-36), handed over their own loaves and fishes (6:38), distributed them to the crowd (6:41), and picked up the leftover pieces (6:43). After all of this experience in 6:30-44, when another hungry crowd again collects around them, out in a desert region, these same disciples ask, "How can one feed these men with bread here in the desert?"

My fellow critics may question whether this verse is ironic. What I know for sure is that countless readers and critics have stumbled awkwardly over 8:4 in the course of their reading experience and found it peculiar and offensive. Many readers and critics alike have found the implicit negative portrayal of the disciples in 8:4 to be too hard to swallow. As a result, the stupidity of the disciples in 8:4 has a long history of being explained away by critics rather than explained. The most common critical strategy has been to claim that the stupidity displayed in 8:4 is the accidental by-product of the flesh-and-blood author's careless use of two different versions of the same story of the miraculous feeding of a multitude. Ctitics argue that the disciples could reasonably be expected to be undiscerning once, as indeed they are throughout Mark 6:30-44, but to think that they could be equally thick-skulled on the second occasion of the feeding of a multitude is "psychologically impossible."[19] The reader-response critic can point out, however, that this explanation is predicated upon the perception, in the course of reading, of a gross incongruity between what the reader expects of the disciples and what they actually do in the story. By calling the unperceptive question of 8:4 "psychologically impossible," one critic has acknowledged but then explained away his experience of reading 8:4. This reaction might not be so bad in itself, but critics have then disregarded the two distinct feeding episodes as a case of a botched editing job on the part of the flesh-and-blood author of the Gospel. As a result, the entire Gospel has often not been taken seriously as a skillfully composed narrative but has instead been regarded as the awkward product of an incompetent editor. The problem here is that critics have considered repetition only as a feature of the story level. They have neglected to consider repetition as a feature of a rhetorical strategy at the discourse level.

19. Ezra Gould, *The Gospel According to St. Mark,* International Critical Commentary (Edinburgh: T. & T. Clark, 1896), 142; Fowler, *Loaves and Fishes,* 93.

Nearly all readers of Mark are taken aback by 8:4, and that reading
experience needs to be acknowledged and discussed by attention to the discourse level and not merely explained away with an obsessive fixation upon
the story level. The way I would explain the common experience of reading
Mark 8:4 runs something like this: Upon reading 8:4 the reader perceives a
profound ironic incongruity within the story itself between what the disciples
should know and yet do not. Furthermore, the reader perceives the additional
ironic incongruity between the blindness of the characters in the story, on the
one hand, and the modicum of insight (at least that the characters in the story
do not have insight) made possible for the narratee by the narrator's discourse,
on the other hand. Often the reader's encounter with these ironic incongruities
has been so shocking that readers, especially modern defenders of the disciples,
have recoiled from their reading experience and endeavored to explain away
the incongruities rather than to face up to them. "Irony" is the best shorthand
label I know to describe what many readers have tacitly reported about their
experience of reading Mark 8:4. At 8:4 the reader discovers both a gross
incongruity within the story and an additional incongruity between what is
understood at story level and what is understood at discourse level. That
experience is dramatic irony.

The two feeding stories provide a good example of the use of matched
pairs of episodes to develop dramatic irony, with the experience of reading
one episode in ironic tension with another.[20] Another use of repetition, the
two incidents about receiving children in 9:36-37 and 10:13-16, is comparatively minor and not so obviously a pair of incidents in which the reader
experiences a turn of dramatic irony. For these reasons, this pair of episodes
is worth a more careful look.

First, note that both of these episodes have to do with receiving and
embracing children and not with being humble and childlike. In both cases
the issue is whether one will embrace a child in Jesus' name (9:37) and thereby
embrace God (9:37) and God's kingdom (10:15). Matthew's Gospel has obscured Mark's interests by changing the issue from embracing children to
becoming childlike. Matthew still has the two separate incidents (18:1-5 and
19:13-15), just as Mark does, but Matthew has performed much editorial
work upon Mark's two incidents: (1) he takes up Mark 10:15 ("Truly, I say
to you, whoever does not receive the Kingdom of God when it approaches
in the form of [hōs] a child, shall not enter it" [RMF, very loosely]); (2) he
completely rewrites it ("Truly, I say to you, unless you turn [straphēte] and
become [genēsthe] like [hōs] children, you will never enter the Kingdom of
heaven. Whoever humbles [tapeinōsei] himself like [hōs] this child, he is the
greatest in the Kingdom of heaven" [Matt. 18:3-4].); (3) he erases all signs

---

20. The two sea stories in 4:35-41 and 6:45-52 play off against each other in a similar way;
Fowler, *Loaves and Fishes*, 100–05. No doubt many other examples could be adduced.

of Mark 10:15 from its original location (see Matt. 19:13-15); and (4) he inserts his new version of Mark 10:15 into the earlier of the two episodes and positions it between Mark 9:36 and 9:37 (see Matt. 18:1-5).

The end result is two passages in Matthew that still have something to do with receiving children, but the sharp ironic edge that Mark hones has been effectively blunted. Matthew's clear and direct concentration on "humbling" oneself, "turning," and "becoming like" a child became the accepted way of reading not only Matthew's version of the two episodes, where this reading is appropriate, but Mark's version as well, where it is deficient. As happens so many times, Matthew seizes upon a small, local ambiguity in Mark, in this case the thoroughly ambiguous *hōs* ("as," "like") in Mark 10:15, and clarifies it, in this case by introducing language about "turning," "becoming," and "humbling oneself." Nevertheless, both incidents in Mark are concerned about the practice of receiving and embracing children, as Mark 9:37, 10:13-14, and 10:16 make clear. My rendering of the elliptical *dexētai tēn basileian tou theou hōs paidion* in Mark 10:15 is therefore "receive the Kingdom of God when it approaches in the form of a child." By contrast, Matthew is concerned about spiritual qualities of humility and childlikeness, which was and is read back into Mark, where it is out of place.

Only after clearing away the overgrowth of Matthew's resolute clarification of Mark and the centuries of reading Mark's Gospel in Matthew's fashion can we begin to appreciate the irony of the disciples' refusal to receive children the second time the opportunity presents itself (Mark 10:13). They are completely oblivious to Jesus' earlier statement that receiving a child in Jesus' name is receiving Jesus, and receiving Jesus is receiving the one who sent him (9:37). Here, as elsewhere in Mark, the disciples run a serious risk of excluding themselves from the Kingdom of God, ironically, by attempting to exclude others, in this case children.

Although repetition can be used for many purposes, especially in the service of reinforcement or direction, Mark frequently employs repetition in the service of erosion or indirection. The more elaborate the repetition, the more likely a reverberatory ironic tension. Such dramatic ironic tension taketh away more than it giveth. Note also that the dramatic irony that is cultivated by elaborate repetition almost always involves the disciples at story level. Significantly, the disciples are usually the unknowing victims of the dramatic irony that is created by means of repetition. Could the victimization of the disciples be merely fortuitous? They are the companions of Jesus through the long haul of the story, and perhaps they are victimized the most merely because they are present the most. That does not explain why they should be victimized at all, however, nor does it explain why their obtuseness grows rather than diminishes. The reader must conclude that the disciples' role as ironic victims is significant not only at the story level but also at the discourse level. As we have seen, Mark's narrative, particularly through dramatic irony, offers us the opportunity to experience the widening distance between Jesus and his closest followers. The chasm between Jesus and the Twelve widens, and we must jump to one side or the other.

Other moments of dramatic irony of wider scope in the reading of the Gospel take virtually the entire narrative to develop. The cloud of ironic incongruity that envelops the passion narrative begins to build already in the earlier chapters. The dramatic irony we experience in reading chapters 14–16 is as powerful as it is because reading chapters 1–13 has prepared us. Again and again in the Passion narrative, we are struck by incongruities within the story itself or between story and discourse that span the entire narrative. The strategies of direction and indirection reach a culmination in the final chapters of Mark, if a narrative so thoroughly committed to indirection can really be said to culminate. For one thing, this narrative may have more than one culmination. In view of the two major plot lines in Mark, I regard the crucifixion scene as the culmination of the story level, the plot of contingency, and the rhetoric of direction, whereas the empty tomb episode is the culmination of the discourse level, the plot of predestination, and the rhetoric of indirection. Even this division is too neat and simple, however. To say that the last scene in the Gospel is the culmination of the rhetoric of indirection may be a lame way of saying that the discourse and the rhetoric of indirection breaks off here, whether it culminates or not. The reality is that the rhetoric of indirection does not achieve resolution within the narrative. Narration ceases at Mark 16:8, but the irony and the other indirect moves of the final scenes of the Gospel continue to reverberate. Paradoxically, the plot of contingency is resolved in the crucifixion scene, but the plot of predestination remains open and unresolved at story's end.

The ironic incongruities of the Passion narrative reverberate backward (also forward) through the gaps, the abruptly juxtaposed episodes, and the various twists and turns of Mark's entire narrative (and beyond). Irony may well be the preeminent strategy in Mark's rhetoric of indirection, but to the extent that Mark's ironies reverberate and do not dissipate, distinguishing them from paradox is difficult. Mark's irony slides over into paradox. This slide is nowhere better illustrated than in the case of the Messianic Secret. As I have suggested, critical concern for the Messianic Secret may be better understood as critical concern for the reader's encounter with the ironic incongruity of a Messiah who attempts to keep his messiahship quiet. Critics have long been perplexed that Jesus is supposedly self-effacing and secretive in this Gospel, yet his commands to secrecy are ignored, his attempts to maintain incognito fall through, and his efforts to find privacy backfire. In short, Jesus' efforts to maintain secrecy fail spectacularly. Considered at story level, this tendency is puzzling; considered at discourse level, it is the shrewdest of rhetorical strategies. The time has come to recognize that the prolonged discussion of the Messianic Secret has moved us no closer to a definitive

solution to this supposed puzzle but has instead demonstrated just how cap-
tivating the weave of Mark's narrative fabric is. We cannot solve the puzzle,
but we never seem to tire of unraveling and reknitting the threads. Should
we not gather from our activity that the act of unraveling and reknitting is
the thing and that the achievement of a final, definitive product is a false
hope? Can we not recognize that Mark's narrative is a puzzle, without sup-
posing that a definitive solution exists?

Less puzzled over by critics is the obverse of the Messianic Secret—
those moments in the narrative where Jesus tries to teach and bring enlightenment to people, especially to the Twelve, but fails. Yet strangers and
outsiders of all kinds do achieve sight, hearing, and intelligent speech, but
unexpectedly, surprisingly, and ironically. The persistent failure of the disciples, coupled with the surprising success of outsiders, might be described
as the rhetorical strategy of the Nonmessianic Revelation, the ironic flip side
of the Messianic Secret. Just as Jesus tries to maintain secrecy or privacy and
fails, he also tries to produce insight and understanding and fails. Where the
reader expects to see the light of understanding, darkness and secrecy seem
to triumph. Conversely, insight, understanding, and faith appear when and
where the reader expects them the least. All of these unexpected twists and
turns are for the reader experiences of dramatic irony, but because Mark's
irony reverberates—and because it appears again and again to the point that
such surprises become familiar and almost predictable—encounters with ironic
incongruity take on a paradigmatic regularity. So when we want to give a
short descriptive label to our reading experience, we reach for paradoxical
expressions such as Messianic Secret to describe the lasting impression we
derived from our repeated encounters with reverberatory dramatic irony.

METAPHOR

Discussions of metaphor have for centuries begun with definitions and comments from Aristotle. "Metaphor," Aristotle said succinctly, "consists in
giving the thing a name that belongs to something else."[21] Two aspects of
this definition deserve notice for historical reasons. One is the assumption
that a metaphor needs to be considered from the vantage point of its creator;
the other is the assumption that understanding a metaphor means understanding
its referential function, how it gives a name to something. Under the influence
of Aristotle, metaphor has more often been considered as a figure of speech
proposed by a speaker rather than as a challenge or invitation taken up by a
hearer, and it has more often been regarded as a phenomenon of semantics
or reference rather than as a phenomenon of pragmatics or rhetorical effect
upon the hearer. To understand the encounter with metaphor in the experience

21. *Poetics* 21/1457b.

of reading Mark's Gospel, we need to find ways to talk about the pragmatic, rhetorical effects that the Markan metaphors have on the reader.

Happily, Aristotle says some other things about metaphor that help us substitute a reader-oriented, pragmatic approach to metaphor for the author-oriented, semantic approach. Aristotle remarks that a metaphor functions like a riddle.[22] Again, he was primarily concerned about the metaphor as a riddle posed by the speaker, but I want to turn it around to consider the metaphor as a riddle taken up by the hearer. Aristotle further observes that "a good metaphor implies an intuitive perception of the similarity in dissimilars."[23] Metaphor derives its power from the tension between dissimilars that are posited to be similar. The sharper the dissimilarity, the more powerful the metaphor. Aristotle's comment is primarily author oriented; he is concerned primarily with the aptitude required of the aspiring creator of metaphors to be able to perceive the hitherto unrecognized similarity of dissimilars. The same aptitude is required of the recipient of metaphor, however: when we encounter metaphors in reading, we accept an implicit invitation to ponder previously uncontemplated similarities between dissimilars.

Already from this insight we can draw a useful contrast between metaphor and irony. Both play heavily on the tension of incongruity, but in different ways. In the encounter with metaphor, we confront an acknowledged or assumed incongruity or dissimilarity and are invited to explore previously unexplored congruities or similarities.[24] In the encounter with irony, the challenge is to perceive the incongruity in the first place, and then to fathom it, to the degree possible. Dealing with metaphor requires moving from an acknowledged incongruity to the realization of congruity; dealing with irony requires uncovering and coming to grips with an incongruity. The movements these two turns of language require of the hearer are by no means mirror reflections of each other, but in a sense they are movements in opposite directions; metaphor requires a movement from incongruity to congruity, and irony a movement into and through incongruity.

Donald Davidson makes the case that a metaphor does not have a referential message or a content, as is so commonly assumed, but rather that it produces an effect upon us.[25] Davidson also argues that metaphors are by

22. *Rhetoric* III.2/1405b; *Poetics* 22/1458a.

23. *Poetics* 22/1459a.

24. The inherent dissimilarity or incongruity in metaphor is much discussed, under a variety of labels. Aristotle speaks of "dissimilarity"; Kenneth Burke of "incongruity" (*A Grammar of Motives*, 504); Gerald L. Bruns, quoting Hans-Georg Gadamer, uses the expression "ambiguity" (*Inventions: Writing, Textuality, and Understanding in Literary History* [New Haven and London: Yale University Press, 1982], 101); Paul Ricoeur speaks of "contradiction," "absurdity," or, following Gilbert Ryle, a "category mistake" (*Interpretation Theory: Discourse and the Surplus of Meaning* [Fort Worth: Texas Christian University Press, 1976], 51).

25. "The common error is to fasten on the contents of the thoughts a metaphor provokes and to read these contents into the metaphor itself" (Donald Davidson, "What Metaphors Mean," in *On Metaphor*, ed. Sheldon Sacks [Chicago and London: University of Chicago Press, 1979], 43).

nature infinite in scope, which is embarrassing for referential approaches to metaphor.[26] For Davidson, only a rhetorical or pragmatic approach to metaphor can possibly take into account the infinite variability of how readers make sense of metaphors. More in keeping with the nature of metaphor is to speak of its rhetorical force on a particular hearer rather than of its abstract referential content.

Few critics have discussed more helpfully than Wayne Booth the rhetorical effects of tropical language upon its recipients. Booth describes, metaphorically, of course, what having a metaphor achieve an effect upon us is like: "The speaker has performed a task by yoking what the hearer had not yoked before, and the hearer simply cannot resist joining him: they thus perform an identical dance step, and the metaphor accomplishes at least part of its work even if the hearer then draws back and says, 'I shouldn't have allowed that!' "[27]

Ted Cohen goes further by describing the "dance steps" that the experience of metaphor puts us through. His description of the three-step dance of the encounter with metaphor is reminiscent of Booth's description of our four-step dance upon encountering irony. Cohen claims that community is created through the experience of metaphor, just as Booth claims that irony welds a tighter bond between speaker and hearer than could ever be achieved through straightforward language. Cohen says that metaphor brings about "the achievement of intimacy. There is a unique way in which the maker and the appreciator of a metaphor are drawn closer to one another. Three aspects are involved: (1) the speaker issues a kind of concealed invitation; (2) the hearer expends effort to accept the invitation; and (3) this transaction constitutes the acknowledgment of a community."[28]

"The achievement of intimacy" is surely what Mark's Gospel is designed to accomplish, through metaphor and all of the other indirect moves it makes on its reader. Indeed, Cohen's three-step dance is by no means descriptive only of metaphor but is essentially a generic description of what we go through whenever we encounter any turn of indirect language. Cohen and Booth agree that indirection is a surprisingly powerful strategy for communication in the sense of community building. How are these observations relevant to a reading of Mark's Gospel?

Turn to Mark 2:15-22, where in rapid succession Jesus offers his listeners the metaphors of physician, bridegroom, new patch on an old garment, and new wine in old wineskins. Just as the verbal irony in Mark is restricted to the speech of characters, so also verbal metaphors are found frequently at story level and seldom in the narrator's commentary on the story. That Jesus

26. Ibid., 44.
27. Wayne Booth, "Metaphor as Rhetoric: The Problem of Evaluation," in *On Metaphor*, ed. Sheldon Sacks, 52.
28. Ted Cohen, "Metaphor and the Cultivation of Intimacy," in *On Metaphor*, ed. Sheldon Sacks, 6.

frequently speaks metaphorically or "in parables" is of course well known. Without doubt, in Mark's story Jesus is a master of metaphor. How do readers make sense of the metaphors they encounter in reading? Mark 2:15-22, with its heavy concentration of metaphors, is instructive regarding how metaphors are employed in Mark's discourse and how readers are invited to take up the invitation to the dance that each metaphor offers.

The first metaphor, the physician, is not hard to fathom because the context in which it is offered in the story is relatively clear and Jesus himself interprets the metaphor at story level. The context is clear because the discourse informs the reader no less than three times in 2:15-16 that Jesus has attracted the critical attention of his opponents by associating with tax collectors and sinners. Thus the three parties to the discussion in the story are Jesus, his opponents, and the tax collectors and sinners. Therefore, when Jesus speaks metaphorically, *"Those who are well* have no need of *a physician,* but *those who are sick"* (2:17a), the three parties in his metaphorical statement neatly match the three parties present in the story. The various additional implications of the physician metaphor are left open for the reader to explore, but at least the parties to whom the metaphor applies are never in doubt. As if doubt still existed, Jesus' own interpretation of the metaphor removes it: *"I* came not to call the *righteous,* but *sinners"* (2:17b). This story-level commentary on a story-level metaphorical statement functions at the discourse level to make emphatic for the reader who the three parties of the metaphor are. Note, however, that much in Jesus' interpretive comment remains unclear. Do we detect a note of irony in his voice when he says he has nothing to do with the "righteous"? Are his "righteous" really righteous and his "sinners" really sinners? Are we entitled to suspect that "righteous" and "sinners" are additional, new turns of metaphor, and perhaps ironic ones at that, in that we may suspect that Jesus is reversing preconceived ideas about the true identity of the righteous and sinners?

Because Jesus himself only occasionally issues an interpretation of his own metaphors at story level, when he does so the reader is given a model to emulate in interpreting the many metaphors that Jesus does not stop to interpret. We are implicitly challenged to interpret all of Jesus' metaphors in the manner in which he himself only occasionally interprets them. Moreover, Jesus' story-level interpretations leave room for or perhaps even demand their own further interpretations. Granted that Jesus did not come to call the righteous but sinners, the question then arises, Who are the "righteous," and who are the "sinners"? The offering of a metaphorical (and maybe ironic) interpretation of a metaphor in the story only begins an interpretive process that the reader is implicitly invited to take up and continue. Interpretations themselves invite interpretation, especially when the interpretation of a metaphor is itself a metaphor.

The second metaphor, the bridegroom (2:19), is also relatively easy to grasp, thanks to its context in the narrative. Asked why his disciples do not fast like the disciples of other masters, Jesus answers that for wedding guests to fast while the bridegroom is with them is inappropriate. The bridegroom can be only Jesus, and the wedding guests (literally, the "sons of the bridal chamber") can be only Jesus' disciples, who participate with him in a celebratory, nonascetic life, to the chagrin of the unspecified questioners. The context renders the referent of the metaphor clear, but the scope of the metaphor remains unclear. If a Christian reader is familiar with the metaphor of the church as the bride of Christ (see John 3:29; 2 Cor. 11:2; Rev. 19:7; 22:17), the reader may think that the metaphor of bridegroom here entails the metaphor of the bride as well, but it is not clear in this context whether the one metaphor implies the other. How to read the comment about the days to come, when the bridegroom will be taken away from the wedding guests, is also ambiguous. Readers may assume that fasting implies a time of mourning for the loss of the bridegroom. After we read to the end of the Gospel, this rereading of the metaphor becomes especially attractive.

Immediately following the bridegroom metaphor are the metaphors of the new patch tearing away from an old garment and the new wine tearing old wineskins (2:21-22). With both of these metaphors, most readers feel they have lost their firm grasp on the referent. If both the physician and the bridegroom are metaphorically identified with Jesus, is Jesus also to be identified with the new patch torn away from the old garment or the new wine that rends the old skin even as it is lost itself? What these two metaphors refer to and the scope of their reference are by no means clear. Even after we grasp them as riddles and pose possible solutions, they remain puzzling. The Gospel has far more open and puzzling metaphors like these two than metaphors that are relatively clear or determined, such as the physician and bridegroom. Yet readers do not cease trying to puzzle through the unclear riddles in Mark 2 because they are inspired by the example of Jesus' own story-level explanation of the physician metaphor and by the narrator's contextual clues as to the referent of both the physician and bridegroom metaphors. Metaphors are by nature enticing, but the urge to take them up as challenging riddles is all the stronger when we observe both the narrator and his protagonist offering us clues and strategies for interpreting certain metaphors. Then when we encounter other metaphors for which the interpretive clues are fewer, we are encouraged to launch out on our own.[29]

29. A number of other metaphors in Mark could be examined: baptism with the Holy Spirit (1:9); the Kingdom of God (1:15 and passim); fishers of persons (1:17); the strong man, his house, and the burglar (3:27); mother, brothers, and sisters (3:33-35); sowers, seeds, and soils (4:1-9 and passim); lamp (4:21); children, bread, and dogs (7:27 and passim); leaven (8:15); cup and baptism (10:38 and passim); fig tree and temple (11:12-25 and passim); the beloved son (12:6 and passim); the rejected stone (12:10); bread and wine (14:22-25 and passim); and the shepherd (14:27 and passim). Most of these are riddlelike, unclear as to scope, and often unclear as to referent.

Another important category of metaphorical expressions in Mark is the nicknames and titles given to various characters at story level. The chief example is Jesus, who receives numerous honorific titles or epithets: "Christ," "Son of God," "Son of man," "Son of David," "King of the Jews," and others. For generations scholars have labored to clarify the meaning of these titles in Mark in the light of their popular usage in first-century Palestine and the broader Mediterranean world,[30] but I shall insist on staying within Mark's Gospel and focusing on the metaphorical, riddlelike nature of the epithets used for Jesus and for other characters.

In Mark's narrative the titles for Jesus are not clearly defined or interpreted, either in the story or in the discourse. The title that gets the most exposure is Son of man, but it remains a metaphorical puzzle to the end. It is the only one of the figurative characterizations of Jesus that Jesus uses freely himself, but always in the third person; readers frequently overlook that Jesus never explicitly identifies himself as the Son of man. No one else in the story uses the expression, and no one in the story ever seems to hear the expression when Jesus uses it. It is a designation for Jesus that supposedly has a place in the story, but it receives uptake only in the discourse. Only Mark's narratee knows that Jesus is the Son of man, by virtue of the narrator's discourse.[31] Anyone who reads Mark's Gospel makes this identification, not on the basis of knowledge of first-century Jewish or Christian usage of the expression "Son of man," but on the basis of having experienced Mark's narrative. I do not deny that knowledge of Jewish or Christian traditions, especially apocalyptic literature and most especially Daniel, deeply enriches our reading of Mark, especially as regards the Son of man. The implied reader of Mark is supposed by the implied author to be familiar with the Jewish Scriptures, including presumably the Son of man passages in Daniel. However, the reader of Mark makes the identification of Jesus as Son of man in the act of reading Mark, and to the extent that the reader is able to fill that expression with meaning, he or she will do so primarily on the basis of the resources supplied by Mark's narrative. The same is equally true of the other epithets for Jesus in Mark.

"Son of man," as well as the other epithets for Jesus in Mark, functions as a metaphor whose primary interpretive context is the narrative in which it is embedded. In order to figure out, to the extent possible, what is at stake when this narrative calls Jesus "Christ," "Son of God," and "Son of man," or for that matter "physician," "bridegroom," "new patch," and "new wine,"

30. See the standard works on christological titles; e.g., Ferdinand Hahn, *Christologische Hoheitstitel: Ihre Geschichte im frühen Christentum*, 2. Auflage (Göttingen: Vandenhoeck & Ruprecht, 1964); idem, *The Titles of Jesus in Christology: Their History in Early Christianity*, trans. H. Knight and G. Ogg (New York and Cleveland: World, 1969); and still very much in this tradition, Kingsbury, *The Christology of Mark's Gospel*.

31. The narrator confirms this identification for the reader in Mark 10:32.

the reader has to deal first and foremost with Mark's narrative. Historical investigation into the background of honorific titles in Jewish, Hellenistic, or Christian usage is eminently defensible on the valid grounds that we are separated in space and time from the first-century Mediterranean world, and to read Mark as a first-century reader would have, we must do all we can to fill the gaps in our knowledge of first-century culture and history. Not only do we have gaps in our historical knowledge of Mark, however, but also gaps and spots of indeterminacy exist in its narrative discourse that even an informed first-century reader would have been challenged to negotiate. For example, first-century readers such as Matthew and Luke were intent upon, among other things, clarifying Mark's ambiguities, filling in his gaps, and straightening out his indirect narrative strategies. Matthew and Luke, as contemporaries of Mark, were not so much bridging a historical gap between themselves and Mark as much as they were taking up and responding to the challenges of Mark's narrative rhetoric. The situation of the modern critical reader is both unlike and like that of Matthew and Luke. We are unlike them in that nineteen centuries separate us from the writing of Mark's Gospel, and we will never know the language and the culture of the first-century Mediterranean world the way Matthew and Luke did. We are like Matthew and Luke, however, in that we still try to read Mark's Gospel and respond to its rhetoric. The modern reader who rushes to fill a gap, clarify a metaphor, or dissolve an irony in Mark primarily on the basis of a historical insight is not merely putting a historical insight to work but also is responding, usually unconsciously, to the challenge of Mark's rhetoric of direction and indirection. Usually we have been aware of our application of historical insights but unaware of our own negotiations with Mark's narrative discourse. One of my goals is to raise to consciousness the act of responding to reading that historically oriented critics of Mark have always engaged in but often without realizing it.

Other metaphorical expressions applied to characters in the story include the nicknames or epithets applied to a few key characters. Most memorable, perhaps, is the nickname that Jesus gives to Simon: *Petros,* or Peter, "the Rock" (3:16). Peter is the only one of the Twelve who appears in enough scenes to give us an inkling of his character, and this leader and spokesperson for the Twelve is anything but a rock in this Gospel. In two critical moments late in the Gospel, the Rock displays his feet of clay: the Gethsemane scene (14:32-42) and the intercalated "trials" of Jesus and Peter (14:53-72). In Gethsemane, Peter's failure to stay awake and to maintain the vigil with Jesus is accentuated when Jesus addresses him, not with the nickname used consistently since 3:16, but with his old name: ". . . and he said to Peter, 'Simon,[32]

---

32. The two names are sharply juxtaposed in the Greek: *kai legei Petrō Simōn. . . .*

are you asleep? Could you not watch one hour?' " (14:37).[33] In the trial scene, Peter steadfastly denies knowledge of Jesus three times, complete with curses, until at last the Rock breaks down and weeps (14:72), but not before he saves his life at Jesus' expense.[34] As severe as his failure is in his last two appearances in the Gospel, Peter actually fares no better earlier in Mark's narrative. At Caesarea Philippi, when faced with Jesus' prediction of suffering and death, Peter rebukes Jesus and then Jesus rebukes Peter by bestowing on him yet another nickname: "Get behind me, Satan! For you are not on the side of God, but of men" (8:33).

Thus, "Peter" is a metaphorical nickname that is deeply ironic in this Gospel, if not in the other Gospels.[35] Recall that Jesus regularly speaks ironically and metaphorically in Mark. Appropriately, the few epithets he applies to other characters (or to himself) are ironic metaphors. Ironic metaphor is surely what we have in the case of "the Sons of Thunder," the nickname Jesus gives to James and John. Little narration in the Gospel characterizes James and John sufficiently to allow us to infer on that basis that this nickname is ironic. Nevertheless, the hyperbole of Sons of Thunder is enough in itself. Hyperbole, because of the inherent incongruity produced by exaggeration, tends naturally toward irony. The Rock and Sons of Thunder are both hyperbolic epithets that have an air of irony about them from the start. The irony then intensifies and becomes unmistakable as the narrative progresses, in the course of which these three leaders of the Twelve regress in insight and understanding.[36]

We now turn from verbal metaphor to extended or dramatic metaphor. As we have noted, the parables of Jesus are essentially extended metaphors,[37] so whenever Jesus is parabolic in the story, the narrator's discourse is also parabolic. Surprisingly, however, Mark's Gospel contains very few of the beloved parables of Jesus. They are not absent because Mark does not appreciate parables. Indeed, Mark is more comfortable with metaphor and other forms of indirection than any other Gospel writer, except perhaps John. Mark

33. See Werner H. Kelber, "The Hour of the Son of Man and the Temptation of the Disciples (Mark 14:32-42)," in *The Passion in Mark: Studies on Mark 14–16*, ed. Werner H. Kelber (Philadelphia: Fortress Press, 1976), 41–60.

34. See Kim E. Dewey, "Peter's Curse and Cursed Peter (Mark 14:53-54, 66-72)," in *The Passion in Mark*, ed. Werner H. Kelber, 96–114.

35. Contrast Mark with Matthew's Gospel, where the irony of the nickname is muted (see Matt. 16:18). For Matthew, Peter may occasionally be "a man of little faith," but he is nevertheless a hero who richly deserves his nickname. See David Rhoads and Donald Michie on the irony of "the Rock" in Mark (*Mark as Story: An Introduction to the Narrative of a Gospel* [Philadelphia: Fortress Press, 1982], 127–29).

36. Other names in Mark that may also be taken as ironic, figurative expressions are Elijah (see especially 9:9-13), Judas Iscariot (3:19 and passim), and Levi, the tax collector (2:13-14).

37. Crossan, *In Parables*, 10–16; idem, "Parables," in *Harper's Bible Dictionary*, gen. ed. Paul J. Achtemeier (New York: Harper & Row, 1985), 747–49.

reserves for himself primarily the privilege of indirect speech. If he is to retain control over his own narrative, he cannot let it be taken over by his protagonist, no matter how highly he may think of him. Mark's Gospel remains fundamentally Mark's discourse and not Jesus', and the true master of indirection in the Gospel is its implied author and narrator, not its protagonist. Readers have been accustomed to giving all of the credit for parabolic speech to the protagonist, which would probably please a master of indirection such as Mark, but that Mark's own use of indirection is masterful should now be brought to light.

If we concentrate on the discourse rather than the story, then we discover that many episodes that seem literal and straightforward at the story level are metaphorical or otherwise figurative at the discourse level (e.g., matched-pair episodes and intercalations). The narrator covertly and indirectly beckons us to grasp his discourse as figurative by presenting to us in his story a Jesus who habitually teaches in parables and then stops to interpret them. At least the narrator *says* that Jesus habitually explains his parables. In the story we read, only rarely does Jesus actually stop to explain one of his parables. Actually, Jesus may very well be interpreting all of his parables in the story, but such interpretations are omitted by the narrator from his discourse, and thus Jesus' illuminating comments take place behind an opaque veil as far as the narratee is concerned. In effect, this strategy is a crafty inducement to us to do the interpretation ourselves. Jesus does not interpret many of his parables in Mark because the narrator wants that to become the narratee's "response-ability."

What little interpretation Jesus does offer in the story is of immense importance for the reader. Just as the reader receives an implicit invitation to explore and interpret verbal metaphors by the example of Jesus' interpretation of the metaphor of the physician (2:17), similarly the reader receives a lesson in the interpretation of extended, dramatic metaphor by the example of Jesus' interpretation of the sower parable (4:1-9, 14-20). The parable of the sower and the rare interpretation that accompanies it are a model, showing readers how to go about reading all of Mark's Gospel. Observe in particular two comments by Jesus in Mark 4: One is that for the outsider (the reader?) "everything" (4:11) is in parables. The other is that if the disciples cannot interpret the sower parable, then they cannot hope to interpret any of the parables (4:13). Apparently the interpretation of this parable is not only the key to the interpretation of all the parables of Jesus *in* the Gospel[38] but also the key to the interpretation *of* the Gospel, because for outsiders such as the reader of the Gospel "everything"—the entire Gospel—is in parables or

---

38. It is legitimate to take 4:14-20 as a glossary of character types that the reader will recognize hereafter in Mark's story, but I would not take this as far as Mary Ann Tolbert does in *Sowing the Gospel: Mark's World in Literary-Historical Perspective* (Minneapolis: Fortress Press, 1989).

riddles. Mark 4:14-20 is a key not only to Jesus' story-level discourse but especially to our narrator's discourse, not because it hands us a ready-made solution to one particular riddle but because it models for us a way of interpreting parabolic discourse generally.

In keeping with a rhetoric of indirection, note that the interpretation of the parable in 4:14-20 is far from clear: it too needs to be interpreted. The sower is said to sow "the word" (*ho logos*). What on earth is that? "The word" figures very nicely both the teaching of Jesus at story level and the narrator's discourse, and therefore "the sower" might be taken as a metaphor for Jesus, for the narrator, for both simultaneously, or for still other sowers of words. Interpreting the sower metaphor by saying that the sower sows "the word" merely introduces another metaphor that requires yet another effort at interpretation. An interpretation requires its own interpretation, especially if metaphor is used to interpret metaphor. The move from the parable of 4:1-9 to the interpretation of it in 4:14-20 is a paradigm of an endless reading and rereading process. I read Mark's narrative figuratively, both in the sense of taking it up as figurative language and in the sense of offering my own new figures to stand in the place of the old, because that is the way the protagonist in Mark "reads" his own narratives.

An implication of taking "everything" in Mark's narrative parabolically is that the entire story is an extended metaphor for what happens in the reader's experience of the discourse. The story level of the narrative figures the experience of reading the narrative, but often ironically. Frequently Mark's story stands in ironic incongruity with what is transpiring at the level of the discourse. Characters in the story do not see, hear, or speak properly, but the reader is instructed and illuminated thereby and therefore does see, hear, or speak properly. Conversely, we are shut out of some moments of enlightenment in the story; their light is our darkness. Ironically, blindness in the story can metaphorically be about the sight achieved through the discourse, and vice versa.

PARADOX

The central turns of indirect language in Mark's discourse are irony and metaphor. When either of these turns makes the most of its inherent incongruity, we find ourselves turned toward paradox. Irony and metaphor regularly slip into paradox. Paradox is also developed and used in its own right, both verbally and dramatically, like other strategies of indirection.

Verbal paradoxes in Mark are oxymoronic turns of phrase, and thus they give the reader an experience different from that of irony or metaphor. Whereas irony invites the reader to see and to see through an incongruity and metaphor invites an exploration of the hitherto unexplored similarities in acknowledged dissimilars, the experience of paradox is the experience of being bracketed between seemingly incompatible but nevertheless coexisting polar opposites. Of all Mark's indirect moves, incongruity is at its sharpest in paradox.

Like the other indirect turns, a paradox is the offering of a "concealed invitation" (Cohen) to perform a "dance step" (Booth), but the dance step often appears at first to be restricted to bouncing back and forth between stark opposites. When the distraught father of the demon-possessed boy says, "I believe; help my unbelief!" (9:24), we can only ponder the mysteries of the coexistence of faith and doubt in the father and in ourselves, dancing back and forth between these conflicting but perhaps even mutually dependent opposites. When ironic mockers say of Jesus, "He saved others; he cannot save himself" (15:31), we can only grant the truth of that seeming contradiction at the story level and perhaps wonder at the same time the reason that, if what they say is true, we cannot bring ourselves to join them in mockery. We grasp the paradox they utter not in the light of the story, but in the light of our experience of the narrator's discourse. The paradox they utter in mockery is true in one way in the story, but true in a much different way at the level of discourse. Sometimes paradox puts us and leaves us between conflicting poles, there to live for a moment, but sometimes we have ways to escape the tension of paradoxical incongruity.

Sometimes other indirect turns lead us into paradox, and sometimes indirect turns provide an escape from a potential prison of paradox. Often the reader's experience of paradox is like taking up and dealing with a complex question.[39] Construing an answer to the implicit question can soften the paradoxical tension. A paradox has a way of getting the reader to ask and try to answer: "How can X and Y both be? How can X be, if Y? How can Y be, if X?" Because incongruity between a certain X and a certain Y is a rough characterization not only of paradox but also of all figurative or double-pronged uses of language, however, an attractive option for negotiating a paradox is to transfigure the paradox into another figure. We can take X, Y, or both metaphorically as indirect instead of direct language and thereby deconstruct our dilemma. Metaphor can lead us into and also out of paradox. A model of this strategy for reading paradox is provided in Mark by Jesus, who offers us both verbal paradoxes and interpretations thereof. This model is demonstrated early in the reading of the Gospel, teaching the reader an important lesson on how to handle paradox.

In Mark 3 we encounter a conflict of interpretations over the source of Jesus' wonder-working power. The first interpretation offered comes from Jesus' family, who think that he has gone crazy (3:21, 31-35). Scribes from Jerusalem offer a second interpretation, that Jesus employs demonic powers

---

39. "These lines turn on a paradox, and it is in the nature of a paradox that a reader who recognizes it is already responding to the question it poses" (Stanley Fish, *Is There a Text in This Class? The Authority of Interpretive Communities* [Cambridge: Harvard University Press, 1980], 124).

to perform exorcisms. Their charge against him is stated in the form of a verbal paradox: "He wields control over Beelzebul; it is by means of the chief of demons that he casts out demons" (3:22, RMF). Jesus takes up their paradoxical charge, transfigures it, and throws it back at them in the form of a question: "How can Satan cast out Satan?" (3:23).[40] Here is one thing a reader can do to escape an uncomfortable paradox: deconstruct it by transforming it into the question it seems to imply. Jesus thus models one strategic move for dealing with paradox. Jesus then proceeds, not to answer the question directly, but to transfigure it further, by means of other metaphors, and by drawing out the logical implications of those metaphors. "Satan casting out Satan" is transfigured into the following: "If a kingdom is divided against itself, that kingdom cannot stand. And if a house is divided against itself, that house will not be able to stand" (3:24-25). Then, taking up a key insight from the new metaphors of divided kingdom and divided house (neither is able to stand), he returns to the question of Satan casting out Satan and applies his insight: "And if Satan has risen up against himself and is divided, he cannot stand, but is coming to an end" (3:26). This reply does not answer the question of 3:23 explicitly, but it does imply that if the scribes really believed what they were saying they would not oppose him; they would instead encourage and congratulate him for hastening the demise of the kingdom of Satan. Jesus demonstrates through the logic of his metaphors that the paradox of Satan casting out Satan leads to conclusions that those putting forward the paradox probably would not accept. This paradox does not make any sense; it is not a paradox at all, but nonsense. Jesus has entered into this apparent paradox only in order to explode it from within. If we grant that paradoxes are seemingly contradictory statements that are nevertheless true, observe that some seemingly contradictory statements are indeed merely contradictory statements, the product of shoddy or dishonest thinking. That not all figurative glitter is gold is a useful lesson. Not all ironies, metaphors, and paradoxes are apt or efficacious. Some are evil. Lessons such as this are vital late in the Gospel when in 15:31 we recognize a paradox that is stated as absurd nonsense at story level and yet is recognized as profound truth at discourse level. One person's paradoxical truth is another person's nonsense (3:23), and one person's nonsense is another person's paradoxical truth (15:31).

The third contribution to the conflict of interpretations in 3:21-35 is Jesus' own typically indirect contribution. In counterpoint[41] to the interpretations that he is crazy or that he possesses demonic power are the words of Jesus in 3:27: "But no one can enter a strong man's house and plunder his goods, unless he first binds the strong man; then indeed he may plunder his house."

40. The Greek word order juxtaposes the nominative and the accusative forms of the word *Satan,* thus sharpening the polarity: *pōs dynatai satanas satanan ekballein?*

41. Mark 3:27 is introduced with the contrastive *alla* ("but," "rather"), which sets 3:27 apart sharply from what precedes it.

No solution for this new riddle is offered, but few readers have had difficulty in discerning that the burglar must surely be Jesus, the strong man Satan, and the house and goods of the strong man somehow the kingdom of Satan. The metaphor of the burglar and the strong man is offered not really as an interpretation of but rather as a metaphorical substitute for the seemingly paradoxical suggestion that Jesus casts out demons by demonic power. In this instance a verbal paradox is supplanted by a metaphorical narrative. Much is clarified thereby, but much remains ambiguous. The burglar metaphor itself is not hard to grasp in broad outline, but the details remain uncertain. When, where, and how does the burglar overpower and bind the strong man? The parable has led us to ask more questions than it has answered for us. Many readers go back and reread the first two chapters of the Gospel in hopes of finding when and where the burglar overpowered the strong man in the story. If this scene actually took place earlier in the story, it was left out of the discourse, so we are not privy to it. For the narratee, the binding of the strong man lies behind an opaque veil. Nevertheless, at least the "how" part of the question has already been asked, if not yet answered, inasmuch as it was essentially the question with which we started back in 3:23. The "how" question now begins to receive an answer in the following verses, where Jesus (3:28-29), as well as the narrator in his commentary (3:30), condemns the scribes for "blaspheming against the Holy Spirit." So, how does Jesus do his exorcisms? The reader now is able to infer an answer: by the power of the Holy Spirit. Yet that interpretation also requires further interpretation, and this new puzzle about the Holy Spirit turns out to receive almost no further illumination in Mark's Gospel. Some questions are answered; others remain open.

The paradox in 3:22 is a false paradox, offered to us only to be repudiated. However, other verbal paradoxes offered in the Gospel as the teaching of Jesus contribute significantly to the indirect exposition of the narrator's conceptual point of view. These paradoxes are not to be rejected but to be pondered, especially when the paradox is accompanied by an interpretation by Jesus. A paradox that is at least partially explained—and not just explained away—must be taken seriously. Choice examples are the verbal paradoxes and the interpretations that accompany them after each of the three Passion predictions in Mark 8–10 (8:31; 9:31; 10:32-34).

Passion Prediction
And he began to teach them that the Son of man must suffer many things, and be rejected by the elders and the chief priests and the scribes, and be killed, and after three days rise again. (8:31)

Paradox
"For whoever would save his life will lose it; and whoever loses his life for my sake and the gospel's will save it." (8:35)

Interpretation

"For what does it profit a man, to gain the whole world and forfeit his life? For what can a man give in return for his life? For whoever is ashamed of me and of my words in this adulterous and sinful generation, of him will the Son of man also be ashamed, when he comes in the glory of his Father with the holy angels." And he said to them, "Truly, I say to you, there are some standing here who will not taste death before they see that the Kingdom of God has come with power." (8:36—9:1)

Passion Prediction

"The Son of man will be delivered into the hands of men, and they will kill him; and when he is killed, after three days he will rise." (9:31)

Paradox

"If any one would be first, he must be last of all and servant of all." (9:35)

Interpretation

And he took a child, and put him in the midst of them; and taking him in his arms, he said to them, "Whoever receives one such child in my name receives me; and whoever receives me, receives not me but him who sent me." (9:36-37)

Passion Prediction

And taking the twelve again, he began to tell them what was to happen to him, saying, "Behold, we are going up to Jerusalem; and the Son of man will be delivered to the chief priests and the scribes, and they will condemn him to death, and deliver him to the Gentiles; and they will mock him, and spit upon him, and scourge him, and kill him; and after three days he will rise." (10:32-34)

Paradox

". . . whoever would be great among you must be your servant, and whoever would be first among you must be slave of all." (10:43-44)

Interpretation

"For the Son of man also came not to be served but to serve, and to give his life as a ransom for many." (10:45)

Several observations are in order here. First, each of the three paradoxical statements is in the form of a "whoever" statement, one of Mark's favorite means of communicating reliable but indirect commentary to the reader. Although relatively few "whoever" statements occur in the first half of the Gospel, by the time we arrive at 8:35 we have probably already perceived that such statements by Jesus are trustworthy. On that basis alone we are well disposed to take seriously these three paradoxes. Furthermore, the reader notices a similarity in theme between the three paradoxical statements. Mark himself states the theme well through Jesus in a "whoever" statement in 8:34: "If any person would come after me, let him deny himself and take up his cross and follow me." Following Jesus means being willing to deny ourselves and to follow him to death. We hear echoes of this daunting challenge in each of the three paradoxical echoes it receives in 8:35, 9:35, and 10:43-44. Thus the three paradoxical "whoever" statements in Mark 8–10 are, because of their familiar form, consistency of theme, and sheer repetition, taken with utmost seriousness by the reader. Mark 8:35, 9:35, and 10:43-44 exemplify the persistence of the paradoxical in Mark's conceptual point of view.

Nevertheless, Mark does not offer these three paradoxes baldly, to be embraced unthinkingly. Rather, each paradox gives rise to thought, and the thinking of readers has frequently turned to devising figures with which to figure out and thereby domesticate one side or the other of the paradox at hand. Each of these paradoxical constructs has ample room for interpretive play, which the narrative itself illustrates conveniently when Jesus himself interprets his paradoxes by means of metaphors. The paradox of 8:35 is interpreted metaphorically in 8:36—9:1, especially in 8:38 (being "ashamed"; an "adulterous" generation; the "Son of man"); the paradox of 9:35 is interpreted metaphorically in 9:36-37, especially in 9:37 (a "child" figures "Jesus," who in turn figures the one who "sent" him); and the paradox of 10:43-44 is interpreted metaphorically in 10:45 (the "Son of man" "serves" by giving his life as a "ransom").

That 8:35, the first of these three paradoxes, receives the most interpretation in the narrative is perhaps not coincidental. Mark 8:36—9:1 shows the reader how to make sense of a paradox, which is useful in view of the two similar paradoxes that come later. In 8:35 what is "saving one's life," that in so doing one "loses one's life"? Conversely, how does one "lose one's life" so as to "save" it? Turning one side or the other of this paradox into a metaphor enables us to make sense of a potentially nonsensical contradiction. The Greek word translated as "life" is *psyche,* which is sufficiently rich in its possible connotations to allow the reader to play with the interpretive options for answering the paradox's implicit question. If "saving" one's *psyche* is taken in the straightforward, literal sense of safeguarding one's physical being, then an easy step is to take the resulting "loss" of one's *psyche* as a figurative expression for the loss of one's ultimate, spiritual existence, the loss of one's soul. Conversely, "losing" one's *psyche* (physically), *for Jesus' sake and the Gospel's,* is "saving" one's *psyche* (spiritually). The reader can make an easy escape via metaphor from this paradoxical interpretive prison. The pressure of the paradoxical contradiction is relieved by figuring out the paradox and by transfiguring it into a statement of contrast that is not at all contradictory.

Note that the paradox is not "Whoever would save his life will lose it; whoever loses his life will save it." Apparently, for Mark saving one's life invariably means losing it, but losing one's life for any cause will not do. Only the losing of one's *psyche* for the sake of Jesus and the *euangelion* will save one's *psyche*. The paradox of 8:35 is thus asymmetrical or skewed. It does not cut the same way in both directions. This asymmetry is to the advantage of the reader, for the phrasing of the paradox in 8:35 bears within itself a signal to the reader of the first step to be taken toward an interpretation of the paradox. "Losing one's life" must first be clearly understood as "losing one's life *for Jesus' sake and the Gospel's.*" With this point clarified, then the interpretive process that has begun already in the very phrasing of the paradox itself is continued for us in 8:36—9:1. The expression "saving one's life" in 8:35 is transfigured in 8:36-37 into "gaining the whole world," which is itself another figure deserving its own interpretation. Transfiguring the remainder of 8:35, but putting it in negative terms, the refusal to "lose one's life for Jesus' sake and the Gospel's" is expressed in 8:38 as "being ashamed of Jesus and his words."[42] Altogether, Mark 8:36—9:1 is a rich lesson in the use of metaphor to create illuminating, figurative interpretations of paradoxical expressions.

In "for Jesus' sake and the Gospel's," I have used an uppercase *G* to suggest that we have here more than a story-level allusion by Jesus to his proclamation of good news. We also have an allusion by the storyteller to his Gospel. Story and discourse reflect each other here. "For Jesus' sake" is the same thing as "for Mark's Gospel's sake." Whoever may be supposed to be telling this story is saying to us that the Jesus presented in this narrative is of utmost importance for the well-being of our spiritual *psyches*. Of course, few readers through the centuries have failed to see that Mark wishes to save our souls by means of his narrative, but few readers have appreciated sufficiently the rhetorical, narrative strategies Mark employs to pursue this aim. Mark's narrative wants to "save" us, yes, but that will happen only, the narrative says, if we are willing to "lose" our ourselves to it.

For the reader of Mark's Gospel, Jesus is the experience of reading Mark's Gospel, and reading Mark's Gospel is experiencing Jesus. That Jesus himself is somehow the focal point of most of Mark's paradoxical constructs, both verbal and dramatic, is therefore appropriate. This focus is evident in 9:37 and 10:45, where the second and third of our three verbal paradoxes are interpreted (by Jesus, of course), one by direct and explicit reference to Jesus (9:37) and the other by indirect reference to himself as "Son of man" (10:45). "Being first" by "being last" means "receiving" Jesus (9:37). "Being great" and "first" by "being servant" and "slave" means following in the footsteps of the "Son of man," who "gives his life as a ransom for many" (10:45; cf. 8:34; 10:32a). Coming to grips with Mark's paradoxes is an interpretive process

42. Continuing the process of interpreting figures with other figures, the "coming of the Son of man in glory" in 8:38 is refigured in 9:1 as the "coming of the Kingdom of God with power."

that opens us up to the process of coming to grips with who and what the Jesus of this Gospel is.

At this point some comments on the extended, dramatic paradoxical turns in Mark's narrative are appropriate. The difficulty here is that Mark's Gospel is so fraught with incongruity that there is no end to what might be identified as moments of extended or dramatic paradox in the reading experience. Mark's propensity for the incongruous has usually led critics to reach for paradoxical expressions in order to summarize Mark's narrative (or their experience of reading Mark's narrative). At the beginning of the twentieth century, William Wrede initiated a scholarly fox hunt for the solution to the Messianic Secret. The hunt continues to this day. Paradoxical expressions comparable to Messianic Secret would be Martin Dibelius's description of Mark as a "book of secret epiphanies" or T. A. Burkill's characterization of Mark as "mysterious revelation." Perhaps even more vivid is Nils Dahl's proposal that the major theme of Mark is the "Crucified Messiah," which does more justice to the prominence of the Passion narrative in Mark and the paradoxical confluence of power and powerlessness we encounter in Mark's Jesus.[43] Note that none of these verbally paradoxical expressions comes directly from the Gospel. Rather, they are each the coinage of a twentieth-century critic. Mark himself would probably not agree that whatever he is trying to accomplish by means of his narrative could be adequately summarized in the form of a single paradoxical expression. Rather, the kind of paradoxical truth that Mark offers us is the truth of paradox lived, not merely described verbally. The modern paradoxical expressions I mentioned are best understood as modern critics' summary descriptions of the end result of their reading experience, during which they experienced countless moments of paradoxical incongruity. Each of these summary statements does some justice to the final perspective gained on the Gospel from the vantage point of the end of the reading experience. They do not, however, do justice to the temporal experience of reading. When reading Mark, we are challenged again and again to find a way for ourselves between polar opposites.

Two other critical readers' comments on Mark's paradoxical nature are of particular interest here. One of the most provocative discussions of Mark in our era is Theodore Weeden's *Mark: Traditions in Conflict*,[44] which has revolutionized our understanding of Mark's story. Perhaps more than any other modern scholar, he has enabled us to discern that at the story level of Mark's narrative the disciples of Jesus are shocking failures. As Weeden himself puts it: "I conclude that Mark is assiduously involved in a vendetta against the

43. Wrede, *The Messianic Secret;* Martin Dibelius, *From Tradition to Gospel,* trans. B. L. Woolf (New York: Scribner's, n.d.), 230; T. A. Burkill, *Mysterious Revelation: An Examination of the Philosophy of St. Mark's Gospel* (Ithaca, N.Y.: Cornell University Press, 1963); Nils Alstrup Dahl, *The Crucified Messiah and Other Essays* (Minneapolis: Augsburg, 1974).
44. Theodore J. Weeden, *Mark: Traditions in Conflict* (Philadelphia: Fortress Press, 1971).

disciples. He is intent on totally discrediting them. He paints them as obtuse, obdurate, recalcitrant men who at first are unperceptive of Jesus' messiahship, then oppose its style and character, and finally totally reject it. As the coup de grace, Mark closes his Gospel without rehabilitating the disciples."[45] Weeden's reading of the role of the Twelve in Mark's story is controversial enough, but he also posits an equally controversial historical and theological explanation for Mark's portrayal of the Twelve. Weeden suggests that the vendetta against the Twelve is a disguised attack by the flesh-and-blood author against his own flesh-and-blood theological opponents, who proclaim the Twelve as their heroes and models.[46] Rather than delving into Weeden's hypothetical first-century theological controversy, in which Mark opposes a "divine man christology" that sees Jesus as a wonder-working divine man of power, glory, and authority, I shall concentrate on the reading experience that lies behind Weeden's hypothesizing about first-century Christian theological controversies.

Crucial to his historical reconstruction is his observation that in the first half of the Gospel Jesus is a figure of great power and authority, but in the second half the emphasis shifts radically to self-denial, self-sacrifice, suffering, and death. Weeden explains this incongruity in the fabric of the narrative by suggesting that Mark is setting up his opponents in the first half of the Gospel by portraying Jesus in a way that is congenial to the opponents' understanding of him as a divine man of power, glory, and authority. Then midway through the Gospel, Jesus begins to insist that his mission is to suffer and die rather than to wield power and authority.[47] The disciples of Jesus, seduced by Jesus' wonder-working power in the first half, are unable to change directions along with Jesus in the second half. In the end, the disciples repudiate and reject Jesus. Their utter failure is a disguised repudiation of Mark's theological opponents.

Weeden argues that the first half of the Gospel sets up the second half and gives way to it.[48] The second half of the narrative supplants the first and

45. Ibid., 50–51.

46. Ibid., 148 and passim.

47. Here is one token of the radical shift that does indeed occur in the middle of the narrative: Early in the Gospel the narrator introduces Jesus to the reader as Son of man in the parenthetical comments in 2:10 and 2:28. Mark 2:10 informs the reader that the Son of man has authority (*exousia*); 2:28 that the Son of man is lord (*kyrios*) of the sabbath. These are both to be taken as reliable, accurate, although perhaps ambiguous, descriptions of Jesus. Then, much later in the Gospel, the topics of authority and lordship arise again in 10:42, but there Jesus warns against the vices of authoritarianism (*katexousiazō*) and lording it over one's subjects (*katakyrieuō*). Apparently *exousia* and the role of *kyrios* are prone to abuse. Consequently, both roles are repudiated by the Son of man, who exemplifies the proper alternative by being servant and slave of all, even giving his life as a ransom for many (10:43-45). The authority and lordship that is evidently his to wield in 2:10 and 2:28 is severely ironized and critiqued in 10:42. Any account of the experience of reading Mark's Gospel must face up to the sharp incongruity of 2:10 and 2:28 versus 10:42.

48. Weeden, *Mark*, 164–65 and passim.

corrects its illegitimate portrayal of Jesus. I affirm Weeden's reading experience: he has grasped significant incongruities between the portrayal of Jesus in chapters 1–8 and in chapters 8–16. I disagree, however, that the second half of the Gospel supplants the first. Weeden has not handled paradoxical incongruity as shrewdly as he might. He has perceived the wide-ranging paradoxical tension in Mark and tried to deal with it by repudiating one pole of the paradoxical incongruity in order to embrace the other pole. Nevertheless, Mark is craftier than Weeden allows. Mark wants us to live through the experience of encountering *both* Jesus' wonder-working power and authority in the first half of the Gospel *and* his self-denial and powerlessness that leads to the cross in the second half. Whereas Weeden ends up with a narrative that is relatively straightforward and clear, thanks to the jettisoning of the conceptual point of view (i.e., theology) of chapters 1–8, I insist that reading chapters 1–16 is from beginning to end a journey through the valley of paradox. In this valley the incongruous and the ambiguous greet us at every turn, up to and beyond the end of the narrative.

Werner Kelber has argued, in response to Weeden, that to do justice to the reading of the whole Gospel we must allow paradoxical incongruities to stand on their own two legs and resist the temptation to amputate one leg or the other. Kelber summarizes the experience of reading Mark's entire paradoxical narrative as follows:

> Jesus announces the Kingdom but opts for the cross; he is King of the Jews but condemned by the Jewish establishment; he asks for followers but speaks in riddles; he is identified as Nazarene but rejected in Nazareth; he makes public pronouncements but also hides behind a screen of secrecy; he saves others but not himself; he promises return but has not returned; he performs miracles but suffers a non-miraculous death; he is a successful exorciser but dies overcome by demonic forces; he is appointed by God in power but dies abandoned by God in powerlessness; he dies but rises from death. His beginning is nebulous and his future status is indefinite, and at the moment of Messianic disclosure he still speaks enigmatically of himself in the third person (14:62; cf. 8:31; 9:31; 10:33-34). If there is one single feature which characterizes the [Markan] Jesus it is contradiction or paradox. It might therefore be argued that "[Mark] presents not two conflicting views of Jesus" but one complex "paradoxical view" ([Kim] Dewey).[49]

With the exceptions of "he saves others but not himself" (cf. 15:31) and "he dies but rises from death" (cf. 16:6), Kelber borrows none of these paradoxical statements directly from the Gospel itself. With these two exceptions, what

---

49. Werner H. Kelber, "Conclusion: From Passion Narrative to Gospel," in *The Passion in Mark: Studies on Mark 14–16*, ed. Werner H. Kelber (Philadelphia: Fortress Press, 1976), 179.

we have here is a catalogue of one reader's insights into moments of extended or dramatic paradox in his experience of reading Mark's Gospel. Kelber has articulated clearly and explicitly moments of paradoxical insight that came to him in his encounter with a discourse that is typically implicit and indirect. This report is a model of one reader's response to a paradoxical narrative.

8

MOVES OF GREATER UNCERTAINTY

Although Mark's rhetoric of indirection occasionally leads us to a moment of clarity, the clarity achieved tends to be paradoxical, two incongruous voices speaking at once. That even in moments of relative clarity Mark's indirection avoids univocality is a reminder of that family characteristic I have called uncertainty. Even in momentary clarity, if discourse is indirect, uncertainty lingers. Frequently, however, our narrator avoids leading us into any kind of clarity whatsoever, and there uncertainty reigns supreme. Uncertainty hovers over irony, metaphor, and paradox, but the moves of greater uncertainty are ambiguity and opacity. Thus I shall now focus on that portion of Mark's spectrum of indirect moves in which clarity is intentionally avoided. As Kenneth Burke might put it, "what we want is *not terms that avoid ambiguity* [or opacity], but *terms that clearly reveal the strategic spots at which ambiguities* [and opacities] *necessarily arise.*"[1]

AMBIGUITY

Reading Mark 8:11-13 is an instructive encounter with uncertainty: "The Pharisees came and began to argue with him, seeking from him a sign from heaven, to test him. And he sighed deeply in his spirit, and said, 'Why does this generation seek a sign? Truly, I say to you, no sign shall be given to this generation.' And he left them, and getting into the boat again he departed to the other side." Modern readers tend to regard this passage as a brief sketch of the Pharisees' opposition to Jesus at story level or as a throwaway transition in the narrator's discourse, an interlude in which the narrator can catch his breath. However, considering the passage more seriously, primarily at the level of discourse, is worthwhile. Mark 8:11 is a request for certainty, resolution, and clear referential ("sign") meaning. The Pharisees ask Jesus for

---

1. Kenneth Burke, *A Grammar of Motives* (New York: Prentice-Hall, 1945), xviii; Burke's italics.

an escape from uncertainty, and he turns them down. This passage demonstrates clearly to the reader that this narrative will not strive for clarity at any price. Clarity is not always its highest priority.

Complicating the reading of 8:11-13 and all moments of ambiguity or opacity in Mark is the modern critical spirit that scorns ambiguity and yearns for clarity. On the subject of clarity, we moderns are closer to the Pharisees in 8:11 than we are to Jesus. We would prefer Mark and his version of Jesus to be clear and direct rather than ambiguous and indirect. For moderns to appreciate the strategic uses of ambiguity in narrative discourse is therefore extraordinarily difficult. The prevailing prejudice concerning ambiguity in language is that it is a defect, a pathological departure from the presumed norms of clarity and directness. Donald N. Levine has discussed what he calls the "flight from ambiguity" in modern Western culture. Along with the rise of science came a bias against figurative, allusive, ambiguous language and a bias in favor of mathematical exactitude and univocality.[2] Levine argues that premodern cultures generally were and are far more comfortable with ambiguity and other forms of indirection than are we, and therefore they are better able to exploit its constructive uses. As a result of his study of the Amhara culture in Ethiopia, Levine posits four major sociological functions of ambiguous discourse: (1) ambiguity can serve as a useful strategy for promoting enlightenment (e.g., teaching through parables, paradox, and other forms of indirection); (2) ambiguity can provide an effective means of achieving affective response; it communicates "expressive overtones and suggestive allusions"; (3) ambiguity can provide a shield of obscurity behind which to hide; and (4) ambiguity in the articulation of social relationships can be a wise way of avoiding rigidity and maintaining flexibility in those relationships.[3] Levine thus suggests that ambiguity has many constructive uses in social relations, and I suggest that these uses have their analogies in narrative discourse.

Others have invited us to consider the possible benefits of ambiguity. Long ago Aristotle noted that ambiguity of expression is not necessarily a faulty use of language; sometimes a situation calls for an ambiguous utterance.[4] In our own time, Ludwig Wittgenstein uses the metaphor of photography— a clear, distinct photograph is not always what we need in a particular situation—to rethink the modern, Western prejudice against ambiguity and for

2. "The movement against ambiguity led by Western intellectuals since the seventeenth century figures as a unique development in world history. There is nothing like it in any premodern culture known to me" (Donald N. Levine, *The Flight from Ambiguity: Essays in Social and Cultural Theory* [Chicago and London: University of Chicago Press, 1985], 21).

3. Ibid., 29–36.

4. The example offered by Aristotle, however, is not very illuminating: fortune tellers who make vague predictions so as not to be caught easily in a false prediction; *Rhetoric* III.5/1407a–b.

clarity and univocality.[5] Once Burke, Levine, Aristotle, Wittgenstein, and others[6] are enlisted to help us to recognize that ambiguity is not necessarily a defect in language and that it can be a very useful tool in one's language toolbox, we are well on our way toward an appreciation of the rhetorical possibilities of ambiguity. The question then becomes, How do readers handle the moments of ambiguity they encounter in the experience of reading Mark's Gospel?

Like Mark's other indirect moves, ambiguity occurs in both verbal and dramatic forms, but distinguishing between the two is difficult. Verbal ambiguity occurs when an utterance can be taken by the hearer in two or more discrete ways or when the hearer has an indefinite range of possibilities from which to choose. With an indefinite range of possibilities, we are faced with the reverberatory extension that is typical of dramatic rather than verbal forms of indirection. So this kind of verbal ambiguity would almost qualify as dramatic ambiguity. Even when the range of possibilities is limited to two or more discrete options, still a verbal ambiguity in the story is always already a verbal ambiguity at the discourse level, and so this usage too almost qualifies as dramatic ambiguity. Verbal ambiguity is never far removed from dramatic ambiguity. We might say that the difference between verbal and dramatic ambiguity is ambiguous, which seems only appropriate.

Unlike Mark's other indirect moves, dramatic ambiguity does not capitalize upon incongruity between story and discourse. Ambiguities tend to function simultaneously and congruently at the story and discourse levels, which distinguishes ambiguity from all of the other indirect moves.[7] Of all the indirect moves, in ambiguity alone the distinction between story and discourse blurs. After all, ambiguity is the business of blurring distinctions and obliterating clear boundary lines. The very possibility of clear critical distinctions, such as those between verbal and dramatic indirection or between story and discourse, is called into question by Mark's affection for ambiguity. The critic who insists on always making clear statements about the experience of reading Mark runs the risk of not hearing what Mark is saying.

These warnings notwithstanding, I shall discuss some notable instances of verbal ambiguity that occur primarily in the story. Following that, I shall examine ambiguities that function primarily at the discourse level.

The chief proponent of indirect speech in the story is Jesus, who, if we can believe the narrator, never speaks without a riddle (*parabolē*) on his lips (4:34), that is, among other things, his speech is persistently ambiguous.

5. Ludwig Wittgenstein, *Philosophical Investigations,* trans. G. E. M. Anscombe (New York: Macmillan, 1953), 34, section 71.

6. See William Empson, who uses the term *ambiguity* far more broadly than I (*Seven Types of Ambiguity* [New York: New Directions, 1947]).

7. This includes opacity, which shares with ambiguity a prominent devotion to uncertainty, but unlike ambiguity involves the sharpest possible incongruity between story and discourse.

Occasionally he provides a modest interpretation of a verbal metaphor (e.g., the physician metaphor in 2:17), but usually he does not (e.g., the leaven metaphor in 8:15[8]). Likewise, Jesus' extended metaphorical discourses only rarely receive interpretive clarification (e.g., the interpretation of the sower parable in 4:14-20), and even this kind of interpretation is an invitation to further interpretation because it substitutes a new ambiguous challenge for the old one. Jesus' metaphorical, ironic, and paradoxical speech always has a shadow of uncertainty about it, but here we are interested in indirect turns that have uncertainty as their foremost characteristic.

A masterpiece of ambiguity occurs in 12:17: "Render to Caesar the things that are Caesar's, and to God the things that are God's." Here Jesus appears to draw a sharp dividing line between the things of Caesar and the things of God, but where is it? What things belong to which side? The line neatly divides reality in two, and yet the silence about where the line actually falls is a master stroke of indirection. Such clarity and yet such ambiguity! Thus do clarity and ambiguity, direction and indirection, often dance together.

Consider the brief conversation between Pilate and Jesus in 15:2. The English translation in the RSV reads: "And Pilate asked him, 'Are you the King of the Jews?' And he answered him, 'You have said so.' " Ancient Greek texts had no question marks, and the phrasing of a question and a declarative statement in Greek is often identical. Pilate's "question," although clearly labeled a question by the narrator, is worded in such a way that it would work perfectly well as a statement of fact: *su ei ho basileus tōn Ioudaiōn.* Moreover, Jesus' "answer" is worded in such a way that it would work equally well as a question: *su legeis?* To grasp the ambiguities of the Greek, an English speaker needs to read the following translation alongside the RSV's: "And Pilate asked him, 'You are the King of the Jews.' And he answered him, 'Are you saying so?' " Any alert reader of Greek would have perceived that Pilate's question to Jesus is simultaneously the narrator's declaration to the reader and that Jesus' declaration to Pilate is the narrator's question addressed to the reader. The ambiguity of both Pilate's and Jesus' utterances allows the language to work at different levels and in different directions simultaneously.

Another example of story-level ambiguity wielded by Jesus is the debate over the son of David in 12:35-37. Here Jesus questions how the Christ can be the son of David, in that David himself calls the Christ his "Lord" (*Kyrios*), according to Jesus' reading of Psalm 110: "David himself calls him Lord; so

---

8. See the impressive clarification of this metaphor in Matt. 16:12 and Luke 12:1. This is a key strategy for discovering early readers' perceptions of ambiguity in Mark: find the clarifications made by Matthew and Luke and work backwards. This is not to say, of course, that we actually undo Matthew's or Luke's clarification and thereby recover a pristine moment of ambiguity in reading Mark. To the contrary, "once clarified, always clarified." I shall discuss in chapter 9 the influence exerted by Matthew and Luke over how all subsequent readers read Mark.

how is he his son?" (12:37). Jesus seems to be challenging the popular first-century Jewish notion that the coming Christ is a (or the[9]) Son of David, so the point of Jesus' rhetorical question in 12:37 may be to reject altogether the idea of the Davidic descent of the Messiah. Then again, maybe he means that the Messiah *is* the son of David but in a sense (figurative?) different from the prevailing one (of literal, physical descent?). The answer to the "how" question of 12:37 remains ambiguous.[10]

Jesus thus uses ambiguity as a rhetorical tool to provoke response from his listeners. At the story level, he is spectacularly unsuccessful. Virtually nowhere is Jesus' rhetoric of indirection fathomed. Other characters in Mark speak just as ambiguously as Jesus, but little note is made of their ambiguous comments at story level. One such example of characters other than Jesus speaking ambiguously may be noted briefly.

One of the many verbal ambiguities in the Passion narrative occurs at Jesus' trial. The priests and elders lose control of themselves and start to abuse the condemned man: "And some began to spit on him, and cover his face, and to strike him, saying to him, 'Prophesy!' " (14:65). "Prophesy what?" we might ask. The answer is by no means clear. Matthew and Luke both take up Mark's ambiguous clue that the abusers covered Jesus' face and use it to clarify the ambiguous command: "Prophesy! [to us, you Christ! (Matthew)] Who is it that struck you?" (Matt. 26:67; Luke 22:64). Matthew and Luke may be making explicit what is implicit in Mark, namely, that a blindfolded Jesus is called upon to identify those striking him, but in specifying carefully what Jesus is supposed to prophesy in the story, Matthew and Luke effectively eliminate further ambiguous reverberations that function at the discourse level in Mark. In the instant that Jesus is challenged to "prophesy!" in the story, the reader realizes that Jesus' most significant prophecy in the Gospel, the prediction of his suffering and death, is in the process of being fulfilled in the story, even though no one in the story takes note of such fulfillment. The verbal ambiguity of "prophesy!" at story level reverberates also at the level of discourse, at least as far back as the Passion prediction in Mark 10:32-34, and perhaps even further. "Prophesy!" entices the reader into a moment of far-ranging retrospection and prospection.

Ambiguity nudges the reader to connect and clarify hitherto unconnected and ambiguous moments in the reading experience. The encounter with ambiguity can be, at one time or another, provocation, question, challenge, encouragement, or opportunity for the reader. Paradoxically, perhaps, the ambiguity in Mark 14:65 offers a richer reading experience than Matthew and

9. "Son of David" is artfully ambiguous because it lacks the definite article in Greek, a topic to which I shall return later.

10. See Vernon Robbins, "The Healing of Blind Bartimaeus (Mark 10:46-52) in the Marcan Theology," *JBL* 92 (1973): 240. In a similar fashion, other unanswered questions posed in the story present the hearer or reader with challenges of ambiguity.

Luke's clarified versions. For one thing, ambiguity both allows and encourages the reader to clarify and connect elements of the narrative for himself, and we take more seriously the connections and clarifications that we ourselves make than those that are handed to us ready-made. Moreover, the reader's labor in clarifying ambiguities creates a more extensive network of narrative fabric than is possible with a clear and direct narrative, which gives the reader less work to do.

Many ambiguities in the story reverberate also in the discourse, but many more are obviously strategies of the narrator's discourse only, to be taken up and experienced by the reader alone. I shall consider here some evidence of ambiguity in the discourse collected by Frans Neirynck and Philip Harner.

In his massive catalogue of editorial changes that Matthew and Luke introduced in their respective re-visions of Mark, Frans Neirynck notes two categories of particular interest.[11] One category is instances in which Matthew or Luke specify the subject of a verb that is unspecified in Mark, and the other category is instances in which they specify a direct or indirect object that is unspecified in Mark.[12] Although many of Matthew and Luke's clarifications are insignificant, the important point to grasp is that Mark often leaves figuring out the subjects and objects of his sentences to the reader. Often any reader can easily clear up such ambiguities, but occasionally they are remarkably intriguing.

Critics have long recognized that Mark likes to use "impersonal plurals"; the narrator says that "they" did this or that but who the "they" are is not instantly obvious to the reader.[13] Frequently Matthew, Luke, or both specify the "they" and thus clarify Mark's ambiguity for their own readers. For example, in Mark 2:18 some unspecified persons ask Jesus about his disciples' not practicing fasting, but Matthew 9:14 specifies that the disciples of John the Baptist did the asking. In Mark 3:2 unspecified persons in a synagogue watch Jesus closely in hopes of catching him violating the sabbath, but Luke 6:7 specifies that Jesus' opponents here were "the scribes and the Pharisees."

Sometimes rather than specifying the unstated subject, Matthew or Luke has resorted to the broader editorial stroke of cutting out the ambiguous word or phrase in Mark. One such example, Mark 3:21, says with artful ambiguity that Jesus' "associates"[14] (hoi par'autou) set out to seize him because they think he has gone crazy. The ambiguity of who these associates are creates

11. Frans Neirynck, with Theo Hansen and Frans Van Segbroeck, The Minor Agreements of Matthew and Luke Against Mark with a Cumulative List, BETL 37 (Leuven: Leuven University Press, 1974).

12. Ibid., 261–72.

13. Ibid., 266; and see my Loaves and Fishes: The Function of the Feeding Stories in the Gospel of Mark, SBLDS 54 (Chico, Calif.: Scholars Press, 1981) 78–79, 207.

14. "His associates" is the "deliberately ambiguous translation" of Sherman Johnson, who tries to preserve the ambiguity of the Greek (A Commentary on the Gospel According to St. Mark [London: Black, 1960], 80).

suspense that engages the reader throughout the metaphor-filled debate over Jesus' exorcisms that follows in 3:22-30. When we reach Mark 3:31, Jesus' mother and brothers arrive to fetch him; it is *they* who think he is crazy and would seize him if they could! *They* are his "associates." Matthew and Luke, who hold Jesus' family in higher esteem than Mark, completely destroy this revelatory moment in the reading of Mark 3:31-35 by deleting Mark 3:21 altogether (see Matt. 12:22-37 and Luke 11:14-23). They object, not to the ambiguity of 3:21, but to the startling clarification that it receives in 3:31-35.[15] In response to Mark, their Gospels paint a far more direct, clear, and positive picture of Jesus' family. They have thus influenced, if not completely controlled, how readers of the Gospels through the centuries have grasped Mark's more indirect and unflattering presentation of Jesus' family.

Turning now to the ambiguity of unspecified objects, consider two tantalizing moments of reading involving Jesus and the temple. The instances I want to consider pivot on the ambiguous or "inexact" use of the third-person personal pronoun *autos* ("he, she, or it").[16] The first occurs in Mark 11:17-18: "And he taught and said to them: 'Is it not written, "My house shall be called a house of prayer for all the nations"? But you have made *auton* a den of robbers.' And the chief priests and the scribes heard and sought how they might destroy *auton*. For [*gar*] they feared *auton*. For [*gar*] all the multitude was astonished at the teaching *autou*" (RMF). *Autos* occurs four times in these two verses, each time ambiguous and each needing clarification. The first *auton* (11:17) presents no problem to the reader; it must have as its antecedent the temple, "the house of prayer for all the nations" that Jesus says has been turned into a "den of robbers." When Jesus makes this metaphorical and ironic identification between the temple of God and a den of robbers, the chief priests and scribes respond immediately by seeking to destroy *auton* (11:18a). Now, does this second *auton* also refer us back to the temple? Do the chief priests and scribes respond to Jesus' criticism of the corrupted temple by seeking to destroy it? As surprising as this may be, 11:18a can be read in exactly that way. We read next that the chief priests and scribes "fear *auton*" (11:18b). Here, too, *auton* is ambiguous, but that they would fear *Jesus,* for whatever reason, seems more likely than fearing their own *temple.* This reading is confirmed when we reach the end of 11:18. We read there that the authorities feared whatever it was that they feared because of the astonishment of the crowd at the teaching of him or it (*autou* is the masculine or neuter genitive singular form of *autos*). Here, at last, we can achieve some clarity and certainty. The temple does not teach, but Jesus does. Working backwards, we can see clearly now that the authorities fear *Jesus* because of

---

15. Besides deleting Mark 3:21, they both carefully dismantle, in different ways, the intercalation in Mark 3:20-21, 22-30, 31-35.

16. The possibilities of "inexact" use of *autos* are noted in BAGD.

the crowd's reception of *his* teaching, and this fear leads the authorities to try to destroy *him,* not their temple. All the *autos*es of 11:17-18 have now been fathomed and clarified. Nevertheless, has not a seed of thought been planted in the mind of the reader that something mysterious and unarticulated connects Jesus and the temple? If the authorities were to destroy Jesus, might they not at the same time in some way be destroying their own temple?

Modern critics have often failed to appreciate the ambiguous *auton* of 11:18a because all readers tend to clarify ambiguities in the act of reading and then read their clarifications back into the text. We do not usually stop to contemplate that we know that the *auton* of 11:18a refers to Jesus only because 11:18b makes this reference perfectly clear in retrospect. We forget that as of 11:18a we did not—and could not—know what that *auton* referred to. The ambiguous *auton* in 11:18a gets us to step with it in one direction (toward the temple) and then in another (toward Jesus), as it leads us through its dance steps. So anxious are we to grasp and hold on to the clear insights that (sometimes) result from working through ambiguity that we have often not appreciated sufficiently the process of working toward those insights. In reading we have often experienced far more than we have been taught to recollect, to put into words, and to appreciate.

Moreover, not only do readers tend to read their clarifications back into the narrative but also they read the text through the record of the clarifications of those who have gone before us. We often merely retrace the footsteps of the readers who have read before us.

For example, how do Matthew and Luke handle the four *autos*es in Mark 11:17-18, especially the critical second one? Matthew deletes Mark 11:18 altogether (Matt. 21:12-13) and so eliminates the ambiguous *auton*. Luke keeps both the *auton* in Mark 11:17 (Luke 19:46) and the crucially ambiguous one in Mark 11:18a (Luke 19:47b), but he inserts a clarifying clause in Luke 19:47a: "And he was teaching daily in the temple." This clause distinguishes Jesus from the temple and at the same time establishes Jesus as the antecedent for the *auton* that will occur in the next clause. Thus do Matthew and Luke exemplify the process of clarifying Mark's narrative that all readers of Mark practice, especially those who have read and been influenced by Matthew and Luke.

A second temple-related ambiguity occurs in the scene in which Jesus dies coincident to the temple suffering serious damage. "And Jesus uttered a loud cry and expired. And the curtain of the temple was torn in two, from top to bottom. And when the centurion, who stood opposite *autou,* saw that he expired like this, he said: 'Truly, this man was son of God' " (15:37-39, RMF). The death cry of Jesus (15:37) and the curtain of the temple being torn in two (15:38) are starkly juxtaposed. The result is a classic case of what

Iser (following Roman Ingarden) calls a spot of indeterminacy[17]: what relationship, if any, we should posit between Jesus' death and the tearing of the curtain is by no means clear. Modern commentators frequently discuss the possible symbolic significance of the tearing of the curtain vis-à-vis the crucifixion of Jesus, but few observe how the narrative all but demands that we explore the ambiguous possibilities. To be sure, Mark's narrative has already hinted several times about possible connections between the death of Jesus and the destruction of the temple (recall the discussion of 11:17-18), so the juxtaposition of Jesus' death and a torn temple curtain does not initiate reflection but rather encourages us to continue previous reflections in this vein.[18]

Because the centurion "who stood opposite *autou*" (*ho parestēkōs ex enantias autou*) is introduced here for the first time in the Passion narrative, we do not know this character or where he is stationed. We may presume that he is the officer in charge of the execution squad, but confirmation comes later, in 15:44. When we are told that the centurion "stood opposite *autou*," therefore, we do not know whether he stands opposite Jesus or the temple.[19] Because the temple in 15:38 is the most immediate masculine or neuter antecedent to the *autou* in 15:39, the reader's first suspicion could be that the centurion is stationed over against the temple, just as Jesus once positioned himself "over against the temple" (*katenanti tou hierou*) on the hill across the Kidron Valley from the temple mount (13:3).

When the narrator goes on in 15:39 to say that the centurion saw that "he expired" (*exepneusen*), that the centurion is observing the death of Jesus becomes clear. An additional ambiguity asserts itself, however. What the centurion saw was "that *thus* he expired" or "that he expired *like this*" (*hoti houtōs exepneusen*), and the allusion is quite unclear. Is the centurion astonished by the exhausted Jesus' loud death cry (often commented upon by modern commentators), by the damage suffered by the temple, *or both?* We must allow Mark to arrange scenery and actors on the stage as he sees fit, and his positioning of the centurion here is provocatively ambiguous vis-à-vis Jesus

17. Wolfgang Iser, *The Act of Reading: A Theory of Aesthetic Response* (Baltimore and London: Johns Hopkins University Press, 1978), 170–73.

18. I hear in 15:38 the echoes of the rending and tearing elsewhere in Mark; e.g., 2:18-22 and 14:63. Michel Clevenot, an interpreter of Fernando Belo's work, agrees. He, like I, argues that tearing in the story is a figure for the effect of the discourse on the narratee. Mark's Gospel, he claims, is itself a disruptive force, a tearing of "symbolic codes" of "social formation" (*Materialist Approaches to the Bible*, trans. William J. Nottingham [Maryknoll, N.Y.: Orbis, 1985], 76).

19. Commentators typically fail to acknowledge the initial ambiguity of the *autou* in 15:39: "[The centurion's] position by the cross is carefully described; he stands by over against Jesus" (Vincent Taylor, *The Gospel According to St. Mark*, 2d ed. [New York: St. Martin's Press, 1966], 597); or "Dem Kreuz gegenüber stehend, beobachtete er den Tod Jesu" (Joachim Gnilka, *Das Evangelium nach Markus*, EKKNT, 2 vols. [Zürich, Einsiedln, Köln: Benziger; Neukirchen-Vluyn: Neukirchener Verlag, 1979] 2:324).

and/or the temple. Regardless of what we make of this ambiguity, no reader
can fail to discern that, as far as the narrator is concerned, Jesus' fate is
somehow linked to the fate of the temple (recall 11:17-18, 14:58, and 15:29).

We have evidence that early readers of Mark recognized the ambiguity
of both *autou* and *houtōs* in Mark 15:39. The scribes who produced early
manuscript copies of Mark often replaced *ex enantias autou* with either the
dative form *autō* ("by" or "with him") or the adverb of place *ekei* ("there").
The former gives us a centurion "who stood by him," the latter a centurion
"who stood there." In either case that the centurion is positioned in relationship
to Jesus and not to the temple is made somewhat clearer. Regarding *hoti
houtōs exepneusen,* a number of copyists added an explicit mention of Jesus'
death cry, which clarifies that the centurion responds to Jesus' death and not
to the temple's calamity. With regard to the *houtōs,* Matthew and Luke handle
the ambiguity much differently. Matthew and Luke both make clear that the
centurion responds not only to the death of Jesus but most especially to the
extraordinary events that accompany it, including the rending of the curtain.
Luke takes up the mention of the torn curtain in Mark 15:39 and relocates it
after Mark 15:33, thus connecting the darkness over the land with the torn
curtain. In Luke the centurion responds to the darkness and the torn curtain,
as well as to the death of Jesus (Luke 23:44-47). Matthew's strategy is to
leave the torn curtain in its place in Mark but to add further supernatural
portents, such as an earthquake and the resurrection of dead "holy ones,"
who then appear in Jerusalem. In Matthew the centurion and his companions
make their collective response *primarily* in response to these portents accom-
panying the death of Jesus (Matt. 27:51-54). In the course of all this clarifying
labor, both Matthew and Luke delete both the ambiguous *ex enantias autou*
and the ambiguous *houtōs* in their revisions of Mark 15:39. They go about
clarifying Mark 15:37-39 differently, but they agree to the extent that they
both see the need to eliminate Mark's ambiguous expressions.

Another ambiguity occurs when the centurion makes his ironic acclamation of Jesus as "son of God" at the end of 15:39. Although critical readers
almost universally regard this statement as the grand denouement in the Gospel,
wherein one who stands opposed to Jesus sees the light and confesses the
Gospel-truth to which Mark's entire narrative is dedicated, I am not so confident about this common reading. Some ironies and ambiguities in the "centurion's confession" need to be recognized and explored.

Philip Harner has discussed the ambiguity of the centurion's confession
in an article on the use of "qualitative anarthrous predicate nouns."[20] Harner
is responding to what has come to be known as Colwell's Rule, a point of
grammar concerning Greek word order discussed in an article by E. C. Colwell

20. Philip B. Harner, "Qualitative Anarthrous Predicate Nouns: Mark 15:39 and John 1:1,"
JBL 92 (1973): 75-87.

in 1933.[21] The question is whether a predicate noun lacking the definite article cannot in fact be understood as a definite noun, if it precedes the copulative verb. Colwell demonstrates that such a sentence structure is common in New Testament Greek, and he formulates the rule that "definite predicate nouns which precede the verb *usually* lack the article."[22] Although he makes a convincing case, he admits that the rule he proposes, like all rules of grammar, has its exceptions. The word *usually* in his statement of the rule thus deserves to be emphasized.

Colwell noted that by applying his rule we can argue that the problematic phrase attributed to the centurion in Mark 15:39 (*alēthōs houtos ho anthrōpos huios theou ēn*) could be translated, "Truly, this man was *the* Son of God," instead of "Truly, this man was *a* son of God." The expression *huios theou* ("son of god") lacks the definite article in the Greek, but it precedes the copulative verb "was" (*ēn*), and so on the basis of Hellenistic Greek grammar we can argue that the definiteness of the noun is implied. Colwell concluded, modestly: "The evidence given in this paper as to the use of the article with predicate nouns *strengthens the probability* that the centurion recognized Jesus as *the* Son of God (so Weymouth and the older English translations), rather than as *a* son of God."[23]

Colwell's carefully qualified rule and his modestly stated conclusions have been reified and turned into Colwell's Rule, which has been brandished like a sword to vanquish ambiguity. Harner helps us to demystify the often unquestioned authority granted to Colwell's Rule. Harner's major concern is something all but ignored by Colwell, anarthrous predicate nouns that are more significant for their qualitative aspect than for either their definiteness or their indefiniteness; that is, often neither definiteness or indefiniteness is what these constructions are about, but rather the "nature or character of the subject."[24] In my language, Harner is saying that Mark and other New Testament writers use anarthrous predicate nouns thoughtfully and intriguingly to engage the reader through the use of ambiguity. The critic's eagerness to find nouns either clearly definite or clearly indefinite reveals more about the modern yearning for clarity than it does about the syntax of Mark's Greek.

Harner discusses eight instances of anarthrous predicate nouns in Mark, several of which are noteworthy here because they apply weighty titles to Jesus with strategic ambiguity.[25] The most important of Harner's passages is

21. E. C. Colwell, "A Definite Rule for the Use of the Article in the Greek New Testament," *JBL* 52 (1933): 12–21.

22. Ibid., 20; emphasis added.

23. Ibid., 21; emphasis added.

24. Harner, "Mark 15:39," 75.

25. The eight instances discussed by Harner are Mark 2:28; 3:35; 6:49; 11:17, 32; 12:35; 14:70; 15:39.

The anarthrous predicate noun in 2:28 is *kyrios* ("lord"), an inherently ambiguous title in

the "centurion's confession" in 15:39. He makes a good start by suggesting that the qualitative significance of the anarthrous *huios theou* matters, and not its definiteness or indefiniteness. I would go further to point out ambiguities and ironies in 15:39 that not even Harner has reckoned with fully.

Harner is on the right track when he notes that if Mark had wanted to have the centurion state unambiguously either that Jesus was "a son of God" or "the Son of God," he could easily have worded the centurion's comment unambiguously. On the basis of a study of Mark's syntax, Harner concludes that Mark is usually careful in his use of both definite and indefinite nouns.[26] In other words, Mark has strategically chosen to employ ambiguity here.

> It is doubtful whether any English translation can adequately represent the qualitative emphasis that Mark expresses in 15:39 by placing an anarthrous predicate before the verb. Perhaps the verse could be best translated, "Truly this man was God's son." This has the advantage of calling attention to Jesus' role or nature as son of God. It minimizes the question whether the word "son" should be understood as indefinite or definite. At the same time it leaves open the possibility that Mark was thinking of Jesus at this point as "a" son of God in the hellenistic sense, or "the" son of God in a specifically Christian sense, *or possibly both.* In all of these ways the translation "God's son" would reflect the various shades of meaning that may be present in Mark's word-order.[27]

In short, Harner recommends an English translation that preserves the ambiguity of the Greek rather than vanquishing it. Where I have italicized above Harner has a footnote in which he points out the direction that I want to explore further. He observes that "some commentators resolve this ambiguity [N.B.] of the phrase by suggesting that it meant a divine being of some kind on the lips of the centurion, but something more than this for Mark."[28] Harner makes this comment only in the footnote and does not pursue it further in his article. What he is acknowledging is that an expression can work one way at story level while working in another way at discourse level. If this possibility is taken seriously, then we can begin to make sense out of what is happening both in story and in discourse in 15:39.

First, we must admit that the phrasing of the centurion's utterance studiously avoids clarity. Therefore, we must admit that we do not know with any degree of certainty what the centurion, at story level, is saying. Moreover,

---

Mark and in other early Christian texts because it is a traditional designation for God in the Septuagint, as well as a confession of faith in Jesus as "Lord," to say nothing of its simple everyday connotation of "sir" or "master."

The noun in 12:35 is *huios Dauid* ("son of David"), another weighty, ambiguous title for Jesus in Mark (cf. Mark 10:47-48; 11:10).

26. Harner, "Mark 15:39," 76–77.

27. Ibid., 81; emphasis added.

28. Ibid., 81–82, n.15.

can we even be sure that, regardless of what he says, he really means what he says? Are we supposed to believe that he is speaking sincerely? I have grave doubts about his sincerity. After all, what reason do we have to trust him? For one thing, as I have noted, virtually every comment uttered by every character in Mark's Passion narrative is an oblique, indirect comment, either ironic, metaphorical, paradoxical, or ambiguous, or a combination of these. Consequently, why should we expect the centurion's utterance in 15:39 to be straightforward? Especially in view of all the mockery of Jesus that takes place at the foot of the cross, why should we think that 15:39 is not more of the same cruel verbal abuse? The narrator does not label the centurion's comment as mockery, but the narrator usually does not explicitly signal ironic speech by characters. Jesus is mocked with honorific titles all the way through the Passion narrative. On what basis do we decide that the honorific title (*if* indeed that is what it is) in 15:39 is sincere, unlike all the rest? We cannot just say that the centurion vows he is speaking "truly" (*alēthōs*) and therefore we may trust him. Insincerity masks itself in claims to truthfulness, just as the Pharisees and Herodians tried to mask their ulterior motive back in Mark 12:14 ("Teacher, we know that you are true . . .").

Besides, have we not already comprehended in our reading the essential qualities of the Roman soldiers, of whom the centurion is probably (we infer) the officer in charge? The attitude of the soldiers is revealed in Mark 15:16-20, where they conduct a mock coronation for Jesus, complete with royal purple and a crown of thorns. Then they take him out to kill him, along with two other troublemakers. While the three dying men dangle from their crosses, the narrator comments that the soldiers, having nothing better to do with their time, gamble to see who gets what from Jesus' few personal effects. Altogether, we get a vivid portrayal of a ruthless, callous execution squad. In light of this description, we can plausibly suggest that the centurion utters the last of all the mockery committed by the soldiers and the passersby. Remember also that the centurion stands "over against" Jesus and/or the temple. Why should we be surprised if he mocks the demise of both with cruel, insincere flattery?

So, in the story the centurion may be speaking insincerely and therefore ironically—or then again he may not. As is typical of irony, uncertainty lingers here as to whether the centurion's comment is ironic. Even if he is sincere, the thrust of what he says ("a son," "the Son," both, or neither?) remains ambiguous. Whichever way we turn, we cannot escape ambiguity in 15:39. If we suppose that the centurion speaks ironically, we remain uncertain about our supposition. If we suppose that he speaks sincerely, then we remain uncertain about what he is supposed to be saying. Neither can we escape some form of irony in 15:39: If the centurion speaks insincerely, then we have verbal irony here. If the centurion speaks sincerely and nonironically, then we have the reverberating, dramatic irony that the person in charge of killing

Jesus acclaims him as son of God by virtue of his death. Another dramatic irony occurs if we conclude that the centurion is speaking ironically, the double irony of a verbal irony in the story turning out to be true at the level of discourse. Thus we cannot escape irony in 15:39; dramatic irony lies in any direction we may go, and verbal irony may be there as well. Any way we read it, ambiguity and irony persist and cooperate in Mark 15:39.

If 15:39 is inescapably ironic and ambiguous, then why have scholars regarded it as the grand denouement of Mark's Gospel, the place in the Gospel where the clearest and most reliable expression of faith in Jesus is to be found? When readers argue that 15:39 is a grand denouement, they are reflecting their own reading experience and their own response to the narrative's discourse. Both what the centurion says (his locution) and what he intends to accomplish by saying it (his intended illocution) remain ambiguous at story level. At discourse level, however, no reader of Mark's Gospel has failed to grasp that the wording of the centurion's utterance can be picked up and used as an appropriate summary of the narrator's own understanding of Jesus. At the level of the narrator's discourse and from the perspective of the narrator's conceptual point of view, that the centurion's statement is "true" is in no doubt whatsoever. At the story level, we have no certainty whatsoever that the centurion's locution is either accurate or sincere. No reader fails to understand at 15:39, however, what the narrator wants him to understand, which is not what the centurian's attitude toward Jesus is but rather what the narrator's attitude toward Jesus is. By the indirect means of ambiguity and irony, the narrator is able to induct the reader into a realization of which she might have been chary, had the narrator proclaimed it boldly and directly. Mark's rhetorical strategy here can be judged only as extraordinarily effective. Only in modern times have critical readers, such as Philip Harner, begun to appreciate the rhetorical strategy employed here.[29]

As with other ambiguities in Mark, early readers took up the indirect challenges of Mark 15:39. Matthew keeps the anarthrous predicate noun (but as *theou huios* instead of *huios theou;* Matt. 27:54) and so retains some of Mark's irony and ambiguity. In Matthew, however, not just the centurion but the entire execution squad is "greatly afraid" when they speak as one voice; they seem too afraid to be mocking, and so they must be speaking sincerely. Matthew has clarified this much at least. How we should understand what the soldiers utter sincerely remains ambiguous, however, as it is in Mark.

Luke changes the centurion's comment entirely: "Now when the centurion saw what had taken place, he praised God, and said, 'Certainly this man was innocent!' " (Luke 23:47). The divine sonship of Jesus has no ambiguity here

---

29. Another scholar who has recognized that 15:39 functions simultaneously on "two levels" is Donald Juel, with James S. Ackerman and Thayer S. Warshaw, *An Introduction to New Testament Literature* (Nashville: Abingdon Press, 1978), 146.

because Luke has dropped this theme entirely. Neither is the sincerity of the centurion's statement in doubt: the reliable Lukan narrator tells us that the centurion "praises" or "glorifies" God (*edoxazen ton theon*). Virtually all of the potential for irony and ambiguity in Mark 15:39 has been dissolved in Luke.

In conclusion, in the course of reading we encounter some ambiguity that we can resolve and some other ambiguity that we cannot. We force the latter, persistent ambiguities into clarity at great risk because we can thereby forfeit the very reading experience the author offers us. Even the ambiguity that can be easily clarified leaves behind it the memories of pathways toward resolution that were considered but rejected, memories of possibilities for clarification that were offered to us but snatched away, and memories of hints and intimations that were whispered in the dark but never uttered boldly in the full light of day. The process of working through ambiguity is more important in its own right—and may be more lasting in its impact—than any clarity or resolution that may or may not be achieved along the way. Precisely when clarity or resolution is not achieved, we realize that the process of wrestling with the ambiguity rather than the final resolution itself is what matters in such an indirect rhetorical strategy. The experience of living in and working through Mark's ambiguity, in the course of reading his narrative, is what Mark's use of ambiguity is "about."

OPACITY

"Opacity" is a useful description for those moments in the reading experience when the narratee "sees" something in the narrative that characters cannot "see," or vice versa.[30] A discussion of opacity is a fitting conclusion to a discussion of the rhetoric of indirection in Mark, for in opacity Mark's repertoire of indirect moves achieves a logical culmination in two different ways simultaneously. On the one hand, moments of opacity present the moments of greatest uncertainty in the narrative; in these moments either characters or the narratee can be placed in the dark concerning what is happening in the story. To the person shut out by the veil of opacity, things in the story are

---

30. At first glance, my interest in "opacity" in Mark may resemble Frank Kermode's discussion of "secrecy" and "obscurity," Perry Kea's claim that "reticence [is] the dominating characteristic of the Gospel," or Werner Kelber's suggestion that Mark is fundamentally "parabolic" and "paradoxical"; see Frank Kermode, *The Genesis of Secrecy: On the Interpretation of Narrative* (Cambridge and London: Harvard University Press, 1979); Perry V. Kea, "Perceiving the Mystery: Encountering the Reticence of Mark's Gospel," PEGLMBS 4 (1984): 191; and Werner H. Kelber, *The Oral and the Written Gospel: The Hermeneutics of Speaking and Writing in the Synoptic Tradition, Mark, Paul, and Q* (Philadelphia: Fortress Press, 1983). What Kermode, Kea, and Kelber are all concerned with is closer to what I have called Mark's "rhetoric of indirection." I use the term "opacity" more narrowly as a label for one reading experience among many in the encounter with Mark's indirection.

not just uncertain, but beyond seeing, hearing, or knowing. Simultaneously, moments of opacity present the moments of greatest incongruity in the narrative, with not merely tension but outright disjuncture between story and discourse. Thus, a moment of opacity is simultaneously more uncertain than ambiguity and more incongruous than paradox. If we were to visualize Mark's rhetoric of indirection as a spectrum of strategies, opacity would bracket the whole spectrum, flanking both the ambiguous left and the paradoxical right, demarcating the limits to which an author can go with indirection. We might even say that in embracing opacity Mark probes not only the limits of indirection but also the limits of language itself.[31]

Opacity occurs in those moments of the reading experience in which either the story or the discourse halts while the other continues. In other words, opacity occurs when there is a manifest discontinuity or gap in either the story or the discourse. As I suggested before, it is the ultimate move in a narrative rhetoric of indirection. Normally in Mark's narrative the story and discourse either cooperate comfortably and directly, or they proceed yoked together in an incongruous tension, the story figuring indirectly the narratee's reception of the discourse. Opacity pushes incongruity to the breaking point, however, with story and discourse momentarily becoming disconnected. Unlike the other indirect moves, opacity is always extended, reverberatory, and dramatic. If a reader is scandalized by a tale that often proceeds indirectly, with story and discourse frequently pulling in different directions, opacity is more shocking still, with either story or discourse not going anywhere at all while the other proceeds by itself. If indeed Mark's narrative operates this way occasionally, then modern readers need to learn a new aesthetic of narrative in order to understand and appreciate how this narrative works. The modern presumption that a narrative's story should fit hand in glove with its discourse—the two levels of the narrative congruent and commensurate one with the other—is severely buffeted by Mark's rhetoric of indirection. To those who like their narrative clear, direct, and realistically referential, a narrative such as Mark's, that (1) is self-referential, if it is referential at all; (2) is figurative and indirect in its self-reference, whenever the story figures the discourse; and (3) is often not referential at all, as for example when the story is put on temporary hold while the discourse continues apace, demands that we learn to read with reading glasses far different from the ones we are accustomed to wearing while reading biblical literature.

The reader's experience of opacity is figured in the narrative in three major ways. The first is the experience of being on this side or that of an imaginary veil or curtain. Those on the favored side see and hear and understand; those on the other side are cut off from seeing, hearing, and understanding. The veil version of opacity is itself figured in Mark in several

---

31. On the limits of language, see the work of John Dominic Crossan, especially *The Dark Interval: Towards a Theology of Story* (Niles, Ill.: Argus Communications, 1975).

ways; for example, when Jesus takes the disciples off to one side for private instruction; when Jesus escorts a deaf-mute away from the crowd to heal him in private; when Jesus seeks solitude by going away, either into deserted regions, across the lake, or up on the mountaintop—in brief, whenever characters in the story make a move of separation or distancing. The questions the critical reader wants to ask concerning such moments are, Who is on which side of the veil? Who sees, hears, and understands, and who does not?

As well as shutting out people, veils and curtains are sometimes drawn aside or ripped open. Opacity sometimes gives way to insight and understanding, which also figures in the narrative: in the splitting of the heavens to allow an unidentified heavenly voice to invade the story (1:10), in Jesus' ambiguous verbal metaphors of the ripped garment and the burst wineskins (2:21-22), and in the hauntingly enigmatic rending of the temple curtain (15:38). These few examples suggest that although opaque veils are frequently lifted or torn in Mark, the results are seldom clear. Opacity in Mark does not easily give way to transparency.

The second major way of figuring opacity in the narrative is the language about "insiders" and "outsiders." The figure is one of being either on the inside or the outside of a hypothetical enclosed space; a privileged inner circle of insight and understanding leaves others on the outside looking in. The most common way this inner circle opacity is figured in the story is in Jesus' habitual retreats "into the house."[32] The imagery of an inside versus an outside is also manifested in movements in or out of villages, in or out of the boat, and eventually in or out of Jerusalem and the temple there. When we read about Jesus retreating into the privacy of "the house," he is usually portrayed as withdrawing there with his disciples, in order to give them private instruction. Seldom is this private tutoring efficacious, however, and more typically outsiders benefit from Jesus' private or inside ministrations on their behalf.[33] Paradoxically, in Mark's narrative the insiders (e.g., Jesus' family and disciples) are often outsiders, and outsiders (e.g., strangers and outcasts) often surprisingly find themselves insiders. That some insiders are really outsiders and some outsiders really insiders is itself an explicit, major theme at the story level in Mark (see 3:31-35 and 4:11), one that ironically and paradoxically figures what is happening at the same time to the narratee at the discourse level.

32. E.g., 3:20, 31-35; 7:17, 24; 9:28.
33. Observe the mercy extended to outsiders in 7:31-37 and 8:22-26. Mark 7:31-37 involves veil opacity—the deaf-mute is taken by Jesus away from the crowd (*apo tou ochlou*), privately (*kat'idian*), in order to be healed. Mark 8:22-26, however, involves circle opacity—the blind man is led outside the village (*exō tēs komēs*) in order to be healed. But as is typical in Mark, in 8:22-26 the inner circle of privilege and insight is turned inside out; only by going "outside" does the blind man become an "insider." "Outside the village" is where the "blind" man can gain his "sight."

The third major way in which opacity is figured in the narrative is the imagery of sense perception and intellectual and spiritual discernment: "seeing" or "not seeing," "hearing" or "not hearing," "understanding" or "not understanding," "speaking clearly and correctly" or not. Not only are people physically blind, deaf, and mute in the story (e.g., in 7:31-37 and 8:22-26), but Jesus also takes up blindness, deafness, and infelicitous speech as metaphors for the intellectual and spiritual deficiencies of his closest followers (e.g., 4:12; 8:16-21; cf. 6:52). If blindness, deafness, infelicitous speech, and deficient understanding are used figuratively within the story, then their function at the level of discourse is even more significant; when blindness, deafness, muteness, and deficient understanding predominate among the characters in the story, the narratee is left to see, hear, understand, and verbalize appropriately what is happening.

This third kind of opacity is perhaps the most interesting because it often crops up just when the narratee thinks that who is on what side of the veil, or who is inside the privileged circle and who is outside, is fairly clear. Just when things seem to be at their clearest, it may suddenly come to light (but usually for the narratee alone) that someone (usually certain characters in the story) did not really see, hear, or understand what we thought they did. Sense perception opacity thus makes its presence felt suddenly and unexpectedly. If we can say that a veil of opacity operates here, it is a veil that pops up unexpectedly, suddenly shrouding one person but not another.

Sense perception opacity is also interesting for two other reasons. For one thing, the variety of ways in which this kind of opacity can be figured (blindness, deafness, muteness, etc.) reveals the limitations of my metaphor of opacity. Opacity is after all a visual metaphor, and it sounds odd when opacity is figured in ways other than visual. Nevertheless, opacity is a serviceable meta-metaphor for metaphors of failed sense perception and understanding.

Second, sense perception opacity is seldom an all-or-nothing experience. Just as literal, physical sense perceptions or intellectual understandings can be warped or otherwise flawed, so also sense perception opacity tends to fall somewhere between total comprehension and no comprehension. For example, in between seeing and not seeing and in between transparency and opaqueness, "blurred vision" (e.g., 6:49; 8:24) is always possible; in between sharp hearing and complete deafness or silence[34] is the possibility of "garbled, misunderstood

34. It is tempting to use the imagery of "silence" instead of "opacity," for as much "blindness" as there is in the narrative, there is also much "deafness." The reading experience I have chosen to call "opacity" would often be better imagined as hearing nothing rather than seeing nothing. Silence figures often in the story, which tips us off that it is at work in the discourse as well. For example, Jesus' efforts to enjoin silence upon those who want to proclaim who he is has long been discussed as a part of the Messianic Secret in Mark. It is no small irony that at the story level of a narrative that obviously is intended to make Jesus known to the reader (e.g., see

sound" (e.g., 15:34); in between complete understanding and an utter lack of comprehension (what Mark calls "hardness of heart"; 6:52; 8:17), "limited" or "correct but defective understanding" (e.g., 8:29) might be found; and in between clear speech and muteness, "jumbled, inarticulate speech" (e.g., 7:32, 35) is possible. All of the examples cited parenthetically are story-level instances of ostensibly physical blindness, deafness, and whatnot, but in the story itself Jesus uses all of them as figures of speech for the intellectual and spiritual perception that the story is apparently really about. Therefore I take them all as figures for what the discourse is really about.

A brief discussion of some of the salient moments of opacity in the reading of the narrative is in order now. I want to look first at moments in which the disciples or other characters in the story are on the privileged side of the veil or on the inside of the circle while the narratee is left on the dark side of the veil or on the outside, looking in. In 4:34 for instance, we are informed that Jesus always speaks parabolically, "but privately to his disciples he explained everything." Reading this verse may be disconcerting because Jesus has just uttered a number of parables for which no explanation is provided in the discourse. We do have Jesus' paradigmatic interpretation of The Sower in 4:14-20, but his other figurative utterances in Mark 4 do not receive the same treatment, at least not in the narrator's discourse. If, however, as 4:34 suggests, Jesus was in the habit of explaining his parables to his disciples privately, as indeed he does in 4:14-20, then we may infer that Jesus has done other private tutoring for the disciples in Mark 4, but offstage, behind a curtain, out of the sight and the hearing of those of us sitting in the audience. To be sure, both verbal and dramatic irony early in Mark 4 draw the reader into a privileged position as an insider, but 4:34 reveals to the narratee that he has also been forcibly shut out of much that was happening in the story by a veil of opacity. More was going on in the story than we could see or hear because of holes or gaps in the discourse.

As troubling as this position might be, the reader's situation could be worse: we could be on the wrong side of the veil and not realize it. At least the reader of Mark often realizes that she has been excluded from understanding the narrative. By contrast, the opacity that excludes story characters is usually impossible for them to discern. The reader is better off than the characters in the story, usually, but, for all we know, we too could be excluded from understanding and never know that we were excluded. The tricky thing about opacity is that the blind, deaf, and mute do not know *what* they are missing

Mark 1:1), Jesus tries to hush up those who would make him known. Of course, it is also ironic that these attempts at silence inevitably fail. Besides the moments of silence that Jesus tries to enjoin but cannot, in some marvelous, pivotal moments in the story silence does indeed resound: 3:4, 9:34, 14:61, 15:5, and 16:8. Usually, the narrator immediately fills the pregnant silence with a silence-breaking comment directed toward the narratee. In such instances silence is an audible opacity that the narrator rushes in to clarify.

or even *that* they are missing anything. If the author were to cast the reader into the role of a blind, deaf, and mute reader, how would we know? Reading Mark's Gospel allows us to see blindness in others and to experience blindness ourselves occasionally, which promotes a chastened, humbled respect for the limitations of our own understanding.

Mark 4:34 points to something else that happens frequently in the discourse of the Gospel. Not only are we regularly deprived of almost all of Jesus' (presumed) private interpretations of his parabolic teachings but also in the first half of the Gospel we are usually cut off from the content of the teaching itself.[35] The scholarly literature notes this absence as a curiosity[36]; referentially oriented critics are at a loss to know what to do with elements of the story that are alluded to in a narrative but not actually narrated. The key, of course, is to consider not only the story but also the discourse. The teaching of Jesus is asserted to be a part of the story, but it is frequently not a part of the visible or audible action in the story because it has been omitted at the level of discourse. The narratee is thus confronted with numerous gaps in the discourse that shut him out of what is supposedly happening in the story. Early blocks of teaching material such as Mark 4:3-32 and 7:6-23 are major exceptions to this rule, which encourages the narratee to pay special attention to them as exemplary instances of Jesus' teaching. In the second half of the Gospel, a great deal of teaching is presented on the lips of Jesus; obviously it is featured now at both story and discourse levels. By this point, apparently the reader has been sufficiently prepared by the reading experience to be deemed worthy to hear what Jesus has to say. The narrator's strategy in the second half of the Gospel is to move us ever more insistently into the privileged circle of awareness and insight that surrounds his protagonist. At the same time, we by now know that the supposed insiders of the first half of the Gospel—those who not only heard the teaching of Jesus that we did not hear but also heard the private explanations that we did not hear—are really outsiders. On the one hand, by shutting us out of Jesus' early teaching, as well as his presumed constant interpretation of it, we are all the more eager to step closer and hear it when it is offered to us late in the Gospel. On the other hand, by reserving teaching and private interpretation primarily for the Twelve in the early chapters, their growing blindness, deafness, and muteness are all the more startling.

Other opacities less often noted by critics, perhaps because the other Gospels have filled or deleted gaps for us, include the prayers of Jesus. Just as in the other Gospels, Mark's Jesus is a man of prayer. Jesus retreats to deserted places, to mountains, and once to an olive grove to pray in private

---

35. See, e.g., 1:21-22, 27; 2:2, 13; 4:33; 6:2, 34; 7:13b.

36. Noted by, among others, Quentin Quesnell, *The Mind of Mark: Interpretation and Method through the Exegesis of Mark 6:52*, AnBib 38 (Rome: Pontifical Biblical Institute, 1969), 139–40; and Augustine Stock, *Call to Discipleship: A Literary Study of Mark's Gospel*, GNS 1 (Wilmington, Del.: Michael Glazier, 1982), 66–68.

(1:35; 6:46; 14:32). He urges his disciples to pray (11:24-25; 13:18; 14:38). He criticizes pretentious public prayer (12:40) and laments that the temple in Jerusalem has been deflected from its purpose of being "a house of prayer for all the nations" (11:17). He says the proper blessing before meals (6:41; 8:6-7; 14:22-23). He even claims to accomplish exorcisms by means of prayer (9:29). We are thus surprised to step back from our reading experience and recollect that the only prayer actually presented in the Gospel is Jesus' agonizing prayer in Gethsemane (14:36).[37] The effect upon the reader of withholding the words of all but the last of Jesus' prayers is not difficult to fathom. By presenting Jesus as a faithful man of prayer but withholding the prayers themselves, the narrator repeatedly carves out gaps in the discourse that the narratee hungers to have filled. If the prayer of 14:36 does not satisfy our hunger, nothing in Mark's narrative will. Of course, thinking that the narrative must necessarily satisfy all the hungers it arouses would be presumptuous. We have no guarantee that narrative will fill the emptiness to which it awakens us.[38]

Actually, the narrator reveals his strategy regarding Jesus' prayers to the sharp-eyed reader long before Gethsemane is reached. In 9:29 Jesus' disciples are told that the exorcism that they had just bungled and that Jesus had performed with ease had been possible only by means of prayer. However, Jesus is not said to have prayed in order to accomplish the exorcism! We have two interpretive options here. One is to suggest that what Jesus *really* meant to say was that only with a rich, regular discipline of prayer can a person hope to be equipped for such spiritual emergencies when they arise, as he had just demonstrated. The other is to accept that the prayer mentioned in 9:29 was indeed prayed and did indeed occur in the story but was withheld by the narrator from the discourse, and therefore we have here a moment of opacity in which the narratee is intentionally excluded from something that really happened in the story.

The latter interpretation offends readers because it implies that the narrative excludes them from grasping what is happening in the story. Yet Mark excludes us more often than we might think. A similar opacity that has perplexed critics is in 14:72, where the narrator says that the cock crowed a second time, with no previous mention having been made of a first crowing. The missing first cock's crow cannot *not* be in the story, but it is obviously missing from the narrator's discourse.

---

37. Unless, of course, Jesus' cry from the cross in 15:34 counts as a prayer, but whether it should or not is beautifully ambiguous.

38. That Mark strategically withholds all but the last of Jesus' prayers is not widely commented upon, I suspect, because the experience of reading Matthew, Luke, and John has effectively overshadowed Mark's strategy. If a reader is familiar with Gospels in which the Lord's Prayer is featured prominently, as in Matt. 6:9-13 and Luke 11:2-4, or with a Gospel that contains a long, sublime prayer, such as the beloved "high-priestly prayer" in John 17, it will be difficult for the reader to see, let alone appreciate, the absence of prayers in Mark.

A weightier example, one that no one has ever been able to solve satisfactorily, is the mystery of the *neaniskos,* the "young man" who runs from Gethsemane undressed in 14:52 and either reappears or is replaced by a *Doppelgänger* in 16:5, this time gloriously dressed, inside a vacated tomb at the crack of dawn. What the reader is supposed to make of the *neaniskos* lies behind an opaque veil.[39] The discourse teases us with bits and pieces of a story about a *neaniskos* that has not been told to us and that therefore we can never fully understand. We may guess at what lies behind the veil, which is a reasonable response to a veil. Some interesting guesses have been made as to what lies behind the *neaniskos* veil, but the veil itself is never lifted or torn asunder in the narrative.[40]

The abrupt mention of a second crow of a cock and the two brief appearances of a *neaniskos* can be enjoyed by readers as challenging narrative puzzles, always good for a spirited if inconclusive readerly debate. Readers attack other gaps in the discourse with far more vigor, however, because more is at stake. Consider the passing allusions to successful teaching or exorcisms conducted by Jesus' disciples. One such reference is made in 3:14-15 and another in 6:12-13 (cf. 6:30); I would also include Jesus' metaphorical statement that Peter and Andrew will become "fishers of people" (1:17). As far as the disciples' ministry of healing and teaching goes, these references are all the Gospel has.[41] These instances are only brief allusions, however; not one single episode of successful healing or teaching by the disciples is actually narrated. In one episode the work of the Twelve is prominently on display, but the outcome is wholly negative. This episode is 9:14-27, the exorcism botched by the disciples and set right by Jesus by the power of prayer.

One bellwether episode demonstrating the failure of the disciples and no episodes whatsoever demonstrating their successes ought to suffice to insinuate the narrator's attitude toward the Twelve. Nevertheless, some critics minimize the failure of the Twelve in 9:14-27 and in many other moments in the Gospel and maximize the allusions to their successes in 3:14-15 and 6:12-13. Many readers do not want to recognize that 3:14-15 and 6:12-13 are not the presentation, but the withholding, of stories of the success of the Twelve. These episodes are announced gaps in the discourse, which many readers eagerly fill and invest with a weight that the narrator himself does not care to give them. A referentially oriented critic may grant a mere reference or allusion

39. For an appreciative discussion of the narrative puzzle of the *neaniskos,* see Kermode's chapter on "The Man in the Macintosh, the Boy in the Shirt," in *The Genesis of Secrecy,* 49–73.

40. An intriguing solution to the *neaniskos* puzzle, the most persuasive with which I am familiar, is proposed by Robin Scroggs and Kent I. Groff, "Baptism in Mark: Dying and Rising With Christ," *JBL* 92 (1973): 531–48.

41. Of course, Mark says nothing at all about a movement, a following, or a "church" that might persist on past the point where the narrative stops. This is a huge gap in the discourse that Matthew and Luke eagerly fill.

great weight, but I take more seriously the narrative I have read than the one that has been alluded to but denied to me. That readers want to fill gaps is understandable, but the repeated absence of episodes demonstrating the disciples' success is a series of gaps that is too huge to be filled so easily and so positively.

Having given some attention to opacities in which characters in the story are "in" and the narratee is "out," I want to look now at instances in which the narratee is on the privileged side of the veil and characters in the story are on the benighted side. An excellent place to start is the beginning of the water-walking episode in 6:45-52.[42] Verse 48 reads as if the narratee stands with Jesus on the lakeshore, sees with him the disciples in the boat struggling against the wind, and begins to walk with him across the water to the boat. The narratee is placed in the position of being with Jesus, distanced from the Twelve. The narratee is privileged to know what Jesus is doing, while the disciples are excluded from insight and understanding. When the narrator then suddenly places us in the boat along with the Twelve in 6:49, we cannot share their ignorance as to who or what approaches them across the waters. They mistake Jesus for a ghost, but we know better and cannot join them in their ignorance and fear. What is opaque to them is perfectly clear to us.

The opacity in 6:48 is figured primarily by means of the physical separation of Jesus from the Twelve. As the episode progresses, however, the veil that enshrouds the Twelve is revealed to be more than just a matter of physical distance. Opacity is also manifest as the narrator informs the narratee that the disciples were fearful (6:49-50), lacking in understanding, and suffering from hardness of heart (6:52). Apparently the disciples are "far" from Jesus in more ways than one. They remain far from him even when they are physically close to him in the boat.

Because the narratee is alone with Jesus in 6:48, it is a clear case of the privileging of the narratee at the expense of characters in the story. Similar privileging of the narratee occurs frequently in Mark, but most instances are less obvious and harder to bring into critical focus. For instance, the demons Jesus encounters in the story regularly recognize him and cry aloud that he is ("a" or "the"?) son of God (1:24; 5:7; cf. 1:34 and 3:12). These loud cries receive no uptake by characters in the story, except of course by Jesus. The demonic cries seem to be smothered by an aural veil that deafens the characters in the story but not the narratee. Similarly, I have noted elsewhere that none of Jesus' comments about the Son of man receives any uptake in the story. The characters in the story are deaf to these sayings, which only the narratee hears.

Whereas earlier I was observing opacities that result from gaps in the discourse that exclude the narratee from portions of the story, here we are

42. See chap. 4.

dealing with moments of opacity that result from gaps in the story that exclude characters from comprehending the very story of which they are a part. In such opacities the discourse proceeds to the benefit of the narratee, while the story, at least as far as the characters within it are concerned, comes to a standstill.

In the history of the reading of Mark's Gospel, readers have had an extraordinarily difficult time comprehending that what is often so clear to the reader, thanks to the narrator's discourse, can be opaque to the characters at the story level. Even though it is said repeatedly in the story itself that characters are blind, deaf, without understanding, and awkward in speech, nevertheless, because *we* see, hear, understand, and speak knowingly about what is going on in the story, we have failed to perceive how little of the story is accessible to the characters in the story. Interestingly, this version of opacity is difficult to discern from either side of the veil. The characters excluded from understanding their own story are oblivious to their plight, and the narratee has trouble believing that the characters could be so obtuse. Neither the characters nor the narratee can see the opaque veil that separates them.

Enough has been said for now about opaque veils that separate narratee from characters, to the exclusion of one party or the other. Often, let us recall, no such veil seems to be in place. Often the narratee stands side by side with the disciples of Jesus as he teaches in public or tutors in private (e.g., 4:2-34; 7:6-23; 8:15-21; 8:31—19:1) or as he performs a miracle or does some other deed (e.g., 4:35-41 and 6:45-52; 6:30-44 and 8:1-10; 9:36-37 and 10:13-16). The narratee tends to presume, unless indications suggest otherwise, that his understanding of Jesus' words and deeds is comparable to that enjoyed by the characters standing alongside him. Sometimes this presumption remains unshaken; in other instances the presumption is shattered in a twinkling. Sometimes a veil of opacity pops up suddenly where none existed an instant before.

To examine such an instance, let us return to Gethsemane and to Jesus' prayer there. In the story Jesus has taken Peter, James, and John (as well as the narratee) off to one side (14:33). Jesus stations the disciples in one spot and tells them to watch (14:34) while he goes on a little farther and begins to pray (14:35). The narratee then sees and hears Jesus pray the only prayer the narratee witnesses in the Gospel (14:36). Then Jesus arises from prayer, comes to the three disciples, and finds them asleep! Sleep had closed their eyes and ears and made them blind, deaf, and unknowing. They missed the prayer that we assumed they were hearing along with us. This realization comes to the reader in a flash, in retrospect. Until 14:37 the reader has no indication that the three disciples have drifted off to sleep and left the reader by himself to remain awake and watching. A silent, unanticipated use of opacity by the narrator has turned the narratee into the only vigilant companion of Jesus in the narrative. The narratee is turned into the narrative's only insider; all others are revealed to be outsiders.[43]

Can everyone—character and narratee alike—be excluded by a veil of opacity? In one place this total exclusion seems to happen: the final episode of the Gospel, where three women discover an empty tomb. This episode is a masterpiece of indirection, and although it is the final episode of the Gospel, it is hardly a conclusion. The story and the discourse break off abruptly and dissonantly at 16:8. The fate of the characters is left up in the air, including the fate of the crucified, said-to-be-risen, said-to-be-proceeding-to-Galilee Jesus. These comments about Jesus are allusions to a story that is not narrated in Mark's Gospel. The narratee is therefore also left up in the air, not knowing where to turn, and not receiving clear guidance from either the narrator or the characters. The last episode of the Gospel shrouds everyone and everything, in story and discourse alike, behind veils of opacity. Because Mark's Gospel is a narrative about inside being outside and outside being inside, however, maybe ending up the narrative on the outside looking in is (ironically, paradoxically, and metaphorically) exactly where we should expect to be.

I have already observed many of the implications of the use of opacity, and in conclusion now I want to draw them out a little further. First, I want to emphasize that although both the characters in the story and the reader outside the story are occasionally shut out by opaque veils, the narrative favors the narratee at the expense of the characters. At one time or another, the narrative casts illumination on everyone, in the story and out; at one time or another, everyone in and out of the story is excluded from understanding. Again and again, however, the reader stands side by side with characters in the story, only to discover subsequently that they did not really see, hear, or understand what we did. By contrast, I can think of no instance of the opposite taking place, where it emerges that we really did not understand what we thought we did while the characters understood more than we thought. Only characters in the story are repeatedly made, retrospectively, victims of opaque exclusion, and only the narratee is repeatedly introduced into a privileged inner circle of insight into the blindness of others. At one point or another, the narrative casts light and darkness on everyone involved with it, but it has a strong tendency to favor the narratee with the greater illumination.

This favoritism for the narratee reinforces my claim that Mark's is an especially reader-oriented narrative. Everything in the narrative does not sooner or later become clear to the diligent reader, however. Some opacity turns

43. Note the dramatic irony that results from the two incongruous turns of opacity in 14:36-37. The words of prayer that have been repeatedly denied to the reader are at last given to us in 14:36, making transparent the opacity that had hitherto excluded us. An instant later we learn that the disciples, who we presume had heard all of those earlier prayers and are hearing this one too, have slept through the prayer we had waited so long to hear. Ironically, the moment of transparency in the discourse at 14:36 is revealed in retrospect to be a moment of opacity in the story.

transparent, some turns translucent, and some remains opaque. This is both a great compliment and a great challenge to the implied reader of this Gospel. This narrative implies that a person should be able to live with uncertainty and gaps in understanding. It gives us practice in living without full illumination.

What is the impact on the reader? Experiencing Mark's opacity is a sobering and humbling experience. After all, we observe characters who cannot see that they cannot see. How do we know that we have not fallen into the same trap? Can we be sure that we really understand the narrative we are reading? How can we remove this nagging uncertainty? The simple answer is that we cannot. Mark's Gospel is designed to guide, direct, and illuminate the reader vigorously and authoritatively, but at the same time challenge, puzzle, and humble its reader. It pulls the reader strongly in opposite directions simultaneously. Can a narrative make these moves and still hope to succeed? I shall address this question further in my final chapter.

PICTURING THE INDIRECT MOVES

As I have worked with Mark's indirection, I have found a diagram helpful in imagining the spectrum of indirect moves.

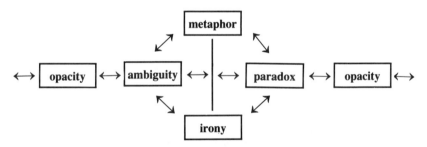

If we take this diagram as a family portrait of Mark's indirect moves, one trait shared in abundance by each member of the family is doubleness. Each move works on two levels simultaneously, usually going in different directions. A characteristic almost as widely shared is the occurrence of both local, limited, verbal versions and more extended, reverberating, dramatic versions of each of these moves, with the possible exception of opacity. Because opacity is the disjuncture of story and discourse, it is essentially always dramatic, even when triggered by an utterance of either a character or the narrator. The distinction between verbal and dramatic versions is extremely relevant in regard to irony, metaphor, and paradox; the distinction becomes weaker when we turn to ambiguity; when we arrive at opacity, it is no longer useful.

The family portrait reflects the greatest diversity in regard to uncertainty and incongruity. To the left are the moves of greater uncertainty. Incongruity is also here, but when uncertainty dominates, it overshadows incongruity. On the other end of the spectrum are the moves of greater incongruity. Uncertainty is also here, but at this end of the spectrum the tension of incongruity is stronger than the shadow of uncertainty.

In the center of the diagram, metaphor and irony strike a rough balance between uncertainty and incongruity, but in dissimilar ways. Metaphor is an invitation to consider a previously unexplored similarity between acknowledged dissimilars; irony offers a challenge to see and to see through an incongruity. Metaphor openly acknowledges uncertainty and incongruity and moves outward from there, in the direction of the resolution of the riddle implied by the metaphor; irony is a veiled invitation to move into and through incongruity and uncertainty, maybe toward resolution but maybe not.

One of the surprises of this family portrait is that opacity somehow got into the photograph at both ends. In opacity we have both the greatest uncertainty in the telling of the story, with one party or another placed behind an opaque veil, but at the same time the incongruity between story and discourse is also at its greatest. My diagram suggests accurately enough that we have a spectrum that ranges from moves of greater uncertainty to those of greater incongruity, but most spectra with which we are familiar (e.g., the spectrum of light wavelengths) do not bend back upon themselves to form a closed loop. To find a figure to represent this family, I would have to abandon a classical, Euclidean, straight-line geometry in favor of a non-Euclidean topological structure, such as a Möbius strip. A Möbius strip is a simple loop made out of a paper strip, but with a single twist in it. Because of the twist in the strip, the inside surface of the strip becomes the outside surface, and vice versa, endlessly. If we draw a line on the strip without lifting the pencil, the line eventually meets itself. The Möbius strip is thus an apt figure for a continuous spectrum of indirection that meets itself coming or going at either end, a strategy of discourse that continually makes insiders out of outsiders by making outsiders out of insiders.

The Möbius strip reminds us of another characteristic of Markan indirection, changeability. Just as the twist in the Möbius strip allows us to move continuously from any spot on the strip to any other, one indirect turn inevitably leads to another. Here my diagram is misleading: the boxes that seem to separate one indirect move from another are deceptively distinct, neat, and static. In reality, indirection in Mark slips back and forth constantly between these boxes.[44] In my previous discussions I could not talk about irony without also talking about paradox and opacity, or about metaphor without talking about ambiguity and irony, and so forth. One indirect turn can prepare for

44. To evoke the characteristic of changeability in Mark's rhetoric of indirection, an illustration much better than my humble diagram would be any of the many visual conundrums of M. C. Escher that involve constant metamorphosis; see J. L. Locher, ed., *The World of M.C. Escher* (New York: Abradale Press/Harry N. Abrams, Inc., 1971).

the coming of another, as, for instance, an ambiguous clue equips us to handle an irony; one indirect turn can be supplanted by another, as, for instance, a paradox is deconstructed by taking one pole or the other of the paradoxical contradiction as a metaphor; one indirect turn can be constructed out of and work hand in hand with another, as, for instance, a striking moment of opacity between story and discourse levels produces a reverberating dramatic irony.

In general, the closer moves are to each other in my diagram, the more affinity they have for each other. Because of the inherent uncertainty of any metaphorical connection, for example, metaphor is particularly close to ambiguity. Irony, because of its heavy investment in incongruity, has a natural affinity for paradox. Contiguous boxes thus often—but not always—represent the most closely related indirect moves.

Sometimes moves that are contiguous can in some ways be far apart. The best example is opacity. As close as opacity is both to ambiguity on the uncertain left and paradox on the incongruous right, it is actually a big step from either ambiguity or paradox to opacity. Because opacity heightens incongruity as well as uncertainty, a move from ambiguity to opacity is almost already a leap all the way to the other end of the spectrum into paradox. Similarly, moving from paradox to opacity is almost leaping from the right side of the spectrum all the way over to the left side. As close as they are in some respects, in other respects large gaps separate ambiguity from opacity from paradox.

At other times the moves that are seemingly the farthest apart actually turn out to work in close connection with each other. Here again opacity plays some funny tricks. By virtue of its intimate association with dramatic irony, opacity is not at all the distant, radical fringe of indirection, but rather its very heart and soul. Dramatic irony is impossible apart from opacity, and opacity similarly lies at the heart of any narrative strategy of indirection that is deeply dramatic.

Anyone discussing Mark's indirection runs the risk of making it clearer than it is. No diagram can do justice to the twists and turns, the gaps and spots of indeterminacy, and the uncertainties and the incongruities of Mark's rhetoric. Nevertheless, a diagram can be a helpful tool for thinking about the spectrum of indirect turns in Mark.

WHAT INDIRECTION ACCOMPLISHES

In Mark's use of indirection, we can see that this Gospel is not so much designed to say as to do something to its reader. The storyteller is not merely conveying the contents of a story but is trying to do something to the audience in the process of telling the story. Indirect language works predominantly along the rhetorical axis of language to affect the reader rather than predominantly along the referential axis of language to convey information. Following

Mark's indirection is a temporal experience of a meaningful event and not the receipt of an abstracted, static content.

To be sure, the Gospel may be said to have a certain referential content, and it is often direct rather than indirect, but even Mark's direction is performative and rhetorical, just like the indirection. However, moderns have difficulty appreciating the rhetorical stance or the audience orientation of direct language because we have been taught to presume that the primary purpose of all language is to convey, as clearly and directly as possible, referential meaning. Nevertheless, a prolonged and powerful encounter with performative, rhetorical language may help us appreciate that language can be something other than referential in purpose, even when it is supposedly clear and direct. Learning to appreciate the rhetoric of indirection in Mark has also helped me appreciate its rhetoric of direction.[45]

Taking a cue from Kierkegaard, who took many of his cues from Socrates,[46] Mark's rhetoric of indirection is maieutic: it performs the role of a midwife, lending encouragement and assistance to the reader's self-development and self-transformation in the experience of reading. Through his study of Socratic irony, Kierkegaard knew well the uses of maieutic irony and other strategies of indirection, especially pseudonymity and writing "hypothetically." Kierkegaard discusses at length the different strategies of direct and indirect communication, and the most illuminating of these discussions are themselves conducted indirectly, written under a pseudonym.[47] The problem with direct communication, he notes, is that it can convey "knowledge" without any subjective, existential appropriation of the knowledge by the recipient. Indirect communication, by contrast, forces the hearer or reader to be actively engaged in the process of communication, which leads to the development of "capability" in the hearer or reader. As "Johannes Climacus," the "author" of *Concluding Unscientific Postscript,* tells us, there are objective truths that can be communicated directly as a "result"; there are subjective truths that can be communicated only indirectly as a "way."[48]

---

45. Clarity is just as much a rhetorical strategy as indirection: "The real deceiver is the plain stylist who pretends to put all his cards on the table. Clarity, then, is a cheat, an illusion. To rhetorical man at least, the world *is* not clear, it is *made* clear. The clear stylist does it with a conjuring trick" (Richard A. Lanham, *The Motives of Eloquence: Literary Rhetoric in the Renaissance* [New Haven: Yale University Press, 1976], 22).

46. Søren Kierkegaard, *The Concept of Irony, with Constant Reference to Socrates,* trans., intro., and notes by Lee M. Capel (Bloomington: Indiana University Press, 1965).

47. For a list of the passages in the Kierkegaard corpus in which indirect communication is discussed see *Søren Kierkegaard's Journals and Papers,* ed. and trans. Howard V. Hong and Edna H. Hong, 7 vols. (Bloomington: Indiana University Press, 1967–78) 2:597.

48. Søren Kierkegaard, *Concluding Unscientific Postscript,* trans. David F. Swenson and Walter Lowrie (Princeton: Princeton University Press, 1941), 72; idem, *Journals and Papers* 1:282; Thomas C. Oden, ed., *Parables of Kierkegaard* (Princeton: Princeton University Press, 1978), xv; C. Stephen Evans, *Kierkegaard's "Fragments" and "Postscript": The Religious Philosophy of Johannes Climacus* (Atlantic Highlands, N.J.: Humanities Press, 1983), 7, 95, 103–4.

According to Johannes Climacus, therefore, the direct communication of knowledge or a result stands over against the indirect communication of capability or a way. Knowledge or a result is exactly what many have gone looking for in Mark's Gospel; nevertheless, capability or a way is what readers experience.

I have already embraced indirection as my own term for the incongruous and uncertain turns of Mark's narrative discourse. Now, too, I embrace capability and way as apt images for what Markan indirection accomplishes. Climacus's way is reminiscent of Mark's way. "The way" (*hē hodos*) in Mark is the road along which much of the action in the story, especially through Mark 8–10, is said to take place. "The way" appears in the story so many times that it seems to become a metaphor for the temporality of experience within the story itself, and it definitely becomes a metaphor of temporality at the discourse level. With the way, as with other things in the Gospel, the story figures the discourse, so that the way on which Jesus walks in the story figures the temporal experience of the reader. At story's end, just when the reader might think that for good or ill certain results must be achieved and destinations reached, the implication within the story is that Jesus is once again on the way, this time back to Galilee (16:7). This is merely an allusion to a story, however; it is not the story itself. The resumed way at the end of the narrative implies that the reader who wishes to continue to follow Jesus on past Mark 16:8—to see where the way might now lead—must continue to read on past where the narrator ceases to narrate. The reader must read right off the bottom of the last page of the Gospel and on into the dark and the silence. Mark's way trails off into realms of enduring opacity, and the reader must decide at the end of the discourse whether to continue the story. If the way to which we have been introduced by reading the Gospel has made its impact deeply enough upon us, we may choose to continue to follow the way even after all of its signposts and landmarks disappear from view.

I am also struck by Climacus's suggestion that indirection promotes "capability." I hear an echo here of another nineteenth-century comment on capability, Keats's line about "negative capability," the capability of "being in uncertainties, Mysteries, doubts, without any irritable reaching after fact and reason."[49] The discourse of Mark's Gospel manifests a remarkable willingness to dwell in uncertainty, mystery, and doubt. The exercise of negative capability in the discourse offers the reader an opportunity to learn negative capability as a way to read this narrative and maybe as a way to live beyond this narrative. This training in a *via negativa* is, as Gilbert Ryle might put it, a "learning how," the development of a capability or knack, rather than a

49. Hyder Edward Rollins, ed., *The Letters of John Keats,* 2 vols. (Cambridge: Harvard University Press, 1958) 1:193.

"learning that," the reception of objective knowledge or results.[50] Again, I do not deny that certain results are achieved and certain knowledge is gained by reading the Gospel. Not only does Mark's direction achieve results and offer knowledge but also much of his indirection also sooner or later leads us to a destination, albeit indirectly. Nevertheless, Mark's persistent and insistent turn to indirection, that is, to doubleness, incongruity, and uncertainty, is calculated to make a deep and lasting impression upon us. Experiencing Mark's indirection gives us the chance to learn various strategies for dealing with indirection. Many of Mark's puzzles we can successfully figure out, which teaches us ways in which some mysteries may be fathomed. The experience of finding other mysteries permanently mysterious teaches us ways in which to live with those mysteries that can never be fathomed.

Learning to live with Mark's indirection also has some interesting side effects on the experience of direct communication and of knowledge or results. The constant encounter with doubleness in Mark's indirection teaches us how to move past surface appearances, for we learn through reading this Gospel that narrative can work on different levels simultaneously; that if we read on one level only, then we may end up as deaf and blind as certain characters in the story. Seeing single, as in seeing one side only of an opaque curtain, is blindness. Seeing double is seeing indeed. If in dealing with Mark's indirection, however, we learn how to see double or hear an utterance in two ways at once, then we may develop the knack of exercising double vision or stereophonic hearing when dealing not only with indirection but with direction as well. Reading Mark's Gospel encourages the development of a frame of mind in which we are inclined to see and see through clarity as well as opacity, certainty as well as uncertainty, and congruity as well as incongruity. In short, Mark's Gospel not only teaches us how to solve the mysteries that can be solved and live with those that cannot but also teaches us thereby to be suspicious of straightforwardness and clarity. Accustomed to Markan doubleness, uncertainty, and incongruity, dare we trust singleness, certainty, and congruity? Should we not suspect that singleness, certainty, and congruity is actually blindness, deafness, and muteness?

Other figures can express the midwifery this narrative practices. To return to Wayne Booth's metaphor for the workings of metaphor, accepting the invitation to read this narrative is accepting an invitation to dance. Every

50. Gilbert Ryle, "Knowing How and Knowing That," *The Concept of Mind* (New York: Harper & Row, 1949), 25–61. Similarly, Donald Davidson contrasts "seeing as" with "seeing that": "Seeing as is not seeing that. Metaphor makes us see one thing as another by making some literal statement that inspires or prompts the insight. Since in most cases what the metaphor prompts or inspires is not entirely, or even at all, recognition of some truth or fact, the attempt to give literal expression to the content of the metaphor is simply misguided" ("What Metaphors Mean," *On Metaphor*, ed. Sheldon Sacks [Chicago and London: University of Chicago Press, 1979], 45).

indirect move is a dance step, which is performed differently by every dancer. Sometimes the dance takes us somewhere, directly or indirectly, but often it takes us nowhere at all. We dance the dance for its own sake, and no further justification is needed.

By dancing we also learn how to dance, a capability that remains with us after the music stops. The capability acquired by dancing Mark's dance is a response-ability, in two senses. First, indirection gives us a multitude of opportunities to respond to incongruous and uncertain stimuli. The narrative places us in circumstances to which, willy-nilly, we must respond, and the more practice we get, the better our chances are of becoming responsive. Second, indirection frequently places on the shoulders of the reader the heavy burden to take up the challenge of indirection and deal with it as best she can. We gain experience in being held answerable to the text; we learn how to shoulder responsibility, in other words. Learning how to be both responsive and responsible is the response-ability promoted by this narrative.[51]

Finally, a sobering thought: indirection is not always a felicitous strategy. Indirection creates its privileged insiders but also its benighted outsiders; it not only has the potential of performing powerful seductions but also runs the risk of abysmal failure. As Wayne Booth and Ted Cohen have observed, turns of indirection can be more successful in shaping a community of like-minded readers than any straightforward declaration of referential meaning. As Booth says of the irony in the crucifixion scene in Mark, "it seems clear that Mark's irony builds a larger community of readers than any possible literal statement of his beliefs could have done"[52]; as Cohen says of metaphor, it is an "achievement of intimacy."[53] When a storyteller tells his tale indirectly, we stick more closely to the indirect paths down which he leads us than we would to clear and direct paths.

51. A concern that must remain outside the scope of this book is the insights that developmental psychology could lend to reader-oriented criticism. I would like to test the hypothesis that Mark's Gospel is aimed at an intellectually, morally, and imaginatively sophisticated audience. In James Fowler's terminology, Mark often operates at the Stage 5 level of Conjunctive Faith, where persons are able to deal comfortably with ambiguity, irony, and paradox (*Stages of Faith: The Psychology of Human Development and the Quest for Meaning* [San Francisco: Harper & Row, 1981], 184–98); see also Mary Wilcox, *Developmental Journey: A Guide to the Development of Logical and Moral Reasoning and Social Perspective* (Nashville: Abingdon Press, 1979), 136–37, 142–43.

This leads to other questions. Can a narrative employing ambiguity, irony, and paradox train its recipient to deal adequately with such indirection? It is debatable whether a narrative can engender in its reader the very skills required to read it with maximum sensitivity. Has Mark effectively limited his audience by using indirection? Matthew and Luke may have perceived that Mark's indirection appealed to or was appreciated by too narrow an audience. Hence, their muting of Mark's indirection may in part be a strategy to win a larger audience.

52. Wayne C. Booth, *A Rhetoric of Irony* (Chicago: University of Chicago Press, 1974), 29.

53. Ted Cohen, "Metaphor and the Cultivation of Intimacy," in *On Metaphor*, ed. Sheldon Sacks (Chicago and London: University of Chicago Press, 1979), 6.

Indirection presents as many or more ways to lose as to win, however. First, when the narrator and narratee win, often someone else has lost. In order to fashion a community of insight and understanding out of those who read the story, Mark's indirection makes victims of many in the story. Second, Mark's readers may decide not to play along with the indirect moves. For one thing, they may be offended that Mark's irony and opacity turn beloved heroes into blind and deaf buffoons in the story, or readers may simply be emotionally unwilling or intellectually unable to play Mark's games of verbal and dramatic ambiguity, metaphor, irony, and paradox. Third, even if Mark's narrative wins a knowing and supportive first generation of readers, the author has no guarantee that later generations of readers will appreciate or even bother to read such a work of indirection. Indeed, a narrative heavily invested in incongruity and uncertainty is especially susceptible to revisionists who retell the story, only more clearly and directly. The master of indirection is always in danger of being supplanted by a clever straight-talker who comes along and says, "Now, what he really meant to say was. . . ." This is, of course, what happened to Mark at the hands of Matthew and Luke. Within one generation of the composition of Mark's Gospel, it had inspired retellings by Matthew and Luke, both of whom clarified and set straight Mark's rhetoric of indirection. Thus the Gospel that by its rhetorical brilliance and novelty inspired the creation of other Gospels was rapidly supplanted by them. That Matthew, Luke, and John undertook to retell *Mark's* story shows how powerful the impact of Mark's Gospel was; that Matthew, Luke, and John undertook to *retell* Mark's story shows how dissatisfied they were with it. In raising the question of how Mark relates to the other Gospels, however, I am anticipating the topic of the next chapter, to which I shall now turn.

9

THE HISTORY OF
READING MARK

A confession is in order. This chapter, which addresses the relationship between Mark and the other canonical Gospels in the history of reading, logically precedes chapters 1 through 8. After all, to be a critic is to stand within a critical tradition, and in the case of the Gospels we have nineteen centuries of reading history with which to contend. The long history of reading Mark is the history of its being eclipsed by other, more illustrative Gospels, however, and we can dispel the shadows that have obscured it only by first discovering the reading of Mark itself. Facing a classic chicken or egg problem, I decided to deal with Mark first and the history of reading Mark afterward.

In the chapters preceding I could not talk about reading Mark without also talking about reading Matthew and Luke. We cannot discuss Mark's rhetoric of indirection without at the same time discussing Matthew and Luke's efforts to undermine Mark's indirection by producing their own more consistently direct narratives. Fathoming what Mark is doing goes hand in hand with fathoming what Matthew and Luke are doing.

Recognizing therefore that our canonical Gospels are unavoidably tangled up with each other, I now address the vexed question of this relationship. I propose to reformulate the puzzle in this chapter, as I have reformulated other puzzles in the preceding chapters, in terms of reader response. The experience of countless readers has been that reading any one of the canonical Gospels apart from the others is virtually impossible, even when the reader is making the critical effort to read one Gospel only. Far more than we have been willing to admit, we have read and continue to read Mark through the distorting lenses we call Matthew, Luke, and John. We are challenged to come to a critical awareness and understanding of our experience of reading not a Gospel, singular, but a tangle of Gospels, plural.

What is the relationship between the four canonical Gospels? This question launched and still drives the modern, critical study of the Gospels. In response to this question, most modern studies of the Gospels have focused on the production of these texts, what we may call the history behind the text. Source criticism tried to answer the question by seeking out the sources behind the Gospels. Attention was directed especially to the Synoptic Gospels of Matthew, Mark, and Luke. The most attractive explanation was the so-called Two-Source Hypothesis: that Mark was the first of our canonical Gospels written, and that Matthew and Luke used as sources Mark and a hypothetical collection of Jesus' teachings, labeled Q for convenience. Today, most biblical critics regard John as independent of the Synoptics—any material John shares with the others can be chalked up to a shared inheritance of early Christian tradition. (I suspect that John knew all three Synoptic Gospels and is responding to them in his own Gospel, just as Matthew and Luke respond to Mark in theirs.) The Two-Source Hypothesis has been accepted by most Gospel critics for generations.[1]

This majority opinion is under attack, most notably in the United States by William R. Farmer.[2] Farmer advocates a return to the Griesbach Hypothesis, which argues that Mark's Gospel is later than—and borrows from—both Matthew and Luke. It suggests, in other words, that Mark is a conflation and a condensation of Matthew and Luke. After many years of protesting what he regarded as an uncritical acceptance of the Two-Source Hypothesis, Farmer and a group of colleagues have succeeded in reminding the scholarly community that the Synoptic Problem has not been settled once and for all. Nevertheless, Farmer and friends have not persuaded the scholarly community to launch a full-scale attack on the Synoptic Problem all over again.

They have not achieved this goal for several reasons. For one thing, few biblical scholars of the late twentieth century are eager to repeat the scholarly battles of the eighteenth and nineteenth centuries. Too much critical history separates us, and the current generation wants to frame the questions in its own way and work toward answers in its own style. Moreover, although we admit that the Synoptic Problem remains unresolved, many of us have a strong intuition that the Two-Source Hypothesis remains the best solution, even though we may not be able to say why. That is, we have a feeling about the relationship of the Gospels that we have so far been unable to express in respectable, critical language. I suggest that the Synoptic Problem is well worth tackling all over again, but with the problem completely reformulated, using the new critical vocabulary of reader response.

I want to offer here a preliminary sketch of how we might go about making a shift in critical focus away from the history of production, the history

---

1. For discussions of the Synoptic Problem, see Werner Georg Kümmel, *The New Testament: The History of the Investigation of Its Problems*, trans. S. McLean Gilmour and Howard Clark Kee (Nashville and New York: Abingdon Press, 1972); and Arthur J. Bellinzoni, ed., assisted by Joseph B. Tyson and William O. Walker, *The Two-Source Hypothesis: A Critical Appraisal* (n.p.: Mercer University Press, 1985).

2. William R. Farmer, *The Synoptic Problem: A Critical Analysis* (New York: Macmillan; London: Collier-Macmillan, 1964).

behind the text, to the history of reception, the history in front of the text.[3] In this chapter I shall consider the experience of reading our four tangled canonical Gospels in a fashion similar to that followed more thoroughly for the reading of Mark in preceding chapters. First, I shall collect some reports from critical readers that offer us clues as to how to reformulate the question of Gospel relationships in terms of reader response. Then I shall discuss some critical language that helps us make sense of this reading experience. Finally, I shall take a look at some texts from the Gospel of Matthew and talk about how reading those texts constrains the way we read Mark's Gospel.

READING TANGLED GOSPELS

To begin, I want to consider some illuminating reports of experiences of reading our tangled Gospels. The first is an infamous passage from B. H. Streeter's classic work on the Two-Source Hypothesis.[4] In the midst of a discussion of the ancient idea that Mark is an abbreviation of Matthew (an idea that finds modern expression in the Griesbach Hypothesis), Streeter lashes out at such a notion: "Now there is nothing antecedently improbable in the idea that for certain purposes an abbreviated version of the Gospel [of Matthew] might be desired; but only a lunatic could leave out Matthew's account of the Infancy, the Sermon on the Mount, and practically all the parables. . . ."[5] This response is not a reasoned argument; it is an emotional outburst. For that reason precisely, it reveals Streeter's genuine concern: assuming the prior existence of the Gospel of Matthew, could the author of Mark realistically expect a reception for his comparatively scanty narrative? What dynamics of reading would be involved in such circumstances of reception?

Other outbursts by supposedly dispassionate scholars abound in the critical literature. In his 1965 review of Farmer's *The Synoptic Problem,* F. C. Grant

3. Paul Ricoeur talks about the worlds "behind" and "in front of" texts in his essay, "The Hermeneutical Function of Distanciation," in *Paul Ricoeur: Hermeneutics and the Human Sciences,* ed. and trans. John B. Thompson (Cambridge: Cambridge University Press, 1981), 131–44; see also Edgar V. McKnight, *The Bible and the Reader: An Introduction to Literary Criticism* (Philadelphia: Fortress Press, 1985), xviii. I am also indebted to Hans-Georg Gadamer's notion of *Wirkungsgeschichte* ("effective-history") and to Hans Robert Jauss and the Konstanz School's concern for *Rezeptionsgeschichte* ("history of reception"); see Hans-Georg Gadamer, *Truth and Method* (New York: Seabury, 1975), 267–74 and passim; Hans Robert Jauss, *Toward an Aesthetic of Reception,* trans. Timothy Bahti, intro. Paul de Man, THL 2 (Minneapolis: University of Minnesota Press, 1982).

4. Burnett Hillman Streeter, *The Four Gospels: A Study of Origins* (London: Macmillan, 1956; orig. 1924). Strictly speaking, Streeter advocated a modified version of the Two-Source Hypothesis, "a four document hypothesis," the four sources being Mark, Q, M (Matthew's special source), and L (Luke's special source). Moreover, he suggested that there was a Proto-Luke that was produced by combining Q and L.

5. Ibid., 158.

asks, rhetorically, "why should anyone wish to substitute Mark's brief narrative, truncated at both ends, for the fuller narratives of Matthew and Luke. . . ?"[6] Grant goes to the heart of the matter: given the existence of Gospel A, how would Gospel B be received, and vice versa? What are the different relationships that arise out of the various possibilities for reading experiences? Should not the critic be able to shed some critical light on such reading experiences?

F. W. Beare provides another clue, in yet another review of Farmer's book:

> It is hard to imagine why Mark should ever have been written, if it was designed for the use of churches which already possessed and were using Matthew and Luke. Who would want this "apocopated" version of the gospel story? *The whole history of the use of the gospels in the church provides a sufficient answer.* Mark was given the smallest place in the liturgy, both in the East and West; until priority was established in the nineteenth century, it was hardly ever treated by commentators; even the history of the text bears witness to its low estate in common usage. If it could thus sink into disuse, even after its acceptance as part of the fourfold gospel canon, how could it ever have achieved recognition in the first place?[7]

Here is a clue of major proportions. When push comes to shove, Beare chooses to talk, not about who has borrowed what from whom in the history of the production of the Gospels, but rather how the Gospels have been used in the life of the church over the course of the centuries. Beare is making inferences about the hazy history of the production of the Gospels by seeing how they have been read or not read, used or not used, over the course of nineteen hundred years.

I want to examine the remarks of one other scholar. Years ago, at a time when the title of his essay would have been thought lunacy by many, Morton Enslin published "The Artistry of Mark." In his introductory paragraph, Enslin mixes metaphors provocatively: "For nearly nineteen hundred years the Gospel of Mark has been *read in the light of* the other three canonical gospels, notably Matthew. In consequence of this it was long *eclipsed* by its rivals. . . . [T]here is still the tendency, however easily we may talk about the 'established priority of Mark,' to continue *to regard it through the lenses* of the other gospels. . . ."[8]

Let us consider these mixed metaphors. Mark has been read in the light of the other Gospels; and Mark has been eclipsed by the others; that is, Mark has been read both in the light of and in the shadows of the other Gospels.

---

6. F. C. Grant, "Turning Back the Clock [review of Farmer, *The Synoptic Problem*]," *Int* 19 (1965): 354.

7. F. W. Beare, review of William R. Farmer, *The Synoptic Problem,* in *JBL* 84 (1965): 297 (emphasis added).

8. Morton Enslin, "The Artistry of Mark," *JBL* 66 (1947): 385 (emphasis added).

The other Gospels simultaneously highlight certain features of Mark's narrative while obscuring others. To turn to the lens metaphor, they simultaneously throw certain features of Mark into sharper focus while throwing other features out of focus.

All of the quotations I have just cited are arguments (or emotional outbursts) based upon observations of the history of the reception of Mark's Gospel. Gospel critics who go looking for evidence of the production of the texts find instead evidence of the texts' reception and then force it into a preconceived source-critical framework. We have always talked about our own personal reception of the text, as well as the history of reception to which we are heirs, but we have done so using language that purports to address the history of the production of the text. We have lacked a vocabulary that would allow us to speak critically about our own experience of reading and about the reading history within which we stand. One such vocabulary is reader-response criticism. Terms in the reader-response vocabulary that can help us to talk about the reading of tangled Gospels are *intertextuality, reading grid, precursor, palimpsest,* and *strong reading* or *misprision.*

TOOLS FOR ANALYSIS

The fundamental fact about the relationship between the Gospels is so obvious that we usually overlook it: whatever relationship is discerned between the Gospels is discerned by a reader in the act of reading. Then what happens? Having perceived in our reading the echoes between the Gospels, modern critics naturally begin to ask questions about "who borrowed what from whom." Source critics have inferred, probably correctly, that a relationship of literary dependence must exist between the Gospels, but neither the Two-Source Hypothesis, the Griesbach Hypothesis, nor any other source-critical explanation of Gospel relationships can be corroborated definitively, given the current state of the evidence. Absolutely indisputable, however, is the fact that countless readers have in the act of reading discerned echoes bouncing back and forth among the Gospels.

INTERTEXTUALITY

In contemporary literary theory, the experience of hearing echoes of one text in another is called *intertextuality*.[9] Intertextuality is an experience known by all readers. It obviously takes place when one reads a text that borrows directly from other texts or quotes them explicitly. Moreover, we also encounter it in the reading of every text, without exception, insofar as every text, in order to be intelligible, must draw upon a culture's accumulated heritage of language

9. See the brief discussion of the intertextuality of Mark and the Jewish Scriptures in chap. 5.

and literature. As Roland Barthes observes, for a text to make sense, it must consist of the *déjà lu*, the already read.[10]

READING GRID

The discussion of intertextuality today is the discovery (or rediscovery, because the ancients knew it intuitively) that texts are never the isolated, autonomous, aesthetic objects that modern criticism has often made them out to be. A text always implicates other texts within itself. Julia Kristeva, a leading theorist of intertextuality, says "every text takes shape as a mosaic of citations, every text is the absorption and transformation of other texts. . . ." Jonathan Culler elaborates: "a work can only be read in connection with or against other texts, which provide a grid through which it is read and structured by establishing expectations which enable one to pick out salient features and give them a structure."[11] That is, not only do we always read a text in relationship to other texts but also the experience of reading one text shapes or constrains the way we view another text. Regarding the Gospels, we encounter a relationship among them in reading them; they are tangled texts, implicated deeply within each other. We should exercise some critical suspicion here, however, for we are likely to be dealing with one or more texts that were intentionally produced to function as a reading grid, with the primary goal of changing our perception of another text. Consequently, when we read one Gospel, we should be on the lookout for ways in which our knowledge of another Gospel exercises its influence. One Gospel, if read through the reading grid provided by another, has certain features blocked out while other features are highlighted. In a sense, an old text is turned into an entirely new one, thanks to the grid that induces us to see the old text with new eyes.

The introduction of a new text can change dramatically and maybe irrevocably our perception of its predecessors. T. S. Eliot provides a classic statement describing this change in perception in his essay "Tradition and Individual Talent":

> No poet, no artist of any art, has his complete meaning alone. His significance, his appreciation is the appreciation of his relation to the dead poets and artists. You cannot value him alone; you must set him, for contrast and comparison, among the dead. . . . what happens when a new work of art is created is something that happens simultaneously to all the works of art which preceded it. The existing monuments form an ideal order among themselves, which is

10. The comment is credited to Barthes by Jonathan Culler, *The Pursuit of Signs: Semiotics, Literature, Deconstruction* (Ithaca, N.Y.: Cornell University Press, 1981), 102.

11. See Culler's quotation and discussion of Kristeva's insights in *Structuralist Poetics: Structuralism, Linguistics, and the Study of Literature* (Ithaca, N.Y.: Cornell University Press, 1975), 139; and see Julia Kristeva, *The Kristeva Reader*, ed. Toril Moi (New York: Columbia University Press, 1986), 36–37, 111.

modified by the introduction of the new (the really new) work of art among them. The existing order is complete before the new work arrives; for order to persist after the supervention of novelty, the *whole* existing order must be, if ever so slightly, altered; and so the relations, proportions, values of each work of art toward the whole are readjusted; and this is conformity between the old and the new.[12]

PRECURSOR

Rather than adopt Eliot's grandiose scope ("all the works of art which preceded it"), let us consider the relationship between a particular text and one or more precursor texts. In discussing the precursors of Kafka, Borges says, "the fact is that each writer *creates* his precursors."[13] No text is produced in anticipation of its serving as a precursor to other texts; it can be turned into a precursor only by a successor. The production of a successor text makes us see things in the precursor text that we had not seen before, because before the successor had been written they had not existed to be seen. The time has come to abandon the notion that texts, once written, never change. At a trivial level, the ink spots on the page may not change,[14] but what readers make of the ink spots never ceases to change. The authors of successor texts are always creating new features to be seen (and to be forgotten) in their precursors. Entertaining the possibility that one or more of the Gospels was intentionally designed as a reading grid for another, the question arises, Does one Gospel create a precursor out of another Gospel? Do we see (or fail to see) certain things in one Gospel because we are familiar with another? Even more intriguingly, once a text has been turned into a precursor by its successor, to what extent can criticism discover and examine the changes wrought in our perception by the successor? What role can and should criticism play in this drama of masking and unmasking precursors and successors?

PALIMPSEST

Another useful term is already familiar to biblical scholars: *palimpsest.* In antiquity writing materials were costly, especially parchment, and occasionally

---

12. T. S. Eliot, "Tradition and Individual Talent," *Selected Essays,* new ed. (New York: Harcourt, Brace, 1950), 4–5.

13. Jorge Luis Borges, "Kafka and His Precursors," *Other Inquisitions: 1937–1952,* trans. Ruth L. C. Simms, intro. James E. Irby (Austin and London: University of Texas Press, 1964), 108.

14. But even this is a dubious supposition, in several ways. For one thing, it is the job of the textual critic to change the ink spots on the printed page; thanks to the textual critics, texts *do* change from generation to generation. Furthermore, texts were even more changeable before the printing press, when no two handwritten copies of a text were ever identical. Texts are more fluid than we have often supposed.

a parchment manuscript would be reused. The original ink would be scraped and washed off, and a new text written on the parchment. Usually, however, the old text was not wholly obliterated; it would still appear faintly through the new text, and with modern techniques using chemicals and ultraviolet light even more of the old text can often be discovered.[15]

The palimpsest, a single writing surface with two texts on it—one wholly visible and the other less than wholly visible—is an apt metaphor for the kind of relationship between texts, experienced in reading, that I have been discussing. Credit for this metaphor goes to the French literary theorist and critic, Gérard Genette. Genette examines that kind of intertextuality wherein one text is written intentionally as a transformation of a specific precursor text.[16] He examines a great variety of literature, both ancient and modern, and categorizes a multitude of techniques that authors use to transform the texts of their precursors. He tries to limit himself to cases in which the transformation of one text in another is "massive" and "declared."[17] One paradigmatic text that he returns to constantly is Homer's *Odyssey,* which has been frequently transformed into new texts, most notably in the twentieth century in James Joyce's *Ulysses.* Playing on the figure of the palimpsest, Genette invents some playful but striking language: Homer's *Odyssey* is a "hypotext"—a text below—while *Ulysses,* by Joyce, is a "hypertext" of it—a text above. Thus Genette proposes "hypertextuality" as an important subcategory of the larger phenomenon of intertextuality.[18] His work is so broad and ambitious that I am surprised that he passes over what may be the best example of hypertextuality in Western literature: the four Gospels. His own guidelines exclude the Gospels from consideration, however, because their relationship is "massive" but not "declared." That is, none of the Gospel writers makes explicit his intention to create a hypertext to be read on top of a particular hypotext. Nevertheless, we can ask, which Gospel, if any, reads like a hypertext, and which Gospel, if any, reads like a hypotext? Which, if any, is a palimpsest of another?

STRONG READING

The figures of the reading grid and the palimpsest are especially instructive when they help us to see that the relationship between precursor and successor is often less a relationship of outgrowth or dependency than one of antagonism

15. Bruce Manning Metzger, *The Text of the New Testament: Its Transmission, Corruption and Restoration,* 2d ed. (New York and London: Oxford University Press, 1968), 12.

16. Gérard Genette, *Palimpsestes: La littérature au second degré,* CP (Paris: Seuil, 1982).

17. Ibid., 16.

18. Genette gets a lot of mileage out of two Greek prepositions, *hypo* and *hyper.* But New Testament critics also know Greek and should be able to use a host of prepositions to describe the multitudinous relationships between texts that are experienced in reading. Must our guild restrict itself to the use of the prepositions *ex* and *eis,* as in "exegesis" and "eisegesis"?

and usurpation. Pushing this insight to its extreme is Harold Bloom, who speaks of the strong poet's misprision, strong reading, or, simply, misreading of his precursor.[19]

For years Bloom has concerned himself with "poetic influence," or "intra-poetic relationships," the wrestling match that a strong poet must engage in with precursors.[20] One of Bloom's own precursors is Freud, so he describes the wrestling match between strong poet and precursor as an oedipal struggle, a son striving to vanquish and to supplant the father.[21] Strong poets supplant the precursor by creative and powerful misreading of the precursor's texts. They must exercise strong reading, "so as to clear imaginative space for themselves."[22] The choice is not whether to read correctly or to misread but whether to misread more or less creatively, more or less interestingly. "Correct readings" of texts do perhaps exist, but only at a trivial and uninteresting level. All strong reading is misreading.

Bloom is also inspired by ancient and medieval gnostic and kabbalistic[23] strong readers, from whom he borrows a vocabulary of tropes with which to describe and discuss the revisionary moves typically made by strong poets. I shall mention only one of his six "revisionary ratios," clinamen:

> *Clinamen* . . . is poetic misreading or misprision proper; I take the word from Lucretius, where it means a "swerve" of the atoms so as to make change possible in the universe. A poet swerves away from his precursor, by so reading his precursor's poem as to execute a *clinamen* in relation to it. This appears as a corrective movement in his own poem, which implies that the precursor poem went accurately up to a certain point, but then should have swerved, precisely in the direction that the new poem moves.[24]

Clinamen is but a sample from Bloom's critical repertoire for exploring the relationships between precursor and successor texts.[25] Bloom's statements about the criticism of poetic tradition could just as easily serve as a programmatic invitation to a revisionary criticism of the Gospels: "Let us give up the

19. Harold Bloom, *The Anxiety of Influence: A Theory of Poetry* (London, Oxford, and New York: Oxford University Press, 1973); idem, *A Map of Misreading* (Oxford and New York: Oxford University Press, 1975); idem, *The Breaking of the Vessels* (Chicago and London: University of Chicago Press, 1982); idem, *Agon: Towards a Theory of Revisionism* (New York and Oxford: Oxford University Press, 1982).

20. "My concern is only with strong poets, major figures with the persistence to wrestle with their strong precursors, even to the death" (*Anxiety of Influence*, 5).

21. *Map of Misreading*, 19.

22. *Anxiety of Influence*, 5; cf. 30.

23. Bloom professes to be "a Jewish Gnostic, an academic, but a party or sect of one"(*Breaking of the Vessels*, 3).

24. *Anxiety of Influence*, 14.

25. See ibid. 14–16 and passim for definition and application of all six revisionary ratios. In subsequent work Bloom expands these into a full "map of misreading" by the addition of poetic images, classical rhetorical tropes, and psychic defenses (*Map of Misreading*, 84 and passim).

failed enterprise of seeking to 'understand' any single poem as an entity in itself. Let us pursue instead the quest of learning to read any poem as its poet's deliberate misinterpretation, *as a poet,* of a precursor poem or of poetry in general."[26]

All together, these various critical terms offer us an embarrassment of riches with which to reformulate the question of the relationship of the Gospels. Instead of asking which Gospel preceded which and which Gospel served as the source for another, we can turn the directional vector of the question around and begin to ask, Which Gospel overlays another, as its reading grid? Which Gospel turns another into its precursor? Which Gospel creatively misreads another and thereby supplants it?

To answer these questions carefully would require nothing less than a complete re-visioning of nineteen centuries of the reading of the four canonical Gospels. Consequently, I shall be able to manage only a token gesture in this direction in the pages that follow. I shall examine a few salient passages from Matthew's Gospel that serve as powerful reading grids or lenses through which to read the parallel passages in Mark. Then I shall comment on how these strong misreadings of Mark by Matthew have prevented us from seeing Mark's text, let alone reading it with any degree of sensitivity.

MATTHEW AS A READING GRID

I want to consider here how Matthew's Gospel stands as a creative and powerful misreading of Mark, how it has served as a reading grid or palimpsest of Mark, how it has turned Mark into its precursor, and how it has vanquished and supplanted Mark. I especially want to consider passages in Matthew that have severely affected our perception of Mark's rhetoric of indirection. Then I shall return to Mark and suggest some ways in which Matthew's gridwork has highlighted and obscured the reading of Mark, especially concerning some of the most common topics of debate in Markan scholarship, including the Messianic Secret, the function of parables, and the role of Jesus' disciples.

A PALIMPSEST OF PARABLES

Matthew 13 is a revision of Mark 4, the so-called parable chapter. Besides overwriting Mark 4, Matthew 13 also constrains how readers grasp other major issues in the interpretation of Mark's Gospel, such as the motif of secrecy or mystery, the understanding and use of parables, and the role of the disciples.

I noted earlier that reading Mark 4:11 is a moment of opacity for the reader. The disciples have supposedly been given the secret of the Kingdom of God, but if they have, the narratee knows nothing of it. The narratee has

26. *Anxiety of Influence,* 43.

been excluded from the giving of any such secret; the narratee is for the moment an outsider. Yet things do not rest there. In Mark 4:12 a rationale for speaking in parables is given that is so incongruous with the stated objective of both the narrator (Mark 1:1) and his protagonist (Mark 1:14-15) that Mark 4:12 must be regarded as verbal irony. Yet things do not rest here, either. In Mark 4:13 Jesus asks the disciples the reason that they do not understand the sower parable; if they cannot understand that parable, they will understand none of Jesus' parables. In this instant a turn of dramatic irony occurs for the narratee because we realize suddenly that the disciples, the supposed possessors of the secret of the Kingdom of God back in 4:11, do not understand. Jesus may already have been speaking ironically about the disciples' lack of understanding in his seemingly complimentary remark in 4:11, but he drops his oblique, ironic demeanor in 4:13 and brings out into the open his criticism of the disciples. The outsider of 4:11—the narratee—suddenly becomes an insider in 4:13, as the supposed insiders of 4:11—the disciples—are revealed as outsiders. Opacity at the discourse level, verbal irony at the discourse level (definitely), verbal irony at the story level (maybe),[27] as well as dramatic irony, which plays upon an incongruity between story and discourse—what does Matthew do to all of these indirect moves in Mark 4?

In framing the question this way, perhaps we can avoid the usual seduction of commenting only upon the changes that Matthew has wrought in Mark's story instead of focusing upon what Matthew is doing at the level of discourse. Far more significant than all the changes in content that we see in Matthew 13 is the repudiation there of a rhetoric of indirection. Most important of all, Matthew eschews incongruous tension between story and discourse. We can see this in Matthew 13 in all the straightforward comments by Matthew's narrator about those who understand and those who do not, that is, those who are insiders and those who are outsiders. In Matthew, everyone plays his role and stays in character: insiders remain insiders and outsiders remain outsiders. In particular, Matthew presents few puzzles to his narratee that would ever cast the narratee into the role of outsider. Matthew's approach is to avoid steadfastly the twists and turns through which Mark likes to put his narratee.

Mark 4:13 makes clear in retrospect that the disciples are really the ones who do not understand Jesus' parables. If we understand that they do not understand, then we have become de facto insiders. Matthew will have nothing to do with such indirect stratagems. Matthew completely overwrites Mark 4:13 to make clear and indelible in Matt. 13:10-11 that the disciples do not ask about the parables for their own benefit but for the sake of the crowd. For Matthew the disciples *do* understand the secrets (plural) of the kingdom

---

27. Recall my argument that Mark 4:12 is an ironic comment from the narrator. That the narratee "hears" the verbal irony in 4:12 is certain; that anyone in the story "hears" 4:12 is far from certain.

and the crowds *do not*—period. Matthew then goes on to contrast, at exhaustive length, the outsiders' lack of understanding versus the blessed gift of understanding that belongs indubitably to the disciples. To stress the benighted condition of the crowd, Matthew quotes at great length and with sincerity the passage from Isaiah to which Mark 4:12 briefly and ironically alludes.[28] To stress that the disciples are blessed with understanding, Matthew substitutes Matt. 13:16-17—hearty congratulations from Jesus on the disciples' unparalleled perspicacity—for Mark 4:13, Jesus' sharp questioning of the disciples' lack of understanding of the parables.

Furthermore, in his version of the explanation of the sower parable, Matthew inserts comments about not understanding (Matt. 13:19) versus understanding (Matt. 13:23), which were absent in Mark's version. As if all these changes were not enough, Matthew ends his version of Mark's parable chapter with an emphatic affirmation of the disciples' comprehension of everything (*panta*) that Jesus has said: " 'Have you understood all this?' They said to him, 'Yes' " (Matt. 13:51).

Matthew uses his narrative discourse clearly and directly to emphasize the polarity that exists between understanding and not understanding in his story. His commitment to clarity and direction sends light pouring into the shadowy recesses of Mark's reticent narrative. Matthew puts his discourse to the faithful and steady service of his story, completely overshadowing Mark's strategy of putting story and discourse into tension with each other. In particular, Matthew repudiates Mark's willingness to cast his own narratee occasionally behind a veil of opacity. In Matthew the disciples in the story understand, other people do not understand, and the narratee hearing the story understands who does and does not understand. In Mark, who understands and who does not understand, both inside and outside the story, is constantly up for grabs. In Matthew clarity and straightforwardness reign to such a degree that we might ask, if everything is as obvious as it seems to be in his version of the story, why does not the whole world enlist in Jesus' cause? Mark

28. Infamous here is Matthew's removal of the *hina* in Mark 4:12 (in Mark Jesus speaks parables *so that* people will not understand!) and his substitution of a *hoti* (in Matthew Jesus speaks parables *because* people do not understand; Matt. 13:13). After substituting the *hoti*, Matthew continues his valiant effort to finesse Mark's irony by quoting Isaiah 6:9-10 at length, suggesting that outsiders do not understand Jesus' parables because the prophet foretold that they would fail to understand. Matthew seems not to like Mark's idea that Jesus would intentionally shut people out in his teaching, but apparently if prophecy says that people will be excluded from understanding, then it is perfectly all right. This seems to suggest, however, that Mark was right after all: some people are simply fated not to understand, so Jesus may use parables to shut them out. But whereas Mark says this with tongue in cheek, Matthew says it with a straight face.

On Matthew's substitution of *hoti* for Mark's *hina,* and on indirection in narrative generally, see Frank Kermode, "Hoti's Business: Why Are Narratives Obscure?," *The Genesis of Secrecy: On the Interpretation of Narrative* (Cambridge and London: Harvard University Press, 1979), 23–47.

displays no such pretensions that the story of Jesus is straightforward and clear.[29]

A STRONG READING OF WATER-WALKING

Matthew's version of the Walking on the Water is an exemplary strong reading (Matt. 14:22-32). Matthew exercises three prominent maneuvers: he preserves some Markan wording almost verbatim (Matt. 14:22-27); he adds a bold new piece to Mark's episode (14:28-33); and he obliterates Mark's ending of the episode (Mark 6:51-52). The result is a revision that changes forever the way we read this story.

As noted earlier (see chap. 4), in Mark's version the narrator adroitly shifts perceptual points of view. Early in the episode we are allowed to see things from Jesus' point of view. Then the perceptual point of view shifts to the disciples struggling in the boat, but we find that we cannot share their point of view, which is one of fear and ignorance as to who or what this apparition is that approaches them through wind and wave. The narrator has manipulated us into the position of knowing more than the disciples in the story, and therefore we find ourselves unable to accept their point of view even as it is thrust upon us. Furthermore, having found ourselves unable to accept the disciples' perceptual point of view, we are unlikely to be eager to embrace the conceptual point of view that it figures. If we have any doubt about the appropriateness of our unfavorable judgment on the Twelve, Mark 6:51b-52 removes it. The narrator is the harshest of all in his judgments on the Twelve.

Matthew echoes almost verbatim the Markan episode through Mark 6:50. Beginning with Mark 6:51, however, Matthew takes a radical departure. He erases the triple negative commentary in Mark 6:51b-52—the disciples were "utterly astounded," "they did not understand," "their hearts were hard-ened"—and introduces the scene where Peter hops out of the boat to join Jesus in walking on the water. True, Peter begins to sink after a few steps; true, Jesus chides Peter for being a man of "little faith." Nevertheless, ap-parently even a little faith is sufficient for water-walking in Matthew. The disciples in Matthew's Gospel know what they are about, and they know with whom they are dealing. When Peter begins to sink, he cries out in the language of Christian piety: "Lord, save me!" (*Kyrie, sōson me;* Matt. 14:30). When Peter and Jesus at last get into the boat together, all of the disciples assume the proper attitude of Christian faith: they "worship" Jesus and confess him

29. Besides the emphatic statement in Matt. 13:51 that the disciples understand everything, one could cite other places where Matthew's narrator insists that the disciples understood Jesus completely, e.g., Matt. 16:12 and 17:13. To the contrary, Mark's narrator frequently states baldly that the disciples did not understand, and such reliable commentary is regularly erased from Matthew's palimpsest of Mark, e.g., Mark 6:52 and 8:17, 21.

as "the Son of God." No one joins Jesus in water-walking in Mark, except the narratee, and, more crucially, no one worships Jesus as the Son of God in Mark's Gospel, although many readers outside the Gospel have.

When Peter hops out of the boat to walk on water, never has a reader been born who could continue to find fault with Peter or the others. We can no longer judge the disciples unfavorably as we did when reading Mark. Rather, in Matthew's story we sit safely in the boat and embrace the perceptual point of view of the eleven as we witness along with them Peter's daring feat. Matthew 14:28-33 gives us both the perceptual and the conceptual point of view of the orthodox Christian disciples in the boat (no longer merely Jewish fishermen companions of Jesus). The narratee has no reason not to embrace both the perceptual and the conceptual point of view of the disciples. Regardless of the distance that may have existed earlier in the episode, in the end no distance at all remains between the narratee and the faithful and discerning Christian disciples among whom the narratee finds himself in the boat.

Most interesting of all is the place of Peter's walk on the water in the history of the reading of the Gospels. Nearly every time I discuss Mark's water-walking episode with a college class or a church group, someone in the class asks where Peter's walk on the water is. Where is the "missing piece"? Paradoxically, by means of an insertion into Mark, Matthew has carved out a gap in Mark. After reading Matthew's water-walking episode, Mark's version inevitably seems incomplete and defective. After reading Matthew, reading Mark's episode without reading into it Matthew's insertion, either consciously or unconsciously, is virtually impossible. Another passage from Matthew that is invariably imported into readings of Mark is found in Matthew's version of the Caesarea Philippi episode (Matt. 16:13-23), which follows.

SIMON BAR-JONA: SATAN OR ROCK?

The narrator of Mark's Gospel favors the narratee in Mark 1:1 with the news that Jesus is the Christ, whereas no one in the story is able to make this identification until Peter does in Mark 8:29. Then, as the narratee must be thinking that Peter and the others finally understand, Jesus silences them (Mark 8:30), begins to talk about suffering and death (8:31), and has a head-to-head clash with Peter (8:33). Peter "rebukes" Jesus, apparently for the prediction of suffering and death,[30] and Jesus "rebukes" Peter, bestowing the name of Satan upon him: "Get behind me, Satan! For you are not on the side

---

30. Matthew has turned this into a certainty in Matt. 16:22. In Mark, what Peter said to Jesus is not narrated; it is a moment of opacity for the narratee. We are supposed to supply on our own a comment something like what Matthew proposes. This is one of many instances where Mark provides the riddle and Matthew the solution.

of God, but of men" (Mark 8:33). Apparently, whatever Peter understood by the epithet Christ did not include the ignominy predicted by Jesus in 8:31. In retrospect, the reader may infer that Jesus suspected that Peter's statement in 8:29 was somehow ill-conceived, and so he hushed the disciples immediately and tried to correct their misunderstanding by speaking of the necessity of suffering.

In the Greek, the language throughout the episode is strong. *Epitimaō,* translated in Mark 8:30 as "to charge" and in 8:32 and 8:33 as "to rebuke," is a term often used in exorcism stories as the exorcist tries to gain control over a powerful spiritual adversary.[31] We have a spiritual battle here, nothing less than a confrontation between the forces of God and the forces of Satan. Jesus is on one side, Peter is on the other, and the narratee must choose between them—we have no alternative. In narrative terms, a clash of conceptual points of view occurs here, and the narratee is pressed into the awkward position of having to choose between the conceptual point of view of the protagonist and that of his chief disciple. This choice is not a happy one, but Mark gives us no other.

What does Matthew do to this episode? Matthew echoes faithfully virtually all of Mark 8:27-33, reminiscent of his preservation of the early verses of Mark's water-walking episode. Also like his revision of the water-walking, Matthew excavates a gaping hole in Mark by the interpolation of Matt. 16:17-19 between Mark 8:29 and 8:30.[32] This famous "Thou art Peter" passage is found exclusively in Matthew's Gospel. The early church knew that Simon, the son of Jona, bore the nickname of Cephas (Aramaic) or Peter (Greek), both of which mean "rock." Mark knows this tradition and mentions early in his Gospel (Mark 3:16) that Jesus himself bestowed this nickname on Simon. At least in Mark, then, that the disciple known as Rock proves to be so unreliable and unsteady is ironic. Matthew sees no irony, of course, nor for that matter does the rest of the New Testament.[33] More than any other text, Matt. 16:17-19 has guaranteed the high esteem with which Peter has been held in Christendom. So strong is Matthew's reading of Mark's Caesarea Philippi episode that readers fail to realize that Mark offers his own strong

31. Howard Clark Kee, "The Terminology of Mark's Exorcism Stories," *NTS* 14 (1968): 232–46.

32. Also reminiscent of the water-walking scene is the expansion that Matthew makes in Peter's confession in Mark 8:29: "You are the Christ, *the Son of the living God.*" This echoes the discerning acclamation Matthew has the disciples make in the boat after Peter's walk on the water (Matt. 14:33).

33. Galatians 2 is an interesting exception. Apparently Paul did not hold Simon Peter in awe. For a critical appraisal, mostly from a historical perspective, of the role of Simon Peter in the New Testament, see Raymond E. Brown, Karl P. Donfried, and John Reumann, eds., *Peter in the New Testament: A Collaborative Assessment by Protestant and Roman Catholic Scholars* (Minneapolis: Augsburg; New York, Paramus, and Toronto: Paulist, 1973).

reading of a name-bestowing scene, namely, Jesus' bestowal of the nickname Satan upon Peter in Mark 8:33.

I suspect that Mark 8:33 is already a strong reading by Mark of one or more precursor narratives told in the early church about how Peter got his name. Nevertheless, he who writes last, writes best. Matthew acknowledges the strength of Mark's audacious reading of Jesus' bestowal of the Satan nickname upon Peter by repeating it almost verbatim. Mark's Satan-nickname scene is too strong a reading to be either forgotten or ignored. It can be vanquished and supplanted by revisionary maneuvers, but it must be dealt with.[34] Matthew tips his hat to Mark by echoing Mark's Satan-nickname story, but he changes forever the way it is experienced by preceding it with an all-the-stronger retelling of the Peter-nickname story.

In Matt. 16:17-19 the narrator glorifies Peter. Jesus pronounces a blessing upon him; he is congratulated for having received nothing less than a divine revelation; he is proclaimed the very "rock" on which the church will be built; he is handed the keys to the kingdom of heaven. Power, honor, and glory are his. In the radiant afterglow of such a scene, Jesus could next call Peter anything and it would not matter.[35] Matthew turns the terrible choice imposed on the reader by Mark—choose between God and Jesus on one side, and Satan and Peter on the other—into an edifying lesson in Christian living: even "the Rock" stumbled occasionally![36]

GRIDDING THE EMPTY TOMB

Matthew takes up Mark's brief and wonderfully indirect episode in which three women discover Jesus' empty tomb (Mark 16:1-8) and replaces it with

34. Mark's Gospel is full of strong readings of many stories from early Christian tradition. Mark has written these episodes on the Christian imagination with indelible ink: the baptism of Jesus, the Feeding of the Five Thousand, the Crucifixion, the Empty Tomb, and so on. We know these narratives only in Mark's version and in the revisions they receive at the hands of other early Christian authors. Matthew and Luke echo Mark as much as they do because Mark has offered many unforgettable episodes that can never be completely erased from any palimpsest of his Gospel. I suspect that all early narrative Gospels (as opposed to Gospels consisting of disconnected sayings of Jesus) have Mark as their precursor. On this point I am essentially in agreement with Werner H. Kelber, "From Aphorism to Sayings Gospel, and from Parable to Narrative Gospel," *Forum* 1 (1985): 23–50.

35. Also, we should not forget that when the reader arrives at the Satan-nickname scene in Matthew, the reader has already observed this "Satan" walk on the water with Jesus. Having witnessed such scenes in Matthew, it will be difficult for the reader to take the Satan epithet seriously. Unfortunately, in this survey of highlights of Matthew's reading grid, I cannot do justice to the cumulative experience of a continuous reading of Matthew.

36. Matthew betrays some nervousness about the relationship between his interpolation in Matt. 16:17-19 and the verses from Mark that follow it. Matthew eases the tension between the Peter-nickname scene in Matt. 16:17-19 and the Satan-nickname scene in 16:22-23 by introducing a time gap between them in 16:21. This helps to avoid making Simon appear schizophrenic: "the Rock" one instant and "Satan" the very next.

a series of episodes in which: (1) a guard is set at Jesus' tomb (Matt. 27:62-66, 28:4, 28:11-15); (2) an angel descends from heaven, rolls the stone away from the (already) empty tomb, and speaks to the women, who witness everything (28:1-3, 5-8); and (3) the resurrected Jesus appears twice to his followers, once to the women (28:9-10) and once to the eleven remaining disciples (28:16-20). The changes Matthew has wrought in Mark's story are so massive that discerning the equally massive changes in narrative strategy at the level of discourse becomes a challenge.

Mark's grand strategy of indirection comes to a head in the last scene of his Gospel. The ending is more inconclusive than conclusive, leaving the reader to provide a conclusion. Matthew takes up Mark's invitation to the reader to complete Mark's narrative. By sharing with us the "end results" of his own reading of Mark, Matthew has made difficult hearing Mark's invitation for ourselves. What are the puzzles that Mark offers the reader in his final episode, puzzles for which Matthew so gladly supplies the answers?

Mark 16:1-8 begins with three women, Mary Magdalene, another Mary, and Salome, coming to Jesus' tomb to anoint his corpse. These women have been mentioned already in 15:40-41 and 15:47. The one Mary is of particular interest. She is first described as Mary the mother of James and Joses (15:41), then Mary the mother of Joses (15:47), and then Mary the mother of James (16:1). The variations in her name call attention to her. In fact, the repetition of the names of all three women suggests that they were persons well known to the original flesh-and-blood readers of this Gospel. Yet Mary the mother of James and Joses was better known to early Christians as Mary the mother of Jesus.[37] The reader remembers that a Mary having sons named James and Joses has already appeared in Mark's narrative (6:3). This Mary is indeed Jesus' mother, and James and Joses are the first two of Jesus' four brothers that Mark names. That Mary is called "the mother of James and Joses" in the final scenes of the Gospel suggests that she is not to be regarded as "the mother of Jesus." Jesus' relationship with his family is still broken. The estrangement that developed in 3:21, 31-35 and deepened in 6:1-6 is still as severe as ever.

Are not Jesus' mother and the other two women performing a commendable act of devotion by coming to the tomb? Are they not portrayed positively by Mark? After all, they did observe Jesus' death on the cross,[38] they witnessed his burial (15:47), and now they come to anoint his body. Is this behavior not worthy of the reader's admiration?

---

37. In making this identification I am in agreement with Werner H. Kelber, John Dominic Crossan, and Thomas Boomershine; see the discussion by Kelber, *The Oral and the Written Gospel: The Hermeneutics of Speaking and Writing in the Synoptic Tradition, Mark, Paul, and Q* (Philadelphia: Fortress Press, 1983), 103–4.

38. But they observe his death "from afar" (15:40), which may suggest to the reader that they are distant in more ways than one.

The reader may entertain this possibility, but when the narrator tells us that the women's purpose in coming to the tomb is to anoint Jesus' corpse, the reader can hardly avoid remembering the episode that opened the Passion narrative, in which an anonymous woman anointed Jesus' body "beforehand for burying" (14:3-9). At that time no one in the story showed any uptake of this strange remark, but anyone reading the story is bound to remember that Jesus has already been anointed for burial. Therefore, when three women come to his tomb expecting to anoint his body, the reader must have a strong suspicion that they will somehow fail to accomplish their goal. Their intentions may be good, but like so many in the story they have failed to understand what was happening in their midst, and so Jesus' anointing passes them by without their knowing it.

That the women would come to the tomb to anoint a body that has already been anointed must strike the reader as a dramatic irony. Also ironic is the women's apparently innocent question to one another: "Who will roll away the stone for us. . . ?" Who indeed? Their unanswered question resonates loudly and cannot help reminding the reader that Jesus had disciples and kinsfolk who could have aided the women.[39] In this story, however, Jesus is abandoned by one and all, with the exception of a few "little people," such as the anonymous woman who anointed him and Joseph of Arimathea, who buried him.

Besides the variety of indirect moves that occur in 16:1-8, Mark also directs the reader with reliable commentary. By inside views we are told the purpose of the women's visit to the tomb, what they said to one another as they approached the tomb, and what they saw when they arrived. Also, at the end of 16:4, the narrator offers us one of his patented awkward *gar* parentheses: *"for it [the stone] was very large."* This clear but awkward comment returns us to indirection because the already-rolled-away stone is a puzzle, a revelation of an earlier moment of opacity that had excluded the reader as well as the women. Both the women in the story and the reader have been denied the experience of witnessing the rolling away of the stone. Who might have rolled the stone away, when, and why are all beyond our seeing, our hearing, and our understanding. The discovery of an already-rolled-away stone is the discovery of a gap both in the story and in the discourse, one that begs to be filled with meaning.

The tomb is not completely empty, however, because inside it we en-counter the additional puzzle of the "young man" (*neaniskos*). Many readers have supposed that he is an angel, but Mark does not say this. Many readers have supposed that he is the same chap who runs naked through Gethsemane

---

39. It is noteworthy that Jesus is buried by a stranger, Joseph of Arimathea (15:42-47). One would have expected either his family or disciples to perform the burial duties, but none of them has anything to do with it. Contrast this to the burial of John the Baptist, which Mark is careful to note was performed by his disciples (6:29).

after Jesus' arrest (14:51-52), but Mark does not confirm this. That he is more unclear than clear, more puzzle than solution, should hardly surprise us at the end of our reading of Mark.

What does the young man have to say? First, let us consider the paradox in the young man's comment to the women in 16:6: "Do not be amazed; you seek Jesus, the Nazarene, the crucified one; he has been raised; he is not here; see the place where they laid him" (RMF). The dead Nazarene, the one shamed by rejection and crucifixion, has been raised up, exalted. This utterance is a verbal paradox, and at the heart of it lies an implicit riddle: If Jesus has been raised, then who or what has raised him? With no help from the narrator, most readers have judged that God is the only appropriate answer. Still, countless other questions about this "raising up" are left unanswered.

The young man's words continue: "But go tell his disciples, even Peter, 'He's going ahead of you to Galilee. There you will behold him, just as he told you' " (R&M). Note that Peter is singled out. Does the distinction drawn between Peter and "his disciples" have an ironic edge? The reader remembers that Peter was not content to abandon Jesus like all the rest, running away into the safety of the night. No, he had to blunder his way into an even more shocking public renunciation of Jesus, denying with oaths that he even knew Jesus (Mark 15:66-72). Therefore, perhaps because his denial of Jesus ran even deeper than that of the others, he is separated from "his disciples" in 16:7.

The question remains, Is this singling out of Peter for good or ill, for blessing or bane? We must not too hastily assume that Peter is being singled out for favorable treatment. Perhaps quite the opposite holds. Our reading of Mark 16:7 remains so constrained by our knowledge of the other Gospels and by nineteen centuries of reading history that I want to shed some new light on the reading of 16:7 by pursuing a line of thought that is seldom if ever pursued here. Putting aside the special attention given to Peter in 16:7 for the moment, let us ask ourselves instead what the status of Judas is in Mark 16:7.[40]

Must not the reader surmise that Judas is included among the disciples in the reference to "his disciples, even Peter"? Nothing here indicates to the reader that Judas is *not* included among "his disciples" in 16:7. If this fact is surprising, it is only because we are familiar with the treatment of Judas in the other Gospels. Matthew, Luke, and even John have constructed reading grids that have effectively blocked from our sight Mark's treatment of Judas.

A full chapter before his version of the empty tomb narrative, Matthew offers us his unique version of Judas' demise: "When Judas, his betrayer, saw that he was condemned, he repented and brought back the thirty pieces of silver to the chief priests and elders, saying, 'I have sinned in betraying

---

40. On the narrative function of Judas in Mark, see Kermode, *Genesis of Secrecy*, 84–95.

innocent blood.' They said, 'What is that to us? See to it yourself.' And throwing down the pieces of silver in the temple, he departed; and he went and hanged himself" (Matt. 27:3-5). Because this episode precedes Matthew's empty tomb narrative, in Matthew's story Judas has clearly been removed from the stage forever by the time the events at Jesus' tomb take place.

Luke narrates a contradictory but equally ignoble demise for Judas at the beginning of the Acts of the Apostles: "Now this man bought a field with the reward of his wickedness; and falling headlong he burst open in the middle and all his bowels gushed out" (Acts 1:18). By delaying this business until Acts 1, Luke has clouded how it relates chronologically to the death and resurrection of Jesus, but clearly Judas has been eliminated from the cast of characters before Acts gets under way.[41]

John's Gospel does not narrate the demise of Judas, but John does add to Judas' infamy by stating that he was a thief (John 12:6) and that he was possessed by Satan[42] (John 13:2, 27). Moreover, John narrates several resurrection appearances, and Judas appears in none of them. We can safely say that he has been removed from the stage by the end of John's Gospel also.

Given the treatment of Judas in Matthew, Luke, and John, we can easily overlook that Judas does not receive his just deserts in Mark. In fact, the astonishing thing about Mark's treatment of Judas at the end of the story is that he is not differentiated from the others; Peter is! Some readers will protest that Judas lies under the curse pronounced by Jesus upon the betrayer of the Son of man (Mark 14:21), and therefore we must suppose that something dreadful will happen to him beyond Mark 16:8. However, such a fulfillment of the curse of 14:21 is not narrated. Moreover, Peter lies under a curse as severe or worse than Judas' curse. By refusing to deny himself (Mark 8:34), by saving his own life (8:35), by being ashamed of Jesus and his words (8:38), Peter can expect the Son of man to be ashamed of him, when the kingdom comes with power (8:38—9:1). Who, after all, takes a stand most directly opposed to what Jesus stands for? Who is the only disciple called Satan in Mark? It is Peter.[43] Just as Judas' fate is not narrated in Mark's Gospel, however, neither is Peter's. At best, Mark 16:7 gestures ambiguously toward a future for the Twelve not narrated in Mark's Gospel. Their future is open, just as it is for the reader, to construe as each one will.

The point of this analysis is to help us see that neither Peter, Judas, nor any other of the Twelve is the principal concern of the author in Mark 16:7.

41. Curiously, there are references to the "eleven" disciples in Luke 24:9 and 24:33, as if Judas has already been disposed of by then, but the timing of Judas' death remains unclear in Luke-Acts.

42. John may borrow this from Luke, who had already suggested that Judas' betrayal was inspired by Satan (Luke 22:3).

43. I suspect that a trajectory runs from Mark to Matthew to Luke to John, in which the burden of the Satan epithet is gradually lifted from Peter's shoulders and transferred over to Judas.

The future that the storyteller is most concerned about is the future of the reader. How the reader responds to the end of Mark's Gospel is what the end of Mark's Gospel is about. That we worry about the incompleteness of the ending of the Gospel—and more in terms of story than of discourse—shows how successfully Mark has been eclipsed by his successors.

More can be said about reading Mark 16:7—"He's going ahead of you to Galilee." Here is marvelous clarity and also marvelous opacity. What is absolutely transparent is that Jesus "goes ahead" (*proagō*[44]). What is absolutely opaque is whether anyone "follows." The implicit, unanswered question here is whether anyone, inside or outside the story, will end up following Jesus. The reader cannot say for sure what the women or the Twelve will do. The reader can only answer for herself.

Another puzzle here is what Galilee is. We might once have thought that we understood what Galilee was, when Jesus began his ministry there back in Mark 1:14-15, but through what kind of Galilee does a crucified and raised Jesus now walk? In retrospect, Galilee may always have been more of a metaphor of space rather than a literal geopolitical region, but all the more so now. Whatever Galilee was before, it is now obviously a figure for wherever it is that the crucified Nazarene "goes ahead" of his disciples.

Many readers have taken "there you will see him" as a prediction that the disciples will soon rendezvous with the risen Jesus in Galilee and see him in his resurrected glory there. Clearly Matthew reads Mark 16:7 this way, but must we? To answer this question, let us first backtrack to the narrator's persistent concern over what the three women in Mark 15:40—16:8 see or do not see in the story.

In Mark 15:40 the three women look upon (*theōreō*) the crucifixion "from afar." Then, in 15:47 two of the three women see (*theōreō*) the place where Jesus was buried. As they approach the tomb early on Sunday morning, they look up (*anablepō*) and see (*theōreō*) that the stone is already rolled away (16:4). They enter the tomb and see (*eidon*) the young man sitting inside. He tells them that they are seeking Jesus of Nazareth, but "he is not here; see (*eidon*) the place where they laid him" (16:6). Then come the young man's instructions to the women in 16:7, which culminate in the words: "he is going before you to Galilee; there you will see (*horaō*) him, as he told you." After all they have "seen," the women come to the wrong place to "see" Jesus. If the women or the Twelve really wish to "see" Jesus, then they must "follow" him, as he "goes ahead" of them to "Galilee." "*There* you will see him," the young man says. Thanks to Matthew's palimpsest of Mark, however, the young man's comment has been read in the sense of "there *you will see him.*" If we can peel away Matthew's reading grid, however, we may

44. Cf. the illuminating use of the verb *proagō* in Mark 10:32. There Jesus "goes ahead" of his disciples, who "follow" (*akoloutheō*) him.

be able to see that the statement in Mark 16:7 was not originally a prediction of a future resurrection appearance but rather an attempt to set straight the women, the Twelve, and most especially the reader, as to where to go to see Jesus. We must not look for him in a tomb. We must instead follow him to Galilee. Presumably, if we do not follow him to Galilee, then we will not see him.[45]

Even a phrase as innocuous as "as he told you" in 16:7 performs a useful service in the discourse, if not in the story. It serves to remind the reader that once already in the story Jesus himself talked about going before his disciples to Galilee. The context for this earlier statement was Jesus' prediction to the disciples that they would all fail him (14:27), and Peter's impassioned protest that even though all of the others might fall away, he would rather die with Jesus (14:29-31). In the midst of this discussion comes the incongruous statement by Jesus: "after I am raised up, I will go before you to Galilee" (14:28). Jesus' statement in 14:28 is echoed faithfully by the young man in the tomb in 16:7.

Neither 14:28 nor its echo in 16:7 receives any uptake in the story, which is in line with my observation earlier that no uptake is ever demonstrated at the level of story for any of Jesus' predictions of his death or resurrection. Such predictions are efficacious only for the reader. Mark 14:28 as well as 16:7 make clear that Jesus will be going ahead, and both leave opaque whether anyone will follow. If Mark had wanted Jesus to predict whether anyone would follow, he could have had Jesus address this topic quite clearly. Frequently in Mark, Jesus issues predictions that are fulfilled before our eyes in the story (e.g., 14:27, 30). Neither 14:28 nor 16:7 says anything about who will follow, however, so we have here no such prediction to be fulfilled.

How does Mark's Gospel end? The last verse[46] reads: "And they went out and fled from the tomb; for trembling and astonishment had come over them; and they said nothing to any one, for they were afraid" (16:8). Literally, the women say "nothing to no one" (*oudeni ouden eipan*); that is, they were

45. The experience of reading Mark's Gospel should by now have taught the reader not to take sense perception ("hearing," "seeing," etc.) too literally. These have all been used figuratively many times in the Gospel. To pull some metaphors together here, as we finish reading Mark we should be able to realize that "Galilee" is *wherever* one "follows" and "sees" Jesus.

46. I assume the original conclusion to Mark's Gospel was 16:8, and that all of the other endings that follow 16:8 in ancient manuscripts are attempts by scribes to bring the text of Mark's Gospel into conformity with its successors by adding appendices to Mark that are essentially pastiches of the resurrection narratives in Matthew, Luke, and John.

The best treatments of the ending of the Gospel with which I am familiar are Thomas E. Boomershine and Gilbert L. Bartholomew, "The Narrative Technique of Mark 16:8," *JBL* 100 (1981): 213–23; idem, "Mark 16:8 and the Apostolic Commission," *JBL* 100 (1981): 225–39; Norman Petersen, "When Is the End Not the End? Literary Reflections on the Ending of Mark's Narrative," *Int* 34 (1980): 151–66; J. Lee Magness, *Sense and Absence: Structure and Suspension in the Ending of Mark's Gospel*, SBLSS (Atlanta: Scholars Press, 1986).

so frightened by their experience that the story of the empty tomb was never told. The story *in* the Gospel seems to preclude the telling *of* the Gospel; Mark's Gospel is the story of a story that was never told. If we read the Gospel with a fixation on the story level, this ending may strike us as an immense problem. No problem exists, however, if we grant that this narrative is more concerned about discourse than story. The women may never tell the story of which they are a part, but the reader has read their story and can respond to it in a multitude of ways, among them the option of telling the story of the story that was never told. The burden of response-ability lies wholly on those of us standing outside the story.

Matthew makes two broad moves in his revision of Mark's empty tomb narrative. For one thing, Matthew shifts the emphasis away from the discourse to the story. Matthew does not somehow avoid using narrative discourse; rather, his heightened emphasis on the story level entails a discourse that is more direct than indirect, seemingly more transparent than opaque. Matthew's second major move is accordingly a move away from indirection to direction. I shall point out later several instances in which Matthew straightens out Markan indirection by reversing an absence of uptake or by clarifying a moment of opacity, which often has the further effect of unraveling a dramatic irony. Features that already were in Mark's empty tomb story but receive new emphasis and clarity in Matthew's story include the tomb itself, the women, the young man, Jesus, and the Twelve.

Symptomatic of Matthew's desire to straighten and clarify Mark's story is what happens to the stone in front of the tomb. In Mark, both the women and the narratee discover the stone already rolled away, and opacity reigns at the level of discourse as well as in the story. By contrast, Matthew makes an effort to remove the opacity from both story and discourse by having the stone rolled away before the eyes of the women and the narratee.

Matthew transfigures the empty tomb from a puzzle in story and discourse alike into a physical fact primarily in the story. He achieves this with an apologetic narrative about a guard set at the tomb. The guard narrative completely surrounds the empty tomb narrative by appearing before, in the middle of, and after Matthew's version of it (Matt. 27:62-65, 28:4, 28:11-14). For all his emphasis on the story level, Matthew is using his own style of narrative rhetoric to lull us into thinking about a tomb surrounded by a guard, so that we will not notice how a tomb story has been gridded roundabout by a guard story.

Matthew's guard story is a strong reading of Mark's tomb story that has to compete with at least one other strong reading of the same story (Matt. 28:13-15)—strong readers often battle each other for exclusive rights to their common precursor. Apparently, opponents of the early Christian movement had read or heard about Mark's tomb story and had pointed out that the story of the empty tomb could be read as a fragment of a larger story about Jesus' disciples stealing his body. By telling a story in which this competing story is dishonestly fabricated, Matthew's reading grid encompasses both Mark's empty tomb narrative and the competing strong reading of it. Matthew's story of the invention of the competing strong reading is the story of a story no honest person would tell; its telling had to be purchased with bribe money. Of course, Matthew's strong reading of Mark is probably just as much a fabrication as the strong reading with which it competes, but it is offered as faithful and true fabrication, protecting Mark's tomb story from the threat of violation posed by the strong reading mentioned in Matt. 28:15. As farfetched as Matthew's guard narrative is as a revision of Mark's narrative, it does effectively disallow competing revisions that are even more farfetched, such as the strong reading of Mark that has the disciples stealing the body. The function of Matthew's guard story is to guard Mark's tomb story from readings that Matthew regards as desecration.

Yet the cost of this protection is high indeed. Matthew has to renounce Mark's narrative tactics in order to protect Mark's narrative contents. To compete with other strong readers of the empty tomb narrative, Matthew treats the empty tomb as if it were an unquestionable piece of public evidence. It can no longer be a puzzle in either story or discourse; it must now be a concrete object—virtually a shrine—in the story. It is no longer open to the reader (or anyone) to enter for purposes of interpretation but is available now only for reverent viewing from a discreet distance. Matthew's text curtails the very thing that Mark's text revels in: the reader's exercise of interpretive freedom, the challenge to respond to the reading experience as we will. The interpretive freedom pressed upon the reader by Mark has led to illegitimate readings, in Matthew's opinion, so he produces a palimpsest of Mark that severely restricts the interpretive options available to the reader. Matthew effectively seals up the empty tomb story, protecting it forever from the threat of illegitimate readings; that is, readings other than Matthew's. Matthew would have us believe that the only way to read Mark's empty tomb story is his way.

A remarkable instance of Matthew's abolition of opacity and absence of uptake occurs toward the beginning of the guard story. In Matt. 27:63-64 the opponents of Jesus come to Pilate and say, "Sir, we remember how that imposter said, while he was still alive, 'After three days I will rise again.' Therefore order the sepulchre to be made secure until the third day, lest his disciples go and steal him away. . . ." In contrast to Mark's typical narrative strategies, in Matthew this speech by the opponents of Jesus is nothing less than astonishing. In Mark no one in the story ever demonstrates any under-standing of any of Jesus' predictions of his death and resurrection. All such predictions by Jesus in Mark take place behind a veil of opacity, as far as characters in the story are concerned. In Matthew, not only do the disciples demonstrate uptake of the Passion predictions (see Matt. 17:23; cf. Mark 9:32) but also even the opponents of Jesus hear and understand his predictions.

They may not believe them, but they grasp their import fully, as indicated in Matt. 27:63. In similar fashion, many puzzles for the narratee in Mark's discourse are turned into public experiences or observable, concrete realities in Matthew's story.

As the principal characters in Mark's tomb story, the women must receive Matthew's attention. First, Matthew masks the identity of Jesus' mother (Matt. 28:1; cf. Mark 16:1). Second, the purpose of the women's visit to the tomb is weakened. Instead of coming to anoint Jesus' body, they come merely "to see the sepulchre" (Matt. 28:1; cf. Mark 16:1). Third, if the women do not come to anoint the corpse, then they no longer need to enter the tomb; they do not have to ask themselves the embarrassing question about who will roll away the stone for them, and thus the narratee is no longer pointedly reminded of the absence of the disciples at the crucifixion and burial of Jesus. By erasing Mark 16:3-5, Matthew erases the dramatic irony that makes unwitting victims of the women and the Twelve. Fourth, instead of being frightened out of their wits by a mysterious young man inside the tomb, the women apparently stand outside the tomb and witness the glorious, unambiguous descent from heaven of an angel, who rolls away the stone before their eyes (Matt. 28:2-4) and then speaks to them (28:5-7). Fifth, the consistent "trembling," "astonishment," and "fear" of the women in Mark is transformed into "fear *and great joy*" by Matthew. The numbing fear that betokens the absence of understanding and faith is preserved by Matthew but transferred from the women to the guards (Matt. 28:4). In Matthew's view, the guards are the narrative's outsiders, and therefore they properly faint away at the sight of heavenly glory, but the women are knowing insiders, and therefore they faithfully witness everything. Sixth, by overlaying the unremitting fear of the women in Mark 16:8 with rapturous joy, the women are no longer fearful and silent, as they are in Mark. Instead, they run to tell the disciples what the angel has just told them (Matt. 28:8-10) but are instantly surprised to encounter the risen Jesus himself, who greets them and repeats the words of the angel.

One verse kept largely unchanged by Matthew is Mark 16:7: "there you will see him."[47] By having it repeated twice, once by an angel from heaven and once again by the risen Lord himself, as well as by going on to narrate the vision of Jesus on a mountaintop in Galilee (Matt. 28:16-20), Matthew has offered us a grid for reading Mark 16:7 that has proven to be overwhelmingly successful in the history of reading the Gospels. The artful uncertainty in Mark 16:7 about who might or might not follow and see Jesus is turned

47. One change worth noting in Matthew's version of Mark 16:7 is the erasure of "even Peter." Matthew's reading grid would probably have been sufficiently strong to have allowed him to keep this embarrassing mention of Peter and still have the reader read it with Matthew's entirely positive outlook on Peter. However, Matthew probably found too distasteful the negative treatment of Peter throughout Mark's Gospel, and so he erases this separation of Peter from "his disciples."

by Matthew into a prediction of a future resurrection appearance, which is then immediately fulfilled in the story.

That Matthew brings Jesus and the disciples back onto the stage at the end of the story is itself a sweeping revision of Mark. Mark ends his Gospel in a bravura turn of indirection, with neither Jesus nor any faithful disciple appearing in the final scene. Yet Matthew's reading grid is so powerful that most readers have difficulty seeing and appreciating that both Jesus and faithful disciples are conspicuous by their absence at the end of Mark. Countless readers acknowledge the success of Matthew's reading grid when they argue that surely Mark implies that everything that Matthew narrates at the end of his Gospel will yet take place beyond Mark 16:8. For nineteen hundred years Mark's Gospel has been "completed" by readers turning consciously or unconsciously to Matthew.

The surprising final absence and silence of Jesus in Mark's narrative is transformed by Matthew into full presence and lordly benediction. The resurrected Jesus is both seen and heard, first by the women running in joy from the tomb (Matt. 28:9-10) and second by the remaining eleven disciples on a mountaintop in Galilee (Matt. 28:16-20). Matthew's story ends as it began, with abundant examples of faithful and true discipleship within the story to provide straightforward and reliable models of discipleship for the reader.

Matthew ties up the loose threads of narrative that he has inherited from Mark into neat and tidy conclusions. He makes sure that Judas receives his just deserts (Matt. 27:3-10). The remaining eleven get to see Jesus in Galilee and receive there the so-called Great Commission. By receiving the Great Commission, Peter will remain "the Rock," continue to hold the keys to the kingdom of heaven (Matt. 16:17-19), and share with his comrades the thrones of judgment over the twelve tribes of Israel (Matt. 19:28). Moreover, the exalted, resurrected Jesus will remain present with his followers "to the close of the age." Few narratives make more grandiose claims for closure than these.

Matthew's narrative insinuates other bold claims for itself. In the scene of the Great Commission, the disciples are commanded to go out into the world to make disciples in Jesus' name, "teaching them to observe all that I have commanded you" (Matt. 28:20). Matthew's Gospel ends with an episode in which faithful disciples of Jesus are mandated to promulgate the teaching of Jesus in the authoritative style of Matthew's Gospel. Whereas the ending of Mark's story seems to preclude the telling of Mark's story, the ending of Matthew's story provides weighty authorization for telling Matthew's story. Whereas Mark's Gospel is indirect and puzzling to the end, Matthew's Gospel is boldly direct to the end; it strives to make impossible imagining that it could not have been narrated or that any other narrative about Jesus could ever again hope to rival it. Matthew's concluding episode stops just short of making an explicit claim that this Gospel has the authority of heaven and earth behind it. Thus does Matthew vanquish and supplant not only the ending of Mark, but the whole of Mark.

REFLECTIONS ON MATTHEW'S GRID

Several perennial problems in the interpretation of Mark take on a new appearance if they are understood as problems that arise because we read Mark through Matthew's reading grid. I have already discussed the overwhelming influence that the ending of Matthew has had on the way we read the ending of Mark. Now I want to consider problems related to the Messianic Secret, the understanding and use of parables, and the role of the disciples that are created by Matthew's reading grid.

THE MESSIANIC SECRET

The Messianic Secret is the rubric under which twentieth-century Markan scholarship has often pursued the problems of Mark's narrative discourse and especially Mark's rhetoric of indirection. Unfortunately, because most biblical scholarship has concentrated on the contents of the story, we have neglected the workings of the discourse. In this book I cannot reformulate the entire scholarly debate concerning the Messianic Secret, but I can offer tools with which it might be done. The first step in such a revisionary project would be to take scholarly discussions of the Messianic Secret as a rich lode of disguised reports of reading experiences from contemporary critical readers of Mark's Gospel.

A dozen passages in Mark have received repeated attention by scholars. They have also been grouped in categories, which also sparks much debate. The passages in Mark traditionally associated with the Messianic Secret are (1) commands to demons to be quiet about Jesus' Messiahship (1:25, 34; 3:12), (2) prohibitions against speaking of the miracles (1:43-45; 5:43; 7:36; 8:26), (3) commands to the disciples to keep silent about Peter's confession (8:30) and the transfiguration (9:9), (4) Jesus' attempts to remain incognito (7:24; 9:30-31), and (5) the incident of the crowd silencing the blind man by the road (10:48).[48]

Of these dozen passages, Matthew erases no less than seven of them in his palimpsest of Mark: 1:25, 34; 5:43; 7:24, 36; 8:26; 9:30-31. Interesting as these erasures are in terms of the content of Matthew's story, they are all the more interesting as a reflection of Matthew's narrative strategies at the level of discourse. That Matthew keeps even five of Mark's Messianic Secret passages is a wonder. Matthew is uncomfortable with all kinds of indirection in Mark; he clarifies opacities, solves riddles implied by metaphors, dismantles

---

48. William Wrede, *The Messianic Secret,* trans. J. C. G. Greig (Cambridge and London: James Clarke, 1971), 34–36.

dramatic ironies, and so on. Given the long-standing success of Matthew's narrative, we cannot be surprised that readers have found Mark's indirection baffling. The befuddlement of critics over the Messianic Secret and their irritation at being befuddled are created as much or more by Matthew's reading grid as by Mark itself. If Matthew's approach to narration is taken as the norm, then Mark's approach appears aberrant, and Matthew has often been taken as the norm, consciously or unconsciously; for centuries it has enveloped Mark in the shadows of its clarifications.

UNDERSTANDING AND USE OF PARABLES

Both Matthew and Luke clarify, straighten out, or erase much of Mark's indirect, figurative language. One form of indirection among many that they avoid is the inherent ambiguity of strong metaphors. One result is that both Matthew and Luke shy away from genuinely parabolic use of parables, which we may find surprising; most of what we know about the parables of Jesus we learn from the Gospels of Matthew and Luke, the two most important collections of the words of Jesus that we have from the early church.[49]

Matthew and Luke are able to incorporate so many of the parables of Jesus into their narratives because they found ways to put them to nonparabolic uses. Typically, Matthew and Luke end a parable of Jesus with a lesson or moral that can be drawn from the story. At other times the parable is followed by an allegorical interpretation[50] or is told in such a way that an allegorical meaning is woven into the fabric of the story itself. Given what we have learned in recent years about how parables work, these occurrences are all essentially nonparabolic uses of parables.[51] A genuine parabolist prefers to weave his own parabolic fabric, which is what Mark does. To be sure, Jesus tells some parables in Mark's story, but the most prominent parabolic discourse that we find in Mark is the discourse level of Mark. Mark has constructed a profoundly parabolic narrative designed to affect its audience by means of intriguing, indirect discourse. Because Mark uses the figures "Jesus" and "the twelve disciples" in his parabolic narrative, however, it lends itself all too easily to being literalized and historicized, once Mark's commitment to indirect discourse has been blunted in subsequent revisions. Matthew represents perhaps the first such revision and the first great step toward the domestication, literalization, and historicization of the parabolic discourse of

49. Next in importance as a repository of the teaching of Jesus is probably the Gospel of Thomas, discovered in the 1940s at Nag Hammadi, in Egypt.

50. To be fair, it should be acknowledged that Mark already uses allegorical interpretation, but Mark's allegorical interpretations are more open-ended, even parabolic, than Matthew's or Luke's.

51. Allegorical interpretation disregards the dynamics of parabolic discourse in order to get at a supposedly hidden story content. Parabolic discourse becomes expendable in the quest for a referential meaning.

the Gospel of Mark. Luke, in his two-volume work of "history," also makes a large contribution to the historicization of Mark's indirect and figurative discourse.

Only in recent decades have we made significant progress in freeing the parables of the historical Jesus from the smothering embrace of Matthew and Luke. A similar rescue mission for Mark's parabolic discourse must also be conducted. Reading grids that have been in place for centuries are difficult to peel away, but in spite of them we have learned that parables are designed to make an impact on the hearer, not to make a point or illustrate a lesson. Parabolic narrative, whether the parables of Jesus or Mark's Gospel, is more discourse oriented than story oriented, more audience oriented than message oriented, more indirect than direct, and more figurative than literal. Given the nonparabolic way that Matthew and Luke use both the parables of Jesus and the Gospel of Mark, however, seeing and appreciating the parabolic qualities of either Jesus' parables or Mark's Gospel are extraordinarily difficult.

THE ROLE OF THE DISCIPLES

The role of the disciples in Mark's Gospel is much debated. This topic also has usually been discussed in terms of story rather than discourse. Even the most thoughtful recent efforts to approach the disciples in Mark as a narrative problem have continued to confuse what happens in the story with what is happening to the narratee thanks to the discourse.[52] Also, we continue to read the role of the disciples in Mark through reading grids. I want to indicate in a few broad strokes how this discussion might be profitably reformulated.

Today the critical discussion of the function of the disciples in Mark's narrative pivots on the question of where the critical reader stands in relationship to the work of Theodore Weeden.[53] Weeden more than anyone else broke the grip of the strong readings of Mark that had enthralled readers for centuries. By arguing that the reader is led to distance himself from the Twelve instead of identifying closely with them, Weeden broke the ancient spell of the earliest and strongest of Mark's readers, namely, Matthew, Luke, and

52. On the narrative function of the disciples in Mark, see Robert C. Tannehill, "The Disciples in Mark: The Function of a Narrative Role," *JR* 57 (1977): 386–405; Joanna Dewey, "Point of View and the Disciples in Mark," *SBLSP* 1982, 97–106; Elizabeth Struthers Malbon, "Fallible Followers: Women and Men in the Gospel of Mark," *Semeia* 28 (1983): 29–48.

53. Although Weeden capitalized upon the work of his own precursors; see Johannes Schreiber, "Die Christologie des Markusevangeliums," *ZTK* 58 (1961): 154–83; idem, *Theologie des Vertrauens: Eine redaktionsgeschichtliche Untersuchung des Markusevangeliums* (Hamburg: Furche, 1967); Joseph B. Tyson, "The Blindness of the Disciples in Mark," *JBL* 80 (1961): 261–68; Alfred Kuby, "Zur Konzeption des Markus-Evangeliums," *ZNW* 49 (1958): 52–64. Weeden does not cite his work, but one must also include among Weeden's precursors David J. Hawkin, "The Incomprehension of the Disciples in the Marcan Redaction," *JBL* 91 (1972): 491–500.

John. Weeden shattered these corrective lenses for reading Mark, but we will take years to get accustomed to reading Mark with uncorrected vision.

Following in Weeden's footsteps, Werner Kelber has explored the story level of Mark with uncorrected vision, with numerous valuable insights offered along the way into the narrative strategies employed in the discourse. Kelber has given us the most honest, unflinching reading of the story level of Mark's Gospel that we have yet seen.[54] The work of Weeden and Kelber has, of course, been severely criticized.[55] I shall not discuss the details of their work here, especially their respective attempts to reconstruct the historical circumstances of the production of the Gospel of Mark, for my interest is the narrative discourse of the Gospel and the history of its reception. Weeden broke the spell of the ancient strong readers of Mark; Kelber relentlessly exposed the story of Mark to scrutiny (with numerous observations along the way regarding Mark's narrative strategies); I have endeavored to fix my critical focus upon the discourse level of the Gospel. Consequently, the contribution I can make here is to place the work of Weeden, Kelber, and their critics into the context of my discussion of Mark's narrative rhetoric.

A common thread runs through many of the critiques of Weeden and Kelber. Their critics often argue that Mark's "pastoral, pedagogical"[56] concern for his reading audience is his reason for portraying the disciples as negatively as he does; Mark is striving to educate his reader about the difficulties of discipleship. As Robert Tannehill puts it: "The composition of Mark strongly suggests that the author, by the way in which he tells the disciples' story, intended to awaken his readers to their failures as disciples and call them to repentance."[57] This statement does not yet contradict anything suggested by Weeden or Kelber; virtually all critics would agree with Tannehill's statement.

Matters get interesting when the critics of Weeden and Kelber go on to say that Weeden and Kelber have exaggerated the negative portrayal of the Twelve. It is much more a "mixed" and "complex"[58] portrayal than Weeden and Kelber have allowed. The reader, after all, gains both positive and negative insights into the demands of discipleship in the course of reading the Gospel. Does this portrayal not suggest, as Elizabeth Struthers Malbon says, that "the disciples are not simply the 'bad guys' "; rather, they are "fallible followers of Jesus"?[59]

54. Most accessible is Kelber's *Mark's Story of Jesus* (Philadelphia: Fortress Press, 1979).

55. In various ways, the works by Tannehill, Dewey, and Malbon are critiques of the Weeden-Kelber axis of interpretation of the narrative role of the disciples in Mark. Kelber responds to his critics in "Apostolic Tradition and the Form of the Gospel," in *Discipleship in the New Testament,* 24–46, ed. Fernando Segovia (Philadelphia: Fortress Press, 1985).

56. See Kelber's response to this line of thought, ibid., 29–30.

57. Tannehill, "Disciples in Mark," 393.

58. Malbon, "Fallible Followers," 33, 45.

59. Ibid., 33.

Malbon supplies an additional clue that illuminates why we all agree that
Mark is using the disciples to educate the reader, and yet many of us go on
to disagree about how the disciples are characterized in the Gospel: "I read
the data Kelber collects for 'discipleship failure' as evidence of Markan
pastoral concern for the difficulty of true discipleship, which affirms both the
power and the suffering of Jesus."[60] Malbon cannot accept the abject failure
of the disciples that Kelber finds at story level because she perceives that the
aim of the narrator at discourse level is to educate the reader as to the trials
and tribulations of discipleship. In other words, granted the pastoral and
pedagogical success of the narrative at discourse level, how can the story
level be as bleak as Kelber suggests? Must not the story march in step with
the discourse?

Here the contents of the story and the aims of the discourse are confused.
Kelber is looking squarely at the story level, but Malbon wants to take up
Kelber's story-level observations as discourse-level observations. At this point
the discussion of the role of the disciples in Mark usually bogs down, with
critics talking past each other. Our conversation slips back and forth between
observations of the story and observations of the discourse; what is happening
in our own reading experience is confused with what is happening in the story.
Not only is the content of the story not the same thing as the aims of the
discourse but also the reader is never guaranteed that story and discourse will
march in step with each other. Critics have had a most difficult time dealing
with Mark, a narrative whose story and discourse are often at odds with each
other. Understanding how a narrative whose story is so full of failure and
stupidity could nevertheless be a narrative "about" insight, understanding,
and success has been difficult. The key is that the success of the narrative
occurs, *if* it occurs, not in the story but at the level of discourse.

So, one problem that Weeden and Kelber have faced is that they have
attempted to focus on the story level of Mark's Gospel, whereas most of us
have continued to slip back and forth between story observations and reading
observations. Another dimension of the controversy stirred up by Weeden and
Kelber is that they are peeling away the reading grids through which Mark
has traditionally been read. Perhaps the best example of the lingering power
of the palimpsests of Mark is the reluctance of scholars to accept the cessation
of Mark's narration at 16:8. All kinds of clever maneuvers are performed at
16:8 to soften the shock of the abrupt ending. Ingenious suggestions are made,
explaining how the narrative that ends at 16:8 really does not end there. Many
of these attempts to evade the abrupt ending of the story are accompanied by
illuminating comments about the experience of reading, which is to say that
critical comments on story and discourse are just as tangled here as elsewhere.

60. Idem, *Narrative Space and Mythic Meaning in Mark* (San Francisco: Harper & Row,
1986), 179, n.26.

We can find, for example, comments galore about how uncertain the future of the disciples is at the end of Mark's story, and how challenging this uncertainty is to the reader of the story. Robert Tannehill says, "The Gospel is open ended, for the outcome of the story depends on decisions which the church, including the reader, must still make."[61] After recognizing this ambiguity and open-endedness, however, Tannehill goes on to argue that Mark 14:28 and 16:7 portend a future meeting between the disciples and the risen Jesus in Galilee. The story beyond Mark 16:8 is hazy, but Tannehill thinks he can discern a glimmer of its outline. I cannot say what reading grids may be in place as Tannehill reads Mark, but the question should be raised whether his understanding that an "anticipated meeting" is "announced"[62] in Mark 14:28 and 16:7 owes much to the influence of Matthew's strong reading of these two verses.

Besides usually finding in 14:28 and 16:7 the announcement of a story beyond the end of the story in 16:8, critics also often refuse to accept the last few words of Mark's story: "and they said nothing to no one, for they were afraid" (RMF). Malbon offers the argument that the women must have reported their experience to someone, because surely someone is presumed to have told it to the narrator: "It would appear that the narrator assumes that the hearer/reader assumes that the women did tell the disciples about the resurrection, because later someone surely told the narrator who now tells the hearer/reader!"[63] Once again, the content of the story and the workings of the discourse are confused here. Apparently, Malbon disallows a storyteller the prerogative of narrating a story in which no one ever understands or tells the story of which she is a part. Nevertheless, this kind of narrative sleight of hand presents no problem whatsoever because story and discourse can function independently or even incongruously with each other. Indeed, the omniscient third-person narrator of Mark's Gospel performs this kind of sleight of hand regularly; an author adopts the strategy of third-person omniscient narration in order to be able to narrate scenes not witnessed by human eyes or, if witnessed, then not understood or reported. The real problem here, I suspect, is an unacknowledged reading grid exerting its influence. Because we observe that the women most definitely *do* run and tell the disciples in Matthew's revision of Mark ("they . . . ran to tell his disciples"; Matt. 28:8), if we read Mark 16:8 ("and they said nothing to no one") and conclude that in Mark also the women run and tell the disciples, must we not entertain the possibility that we are perhaps actually reading Matthew's strong reading of Mark rather than Mark itself?

Because Mark is willing to put story and discourse into tension with each other, he is able to offer a narrative that instructs the narratee in the challenges

61. Tannehill, "Disciples in Mark," 404.
62. Ibid., 403–4.
63. Malbon, "Fallible Followers," 45.

of discipleship without a full and explicit portrayal of successful discipleship in the story.[64] In Mark the Twelve are foils to Jesus at story level so that at discourse level the narratee can observe their mistakes and inadequacies and learn to behave differently. In Matthew and Luke, where story and discourse are more congruous, what the narratee sees in the story is what he gets in the discourse, and vice versa. In Matthew and Luke, therefore, readers have no doubt that the Twelve (or at least the eleven) are exemplary models for the narratee. In Matthew, for example, the disciples are human and fallible, "men of little faith," but men of faith nonetheless. They are favored by Jesus with the bestowal of his divine authority.[65] Given the positive function of the Twelve as exemplary role models in Matthew and in each of the other Gospels, we have extraordinary difficulty seeing, let alone appreciating, how they function negatively in Mark. Once again, our perception of a persistent problem in Markan scholarship, in this case the role of the disciples in Mark, is created as much or more by the palimpsests of Mark as by Mark itself.

64. In the literary context of the Hellenistic Age, this is an unusual narrative treatment of the topic of discipleship. See Vernon Robbins's observations that Mark's negative portrayal of Jesus' disciples is virtually unique among all portrayals of disciples in Greco-Roman literature (*Jesus the Teacher: A Socio-Rhetorical Interpretation of Mark* [Philadelphia: Fortress Press, 1984], 204–9. I insist, however, that at least one character in Mark is a successful disciple from beginning to end. This is none other than the greatest disciple of John the Baptist, a certain Jesus of Nazareth. Thus the further irony that in Mark's story only one faithful disciple of John is portrayed (others are mentioned, but not portrayed), but none for Jesus.

65. See the "Thou art Peter" passage in Matt. 16:17-19, the passage about the disciples' twelve thrones of judgment in 19:28, and the Great Commission in 28:16-20.

An Ambivalent Narrative?

I am frustrated in not being able to say, all at once, everything that needs to be said about reading Mark. For instance, in my emphasis on indirection in the latter chapters of this book I may have inadvertently encouraged my reader to forget the abundance of direction discussed in earlier chapters. To neglect either direction or indirection would lead to an impoverished understanding of Mark's narrative rhetoric. Mark's rhetoric is powerfully, insistently direct *and* tantalizingly, intriguingly indirect. This narrative pulls (and entices) the reader so vigorously (and seductively) in different directions simultaneously that it is ultimately an ambivalent narrative. This narrative seems not quite able to make up its mind about what it wants to do to us.

When its rhetoric of direction is particularly compelling, this narrative tells us exactly and unquestionably what to see, hear, understand, think, and believe. When its rhetoric of indirection is particularly enticing, it lures us into pondering puzzles and clarifying opacities for ourselves, an impressive advocacy of the exercise of readerly freedom and response-ability. This narrative is repetitive and yet full of gaps; frequently clear and determinate in meaning and yet frequently ambiguous and even opaque; filled with reliable narrative commentary and yet imposing all manner of mysteries, riddles, and puzzles upon the reader; and at once overbearingly direct and maddeningly obscure. At one extreme, the narrative seems to strike an authoritarian pose, dictating our perceptual and conceptual points of view. At the other extreme, the narrative strikes a libertarian pose, championing the freedom of the reader to plot her own course through the reading experience. Direct and indirect, authoritarian and libertarian—can a narrative have it both ways? Can a person (or a person's text) authentically command another person to live a life of freedom and response-ability? Is this attempt to dominate the reader and at the same time sponsor the reader's freedom and independent judgment a case of oxymoronic nonsense or paradoxical truth?

These questions are easier asked than answered. In the end, I find that the Gospel is ambivalent. Nevertheless, I enjoy reading it, I appreciate being read by it, and I hear among its ambivalent voices at least one subversive, antiauthoritarian voice that I welcome and that I would like others to hear as well. This is enough to keep me reading this narrative and talking about reading it.

Is the Gospel's ambivalence another face of its indirection? Perhaps the Gospel's ambivalence is like parental concern for offspring nearing maturity. In the end the Gospel beckons us to leave the relative security of its nest behind and to try out our new wings, by plunging ahead into the void beyond Mark 16:8. At the same time, the Gospel displays a conflicting tendency to pull us back to it and to clutch us to its bosom forever. If a parent can reasonably display such conflicting tendencies, can a narrative also?

Recall two ways in which conflicting tendencies are displayed in Mark. One is Mark's ambivalent use of apocalyptic language, with which he speaks of Jesus' careers and titles, past and future. On the one hand, Mark's narrative is a retrospective narrative, placing Jesus unambiguously and forever in the reader's past. People who proclaim that the Christ has returned here and now are deluded, Mark says (13:6, 21-22). On the other hand, Jesus in the past time of Mark's narrative spoke repeatedly of a coming Son of man, who would usher in the Kingdom of God with power (9:1; 14:62). The coming of this Son of man lies somewhere in the near future beyond Mark 16:8. Apparently the Jesus who was present in the past will again be present in the future, but he is not present in the present. Yet does that make sense? This puzzle may be less irksome if we consider that perhaps again we have confused story content with narrative discourse because the Jesus of Mark's past, present, and future is always *Mark's* Jesus. The suspicion arises that ambivalence over the past, present, or future of Jesus may be another of those Markan narrative illusions or sleights of hand, another of those apparent puzzles in the story that is really a strategy in the discourse.

The second Markan ambivalence that I want to consider is the treatment of Galilee at the end of the Gospel. In one sense the Galilee alluded to in 14:28 and 16:7 is the experience beyond 16:8 of following Jesus on the way into an unknown future. In another sense, what is Galilee but the way in which we have already followed Jesus through the experience of reading the sixteen chapters of Mark's Gospel? Could not the very last word of the Gospel (the awkwardly placed conjunction *gar*) be analogous to the musical notation of a coda, which signals the musician to return to a marked passage and to keep on playing?[1] Thus, the awkward *gar* at Mark 16:8, coupled with the ambiguous allusion to Galilee in 16:7, signals the reader to return to the beginning of the Gospel, to begin reading all over again. Again, if Galilee is understood less in terms of story and more in terms of discourse and reading experience, then perhaps the ambivalence over Galilee is no more of a problem

---

1. For the figure of the coda I am indebted to Joseph L. Price and his unpublished paper "*Gar* as the Sign of Coda: An Aesthetic and Theological Interpretation of Mark 16:8."

than the supposed ambivalence over the past, present, and future of Jesus. If Galilee is perceived as the experience of following Jesus on beyond Mark 16:8, should not it already have been figured reliably by the Galilee through which the reader followed Jesus from Mark 1:1 through 16:8? The Jesus and the Galilee of past, present, and future are both figurative tokens of this narrative's conviction that we can acknowledge Mark's reliable, authentic authority and still have our own genuine personal freedoms too, that we can have a secure textual fabric on which to stand, and from which to venture forth freely, but also to which we can return again. To want to read Mark's Gospel is to want to believe that authority and freedom are not mutually exclusive.

So far the ambivalences I have discussed have been those that I have found in reading the Gospel itself. As a critic, I, too, have my own ambivalences. For one thing, I am ambivalent about what this book has accomplished, both for my reader and for the Gospel of Mark. The responses and judgments of my readers I will surely receive, but what I have done or not done for Mark's Gospel will remain an open question. I ask myself, By exposing Mark's rhetorical strategies to critical scrutiny, have I undermined Mark's narrative, given it a modest helping hand, or maybe done a little of both?

After all, exposing rhetorical strategies is often the way a critic goes about undermining someone's rhetoric. In this case, however, I could reveal Mark's rhetoric only by revealing the ways other authors have eclipsed Mark's rhetoric. Mark's rhetorical strategies have been covered up, and so I have tried to discover them. By discovering Mark's rhetoric, I do not so much undermine it (that was done far better than I ever could by Matthew and Luke) as give Mark's Gospel a better chance to be approached on its own terms once again.

Paradoxically, to be able to read Mark rather than a reading grid of it, we must first practice criticism. Although I agree in principle with George Steiner that reading precedes criticism and must take precedence over it, we can read a text with a long reading history only by means of criticism of the reception history of that text. If we do not peel away venerable reading grids, then we will be reading, not the ancient text itself, but its palimpsests. Even with the powers of criticism, we cannot magically work our way back through the centuries of reading history to recapture the experience of the first flesh-and-blood readers of the Gospels. To think that we can read Mark as it was first read is a delusion. We never read the text itself, only the history of the reading of the text. The choice is either to read the history of reading with sensitivity and imagination, which is the vocation of Steiner's "critic," or to be read by the history of reading, which is the fate of the "reader."

I am reprising an ambivalence addressed at the beginning of this book, the perpetual tension between the roles of the reader and the critic. In spite of the inherent conflict between these two roles, we need both. Apart from the ecstasy of reading, we have no reason to deepen and illumine the reading experience through criticism. The reason for doing criticism is to enrich the experience of reading. However, reading is in peril if it eschews criticism. Without criticism, we are read blindly by powers and principalities that we cannot comprehend. Reading and criticism are shortsighted and dangerous without each other, so long live the uneasy conversation between the reader and the critic! May that uneasy conversation take place within each of us.

My final expression of ambivalence arises out of a belated word of respect that I must express for the strongest and most influential reader of Mark ever. As is the custom in scholarly treatments of Mark, I have thus far completely neglected this strong reader, even though his palimpsest of Mark has been more frequently "read" and has been more influential than any other in history, in spite of the fact that no copies of his palimpsest have existed for many centuries. Obviously, I am spinning out a riddle, so what is the answer?

This powerful reading grid is the Diatessaron of Tatian, written sometime in the middle of the second century C.E.[2] The history of the production of the Diatessaron remains obscure. Because only fragments survive—and these in several ancient languages—scholars are not even in agreement over the language in which it was originally written. Tatian appears to have constructed the Diatessaron by piecing together phrases lifted from each of the four canonical Gospels. He took one phrase out of one Gospel, another phrase out of another, and so on, until he had created a single, continuous narrative from the four Gospels. Thus the name given to his work, *dia tessaron,* means literally "[one created] through four." Tatian's work was enormously popular, was translated into many languages, and influenced the production of numerous medieval Gospel harmonies in various European languages. In spite of its great popularity and influence, no complete copy of the Diatessaron has survived. Tatian was judged a heretic by the early church, and zealous, orthodox Christians destroyed copies of the Diatessaron wherever they were discovered. In 423 C.E., Bishop Theodoret of Cyrrhus on the Euphrates learned that many copies of the Diatessaron were being used in his diocese. He sought out and destroyed as many copies as he could find, more than two hundred.

Although Tatian's work was lost to history, in another sense it never left us. The narrative that Tatian produced was a reading grid in the tradition of the strong readers who had preceded him. Just as Matthew and Luke each created a grid for reading Mark, and John perhaps wrote his Gospel to grid all three Synoptics, Tatian does John one better by gridding all four canonical Gospels. The Diatessaron is thus the logical outcome of a history of strong

2. On the Diatessaron, see Bruce Manning Metzger, *The Text of the New Testament: Its Transmission, Corruption and Restoration,* 2d ed. (New York and London: Oxford University Press, 1968), 89–92; and Howard Clark Kee, *Jesus in History: An Approach to the Study of the Gospels,* 2d ed. (New York: Harcourt Brace Jovanovich, 1977), 280–92.

reading among a particular family of texts that are deeply implicated in each other. If Tatian had not written the Diatessaron, someone else would have. As a person reads the four canonical Gospels, a gravitational attraction between the four all but demands the reader to read them together. Tatian acceded to this gravitational pull and conflated the four Gospels; he did consciously and explicitly what most readers of the Gospels have done unconsciously and implicitly for nineteen hundred years. Many diatessarons have been created through the centuries, a few dependent upon Tatian's and many more independent of it, and diatessarons are still published today. Every few years, it seems, I receive an announcement of the publication of a new version of the Gospels, in which all four canonical Gospels are merged to form one continuous story. The creators of these modern-day diatessarons always seem blissfully unaware that this work has all been done before, thousands of times.[3]

Consequently, I claim that the Diatessaron is the best known and most beloved of all strong readings of Mark's Gospel. Readers and critics alike read an imaginary "Gospel according to Tatian" more than any of us would care to admit. Therefore, despite the value of peeling away Matthew's reading grid from Mark, that effort is only the beginning of the critical task of peeling away reading grids. To read Mark and not someone's revision of Mark, we would need to peel away Matthew, Luke, John, and, most difficult of all, the "one Gospel through four," that invisible, omnipresent version of Mark that we tend to read whenever we read any of the Gospels. Therefore, although I have tried to read—and to talk about reading—only one Gospel in this book, I am ambivalent about whether this task can be done. Reading one Gospel is almost impossible without somehow reading all of the others at the same time.

I have doubts, therefore, about what we can accomplish by penetrating the layers of reading grids to get as close as possible to a supposed precursor. This rather backward-looking enterprise stands in tension with a prominent tendency of Mark's Gospel. Although one tendency of Mark is to clutch us to its bosom, another conflicting tendency is to urge us to exercise the freedom and response-ability to move forward, leaving Mark behind us. Matthew, Luke, John, and Tatian were all, in their own way, respectful of both tendencies in Mark. They each left Mark behind by creating their own new narratives, but the narratives they created were revisions of Mark. Mark survives in their new narratives, but transfigured.

---

3. Typical is the following announcement I received several years ago:
This watershed work represents a milestone in religious literature—the life of Jesus Christ presented in one unified Gospel.

   The original four Gospels of Matthew, Mark, Luke, and John contain much similar and overlapping information. At the same time, each by itself is incomplete and somewhat weighted in favor of the special interests of its author. By combining and corroborating details, however, and adding information about Jesus contained in other parts of the New Testament, such as the Letters of Paul and the Book of Acts, it is possible to derive a complete picture of the real Jesus. This is what [the author] has done, and it is an impressive achievement.

This process of transfiguration is typical of the history of biblical literature generally. The Bible is replete with narratives that have been turned into new versions of themselves. In biblical tradition Jews and Christians have constantly practiced revision. If we were to be faithful today to what Matthew, Luke, John, and Tatian did to Mark's narrative, would we not do to them what they did to Mark? Would we not transfigure their narratives through strong reading and turn them into our precursors?

Yet my own vocation is not storyteller but critic. If I were a storyteller, I would like to write a Gospel that places Mark's successors in such a light that the shadows they have cast upon Mark for centuries would be dispelled and the highlights they have shone upon Mark would be muted. I would like to construct a grid for reading Matthew that blocks out Matthew and allows only Mark's Gospel to be seen as it was before Matthew came along. Nevertheless, such a reading experience is a pipe dream—no such magical reading grid will ever be produced—so I shall continue to trust the powers of criticism to serve reading.

SUBJECT INDEX

Adverbs, 110–12
Ambiguity, 16, 17, 18, 22, 58, 81, 89, 95, 103,
    106, 111, 119, 122, 129, 131, 148, 153,
    158–62, 164–67, 173, 179, 181, 192,
    195–209, 210, 211, 215, 221–22, 226,
    247, 255, 259, 261, 262
    dramatic, 166, 197, 200–209, 227
    verbal, 166, 197–200, 227
Ambivalence, 261–66
Anacoluthon, 91–92, 112–16, 118
Anachrony. *See* Violation of chronological
    sequence
Anagnostes, 84–85
Analepsis, 94, 111, 139
    See also Retrospection
Anthropology, 58
Anthrōpos ("a person"), 76
Anticipation. *See* Prospection
Apposition, 92, 116, 117, 120
Aristotle, 135, 139, 175–76, 196–97
Audience–oriented. *See* Reader–oriented
Authority, 61–64, 65, 66, 73–77, 78, 104, 106,
    116, 119, 126, 127, 131, 133, 142, 220,
    253, 263
Autos ("he, she, it"), 201–2

Bacchae, The, 162
Beginning of the Gospel, 19, 71, 87, 90, 91, 98,
    111, 120, 153–54, 213, 238, 241
Blanks, 34, 135, 148–49

Capability, 163, 224
Chiasm, 151–52
Changeability, 166–67, 221–22
Clarity, 124, 158, 195, 198, 223, 225, 239, 240,
    246, 248, 250, 261
Clarification, 16, 17, 173, 181, 190, 198, 199–
    202, 204, 208-9, 213, 227, 250, 255,
    261

Closed Narrative. *See* Text: and closed
Closure, 253
Commentary, 64, 167
    explicit, 81–126, 140, 154, 156–60, 162
        on discourse, 81, 82–91, 153
        on story, 82, 91–126, 153
    implicit, 81–82, 91, 127–54, 169, 178, 188
        by means of characters, 82, 127–34
        by means of plotting, 82, 127, 134–47
Container metaphor. *See* Language: and container
    metaphor of
'Critic'/'Reader,' 4–5, 18, 34, 38, 41, 44, 135,
    167, 168, 171, 263–64, 266
Critical compasses. *See* Language: and critical
    compasses of
Critical reading. *See* 'Critic'/'Reader'

De ("and, but"), 92, 103, 116–17
Defamiliarization, 134
Developmental psychology, 226
Dia ("because of"), 92, 93, 101
Diatessaron, 264–66
Direction, 3, 4, 58, 81–154, 155, 174, 198, 223,
    225, 239, 250, 253, 256, 261
Disciples, role of the, 20, 70–73, 79, 173–74,
    192, 216–17, 237, 254, 256–60
Discourse level, 2, 3, 4, 16, 17–20, 22–23, 57,
    70, 72, 74–79, 81, 85, 86, 88, 90, 92,
    95, 96, 97, 98, 99, 100, 102, 103, 109,
    111, 112, 118, 119, 122, 128, 129, 130,
    132, 137, 139, 141, 143, 146, 150, 152,
    153–54, 156, 160, 164—65, 168–70,
    171–72, 174, 178, 180, 183–84, 186,
    190, 195, 197, 199, 200–220, 222, 238–
    39, 244, 248–52, 254, 255–60, 262
Distance, 32–33, 44, 70, 71, 72, 77–80, 146,
    148, 174, 211, 217, 241, 244, 256

267

Author Index

272

Scripture Index